The ARPANET Sourcebook

The Unpublished Foundations of the Internet

PETER H. SALUS, SERIES EDITOR

Packet Communications

Lions' Commentary on UNIX

The ARPANET Sourcebook:
The Unpublished Foundations of the Internet

The ARPANET Sourcebook

The Unpublished Foundations of the Internet

The ARPANET Sourcebook: The Unpublished Foundations of the Internet

Selection and compilation of materials in this volume Copyright © 2008 by Peter H. Salus. All rights reserved. Please see the Acknowledgments page regarding permissions for individual documents in this collection. This book may not be reproduced, in whole or in part, including illustrations, in any form (beyond that copying permitted by Sections 107 and 108 of the U.S. Copyright Law and except by reviewers for the public press) or by any means, without the advance written permission of the publisher.

COMPUTER CLASSICS REVISITED SERIES
Series Editor: Peter H. Salus

Published by:
Peer-to-Peer Communications LLC
PO Box 6970
Charlottesville, VA 22906–6970
United States
Website: http://www.peerllc.com
Email: info@peerllc.com

The publisher offers discounts on this book when ordered in bulk quantities.

Cover Design and Illustration: Gordon Haber and Chris Harrison.
Production: Chris Harrison

Manufactured in the United States of America
1st Edition
Paper: ISBN-13: 978-1-57398-000-5
ISBN-10: 1-57398-000-5
Cloth: ISBN-13: 978-157398-006-7
ISBN-10: 157398-006-4

IN MEMORIAM

Jon Postel
6 August 1943–16 October 1998

Jonathan Bruce Postel was a graduate student in Len Kleinrock's lab when the ARPANET was nascent. When Steve Crocker wrote RFC 1, Jon offered to edit it. He was the RFC editor for over 30 years. Jon was IANA. He managed the .us domain. He was on the Board of the Internet Society.

If you use the Internet, you are indebted to Jon.

PHS, 2007

Contents

Acknowledgments ix
Preface xi

PART A "IMAGINING THE ARPANET" 1
   Myth and History Peter H. Salus (*Matrix News* 2/2000) 2
   Paul Baran's Reports Peter Salus (*Matrix News* 3/2000) 3
   On Distributed Communications Paul Baran (1964)
       Memorandum I: Introduction to Distributed Communications Networks 5
       Memorandum XI: Summary Overview 46
   The Truth about Baran Willis H. Ware (*Matrix News* 4/2000) 70
   The Computer as a Communication Device J.C.R. Licklider/Robert Taylor (1968) 72

PART B "PLANNING THE ARPANET" 93
   Memoirs of the Sixties Leonard Kleinrock 94
   Retrospective on the Arpanet Protocols and RFCs Steve Crocker 97
   A Study of Computer Network Design Parameters Elmer Shapiro (1968) 103
   ORIGINAL RFC REPRINTS
     1. Host Software 177
     2. Links 186
     3. Documentation Conventions 195
     4. Network Timetable 197
     5. DEL 204
     6. Conversation with Bob Kahn 223
     7. Host-Imp Interface 224
     8. ARPA Network Functional Specifications 237
     9. Host Software 249
    10. Documentation Conventions 264
    11. Implementation of the HOST-HOST Software Procedures in Gordo 267
    12. IMP-HOST Interface Flow Diagrams 321
    13. Referring to RFC 11 326
    15. Network Subsystem for Time Sharing Hosts 327
    16. M.I.T. 336
    17. Some Questions Re: HOST-IMP Protocol 337

   17a. Robert Kahn Responses to John Kreznar's Questions   338
    18. IMP-IMP and HOST-HOST Control Links   339
    51. Proposal for a Network Interchange Language   340

PART C   "BUILDING THE ARPANET"   359
   Looking back at the ARPANET effort decades later David C. Walden (2006)   360
  BOLT BERANEK AND NEWMAN TECHNICAL REPORTS
   BBN Report 1763 (January 1969, Initial Hardware Design for IMP)   363
   BBN Report 1765 (excerpt, Figure 1: IMP Program Schedule)   444
   BBN Report 1783 (April 1969: Quarterly Technical Report No. 1, January-March 1969)   445
   BBN Report 1837 (July 1969: Quarterly Technical Report No. 2, April-June 1969)   461
   BBN Report 1890 (October 1969: Quarterly Technical Report No. 3, July-September 1969)   478
   BBN Report 1928 (January 1970: Quarterly Technical Report No. 4, October-December 1969)   490

APPENDIX   HISTORICAL MUSINGS FROM *MATRIX NEWS*
   And they argued all night Michael A. Padlipsky (*Matrix News* 2/2000)   504
   Response to Padlipsky Les Earnest (*Matrix News* 4/2000)   510

Acknowledgments

I need to thank a great many people for aiding and abetting this effort.

First and foremost, Dan Doernberg, the publisher, for a decade's persistence.

Second, Mike O'Dell, who has been encouraging my historical bent for twenty years.

Where this book is concerned, Steve Crocker, Les Earnest, Len Kleinrock, Bob Taylor, Jennie Connolly, Mike Padlipsky, and Dave Walden are each owed an unrepayable debt.

I'm grateful to the following individuals and companies for their generous permission to reprint copyrighted materials in this volume:

The individual authors of the Forewords (Steve Crocker, Len Kleinrock, David Walden) and of the essays that first appeared in *Matrix News*: Michael Padlipsky, Les Earnest, and Willis Ware.

Robert Taylor, for allowing us to reproduce a lengthy email in the Preface and for helping us obtain permission (years ago!) to reprint "The Computer as a Communication Device."

BBN Technologies, successor to Bolt, Beranek and Newman (BBN), to reprint selected ARPANET technical reports. We are indebted to Dave Walden and Alex McKenzie, former Vice Presidents of BBN, and Jennie Connolly, for many years BBN and BBN Technologies librarian, for their aid and support.

Digital Equipment Corporation (now part of Hewlett-Packard) for permission to reprint J.C.R. Licklider/Robert Taylor's "The Computer as a Communication Device."

The Franklin Institute for permission to reprint two pages contained in Paul Baran's Summary Overview paper (below).

The Internet Engineering Task Force (IETF) for permission to reprint the RFCs. Joe Touch, Director of the Postel Center at the USC Information Sciences Institute and Paula Jabloner of the Computer History Museum were extremely gracious about helping fill in gaps in our collection of legible copies. Thanks also to Prof. Chris Edmondson-Yurkanan (University of Texas at Austin) for several helpful suggestions.

RAND Corporation for permission to reprint the introductory and summary overview chapters of Paul Baran's "Introduction to Distributed Communications Networks." Thanks to Lauren Skrabala for "going the extra mile."

SRI International for permission to reprint E.B. Shapiro's "A Study of Computer Network Design Parameters." We are indebted to Marty Mallonee (Manager, Corporate and Marketing Communications), Lisa Beffa (Manager, Archiving and Research), and Richard A. Cramer (Assistant General Counsel).

PHS, Toronto, September 2007

Preface

"The longer you look back,
the farther you can look forward"
WINSTON CHURCHILL

If you're reading this, you're probably "on" the Internet. And you use a telephone. But while the phone's story and Alexander Graham Bell are reasonably well-known, that of the net is not.

Several hundred people were involved in the creation of what we think of as the ARPANET,* which was to become the Internet.

While the ARPANET was born at the end of 1969, with four interconnected nodes in the western United States, the seeds were sown nearly a decade earlier. And while several individuals, with a good deal of fanfare and publicity, have declared themselves (or been declared) the "Father of the Internet" (sometimes, "one of the Fathers of the Internet"), many of the most important individuals have gone without laurels.

This book contains a number of original documents. Only the article by Licklider and Taylor, a few of the early RFCs and the four articles (one by me and one each by Willis Ware, Les Earnest and Mike Padlipsky) have been somewhat available. And the names of most of the authors are not household words.

The ARPANET was the brainchild of J.C.R. Licklider, the original director of the IPTO (DARPA's Information Processing Techniques Office), appointed in 1962; he left to return to IBM in 1964. The project was launched in 1966 and nourished by just over a million dollars from Bob Taylor (Lick's successor but one) at ARPA. I have no doubt that only the purchase of "Seward's Icebox" comes close to that bargain.

The documents in this volume are important not merely because of what the ARPANET grew into, but because they represent the reality of what was instantiated in 1969, not what participants claim or wish or embroider.

Bob Taylor sent me his version of events:

> A note on ARPANET history
> A couple of years ago in response to some uninformed postings on Dave Farber's list [IP] regarding ARPAnet history I wrote the following:
>
> In February of 1966 I initiated the ARPAnet project. I was Director of ARPA's Information Processing Techniques Office (IPTO) from late '65 to late '69. There were only two people involved in the decision to launch the ARPAnet: my boss, the Director of ARPA Charles Herzfeld, and me.
>
> From 1962 to 1970, beginning with J.C.R. Licklider, Ivan Sutherland, and then me, IPTO funded several of the first projects devoted to the creation of interactive computing—then referred to as time-sharing.
>
> In '64–'65, I witnessed that within each local site when users were first connected by a time-sharing system, a community of people with common interests began to discover one another and interact

---

* DoD directive 5105.15 (7 February 1958) set up "The Advanced Research Projects Agency" (ARPA) as a result of the USSR's launches of Sputnik 1 and Sputnik 2 on October 4, 1957 and November 3, 1957 respectively. On 23 March 1972, by DoD directive, the name was changed to DARPA. On 22 February 1993, DARPA was "redesignated" ARPA, and on 22 February 1996, Public Law 104–106 (Title IX of the FY 1996 Defense Authorization Act) directed an "organizational name change" to DARPA. —PHS

through the medium of the computer. I was struck by the fact that this was a wonderfully new and powerful phenomenon.

The next obvious step was to connect those sites with an interactive network. To me, computing was about communication, not arithmetic.

Hence the ARPAnet.

This theme is elaborated in a paper Lick and I wrote in 1968 entitled, *The Computer as a Communications Device*. Google can find it for you. [It's included in this volume — PHS] On the last couple of pages there is a scenario that is reminiscent of today's Internet.

The theoretical basis for the distributed system arose from the work of Len Kleinrock, whose 1964 *Communication Nets* (based on his 1962 MIT dissertation) is of fundamental importance). The first (abortive) attempt at a network was by Donald Davies and Roger Scantlebury at the NPL in Cambridge, UK, but this was a "star" network, and while Davies spoke of switching, they lacked the necessary funding to go further.

Bob Taylor wrote: "As the ARPAnet was being designed ('67–'69) we all believed that Baran and Donald Davies in England, independently, invented packet switching. Most of us still believe that; but 30 years later, in 1995, Kleinrock and [Larry] Roberts claimed that Kleinrock invented it. Following this, Davies wrote, "An Historical Study of the Beginnings of Packet Switching," and asked that it be published posthumously. It was, by the British Computer Society's, *The Computer Journal* (Vol. 44, No.3, 2001, pp 152–162).

Taylor's is an extreme position; I'd say that while many agree with his view, many others concur with Len Kleinrock. And many hold to Davies' posthumous brief, which is closer to Taylor's than to Kleinrock's.

Les Earnest, of SAGE, SAIL, and cycling fame, wrote me in December 2006: "I agree that Baran had worked out a lot of the theory for packet switching but believe that the fact that some of his reports were classified 'Secret' was not significant. After all, Larry Roberts had a security clearance, as did I and some others in the ARPAnet startup committee. The problem was that none of us learned of his work until Roberts met Roger Scantlebury, a colleague of Donald Davies, at an ACM conference in October 1967 and through him learned of both Davies' and Baran's work."

Historical credit for various aspects of the ARPANET's architecture is similarly contentious.

The hardware, connections and IMP software were the result of devoted work by a team of six run by Frank Heart at BBN (Bolt, Beranek and Newman of Cambridge, Massachusetts) with Severo Ornstein and Will Crowther as his lieutenants. The host software grew out of the efforts of the graduate students at UCLA, UC-Santa Barbara, SRI (the Stanford Research Institute), and the University of Utah. The IMP (Interface Message Processor) was the result of a brilliant insight on the part of Wes Clark. Taylor said: "The singularly most important contribution to the architectural design of the ARPAnet/Internet came from Wesley Clark: the interface message processor (IMP). Wes' ARPAnet concept ensured the critically valuable distributed architecture of the ARPAnet. Wes was the designer of the LINC which was arguably the first personal computer."*

I (and others) might quibble as to whether Clark's was "the most important contribution," but not as to whether Wes' role was crucial to the ARPANET.

Les Earnest's view is: "The most important contribution to the architectural design of ARPAnet was clearly the insight that a multipath network in which each node is connected to only a few neighbors can provide effective communication between all nodes. Of course, that idea evidently also occurred to Baran and Davies independently

---

* The LINC was a 12-bit, 2048-word computer, designed at Lincoln Lab by Clark and Charles Molner; it sold for about $50,000. The software was written by Sir Maurice V. Wilkes, who in May 1949 designed and built the first stored program computer, the EDSAC. In 1951, he developed the concept of microprogramming. His lab at Cambridge developed the Titan for Ferranti, introducing password encryption. His contributions to computing are too numerous to elaborate further here. —PHS

though they were unable to get their schemes implemented. The use of IMPs was an improvement on this idea in that it allowed the packet switching software to be simplified and standardized and would allow network services to continue to flow through the node even when the host was taken off-line for maintenance or experimentation. However that was an embellishment on the fundamental network architecture."

History, I suppose, is made up of "dire combustion and confused events/New hatch'd to the woeful time." (Macbeth, 2.3.73f.) This is not to denigrate or demean what some claim, but to elevate those who have been less publicized. "The one duty we owe to history," said Oscar Wilde,"is to rewrite it."

Part A of this book, "Imagining the ARPANET," contains an article by me, introducing Paul Baran's work, the first and final sections of Baran's work, and an article (*The Truth about Baran*) by Willis Ware, senior computer scientist emeritus at RAND. Unfortunately, the innovative work of Baran was executed as an Air Force contract and reported by RAND to the DoD. It was not widely circulated; the planners at ARPA only became aware of it (as well as the work of Davies) after a meeting in 1967 in Gatlinburg, TN.

The contract had arisen as the result of a military panic, as described in my *Myth and History* (originally published in 2000). Baran deserves fuller study: not only were his ideas on redundancy and packet switching formative, but he was involved in the development of packet voice technology and Telebit's multitone modem, founded Metricom (the first wireless Internet company), and developed the technology used in the airport metal detector.

Baran's work is followed by the essay by Licklider and Bob Taylor mentioned earlier. The article struck me as science fiction when I read it in the late 1960s, at which time I truly believed that computers were just for calculation (I didn't realize that Les Earnest had written the first spell-checker in 1961). Lick and Bob told me what we all know 40 years later: computers are communication devices.

Part B, "Planning the ARPANET," begins with retrospective essays by Len Kleinrock, the most notable expert on queuing theory and whose UCLA lab hosted the first ARPANET node, and Steve Crocker, then a grad student of Kleinrock's, who wrote RFC 1 and instituted the RFC process.

There are now well over 4000 Requests for Comment. The first few of these are, as Sam Spade puts it, "the stuff that dreams are made of" (The Maltese Falcon). This volume reprints RFCs 1–18, those RFCs published before the ARPANET went "live." Most were typewritten, though RFCs 7 and 8 are in longhand and all the diagrams are hand drawn. Crocker's RFC 1, among other things, defined the size of network addresses; Shapiro's RFC 4 contains the first network map (a straight line between SRI in Menlo Park and UCLA). RFC 14 was never issued. Under a dozen copies of each RFC were circulated, and all three of the surviving sets of copies we've been able to find are nth generation photocopies, sometimes heavily banded, with occasionally barely legible text. They are reproduced here as best we could; to make the text as legible as possible banding and dark areas on some pages had to be left in. Overall they came out well, almost always more legible than the photocopies we started with.

Even true visionaries have only a blurry image of the future. For this reason, RFC 1's assignment of 5 bits to address space is significant. It provided for a network of 31 "hosts" (0 wasn't used). By September 1969, address space had expanded to 6 bits (63 hosts). But the ARPANET was waxing. By January 1976 there were 63 hosts, but BBN had altered the software to provide for 8 bits of address space (255 hosts). Host Table #166 in May 1982 had 235 entries. A new system was established; but it was soon clear that the Internet Protocol needed to be pushed yet further. Today, we are in the process of instantiating IPv6—a version that allows 128 bit addressing.

But don't laugh at Crocker and his colleagues. As late as 1972 there were predictions that the network might grow to as many as 2000 users. Thirty years later, guesses placed the number of actual users at over 500 million. At the end of 2006, my estimate would be over a billion people with Internet access.

People jeered Robert Fulton's "folly," the paddlewheel steamship; in 1876 Alexander Graham Bell said that the telephone was purely a business tool, that no one would ever want an instrument at home; a century later, Ken Olsen, founder of DEC, said that no one would want a computer at home. But remember, it was Niels Bohr who said, "Prediction is very difficult, especially if it's about the future."

Part C, "Building the ARPANET," is made up of an essay by Dave Walden, formerly a Vice President at BBN, and six BBN reports from 1969. Taylor says: "The most significant role in actually building the ARPAnet was played by Frank Heart and his Bolt, Beranek & Newman team: Severo Ornstein, Will Crowther, Ben Barker, Bernie Cosell, Dave Walden, and Bob Kahn." Here I agree entirely with Bob.

The Appendix contains two retrospective articles from *Matrix News* in 2000. *MN* is no more, killed off in 2003 by venture capitalists who saw no use in a monthly that merely broke even. The essays disagree with one another and with some of the introductory essays and some of the documents. That's the problem with reality. It doesn't come neat and smooth, like the history we're taught in school. And memory isn't perfect—even the memories of participants.

I have also chosen to add RFC 51 (1970) by Michel Elie to Section B because it is nearly unknown (I wrote a note about it in 1998). When James Gosling began Java (then "Oak") in 1991, the concept of "write once, run anywhere" was a remarkable innovation. Elie had the notion of a Network Interchange Language 20 years earlier, while a graduate student at UC Berkeley. He's now in semi-retirement, but runs the "Observatoire des usages de l'Internet" at the University of Montpellier. He was far ahead of his time.

The ARPANET, the Internet, the World Wide Web grew from the visions of a handful of folks, through the work of several hundred, to become the tool and plaything of nearly a billion people.

The foundation is here: the dream, the theory, the construction.

Peter H. Salus, Toronto, 2007

SOME FURTHER READING

For those interested, details can be found in

Peter H. Salus, *Casting the Net* (1995), ISBN 0201876744.

Katie Hafner & Matthew Lyon, *Where Wizards Stay Up Late* (1996), ISBN 0684812010.

John Naughton, *A Brief History of the Future* (1999), ISBN 1585670324

The ARPANET Sourcebook

The Unpublished Foundations of the Internet

PART A

Imagining the ARPANET

Myth and History

Peter H. Salus <peter@mids.org>

Copyright © 2000 Matrix Information and Directory Services (MIDS)

[*Recently, a number of contributors to the cyberhistory mailing list have brought up the "myth" of the roots of the ARPANET being in nuclear fear. Another version of this was posted there.*]

It seemed to me that there are a number of questions embedded in this thread which are getting ensnarled. The "why study myth?" is part of this. If, indeed, history is what we remember, then myth is part of that history (in fact it may be *more* important: we all recall Washington's "cannot tell a lie," but who knows the names of his cabinet members? But the more basic question of what is fact and what myth remains.

Another problem is that most of the contributors to this discussion appear to believe that what the creators of the ARPANET in 1968-1973 recall, is what motivated the DoD in 1961/62.

In 1994, after a talk with Alex McKenzie (then a VP at BBN) in which he alluded to the nuclear war myth, I spent a day in the newspaper archives of the Boston Public Library. Much to my surprise, three microwave towers in Utah were indeed bombed by the American Republican Army. The *New York Times* carried the story on May 29, 1961:

> Three microwave relay stations in Utah shattered by mysterious explosions -- widespread communications disruption results; national defense circuit shifts automatically to alternate routes; FBI opens probe.

On June 19 there were four arrests and on November 3, the *Times* published a piece on the sentences.

The Times also reported that the DoD believed that there might be a "heavily manned bomber attack against this country in the next few years."

The DoD contract to RAND which resulted in Paul Baran's reports in 1962 was the direct result. And it was Baran who introduced the concept of the "message block."

It was five years later that Wes Clark came up with his notion of the IMP, another year before BBN got the contract, and another year until there were four hosts.

That the BBN folks and the UCLA students (Cerf, Postel, Crocker, etc.) didn't see the 1961 events as causal is not unreasonable. It was only in 1962 that Lick went from BBN to ARPA to run CCR (which became the IPTO in 1964). His famous memo to the "Intergalactic Computer Network" is dated "April 25, 1963." In 1964, Lick was succeeded by Sutherland, who served till 1966; he was followed by Taylor (66-69), Roberts (69-73), and Lick (again) 74-76.

There are a vast number of books and articles on this stuff: mine, Abbate's, Norberg & O'Neill, Zachary on Lick, Hafner & Lyon, etc. There is a vast amount of material still to be collected first hand.

To that end, we've begun publishing "memoirs" in *Matrix News*. Last August, a piece by Len Kleinrock; last month, part of an autobiography by Les Earnest; this issue, an essay by Mike Padlipsky (who says he doesn't believe that writing technohistory is possible); with more to come.

Last year, Alex McKenzie (BBN 1967-1976) posted the following:

> While it is true that the design of the ARPANET was not at all influenced by concerns about surviving a nuclear attack, it is also true that the designers of the ARPANET and other ARPA-sponsored networks were *always* concerned about "robustness", which means the ability to keep operating in spite of failures in individual nodes or the circuits connecting them. A key design feature of the ARPANET from its inception was the use of a distributed adaptive routing algorithm. "Distributed" in this context means that each node computed the routing it would use on the basis of inputs from its neighbors; thus there was no central "routing engine" whose failure or isolation would impare the ability of the nodes to use the current best route to a destination. "Adaptive" in this context means that so long as there was any path to a given destination a node would find it, and if there were multiple paths the node would find the "best" one. Thus the ARPANET was "survivable" from the beginning, although its modes of connectivity and number of alternate paths were insufficient to survive even a modest nuclear attack. It was an explicit goal of the ARPANET topologic design from 1969 through the decommisioning of ARPANET in the early 1990's that no single node or circuit failure would partition the network into two separate pieces (this goal was occasionally violated, notably for the connections to Hawaii and Europe, for the sake of expediency and it always caused trouble given the MTBF of both circuits and nodes in the 70's and 80's.

Paul Baran's Reports

Peter H. Salus <peter@mids.org>

Copyright © 2000 Matrix Information and Directory Services (MIDS)

In 1962, the Department of the Air Force asked the RAND Corporation to study the design parameters of digital data communications networks. [Project RAND-Contract No. AF 49(638)-700; monitored by the Directorate of Development Plans, USAF.] In 1964, RAND issued a dozen reports by Paul Baran (with some collaborators) under the group title *On Distributed Communications*. Baran had earned a BS in Electrical Engineering from Drexel, in his native Philadelphia, and an MS from UCLA. Among other things, he is the recipient of the IEEE's Alexander Graham Bell medal.

The final section of report 1 reads:

> Although it is premature at this time to know all the problems involved in such a network and understand all costs, there are reasons to suspect that we may not wish to build future digital communication networks exactly the same way the nation has built its analog telephone plant.
>
> There is an increasingly repeated statement made that one day we will require more capacity for data transmission than needed for analog voice transmission. If this statement is correct, then it would appear prudent to broaden our planning consideration to include new concepts for future data network directions. Otherwise, we may stumble into being boxed in with the uncomfortable restraints of communications links and switches originally designed for high quality analog transmission. New digital computer techniques using redundancy make cheap unreliable links potentially usable. A new switched network compatible with these links appears appropriate to meet the upcoming demand for digital service. This network is best designed for data transmission and for survivability at the outset.

The Reports are available to "qualified requestors" from the Defense Documentation Center

In an interview with the *Philadelphia Inquirer* last year, Baran remarked:

> Since the late 1950s, Baran had been theorizing on details of a communications system that might survive nuclear attack by shuttling digital data among interconnected computers spread all over the country.
>
> "It was the height of the Cold War," Baran recalled of the atmosphere that drove his research at the time. "There were threats going back and forth, and we were entering the Cuban missile crisis. They were crazy times."
>
> He said he didn't regard packet switching "as any great achievement." It just happened to be "the only solution I could think of for survivability," he said. [*5 May 1999*]

This having been said, what did the Reports contain? Here is the listing for all but the final one. This was "Security," and it is unavailable.

I. Introduction to Distributed Communications Networks, Paul Baran, RM-3420-PR.

> Introduces the system concept and outlines the requirements for and design considerations of the distributed digital data communications network. Considers especially the use of redundancy as a means of withstanding heavy enemy attacks. A general understanding of the proposal may be obtained by reading this volume and Vol. XI.

II. Digital Simulation of Hot-Potato Routing in a Broadband Distributed Communications Network, Sharla P. Boehm and Paul Baran, RM-3103-PR.

> Describes a computer simulation of the message routing scheme proposed. The basic routing doctrine permitted a network to suffer a large number of breaks, then reconstitute itself by rapidly relearning to make best use of the surviving links.

III. Determination of Path-Lengths in a Distributed Network, J. W. Smith, RM-3578-PR.

> Continues model simulation reported in Vol. II. The program was rewritten in a more powerful computer language allowing examination of larger networks. Modification of the routing doctrine by intermittently reducing the input data rate of local traffic reduced to a low level the number of message blocks taking excessively long paths. The level was so low that a deterministic equation was required in lieu of Monte Carlo to examine the now rare event of a long message block path. The results of both the simulation and the equation agreed in the area of overlapping validity.

IV. Priority, Precedence, and Overload, Paul Baran, RM-3638-PR.

The creation of dynamic or flexible priority and precedence structures within a communication system handling a mixture of traffic with different data rate, urgency, and importance levels is discussed. The goal chosen is optimum utilization of the communications resource within a seriously degraded and overloaded network.

V. History, Alternative Approaches, and Comparisons, Paul Baran, RM-3097-PR.

A background paper acknowledging the efforts of people in many fields working toward the development of large communications systems where system reliability and survivability are mandatory. A consideration of terminology is designed to acquaint the reader with the diverse, sometimes conflicting, definitions used. The evolution of the distributed network is traced, and a number of earlier hardware proposals are outlined.

VI. Mini-Cost Microwave, Paul Baran, RM-3762-PR.

The technical feasibility of constructing an extremely low-cost, all-digital, X- or Ku -band microwave relay system, operating at a multi-megabit per second data rate, is examined. The use of newly developed varactor multipliers permits the design of a miniature, all-solid-state microwave repeater powered by a thermoelectric converter burning L-P fuel.

VII. Tentative Engineering Specifications and Preliminary Design for a High-Data-Rate Distributed Network Switching Node, Paul Baran, RM-3763-PR.

High-speed, or "hot-potato," store-and-forward message block relaying forms the heart of the proposed information transmission system. The Switching Nodes are the units in which the camplex processing takes place. The node is described in sufficient engineering detail to estimate the components required. Timing calculations, together with a projected implementation scheme, provide a strong toundation for the belief that the construction and use of the node is practical.

VIII. The Multiplexing Station, Paul Baran, RM-3764-PR.

A description of the Multiplexing Stations which connect subscribers to the Switching Nodes. The presentation is in engineering detail, demonstrating how the network will simultaneously process traffic from up to 1024 separate users sending a mixture of start-stop teletypewriter, digital voice, and other synchronous signals at various rates.

IX. Security, Secrecy, and Tamper-Free Considerations, Paul Baran, RM-3765-PR

Considers the security aspects of a system of the type proposed, in which secrecy is of paramount importance. Describes the safeguards to be built into the network, and evaluates the premise that the existence of "spies" within the supposedly secure system must be anticipated. Security provisions are based on the belief that protection is best obtained by raising the "price" of espied information to a level which becomes excessive. The treatment of the subject is itself unclassified.

X. Cost Estimate, Paul Baran, RM-3766-PR.

A detailed cost estimate for the entire proposed system, based on an arbitrary network configuration of 400 Switching Nodes, servicing 100,000 simultaneous users via 200 Multiplexing Stations. Assuming a usable life of ten years, all costs, including operating costs, are estimated at about $60,000,000 per year.

XI. Summary Overview, Paul Baran, RM-3767-PR.

Summarizes the system proposal, highlighting the more important features. Considers the particular advantages of the distributed network, and conuents on disadvantages. An outline is given of the manner in which future research aimed at an actual implementation of the network might be conducted. Together with the introductory volume, it provides a general description of the entire system concept.

MEMORANDUM
RM-3420-PR
AUGUST 1964

ON DISTRIBUTED COMMUNICATIONS:
I. INTRODUCTION TO DISTRIBUTED COMMUNICATIONS NETWORKS

Paul Baran

This research is sponsored by the United States Air Force under Project RAND—Contract No. AF 49(638)-700 monitored by the Directorate of Development Plans, Deputy Chief of Staff, Research and Development, Hq USAF. Views or conclusions contained in this Memorandum should not be interpreted as representing the official opinion or policy of the United States Air Force.

DDC AVAILABILITY NOTICE
Qualified requesters may obtain copies of this report from the Defense Documentation Center (DDC).

The RAND Corporation
1700 MAIN ST · SANTA MONICA · CALIFORNIA · 90404

PREFACE

This Memorandum is one in a series of eleven RAND Memoranda detailing the Distributed Adaptive Message Block Network, a proposed digital data communications system based on a distributed network concept. Various items in the series deal with the concept in general and with its specific features, results of experimental modelings, engineering design considerations, and background and future implications.[*]

The series, entitled <u>On Distributed Communications</u>, is a part of The RAND Corporation's continuing program of research under U.S. Air Force Project RAND, and is related to research in the field of command and control and in governmental and military planning and policy making.

The present Memorandum, the first in the series, introduces the system concept and outlines the requirements for and design considerations of a digital data communications system based on the distributed concept, especially as regards implications for such systems in the 1970s. In particular, the Memorandum is directed toward examining the use of redundancy as one means of building communications systems to withstand heavy enemy attacks.

While highly survivable and reliable communications systems are of primary interest to those in the military concerned with automating command and control functions, the basic notions are also of interest to communications systems planners and designers having need to transmit digital data.

Various aspects of the concept as reported in this Memorandum were presented before selected Air Force audiences in the summer of 1961 in the form of a RAND briefing (B-265), and contained in RAND Paper P-2626, which this Memorandum supersedes.

---

[*] A list of all items in the series is found on p. 35.

SUMMARY

This Memorandum briefly reviews the distributed communications network concept and compares it to the hierarchical or more centralized systems. The payoff in terms of survivability for a distributed configuration in the cases of enemy attacks directed against nodes, links, or combinations of nodes and links is demonstrated.

The requirements for a future all-digital-data distributed network which provides common user service for a wide range of users having different requirements is considered. The use of a standard format message block permits building relatively simple switching mechanisms using an adaptive store-and-forward routing policy to handle all forms of digital data including "real-time" voice. This network rapidly responds to changes in the network status. Recent history of measured network traffic is used to modify path selection. Simulation results are shown to indicate that highly efficient routing can be performed by local control without the necessity for any central--and therefore vulnerable--control point.

A comparison is made between "diversity of assignment" and "perfect switching" in distributed networks. The high degree of connectivity afforded allows the use of low-cost links so unreliable as to be unusable in present type networks.

Note: page vi in the original document was blank.

FOREWORD

The series that this Memorandum introduces describes work on distributed communications. Originally, it was thought that each of the eleven volumes would be able to stand by itself. But, somewhere downstream it became clear that this goal could not be fully met, as each part hinged upon others. Therefore, publication of the individual Memoranda of the series was delayed in order to release the set as a whole.

While the resulting mound of paper forms a frightening pile, it need not all be read in depth, nor will all readers be interested in all the volumes. It is suggested that the present volume be read first especially if the reader is not familiar with its antecedents, B-265 or P-2626. Then the reader should advance directly to the summary overview in Vol. XI. Once in context, it will be easier to selectively examine the other papers of the series in more detail.

Two types of papers will be found. The first set, Vols. I, IV, V, IX, and XI, describes in general terms the underlying system philosophy and what this system approach has to offer. The second set, Vols. II, III, VI, VII, VIII, and X, describes in nuts-and-bolts detail one possible way of implementing the proposed mechanisms. The purpose of this second set is to supply the technical details of the proposed system in sufficient detail, it is hoped, to permit the reader to focus his questions on the potential feasibility of the system in a meaningful manner.

It should be stated at the outset that we are dealing with an extremely complicated system and one that is even more complicated to describe. It would be treacherously easy for the casual reader to dismiss the entire concept as impractically complicated--especially if he is unfamiliar with the ease with which logical transformations can be performed in a time-shared digital apparatus. The temptation to throw up one's hands and decide that it is all "too complicated," or to say, "It will require a mountain of equipment which we all know is unreliable," should be deferred until the fine print has been read.

In the interim, let us agree on what we mean when we speak of "complexity." It can be defined in several ways; for example, by size, by flexibility, or by number of components. But these are not identical measures. Consider an ancient electro-mechanical computer composed of bays of clacking relays. The logical diagrams are simple-- a few conceptually simple boxes perform almost trivial logical functions. But the physical dimensions of the package and the amount of maintenance effort required constitute a frightening aspect of complexity.

Conversely, consider a "shoe-box" of electronic equipment that performs all the functions the larger unit did, plus many new ones, and does them more quickly. It's smaller, more reliable, quieter, and requires less maintenance. But it may actually contain more components and its logical equations may be more difficult to comprehend. Is the shoebox more complex or less complex than its room-size electro-mechanical counterpart?

ACKNOWLEDGMENTS

In developing this work, I received a large number of excellent ideas and suggestions--so many, in fact, that it has become impossible to fully acknowledge each person who has contributed in some way without unduly lengthening these manuscripts.

I wish to take this opportunity to thank the following contributors, each of whom reviewed one or more of the Memoranda in the series and who offered highly appreciated and accepted suggestions. The process of review of a manuscript does not necessarily imply full agreement with all that is said, so I alone must accept responsibility for any mistakes in the work.

Reviewers included:[*] Marvin Adelson (National Academy of Sciences), C. L. Baker, Edward Bedrosian, Sharla Boehm, J. L. Bower, J. B. Carne, L. J. Craig, J. I. Derr, F. E. Eldridge (Office of the Assistant Secretary of Defense, Comptroller), T. O. Ellis, James Farmer, N. E. Feldman, H. Hambrock (North Electric Company), W. B. Holland, J. L. Hult, C. B. Laning (System Development Corporation), C. R. Lindholm, I. S. Reed, E. E. Reinhart, R. H. Scherer (Office of the Director of Defense Research and Engineering), J. W. Smith, Harold Steingold, C. G. Svala (North Electric Company), Rein Turn, K. W. Uncapher, T. G. Williams (Philco Corporation).

---

[*]Unless otherwise noted, those listed are with The RAND Corporation.

Note: page x in the original document was blank.

CONTENTS

PREFACE iii

SUMMARY v

FOREWORD vii

ACKNOWLEDGMENTS ix

Section
- I. INTRODUCTION 1
- II. EXAMINATION OF A DISTRIBUTED NETWORK 3
  - Node Destruction 6
  - Link Destruction 9
  - Combination Link and Node Destruction 9
- III. DIVERSITY OF ASSIGNMENT 13
  - Simulation 13
  - Comparison with Present Systems 15
- IV. ON A FUTURE SYSTEM DEVELOPMENT 16
  - Future Low-Cost All-Digital Communications Links 17
  - Variable Data Rate Links 19
  - Variable Data Rate Users 19
  - Common User 20
  - Standard Message Block 20
  - Switching 23
  - Forgetting and Imperfect Learning 30
  - Lowest-Cost Path 33
- V. WHERE WE STAND TODAY 34

LIST OF PUBLICATIONS IN THE SERIES 35

I. INTRODUCTION

Let us consider the synthesis of a communication network which will allow several hundred major communications stations to talk with one another after an enemy attack. As a criterion of survivability we elect to use the percentage of stations both surviving the physical attack and remaining in electrical connection with the largest single group of surviving stations. This criterion is chosen as a conservative measure of the ability of the surviving stations to operate together as a coherent entity after the attack. This means that small groups of stations isolated from the single largest group are considered to be ineffective.

Although one can draw a wide variety of networks, they all factor into two components: centralized (or star) and distributed (or grid or mesh) (see Fig. 1).

The centralized network is obviously vulnerable as destruction of a single central node destroys communication between the end stations. In practice, a mixture of star and mesh components is used to form communications networks. For example, type (b) in Fig. 1 shows the hierarchical structure of a set of stars connected in the form of a larger star with an additional link forming a loop. Such a network is sometimes called a "decentralized" network, because complete reliance upon a single point is not always required.

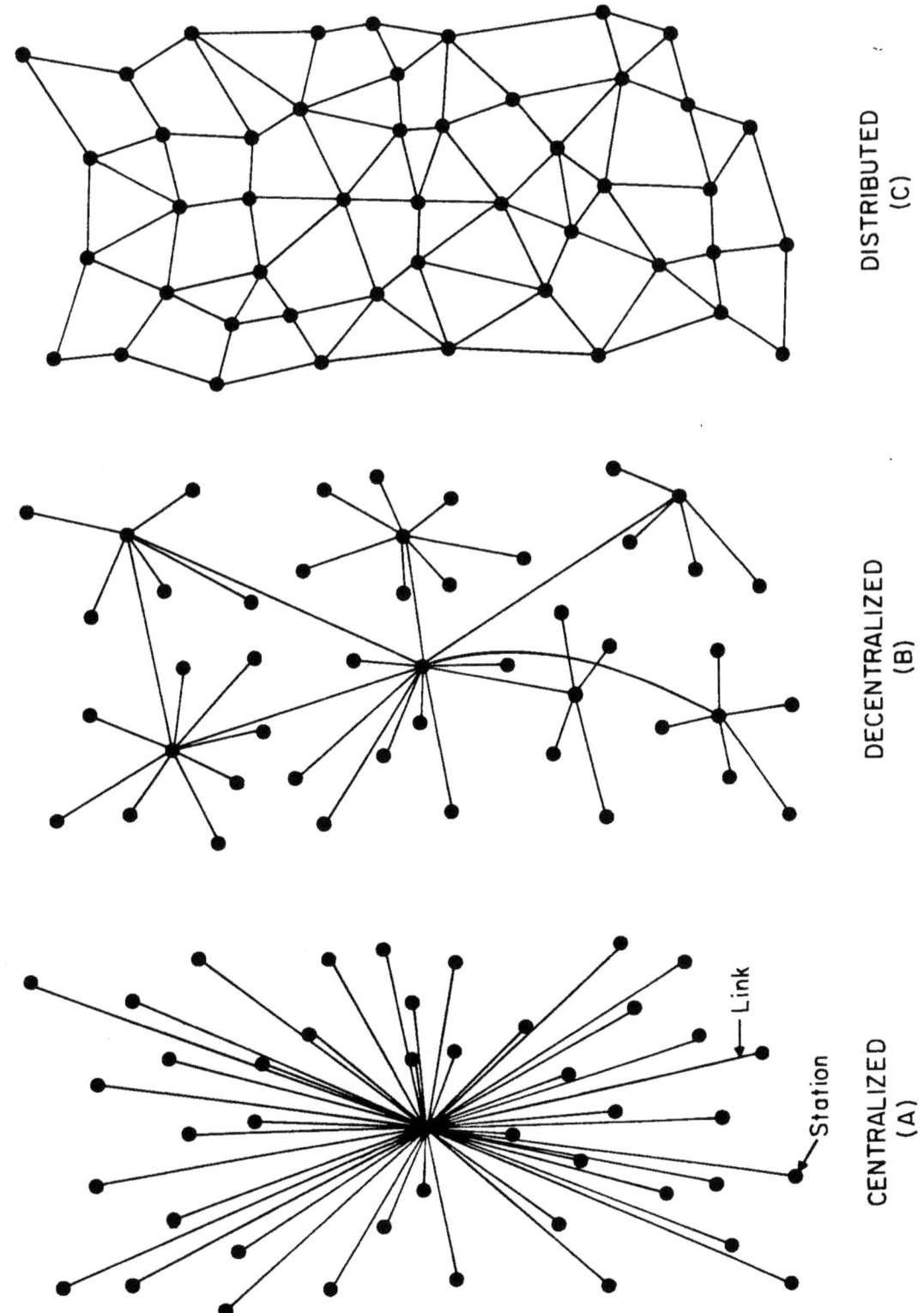

FIG. 1 — Centralized, Decentralized and Distributed Networks

II. EXAMINATION OF A DISTRIBUTED NETWORK

Since destruction of a small number of nodes in a decentralized network can destroy communications, the properties, problems, and hopes of building "distributed" communications networks are of paramount interest.

The term "redundancy level" is used as a measure of connectivity, as defined in Fig. 2. A minimum span network, one formed with the smallest number of links possible, is chosen as a reference point, and is called "a network of redundancy level one." If two times as many links are used in a gridded network than in a minimum span network, the network is said to have a redundancy level of two. Figure 2 defines connectivity of levels 1, 1½, 2, 3, 4, 6, and 8. Redundancy level is equivalent to link-to-node ratio in an infinite size array of stations. Obviously, at levels above three there are alternate methods of constructing the network. However, it was found that there is little difference regardless of which method is used. Such an alternate method is shown for levels three and four, labelled R'. This specific alternate mode is also used for levels six and eight.*

Each node and link in the array of Fig. 2 has the capacity and the switching flexibility to allow transmission between any ith station and any jth station, provided a path can be drawn from the ith to the jth station.

Starting with a network composed of an array of stations connected as in Fig. 3, an assigned percentage of nodes and links is destroyed. If, after this operation, it is still possible to draw a line to connect the ith station to the jth station, the ith and jth stations are said to be connected.

---

*See Craig, L. J., and I. S. Reed, "Overlapping Tessellated Communications Networks," *IRE Trans. Comm. Sys.*, CS-10 (1962) 125-129.

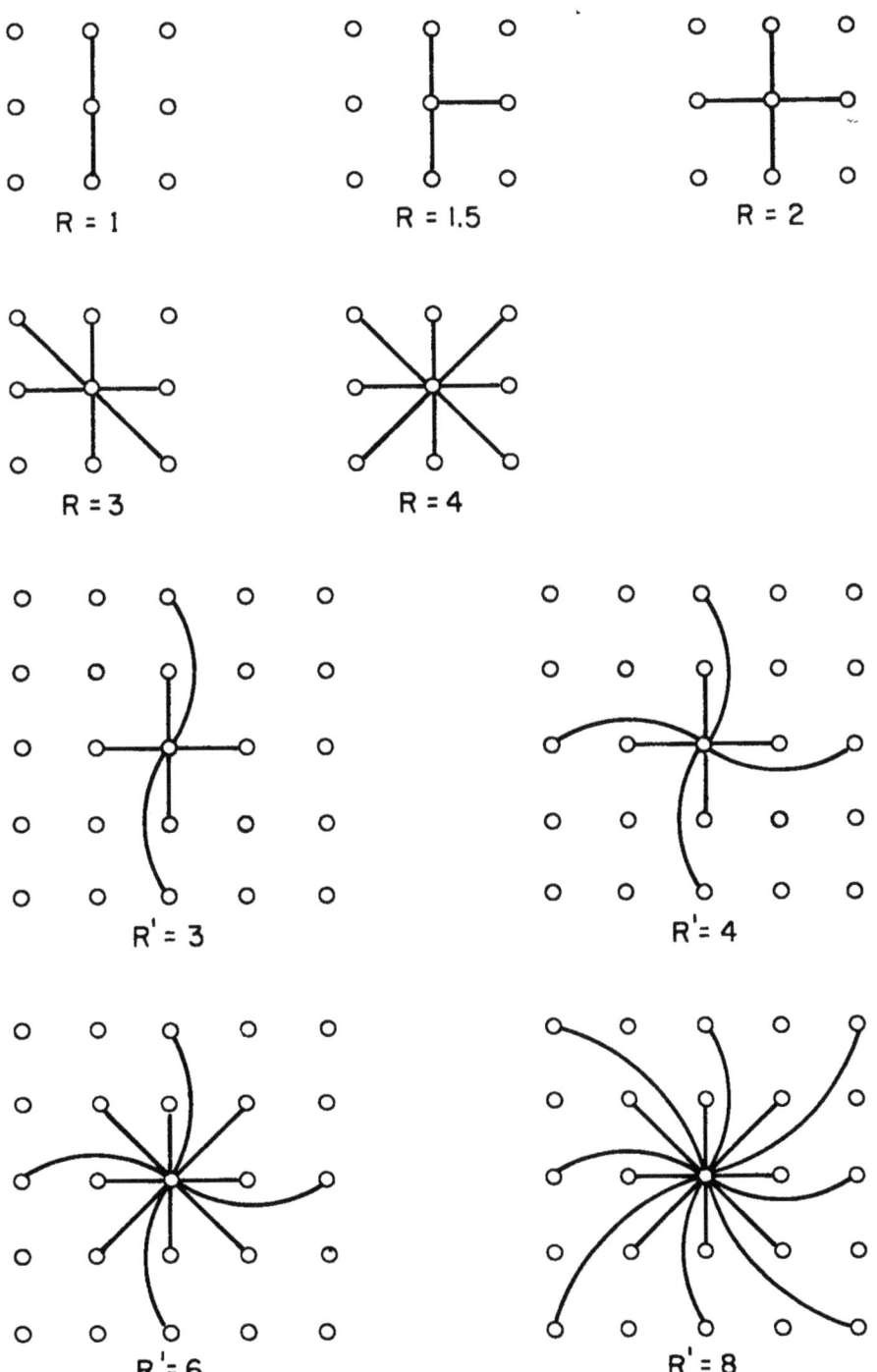

FIG. 2 — Definition of Redundancy Level

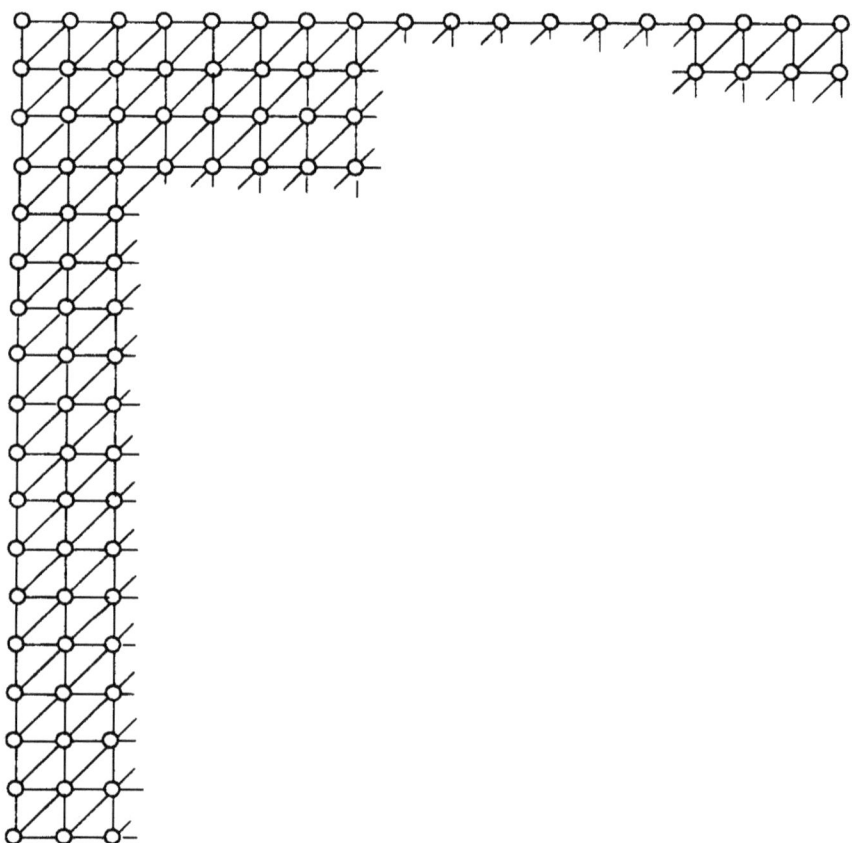

FIG. 3 — An Array of Stations

NODE DESTRUCTION

Figure 4 indicates network performance as a function of the probability of destruction for each separate node. If the expected "noise" was destruction caused by conventional hardware failure, the failures would be randomly distributed through the network. But, if the disturbance were caused by enemy attack, the possible "worst cases" must be considered.

To bisect a 32-link network requires direction of 288 weapons each with a probability of kill, $p_k = 0.5$, or 160 with a $p_k = 0.7$, to produce over an 0.9 probability of successfully bisecting the network. If hidden alternative command is allowed, then the largest single group would still have an expected value of almost 50 per cent of the initial stations surviving intact. If this raid misjudges complete availability of weapons, or complete knowledge of all links in the cross section, or the effects of the weapons against each and every link, the raid fails. The high risk of such raids against highly parallel structures causes examination of alternative attack policies. Consider the following uniform raid example. Assume that 2,000 weapons are deployed against a 1000-station network. The stations are so spaced that destruction of two stations with a single weapon is unlikely. Divide the 2,000 weapons into two equal 1000-weapon salvos. Assume any probability of destruction of a single node from a single weapon less than 1.0; for example, 0.5. Each weapon on the first salvo has a 0.5 probability of destroying its target. But, each weapon of the second salvo has only a 0.25 probability, since one-half the targets have already been destroyed. Thus, the uniform attack is felt to represent a known worst-case configuration in the following analysis.

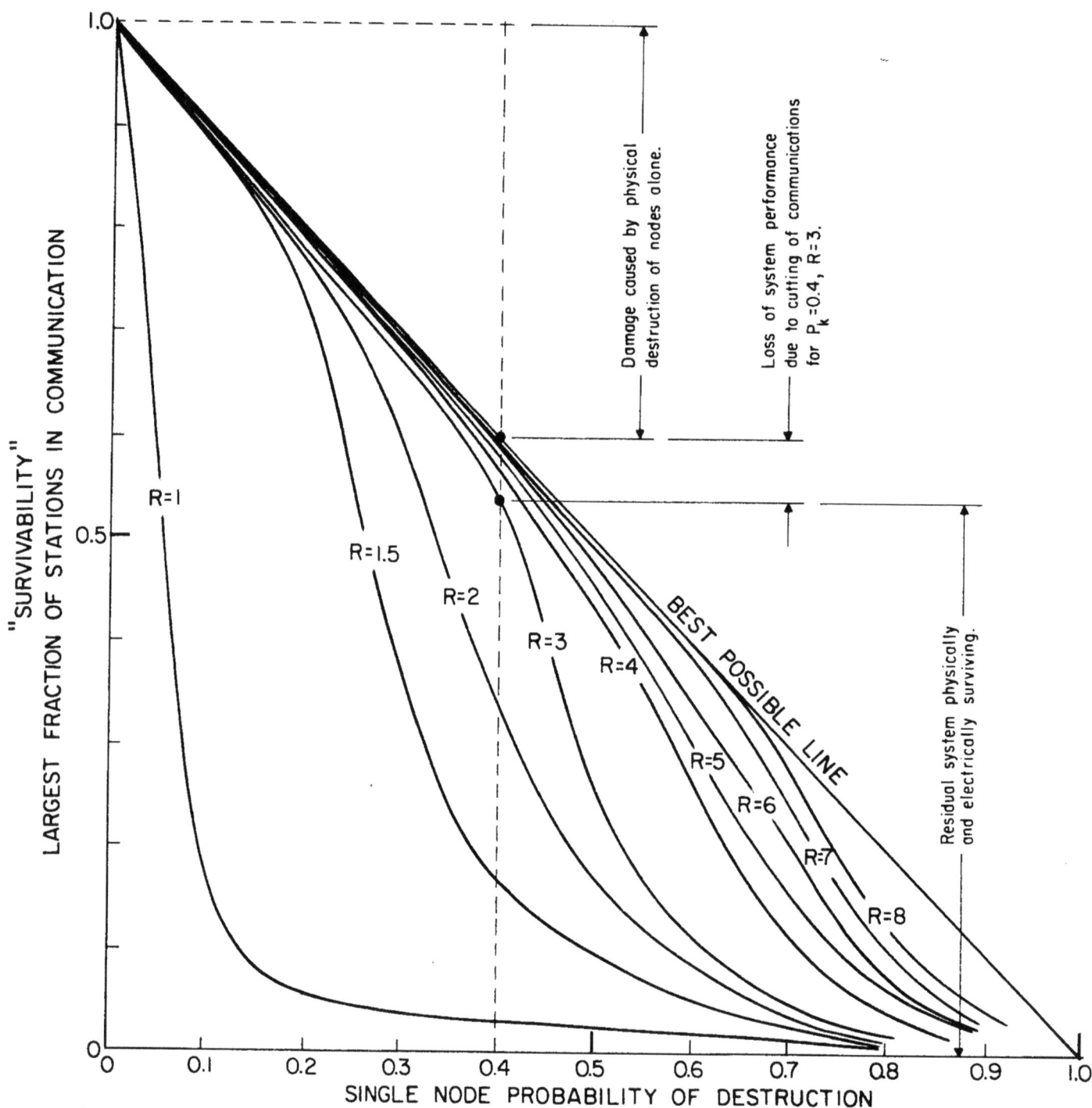

FIG. 4 — Perfect Switching in a Distributed Network — Sensitivity to Node Destruction, 100% of Links Operative.

Such worst-case attacks have been directed against an 18x18-array network model of 324 nodes with varying probability of kill and redundancy level, with results shown in Fig. 4. The probability of kill was varied from zero to unity along the abscissa while the ordinate marks survivability. The criterion of survivability used is the percentage of stations not physically destroyed and remaining in communications with the largest single group of surviving stations. The curves of Fig. 4 demonstrate survivability as a function of attack level for networks of varying degrees of redundancy. The line labeled "best possible line" marks the upper bound of loss due to the physical failure component alone. For example, if a network underwent an attack of 0.5 probability destruction of each of its nodes, then only 50 per cent of its nodes would be expected to survive--regardless of how perfect its communications. We are primarily interested in the additional system degradation caused by failure of communications. Two key points are to be noticed in the curves of Fig. 4. First, extremely survivable networks can be built using a moderately low redundancy of connectivity level. Redundancy levels on the order of only three permit withstanding extremely heavy level attacks with negligible additional loss to communications. Secondly, the survivability curves have sharp break-points. A network of this type will withstand an increasing attack level until a certain point is reached, beyond which the network rapidly deteriorates. Thus, the optimum degree of redundancy can be chosen as a function of the expected level of attack. Further redundancy buys little. The redundancy level required to survive even very heavy attacks is not great--on the order of only three or four times that of the minimum span network.

LINK DESTRUCTION

In the previous example we have examined network performance as a function of the destruction of the nodes (which are better targets than links). We shall now re-examine the same network, but using unreliable links. In particular, we want to know how unreliable the links may be without further degrading the performance of the network.

Figure 5 shows the results for the case of perfect nodes; only the links fail. There is little system degradation caused even using extremely unreliable links—on the order of 50 per cent down-time—assuming all nodes are working.

COMBINATION LINK AND NODE DESTRUCTION

The worst case is the composite effect of failures of both the links and the nodes. Figure 6 shows the effect of link failure upon a network having 40 per cent of its nodes destroyed. It appears that what would today be regarded as an unreliable link can be used in a distributed network almost as effectively as perfectly reliable links. Figure 7 examines the result of 100 trial cases in order to estimate the probability density distribution of system performance for a mixture of node and link failures. This is the distribution of cases for 20 per cent nodal damage and 35 per cent link damage.

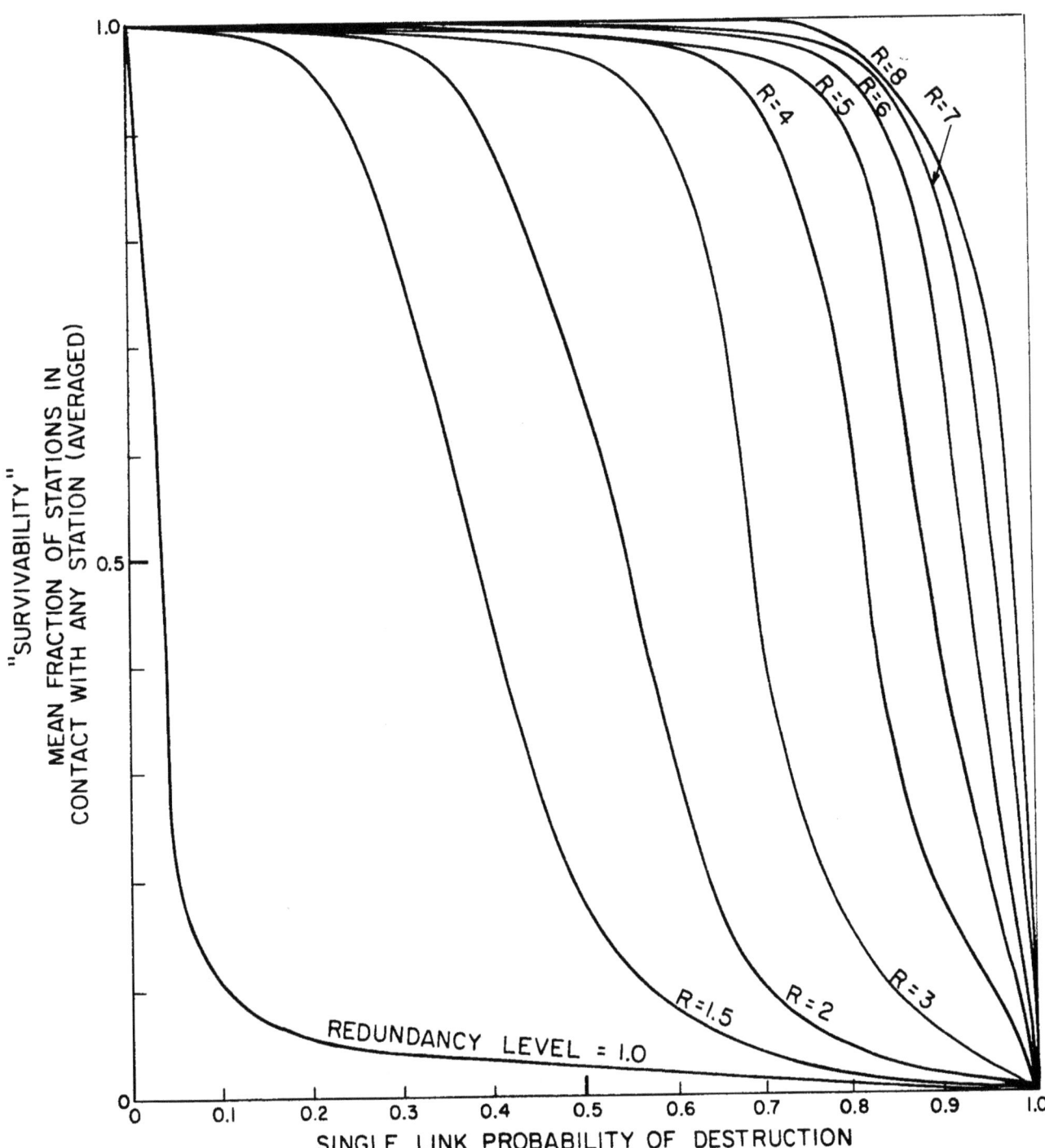

FIG. 5 — Perfect Switching in a Distributed Network — Sensitivity to Link Destruction, 100% of Nodes Operative.

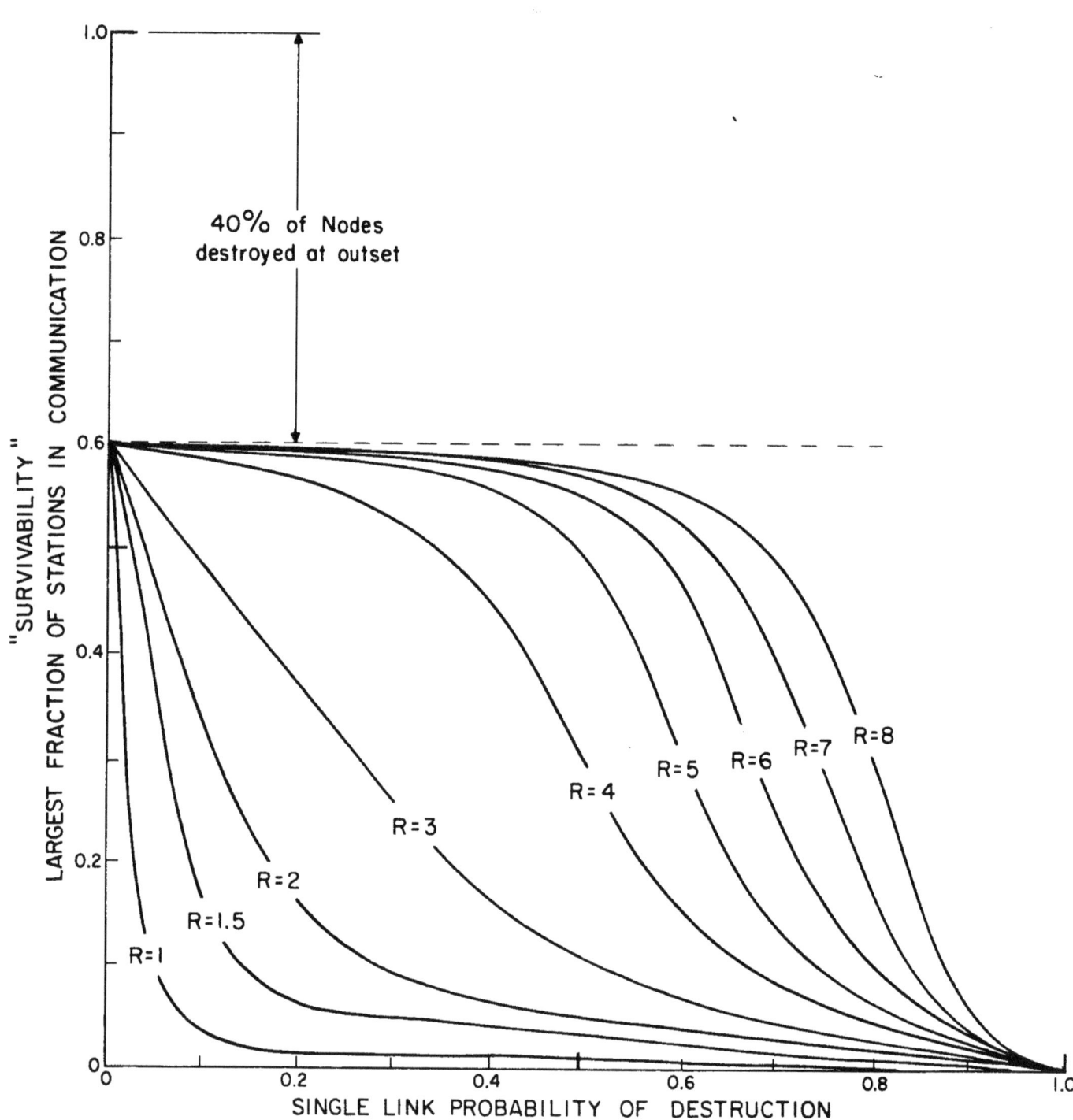

FIG. 6 — Perfect Switching in a Distributed Network — Sensitivity to Link Destruction After 40% Nodes Are Destroyed.

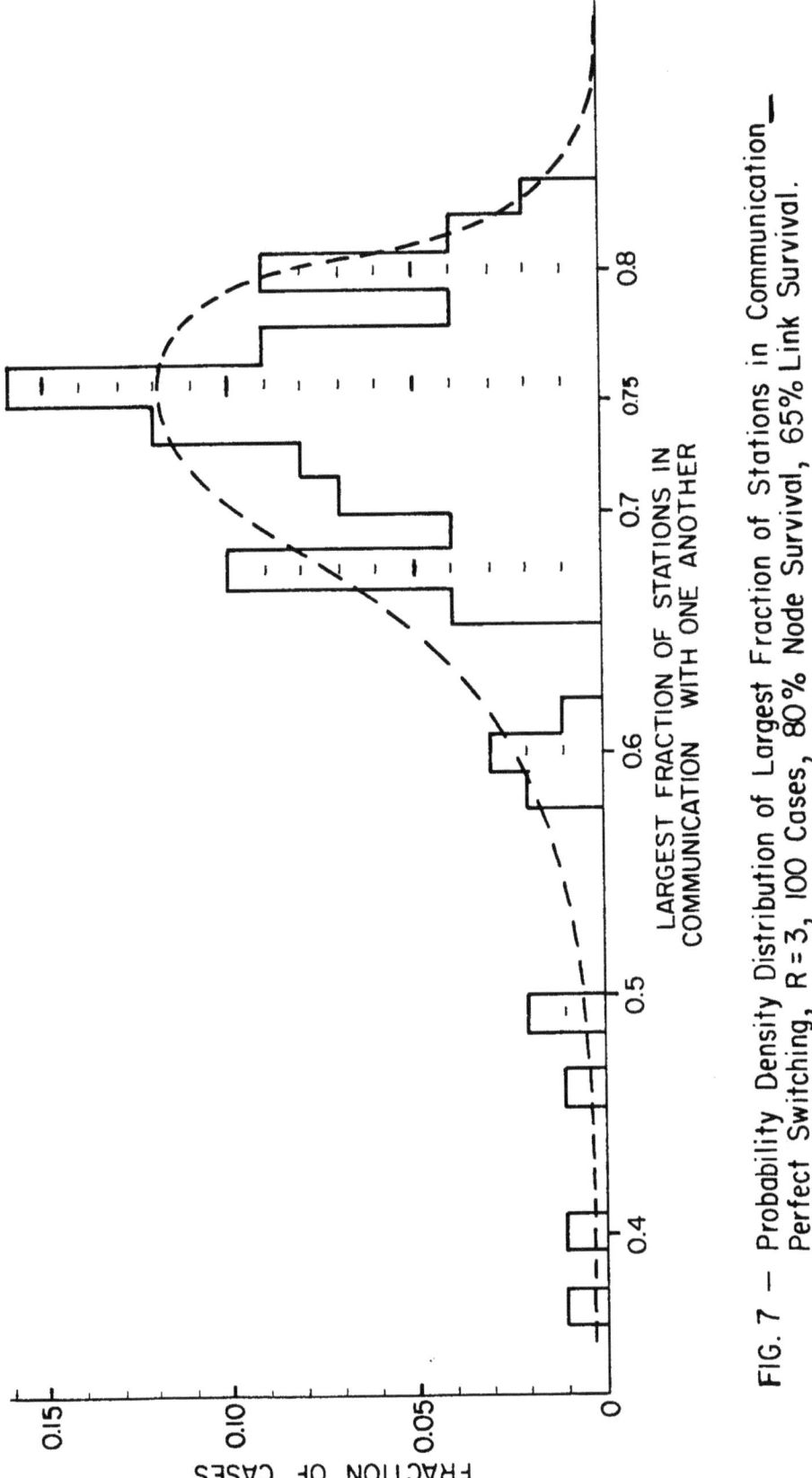

FIG. 7 — Probability Density Distribution of Largest Fraction of Stations in Communication Perfect Switching, R = 3, 100 Cases, 80% Node Survival, 65% Link Survival.

III. DIVERSITY OF ASSIGNMENT

There is another and more common technique for using redundancy than in the method described above in which each station is assumed to have perfect switching ability. This alternative approach is called "diversity of assignment." In diversity of assignment, switching is not required. Instead, a number of independent paths are selected between each pair of stations in a network which requires reliable communications. But, there are marked differences in performance between distributed switching and redundancy of assignment as revealed by the following Monte Carlo simulation.

SIMULATION

In the matrix of N separate stations, each $i\underline{th}$ station is connected to every $j\underline{th}$ station by three shortest but totally separate independent paths ($i=1,2,3,...,N$; $j=1,2,3,...,N$; $i \neq j$). A raid is laid against the network. Each of the pre-assigned separate paths from the $i\underline{th}$ station to the $j\underline{th}$ station is examined. If one or more of the pre-assigned paths survive, communication is said to exist between the $i\underline{th}$ and the $j\underline{th}$ station. The criterion of survivability used is the mean number of stations connected to each station, averaged over all stations.

Figure 8 shows, unlike the distributed perfect switching case, that there is a marked loss in communications capability with even slightly unreliable nodes or links. The difference can be visualized by remembering that fully flexible switching permits the communicator the privilege of ex post facto decision of paths. Figure 8 emphasizes a key difference between some present day networks and the fully flexible distributed network we are discussing.

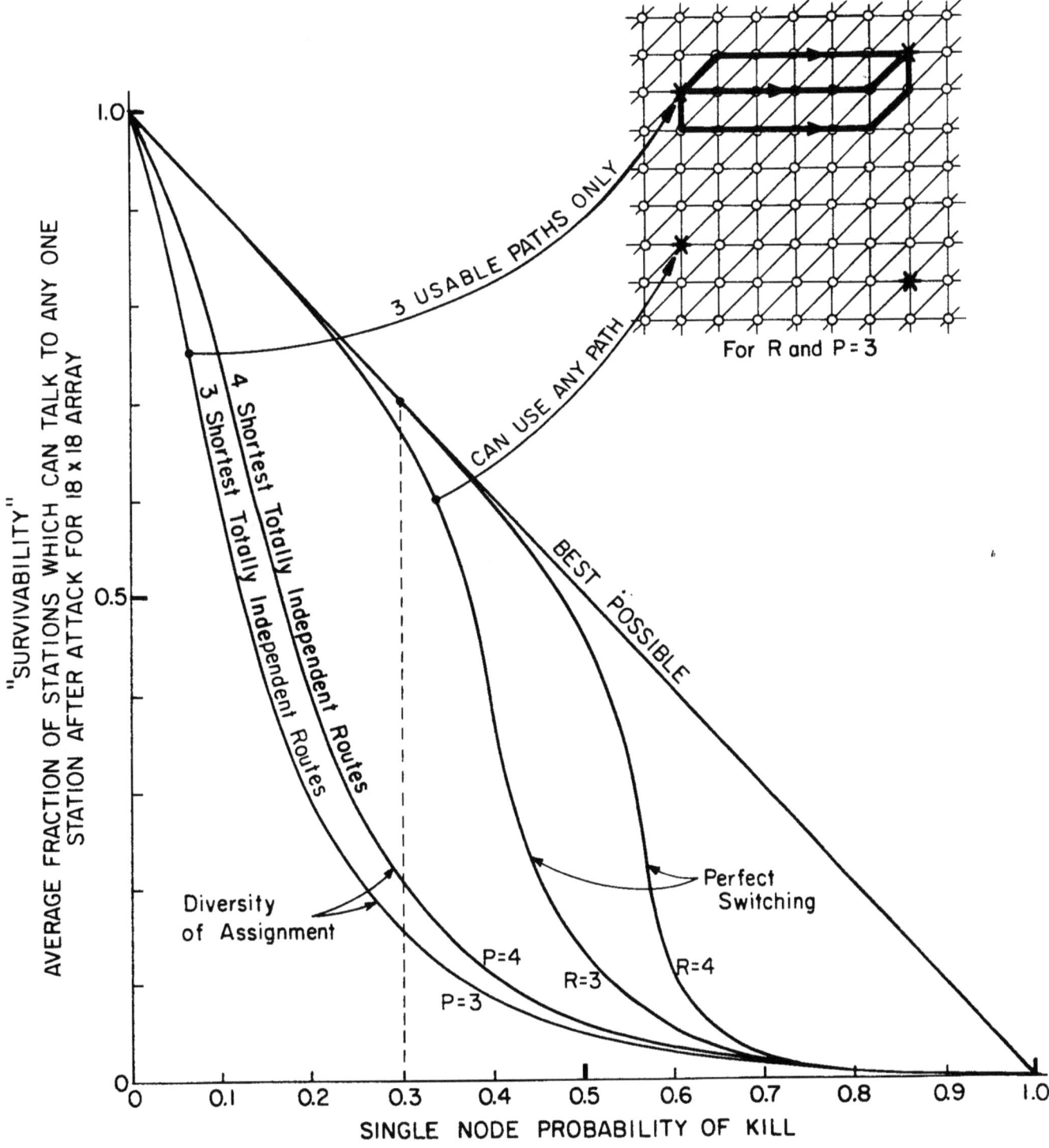

FIG. 8 — Diversity of Assignment vs. Perfect Switching in a Distributed Network.

COMPARISON WITH PRESENT SYSTEMS

Present conventional switching systems try only a small subset of the potential paths that can be drawn on a gridded network. The greater the percentage of potential paths tested, the closer one approaches the performance of perfect switching. Thus, perfect switching provides an upper bound of expected system performance for a gridded network; the diversity of assignment case, a lower bound. Between these two limits lie systems composed of a mixture of switched routes and diversity of assignment.

Diversity of assignment is useful for short paths, eliminating the need for switching, but requires survivability and reliability for each tandem element in long haul circuits passing through many nodes. As every component in at least one out of a _small_ number of possible paths must be simultaneously operative, high reliability margins and full standby equipment are usual.

IV. ON A FUTURE SYSTEM DEVELOPMENT

We will soon be living in an era in which we cannot guarantee survivability of any single point. However, we can still design systems in which system destruction requires the enemy to pay the price of destroying n of n stations. If n is made sufficiently large, it can be shown that highly survivable system structures can be built--even in the thermonuclear era. In order to build such networks and systems we will have to use a large number of elements. We are interested in knowing how inexpensive these <u>elements</u> may be and still permit the <u>system</u> to operate reliably. There is a strong relationship between element cost and element reliability. To design a system that must anticipate a worst-case destruction of both enemy attack and normal system failures, one can combine the failures expected by enemy attack together with the failures caused by normal reliability problems, provided the enemy does not know which elements are inoperative. Our future systems design problem is that of building very reliable systems out of the described set of unreliable elements at lowest cost. In choosing the communications links of the future, digital links appear increasingly attractive by permitting low-cost switching and low-cost links. For example, if "perfect switching"[*] is used, digital links are mandatory to permit tandem connection of many separately connected links without cumulative errors reaching an irreducible magnitude. Further, the signaling measures to implement

---

[*]See ODC-V. (ODC is an abbreviation of the series title, <u>On Distributed Communications</u>; the number following refers to the volume in the series. See list on p. 35.)

highly flexible switching doctrines always require digits.

FUTURE LOW-COST ALL-DIGITAL COMMUNICATIONS LINKS

When one designs an entire system optimized for digits and high redundancy, certain new communications link techniques appear more attractive than those common today.

A key attribute of the new media is that it permits formation of <u>new routes</u> cheaply, yet allows transmission on the order of a million or so bits per second, high enough to be economic, but yet low enough to be inexpensively processed with existing digital computer techniques at the relay station nodes. Reliability and raw error rates are secondary. The network must be built with the expectation of heavy damage, anyway. Powerful error removal methods exist.

Some of the communication construction methods that look attractive in the near future include pulse regenerative repeater line, minimum-cost or "mini-cost" microwave, TV broadcast station digital transmission, and satellites.

Pulse Regenerative Repeater Line

Samuel B. Morse's regenerative repeater invention for amplifying weak telegraphic signals has recently been resurrected and transistorized. Morse's electrical relay permits amplification of weak binary telegraphic signals above a fixed threshold. Experiments by various organizations (primarily the Bell Telephone Laboratories) have shown that digital data rates on the order of 1.5 million bits per second can be transmitted over ordinary telephone line at repeater spacings on the order of 6,000 feet for #22 gage pulp paper insulated copper pairs. At present, more than 20 tandemly connected amplifiers have been used in the Bell System T-1 PCM multiplexing system without retiming synchronization problems. There appears to be no fundamental reason why either lines of lower loss, with corresponding further repeater spacing, or more powerful resynchronization methods cannot be used to extend link distances to in excess of 200 miles. Such distances would be desired for a possible national distributed network.

Power to energize the miniature transistor amplifier is transmitted over the copper circuit itself.

"Mini-Cost" Microwave

While the price of microwave equipment has been declining, there are still untapped major savings. In an analog signal network we require a high degree of reliability and very low distortion for a long string of tandem repeaters. However, using digital modulation together with perfect switching we minimize these two expensive considerations from our planning. We would envision the use of low-power, mass-produced microwave receiver/transmitter units mounted on low-cost, short, guyed towers. Relay station spacing would probably be on the order of 20 miles. Further economies can be obtained by only a minimal use of standby equipment and reduction of fading margins. The ability to use alternate paths permits consideration of frequencies normally troubled by rain attenuation problems reducing the spectrum availability problem.

Preliminary indications suggest that this approach appears to be the cheapest way of building large networks of the type to be described (see ODC-VI).

TV Stations

With proper siting of receiving antennas, broadcast television stations might be used to form additional high data rate links in emergencies.*

Satellites

The problem of building a reliable network using satellites is somewhat similar to that of building a communications network with unreliable links. When a satellite is overhead, the link is operative. When a satellite is not overhead, the link is out of service. Thus, such links are highly compatible with the type of system to be described.

VARIABLE DATA RATE LINKS

In a conventional circuit switched system each of the tandem links requires matched transmission bandwidths. In order to make fullest use of a digital link, the post-error-removal data rate would have to vary, as it is a function of noise level. The problem then is to build a communication network made up of links of variable data rate to use the communication resource most efficiently.

VARIABLE DATA RATE USERS

We can view both the links and the entry point nodes of a multiple-user all-digital communications system as elements operating at an ever changing data rate. From instant to instant the demand for transmission will vary.

---

*Baran, P., <u>Coverage Estimate of FM, TV and Power Facilities Useful in a Broadband Distributed Network</u> (UFOUO), The RAND Corporation, RM-3008-PR, March 1962.

We would like to take advantage of the average demand over all users instead of having to allocate a full peak demand channel to each. Bits can become a common denominator of loading for economic charging of customers. We would like to efficiently handle both those users who make highly intermittent bit demands on the network, and those who make long-term continuous, low bit demands.

COMMON USER

In communications, as in transportation, it is more economical for many users to share a common resource rather than each to build his own system--particularly when supplying intermittent or occasional service. This intermittency of service is highly characteristic of digital communication requirements. Therefore, we would like to consider the interconnection, one day, of many all-digital links to provide a resource optimized for the handling of data for many potential intermittent users--a new common-user system.

Figure 9 demonstrates the basic notion. A wide mixture of different digital transmission links is combined to form a common resource divided among many potential users. But, each of these communications links could possibly have a different data rate. Therefore, we shall next consider how links of different data rates may be interconnected.

STANDARD MESSAGE BLOCK

Present common carrier communications networks, used for digital transmission, use links and concepts originally

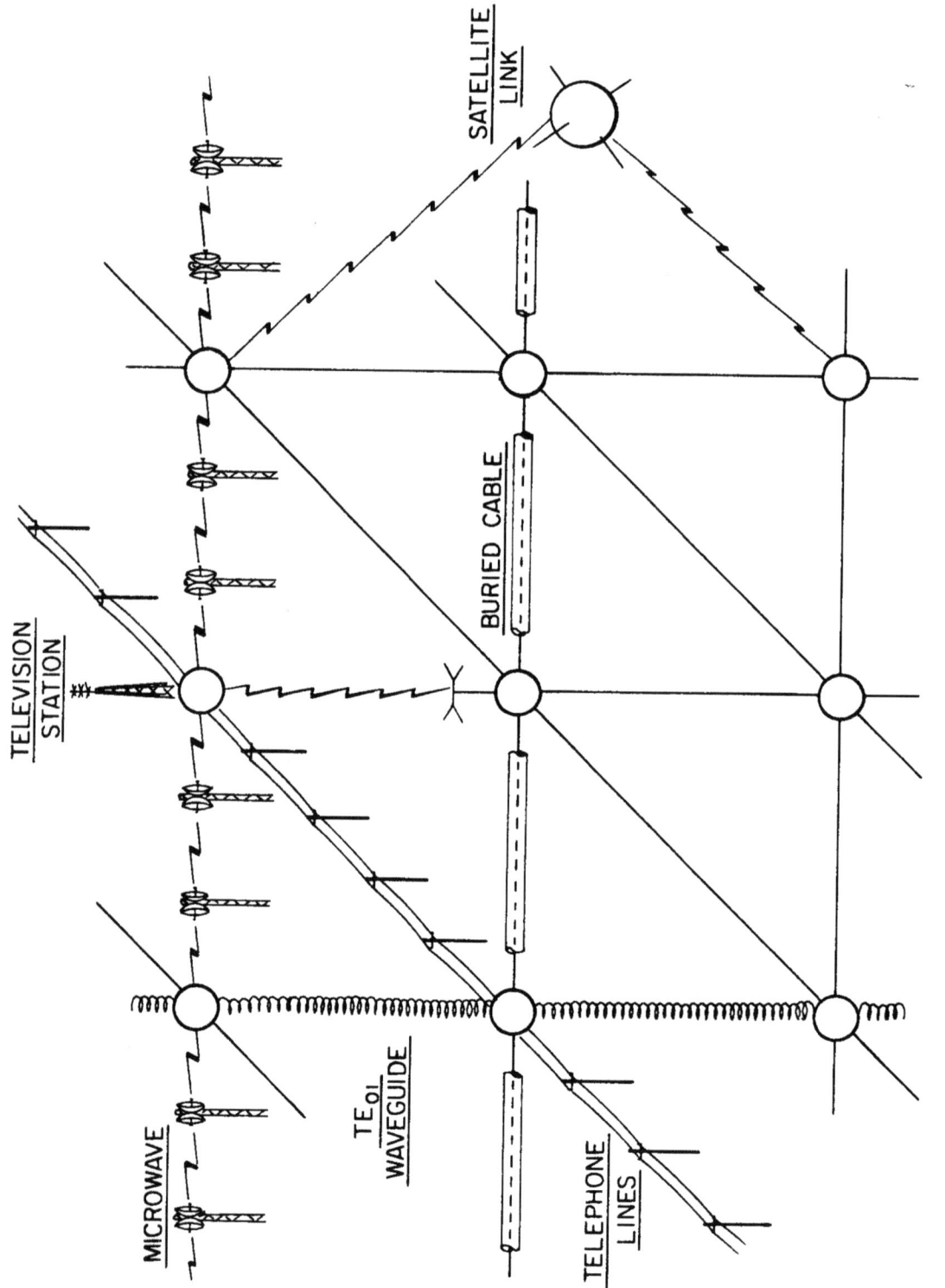

FIG. 9 – All Digital Network Composed of Mixture of Links

designed for another purpose--voice. These systems are built around a frequency division multiplexing link-to-link interface standard. The standard between links is that of data rate. Time division multiplexing appears so natural to data transmission that we might wish to consider an alternative approach--a standardized message block as a network interface standard. While a standardized message block is common in many computer-communications applications, no serious attempt has ever been made to use it as a universal standard. A universally standardized message block would be composed of perhaps 1024 bits. Most of the message block would be reserved for whatever type data is to be transmitted, while the remainder would contain housekeeping information such as error detection and routing data, as in Fig. 10.

As we move to the future, there appears to be an increasing need for a standardized message block for all-digital communications networks. As data rates increase, the velocity of propagation over long links

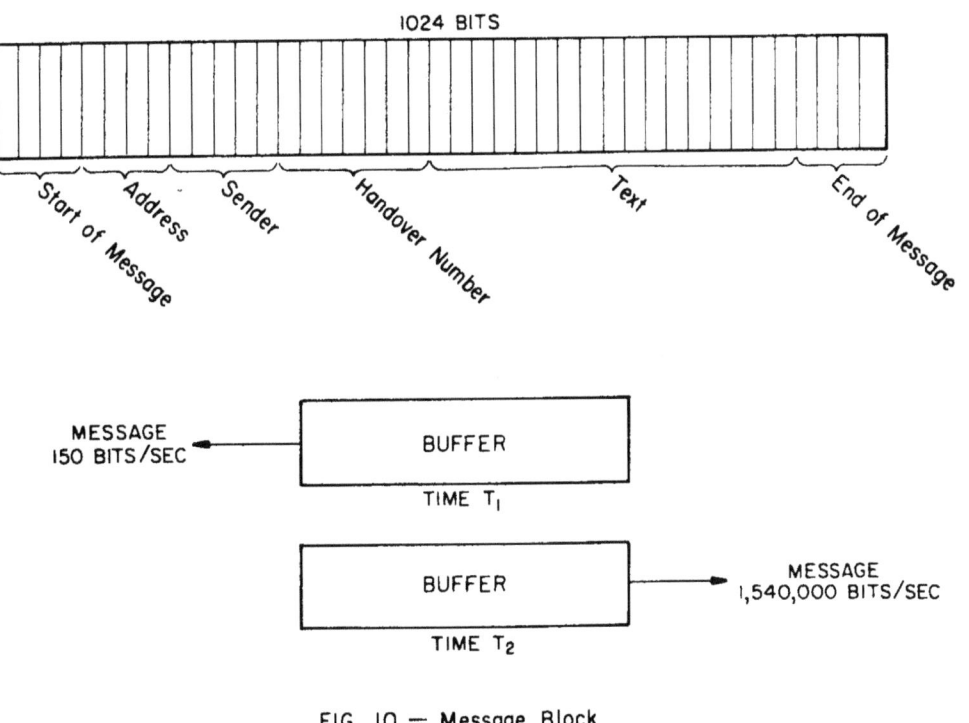

FIG. 10 — Message Block

becomes an increasingly important consideration.* We soon reach a point where more time is spent setting the switches in a conventional circuit switched system for short holding-time messages than is required for actual transmission of the data.

Most importantly, standardized data blocks permit many simultaneous users each with widely different bandwidth requirements to economically share a broadband network made up of varied data rate links. The standardized message block simplifies construction of very high speed switches. Every user connected to the network can feed data at any rate up to a maximum value. The user's traffic is stored until a full data block is received by the first station. This block is rubber stamped with a heading and return address, plus additional housekeeping information. Then, it is transmitted into the network.

SWITCHING

In order to build a network with the survivability properties shown in Fig. 4, we must use a switching scheme able to find any possible path that might exist after heavy damage. The routing doctrine should find the shortest possible path and avoid self-oscillatory or "ring-around-the-rosey" switching.

We shall explore the possibilities of building a "real-time" data transmission system using store-and-forward techniques. The high data rates of the future

---

*3000 miles at $\simeq$ 150,000 miles/sec. $\simeq$ 50 milliseconds transmission time, T.
  1024-bit message at 1,500,000 bits/sec. $\simeq$ 2/3 millisecond message time, M.
  $\therefore$ T>>M

carry us into a hybrid zone between store-and-forward and circuit switching. The system to be described is clearly store-and-forward if one examines the operations at each node singularly. But, the network user who has called up a "virtual connection" to an end station and has transmitted messages across the United States in a fraction of a second might also view the system as a <u>black box providing an apparent circuit connection</u> across the U.S. There are two requirements that must be met to build such a quasi-real-time system. First, the in-transit storage at each node should be minimized to prevent undesirable time delays. Secondly, the shortest instantaneously available path through the network should be found with the expectation that the status of the network will be rapidly changing. Microwave will be subject to fading interruptions and there will be rapid moment-to-moment variations in input loading. These problems place difficult requirements upon the switching. However, the development of digital computer technology has advanced so rapidly that it now appears possible to satisfy these requirements by a moderate amount of digital equipment. What is envisioned is a network of unmanned digital switches implementing a self-learning policy at each node so that overall traffic is effectively routed in a changing environment--without need for a central and possibly vulnerable control point. One particularly simple routing scheme examined is called the "hot-potato" heuristic routing doctrine and will be described in detail.

Torn-tape telegraph repeater stations and our mail system provide examples of conventional store-and-forward switching systems. In these systems, messages are relayed from station-to-station and stacked until the "best" outgoing link is free. The key feature of store-and-forward transmission is that it allows a high line occupancy factor by storing so many messages at each node that there is a backlog of traffic awaiting transmission. But, the price for link efficiency is the price paid in storage capacity and time delay. However, it was found that <u>most of the advantages of store-and-forward switching could be obtained with extremely little storage</u> at the nodes.

Thus, in the system to be described, each node will attempt to get rid of its messages by choosing alternate routes if its preferred route is busy or destroyed. Each message is regarded as a "hot potato," and rather than hold the "hot potato," the node tosses the message to its neighbor, who will now try to get rid of the message.

The Postman Analogy

The switching process in any store-and-forward system is analogous to a postman sorting mail. A postman sits at each switching node. Messages arrive simultaneously from all links. The postman records bulletins describing the traffic loading status for each of the outgoing links. With proper status information, the postman is able to determine the best direction to send out any letters. So far, this mechanism is general and applicable to all store-and-forward communication systems.

Assuming symmetrical bi-directional links, the postman can infer the "best" paths to transmit mail to any station merely by looking at the cancellation time or the equivalent handover number tag. If the postman sitting in the center of the United States received letters from San Francisco, he would find that letters from San Francisco arriving from channels to the west would come in with later cancellation dates than if such letters had arrived in a roundabout manner from the east. Each letter carries an implicit indication of its length of transmission path. The astute postman can then deduce that the best channel to send a message _to_ San Francisco is probably the link associated with the latest cancellation dates of messages _from_ San Francisco. By observing the cancellation dates for all letters in transit, information is derived to route _future_ traffic. The return address and cancellation date of recent letters is sufficient to determine the best direction in which to _send_ subsequent letters.

Hot-Potato Heuristic Routing Doctrine

To achieve real-time operation it is desirable to respond to change in network status as quickly as possible, so we shall seek to derive the network status information directly from each message block.

Each standardized message block contains a "to" address, a "from" address, a handover number tag, and error detecting bits together with other housekeeping data. The message block is analogous to a letter. The "from" address is equivalent to the return address of the letter.

The handover number is a tag in each message block set to zero upon initial transmission of the message block into the network. Every time the message block is passed on, the handover number is incremented. The handover number tag on each message block indicates the length of time in the network or path length. This tag is somewhat analogous to the cancellation date of a conventional letter.

The Handover Number Table. While cancellation dates could conceivably be used on digital messages, it is more convenient to think in terms of a simpler digital analogy—a tag affixed to each message and incremented every time

	LINK NUMBER							
	1	2	3	4	5	6	7	8
	HANDOVER NUMBER ENTRIES							
A	22	∞	12	10	9	9	8	13
B	5	3	2	2	4	5	12	2
C	7	8	13	9	22	10	7	8
D	21	23	19	21	12	10	12	13
E	7	10	12	14	12	13	13	15
F	7	10	12	13	14	21		
G	6	4	10					
Z	15	20	7	3	10	8	5	10

BEST CHOICE				
1st	2nd	3rd	4th	5th
LINK NUMBER for DECISION CHOICE				
7	5	6	4	3
3	4	8	2	5
1	7	2	8	4
6	5	7	8	3
1	2	3	5	6
1	2	3	4	8
5	2	1	6	
4	7	3	6	5

Each Switching Node contains a table used to record handover numbers of traffic en route. The entries on the table represent the lowest recently measured handover numbers <u>from</u> stations A, B, C, etc., on each of the eight links feeding the node. For example, station E's traffic had a handover number of 7 on link number 1. The table to left orders the preference of the routes <u>to</u> the stations shown. Thus, if traffic were addressed <u>to</u> station E, link number 1, the shortest measured route, will be the first choice. If link 1 is busy or destroyed, the next highest handover number is found on link 2, which then becomes the preferred choice.

FIG. 11 — The Handover Number Table

the message is relayed. Figure 11 shows the handover table located in the memory of a single node. A row is reserved for each major station of the network allowed to generate traffic. A column is assigned to each separate link connected to a node. As it was shown that redundancy levels on the order of four can create extremely "tough" networks and additional redundancy brought little, only about eight columns are really needed.

Perfect Learning. If the network used perfectly reliable, error-free links, we might fill out our table in the following manner. Initially, set entries on the table to high values. Examine the handover number of each message arriving on each line for each station. If the observed handover number is less than the value already entered on the handover number table, change the value to that of the observed handover number. If the handover number of the message is greater than the value on the table, do nothing. After a short time this procedure will shake down the table to indicate the path length to each of the stations over each of the links connected to neighboring stations. This table can now be used to route new traffic. For example, if one wished to send traffic _to_ station C, he would examine the entries for the row listed for station C based on traffic _from_ C. Select the link corresponding to the column with the lowest handover number. This is the shortest path to C. If this preferred link is busy, do not wait, choose the next best link that is free.

Digital Simulation

This basic routing procedure was tested by a Monte

Carlo simulation of a 7x7 array of stations. All tables were started completely blank to simulate a worst-case starting condition where no station knew the location of any other station. Within ½ second of simulated real world time, the network had learned the locations of all connected stations and was routing traffic in an efficient manner. The mean measured path length compared very favorably to the absolute shortest possible path length under various traffic loading conditions. Preliminary results indicate that network loadings on the order of 50 per cent of link capacity could be inserted without undue increase of path length. When local busy spots occur in the network, locally generated traffic is intermittently restrained from entering the busy points while the potential traffic jams clear. Thus, to the node, the network appears to be a variable data rate system, which will limit the number of local subscribers that can be handled. If the network is carrying light traffic, any new input line into the network would accept full traffic, perhaps 1.5 million bits per second. But, if every station had heavy traffic and the network became heavily loaded, the total allowable input data rate from any single station in the network might drop to perhaps 0.5 million bits per second. The absolute minimum guaranteed data capacity into the network from any station is a function of the location of the station in the network, redundancy level, and the mean path length of transmitted traffic in the network. The "choking" of input procedure has been simulated in the network and no signs of instability under overload noted. It was found that most of the advantage of store-and-forward transmission can be provided in a system having relatively little memory capacity. The network "guarantees" very rapid delivery of all traffic that it has accepted from a user (see ODC-II, -III).

FORGETTING AND IMPERFECT LEARNING

We have briefly considered network behavior when all links are working. But, we are also interested in determining network behavior with real world links--some destroyed, while others are being repaired. The network can be made rapidly responsive to the effects of destruction, repair, and transmission fades by a slight modification of the rules for computing the values on the handover number table.

Learning

In the previous example, the lowest handover number ever encountered for a given origination, or "from" station, and over each link, was the value recorded in the handover number table. But, if some links had failed, our table would not have responded to the change. Thus, we must be more responsive to recent measurements than old ones. This effect can be included in our calculation by the following policy. Take the most recently measured value of handover number; subtract the previous value found in the handover table; if the difference is positive, add a fractional part of this difference to the table value to form the updated table value. This procedure merely implements a "forgetting" procedure--placing more belief upon more recent measurements and less on old measurements. This device would, in the case of network damage, automatically modify the handover number table entry so as to exponentially and asymptotically approach the true shortest path value. If the difference between measured value minus the table value is negative, the new table value would change by only a fractional portion of the recently measured difference.

This implements a form of sceptical learning. Learning will take place even with occasional errors. Thus, by the simple device of using only two separate "learning constants," depending whether the measured value is greater or less than the table value, we can provide a mechanism that permits the network routing to be responsive to varying loads, breaks, and repairs. This learning and forgetting technique has been simulated for a few limited cases and was found to work well (see ODC-II, -III).

Adaptation to Environment

This simple simultaneous learning and forgetting mechanism implemented independently at each node causes the entire network to suggest the appearance of an adaptive system responding to gross changes of environment in several respects, without human intervention. For example, consider self-adaptation to station location. A station, Able, normally transmitted from one location in the network, as shown in Fig. 12(a). If Able moved to the location shown in Fig. 12(b), all he need do to announce his new location is to transmit a few seconds of dummy traffic. The network will quickly learn the new location and direct traffic toward Able at his new location. The links could also be cut and altered, yet the network would relearn. Each node sees its environment through myopic eyes by only having links and link status information to a few neighbors. There is no central control;

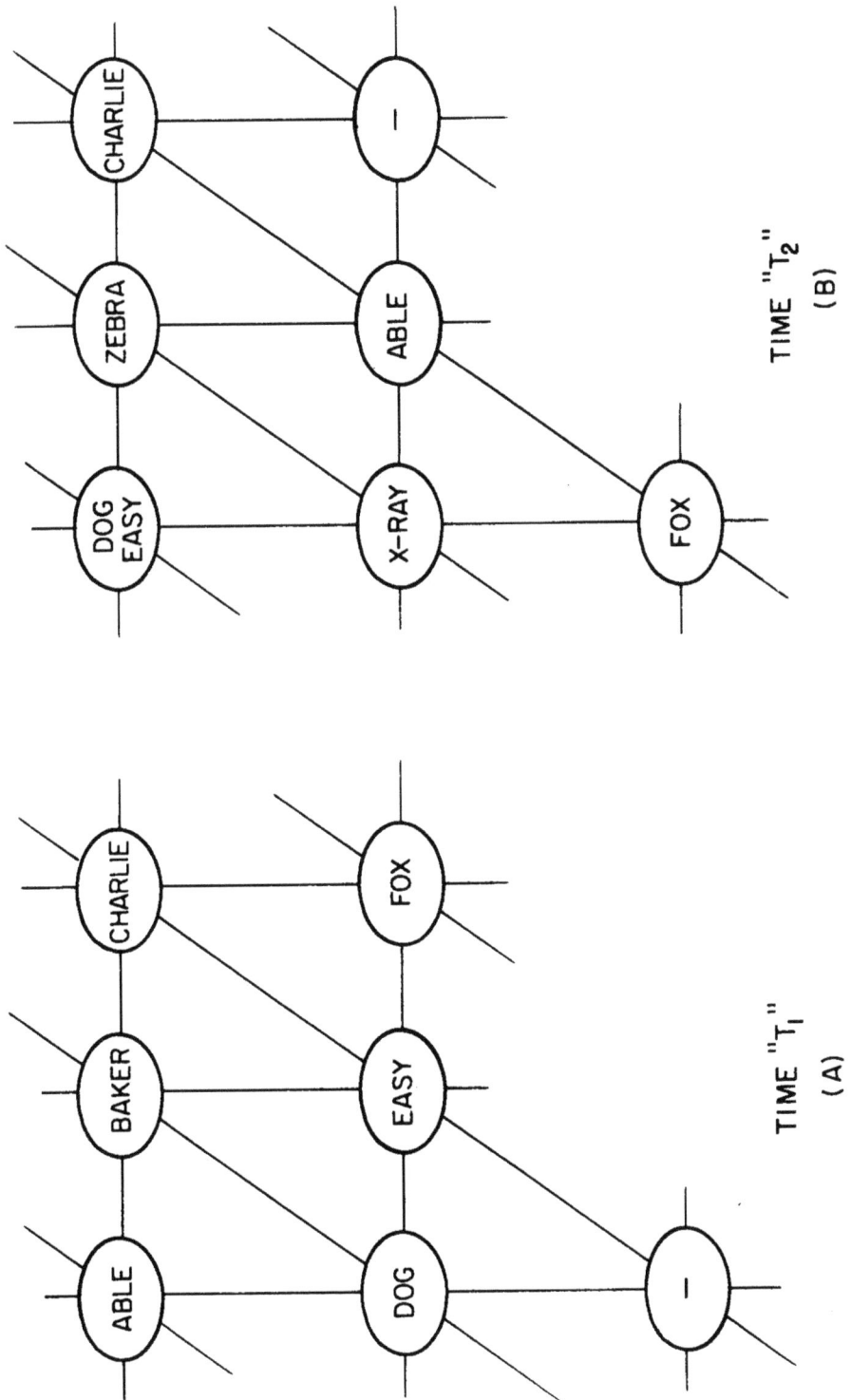

FIG. 12 — Adaptability to Change of User Location

only a simple local routing policy is performed at each node, yet the overall system adapts.

LOWEST-COST PATH

We seek to provide the lowest-cost path for the data to be transmitted between users. When we consider complex networks, perhaps spanning continents, we encounter the problem of building networks with links of widely different data rates. How can paths be taken to encourage most use of the least expensive links? The fundamentally simple adaptation technique can again be used. Instead of incrementing the handover by a fixed amount, each time a message is relayed, set the increment to correspond to the link-cost/bit of the transmission link. Thus, instead of the "instantaneously shortest non-busy path" criterion, the path taken will be that offering the cheapest transportation cost from user to user that is available. The technique can be further extended by placing priority and cost bounds in the message block itself, permitting certain users more of the communication resource during periods of heavy network use.

V. WHERE WE STAND TODAY

Although it is premature at this time to know all the problems involved in such a network and understand all costs, there are reasons to suspect that we may not wish to build future digital communication networks exactly the same way the nation has built its analog telephone plant.

There is an increasingly repeated statement made that one day we will require more capacity for data transmission than needed for analog voice transmission. If this statement is correct, then it would appear prudent to broaden our planning consideration to include new concepts for future data network directions. Otherwise, we may stumble into being boxed in with the uncomfortable restraints of communications links and switches originally designed for high quality analog transmission. New digital computer techniques using redundancy make cheap unreliable links potentially usable. A new switched network compatible with these links appears appropriate to meet the upcoming demand for digital service. This network is best designed for data transmission and for survivability at the outset.

It is the purpose of the other volumes in this series to consider this new direction in more detail. The reader may wish to review ODC-XI as a more recent overview before reading the intervening papers.

MEMORANDUM
RM-3767-PR
AUGUST 1964

ON DISTRIBUTED COMMUNICATIONS:
XI. SUMMARY OVERVIEW

Paul Baran

This research is sponsored by the United States Air Force under Project RAND—Contract No. AF 49(638)-700 monitored by the Directorate of Development Plans, Deputy Chief of Staff, Research and Development, Hq USAF. Views or conclusions contained in this Memorandum should not be interpreted as representing the official opinion or policy of the United States Air Force.

DDC AVAILABILITY NOTICE
Qualified requesters may obtain copies of this report from the Defense Documentation Center (DDC).

1700 MAIN ST. · SANTA MONICA · CALIFORNIA · 90406

PREFACE

This Memorandum is one in a series of eleven RAND Memoranda detailing the Distributed Adaptive Message Block Network, a proposed digital data communications system based on a distributed network concept, as presented in Vol. I in the series.* Various other items in the series deal with specific features of the concept, results of experimental modelings, engineering design considerations, and background and future implications.

The series, entitled On Distributed Communications, is a part of The RAND Corporation's continuing program of research under U.S. Air Force Project RAND, and is related to research in the field of command and control and in governmental and military planning and policy making.

The present Memorandum, the eleventh and final volume in the series, summarizes the development of the system proposal. The more salient features of the system, presented in much greater detail in the other Memoranda in the series, are gisted, allowing the casual reader to obtain a general overview of the network. A reading of the introductory Memorandum in the series and the present Memorandum should suffice for a general understanding of the proposed Distributed Adaptive Message Block Network.

Additionally, the advantages and disadvantages of the system are given, which will greatly facilitate critical evaluation of the system's feasibility.

---

*A list of all items in the series is found on p. 21.

Note: page iv in the original document was blank.

SUMMARY

Progress in synthesizing the Distributed Adaptive Message Block Network is reviewed in this Memorandum, and conclusions are drawn with respect to its anticipated characteristics. The advantages and disadvantages of the proposed system are listed in a comparison with traditional approaches to communication networks.

An outline of critical key tasks required for further development of these concepts is given.

Summarizing the last few years' work in this field:

1) It appears theoretically possible to build large networks able to withstand heavy damage whether caused by unreliability of components or by enemy attack.

2) Highly reliable and error-free digital communication systems using noisy links and unreliable components can be built without exceeding the present-day state-of-the-art of electronic components--provided we use digital modulation.

3) We are beginning to understand, or at least to appreciate, the cause of time delays and overloading phenomena in communication systems handling competing users with different levels of importance. There is a basis for hope that one day we may be able to automate highly sophisticated priority systems. Such systems may even be so effective as to provide the operational equivalent of exercised judgment.

4) It appears that a proper direction in which to move in attacking the secrecy problem in large military and commercial communication systems, is to design the

cryptographic provisions as an integral part of the digital switching system.

5) Digital communication systems able to serve highly automated sources can be more readily designed from the viewpoint of bit-transportation systems rather than the conventional approach of a tandem connection of real-time links.

6) One day in the future (and we are not foolhardy enough to predict an exact date), for economic reasons alone in the military environment it may be <u>necessary</u> to break away from existing analog signal communication network concepts in favor of all-digital networks.

7) It is appropriate to redesign user input-output instruments, such as telephones and teletypewriters, for the described system in order to gain the full benefit that accrues to an all-digital communications network.

CONTENTS

PREFACE iii

SUMMARY v

Section
- I. INTRODUCTION 1
  - The Goal 1
  - Synthesis 2
- II. DISADVANTAGES OF THE DISTRIBUTED ADAPTIVE MESSAGE BLOCK NETWORK 6
- III. SOME POSITIVE ATTRIBUTES OF THE DISTRIBUTED ADAPTIVE MESSAGE BLOCK NETWORK 8
- IV. SUGGESTED DEVELOPMENT 12
- V. NEXT-GENERATION RESEARCH 15
- VI. CONCLUSIONS 17

POSTSCRIPT--A POSSIBLE PITFALL 18

LIST OF PUBLICATIONS IN THE SERIES 21

I. INTRODUCTION

The introductory Memorandum in the series <u>On Distributed Communications</u> described a set of basic concepts, the details of which have been greatly expanded in the intervening Memoranda in the series. The series as a whole is an examination of the feasibility of any digital communications system utilizing "hot-potato routing" and automatic error detection. While preparing the draft of this concluding number, it became evident that a distinct and specific system was being described, which we have now chosen to call the "Distributed Adaptive Message Block Network," in order to distinguish it from the growing set of other distributed networks and systems, as described in ODC-V.[*]

THE GOAL

An <u>ideal</u> electrical communications system can be defined as one that permits any person or machine to reliably and instantaneously communicate with any combination of other people or machines, anywhere, anytime, and at zero cost.

It should effectively allow the illusion that those in communication with one another are all within the same soundproofed room--and that the door is locked.

Almost by definition, all electrical communications systems will fall short of meeting these goals, the

---

[*]ODC is an abbreviation of the series title, <u>On Distributed Communications</u>; the number following refers to the particular volume within the series. A list of all items in the series is found on p. 21.

shortcomings we are content to live with being determined on the basis of intended application and price. Present-day networks are designed to do one particular set of tasks well. In the future, we shall make even greater demands upon our networks and shall consider new ways of building communications networks taking advantage of the newly emerging computer-based technology.

SYNTHESIS

Let us consider one way we might go about building a new system to meet the requirements of the future. We shall attempt to start from scratch and ignore the traditional approach of existing communications systems. We shall first focus upon those requirements--particularly military--not being fully satisfied by today's systems.

For example, in their outstanding study of Army communications, Bloom, Mayfield, and Williams, of the Franklin Institute,[*] conducted a survey among Army Officers on shortcomings of present-day Army communications. Their findings are shown in Fig. 1.

We have used the Bloom, Mayfield, and Williams data as a check list against which the distributed network has been evaluated. The separate mechanisms included within the distributed system to match these "problems" are presented in Table I.

---

[*] Bloom, Joel N., Clifton E. Mayfield, and Richard M. Williams, People, Organizations, and Communications, Final Report, F-A2312. Prepared for Army Communications Systems Division by the Franklin Institute Laboratories for Research and Development, Philadelphia, January 1962.

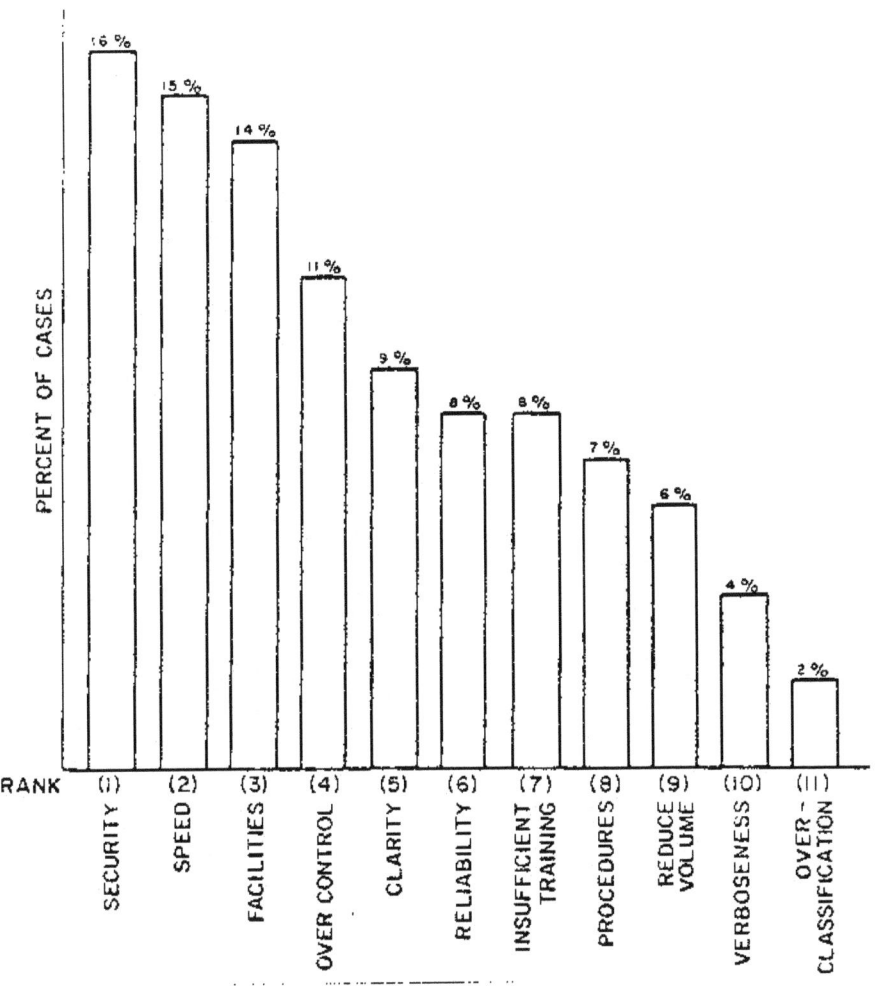

Fig. 1--Principal Problems in Army Communications*

---
*From: Bloom, et al., ibid, p. 30.

Table I

THE DISTRIBUTED SYSTEM'S HANDLING OF PRINCIPAL MILITARY COMMUNICATIONS PROBLEMS

	Problem*	Number of Cases, %	Possible Solutions Included in Distributed Network
1	Security	16	Built-in cryptographic protection services as an integral part of the system. All traffic is treated on a cryptographically secure base.
2	Speed	15	Design for a maximum of two seconds initial connection time. Permit quasi-real-time operation--even for store-and-forward traffic.
3	Facilities	14	Design for "area availability." Many tie-in points; many stations.
4	Over Control (Administrative Censorship)	11	User-to-user rather than emphasis on center-to-center operation.
5	Clarity	9	Error-free end-to-end "quasi-circuits." (Clarity may not be a technical problem.)
6	Reliability	8	Spatially organized parallel redundancy to buy high reliability using lesser-reliability subsystems.
7	Insufficient Training	8	Capability for unmanned operation; automatic fault location.
8	Procedures	7	Reduced cost of long-haul communications bandwidth. Allows cryptographic conference calls.
9	Reduce Volume	6	Automatic priority control, responsive to changing loads and demands.
10	Verboseness	4	Fast feedback to user to establish context. (Verboseness may not be a technical problem.)
11	Over-classification	2	Allow wider access to user-to-user cryptographic "circuits." All network traffic is treated as if it were highly classified.

*From Bloom, Mayfield, and Williams, ibid.

This list wasn't available at the time the system synthesis was initiated, and we chose a somewhat different, but similar, set of criteria. (Survivability was placed at the top of our list.)

The aim was towards an "ideal" electrical communication system. But a real-life system is a collection of compromises, and this system is no exception. The author believes, though, that it represents an acceptable price to have to pay for a national communications system able to meet the extreme demands of survivability in the face of a determined enemy. Some of the system's disadvantages and advantages are summarized in the next sections, together with references to the volumes in the series in which the particular topic is detailed.

II. DISADVANTAGES OF THE DISTRIBUTED ADAPTIVE MESSAGE BLOCK NETWORK

1. The system concept is difficult to explain and to comprehend. (ODC-I, -III, -VII, -VIII)

2. There is an almost fixed 0.5-sec time delay in voice transmission. (ODC-III, -VIII)

3. A <u>small</u> distributed network is a meaningless entity--only large networks are capable of emulating the system's desired properties. (ODC-I, -II)

4. No one has ever built or even fully designed all the hardware components required. (ODC-VII, -VIII)

5. It is an expensive system to simulate. (ODC-II, -III, -VIII)

6. The concept is especially sensitive to poor system design. A brute-force, massive-organization approach can easily end up with an expensive, fractional-GNP-priced kluge. (ODC-VII, -VIII, -X)

7. An understanding of digital computer design is mandatory to adequately evaluate feasibility. (ODC-VII, -VIII)

8. The cryptographic features have not yet been reviewed by those well-versed in the secrecy business and responsible for determining the acceptability of the proposed generalized secrecy arrangements. The analyses made on secrecy have been limited to information found in the open literature (plus a little common sense). (ODC-IX)

9. Analog-to-digital conversion is required. (While such transformation is apparently necessary in conventional cryptography, its present cost is high.)

10. The distributed system, at this time, is designed primarily for communications among large key military installations wherein it is possible to maintain secure areas for cryptographic material adjacent to the Multiplexing Stations. A later logical step in the development of the overall approach is to extend cryptographic protection to remote telephones, a facility not included in the present design. (Some preliminary work has been started on this problem.)

11. Another possible difficulty is that our present voice telephone plant usually provides excellent service for peacetime civilian communications, and the need for special communications capabilities for the military has not always been widely appreciated. Many tend to evaluate potential performance under combat conditions from the standards of their own civilian voice telephone experience. This is not the best measure for realistically determining the suitability of a military communications system.

III. SOME POSITIVE ATTRIBUTES OF THE DISTRIBUTED ADAPTIVE MESSAGE BLOCK NETWORK

1. The system uses automatic learning to obtain "perfect switching"* in its fully-distributed network configuration. Thus, it is less vulnerable to enemy attack than conventional networks. (ODC-I, -II, -III)

2. The system has been designed completely from scratch to meet future requirements of military security, physical survivability, digital data flexibility, and ease of adding new services. (ODC-I, -IV, -V, -VIII, -IX)

3. The system handles start-stop teletype, as well as standard "high-speed" binary-stream synchronous data rates of 600, 2400, 4800, 9600, and 19,800 bits/sec. It could easily be adapted to handle very-high-speed data, if required. (ODC-VIII)

4. Each of the up to 1024 Multiplexing Stations simultaneously handles some 128 cryptographically-secure telephone subscribers, together with 866 other simultaneous subscribers using other data input devices. (ODC-VIII, -IX)

5. Automatic user-to-user cryptography is integrated into the network switching apparatus to eliminate the need for slow, manual cryptographic synchronization. (ODC-VII, -VIII, -IX)

6. User-to-user information flows through the network only during _actual_ transmission of information. For example, after a "pseudo-circuit" is established, blank spots lasting longer than 1/20 sec in speech modes are

---

*See ODC-IV, p. 12.

not transmitted. Thus, high-quality speech need only load the transmission plant to an average equivalent data rate of about 5000 bits/sec. (ODC-VIII)

7. The system is readily amenable to the use of satellites as links. (ODC-VII)

8. The system is able to withstand heavy network damage without interruption of on-going, end-to-end traffic. (ODC-I, -II, -III, -IX)

9. From the user's viewpoint, the system appears to be virtually noise- and error-free when handling data. (ODC-VIII, -IX)

10. No cumulative distortion occurs on voice circuits (whether 1 mi or 10,000 mi long) other than a fixed initial quantization noise. (ODC-III, -VIII, -IX)

11. Undetected digital errors are expected to be extremely rare. (ODC-III, -VIII, -IX)

12. The network is designed to handle a broad mixture of input/output devices. (ODC-III, -VIII, -IX)

13. Automatic error detection and repeat transmission is built into the system on a link-by-link basis, simplifying the design of highly automated, low-cost digital input devices. (ODC-I, -VII)

14. Multi-level cryptography and automatic error-tracking procedures make the system far more immune to sophisticated sabotage than any other known communications system. (ODC-VII, -VIII, -IX)

15. Instantaneous, multi-station, cryptographically-secure conference calls can be set up even after the conversation is underway. (ODC-VIII)

16. The potentially high degree of security protection provided permits a mixing of classified and unclassified traffic, both military and civilian, over the same facilities. (ODC-VII, -VIII, -IX)

17. As Message Blocks usually travel by different routes, it appears impossible for an eavesdropper to decrypt traffic unless <u>all</u> preceding Message Blocks are received. (ODC-II, -III, -VIII, -IX)

18. The system appears to be highly resistant to overload--even when subjected to heavy damage. (ODC-V)

19. The overall system reliability offers hopes of being far better than today's systems; and, it can be built of elements of lower-reliability than presently used. (ODC-I, -III, -VII, -X)

20. The system uses regenerative (saturated) amplification to circumvent the effects of cumulative distortion, thereby permitting the use of inexpensive, high-data-rate links. (ODC-VIII, -X)

21. The system uses the "mini-cost" microwave to build new high-data-rate links at very low cost; 4.5-megabit/sec rates appear feasible at a link cost a decimal order of magnitude lower than in conventional systems. (ODC-VI)

22. Cost, even on a per-subscriber basis, appears roughly comparable to that of present-day conventional networks. (ODC-VIII, -X)

23. Signaling symbols are transmitted as repetitive binary patterns at the same bit rate as the data information, permitting additional signaling, if desired, while the receiver is "off-hook." This feature can be used to

simplify future automatic computer-to-computer conversation. (ODC-VIII)

24. Automatic error detection and analysis is easily implemented by virtue of the all-digital nature of the equipment, facilitating the locating of possible sources of trouble. (ODC-VII, -IX)

25. This system has the security, speed, and low-error characteristics to make it useful as a signaling network to set circuit switches for possible extremely-high-data-rate circuit-switched systems in the far future.

26. The system allows ready implementation of sophisticated automatic priority, precedence, and overload controls. (ODC-IV)

IV. SUGGESTED DEVELOPMENT

To this point we have spoken primarily of a system <u>concept</u>. In order to evolve a <u>hardware</u> system, more study and prototype development is indicated. Only after this series has been carefully scrutinized and only after we have ironed out possible flaws in the concept, should such further development be considered.

Such a development program might include the following items. These items are merely "guesstimates" based on the writer's judgment of what work must be done.

Study and Research Phase	Cost ($ in millions)
1. Investigate new problems that may be encountered in a bit-transportation communications system.	.25
2. Perform a traffic analysis for this future system and recommend a detailed system growth plan.	1.00
3. Study the precise degree of secrecy required in future systems.	.50
4. Amplify the detailed description of the mechanisms used for automating precedence.	.50
5. Simulate entire system operation in maximum depth with emphasis on reliability.	2.00
6. Investigate some of the better analog-to-digital modulation schemes, such as High Information Delta Modulation, applicable to this system.	.25
7. Perform cost-comparison studies	.50
Total	5.00

	Cost ($ in millions)
<u>Design Phase</u>	
1. Design a low-cost all-digital telephone with push-button signaling.	.20
2. Design the Switching Node in full detail.	1.50
3. Design the Multiplexing Station in full detail.	3.00
4. Design the "Mini-Cost" microwave in full detail.	.20
5. Design of low-cost high-data-rate plowed cable line in full detail.	.20
6. Design low-cost graphic and text input/output devices suitable for user-to-user service in this system.	1.50
Total	<u>6.60</u>
<u>Hardware Test Phase</u>	
1. Build and test mini-cost microwave.	.25
2. Build and test low-cost plowed cable line.	.20
3. Build and test critical assemblies proposed for the Switching Node.	.50
4. Build and test critical assemblies proposed for the Multiplexing Station.	.75
5. Build and test low-cost text handling devices.	2.00
6. Build and test teletype and voice High Information Delta Modulation data modems.	.40
Total	<u>4.10</u>

Development Phase	Cost ($ in millions)
1. Build and test three Switching Nodes.	2.00
2. Build and test three Multiplexing Stations.	4.00
Total	6.00

Final Test Phase	
1. Evaluate performance of test units before proceeding.	2.00
Total	2.00

The expenditure milestone points that can be earmarked for system evaluation would occur at about the $1.25-million level (during the Study and Research Phase), after the $5-million point (at the conclusion of the entire Study and Research Phase), at the $11.6-million level (at the end of the Design Phase), at the $15.7-million mark (at the end of the Test Phase), at the $21.7-million level (at the end of the Development Phase), and at the $23.7-million point (at the end of the Final Test Phase). Thus, there are many early opportunities to re-evaluate and redirect this program upon discovery of unforeseen difficulties or better alternative approaches.

V. NEXT-GENERATION RESEARCH

Even though the system has yet to be studied in actual implementation detail, it is felt appropriate to start thinking about further development of the system notion. Consideration today of a next-generation system will simplify orderly system evolution tomorrow.

New areas for research, for example, might include the investigation of the feasibility of using links in the 15- to 150-megabit/sec range. Or, we might study the possibility of forming links of low-cost infrared lasers.

Very-low-cost microwave is also a possible avenue to reduce the feeder network cost.

The technology upon which the system is based is developing at an explosive rate. For instance, our design examination of the Switching Node (ODC-VII) indicated a physical size of about 72 cu ft, using late-1962 digital computer technology. Autonetics Division of North American Aviation, Inc., however, has announced a new microminiaturized computer (see Table II) in late stages of development. This unit appears to have a computing capacity almost as great as that we have proposed in 72 cu ft, but in a package of about 0.3 cu ft--and, at a comparable cost.

The implication of what the changing computer technology offers the communications designer has not always been fully appreciated in the past. Therefore, we should strive to become better prepared to take advantage of this developing technology by continuing the research

Table II

COMPARISON OF THE MONICA-C COMPUTER
WITH THAT PROPOSED FOR THE SWITCHING NODES

	Monica-C[a]	Proposed Switching Node
Words, core storage	8192	4000
Word length, bits	30	32

Memory cycle (μsec):
  Main memory
  Scratch pad
  (256 words)
	6
	1
		1
		-

Clock rate (mc)	1.0	1.5
MTBF[b] (hr)	19,500	720
Size (cu ft)	0.3	72
Power (kw)	0.19	5
Temperature (°C)	65	40
Cost (in production quantities)	<$100,000 (?)	~$100,000 to $150,000

[a] North American Aviation, Inc., Autonetics Division.
[b] Mean-Time Between Failures.

effort, even while building the hardware.

In retrospect, the designs described in ODC-VII and -VIII are now somewhat out of date, in light of the microminiature developments of the past year.

VI. CONCLUSIONS

A new system has been described offering much promise in solving many military communications problems. It is, however, a difficult system to understand and further research is necessary in order to achieve sufficient confidence in the notion to permit investment of large sums for its construction. Some paths leading to further examinations of these concepts have been described. The amount of work and its nature is such that it is beyond the scope of work appropriate to RAND.

Thus, the majority of the future work will have to come from other organizations and agencies. Now the hard work must begin.

POSTSCRIPT--A POSSIBLE PITFALL

There is the human tendency for those who would suggest new systems to overstate the value of their projects and to understate the problems.

The writer believes that he has called attention to the individual technical problems as they have arisen within each of the Memoranda describing the system. However, there are still a few problems that are not so specifically elucidated.

These are not technical problems in the usual sense, but will probably be the key problems which will set the upper bound upon the speed of development of the proposed system. They include: the limited diffusion of technical competence in the computer/communications art; a very human fear of "complicated" systems; the right of free access between existing communications networks; etc.

We would like to discuss briefly one of these key problems. In this series we have proposed a radically different communications system--one that started with a difficult military goal and has been shown to require complex equipment to satisfy a large set of military "needs."

We have discussed a new large communication system, one markedly different from the present in both concept and in equipment, and one which will mean a merging of two different technologies: computers and communications. People with competence in both these fields are not numerous. Our concern is whether we will have enough well-trained people capable of understanding both the communications and digital computer techniques to make this venture a success. Here may lie the real question of feasibility. Our present-day components are fully adequate. The difficult problems lie in hooking them together.

This is not to say that there will be a dearth of organizations happy to bid on providing such a system on a cost-plus-fixed-fee basis. There may even be some foolhardy enough to have a go at a fixed cost (banking on the returns from the inevitable engineering changes to bail them out). The skills that we need are exactly those which are most heavily advertised in the help-wanted pages of our newspapers and magazines. Thus, where we can go and what we can do may be substantially limited by the breadth and extent of our computer technology manpower base.

Historically, we upgrade the level of responsibility of each of the engineers on a "Big-L" military electronics project--or fracture the project into enough small pieces, in hopes that sheer numbers of warm bodies alone will make up for an acknowledged lack of technical foundations.

But, in the development of a system of this type, numbers alone will not substitute for competence.

The Truth about Baran

Willis H. Ware <willis@rand.org>
Copyright © 2000 by the author.

[Willis H. Ware is senior computer scientist emeritus with the RAND Corporation. After a long career, he was awarded the IFIP's Kristian Beckman Award (named after the first chair of TC11) last year. He is also a member of the National Academy of Engineering, a Fellow of IEEE, and the recipient of the Air Force Exceptional Civilian Service Medal (1979), the IEEE Centennial Medal (1984), the National Computer System Security Award (1989), and the IEEE Pioneer Award (1993). - Ed.]

In a discussion, Les Earnest commented that Paul Baran's work had been classified and therefore, was generally unknown to the world at large.

I was in the management structure of RAND's Computer Sciences Department at the time of Paul's work, and interacted with him continuously. I can do what Sgt. Joe Friday always demanded: (in paraphrase) "Give me the facts; just the facts."

1. First, contract support. In the period of interest (1960s) RAND's two major contracts were with the USAF and the AEC. However, all the work on distributed communications was done under Project RAND (USAF) funding.

2. Next, the question of classification; here's the publication chronology.

a. The first - and unclassified -- publication to discuss the payoff from redundancy in a communications system was:

May 27, 1960, Reliable Digital Communications Systems Using Unreliable Network Repeater Nodes, P. Baran, The RAND Corporation Paper P-1995.

It suggested a fishnet-like structure for a network and introduced (in 1960) the idea of "hot potato routing" for fixed length message blocks (described in more detail in documents noted below.

b. Another slightly later unclassified paper of relevance was:

September 1962, On Distributed Communications Networks, P. Baran, The RAND Corporation. Paper P-2626.

This paper spelled out the distributed communications system and specifically described the main characteristics commonly associated with packet switching; including packet housekeeping and separation of the physical address from the logical address to allow users moving in the network to maintain their addresses.

Concurrently with the above a longer series of documents was in preparation and we intentionally withheld publication of any until all could be released concurrently in August 1964.

c. The series, often referred to as the "dozen research memoranda" were:

August 1964, On Distributed Communications

Vol. I. Introduction to Distributed Communications Networks, P. Baran, RAND Corporation, RM-3420-PR.

Vol. II. Digital Simulation of Hot-Potato Routing in a Broadband Distributed Communications Network; Sharla P. Boehm, and P. Baran, RM-3103-PR.

Vol. III. Determination of Path Lengths in a Distributed Network, J. W. Smith, RM-3578-PR.

Vol. IV. Priority, Precedence and Overload, P. Baran, RM-3638-PR.

Vol. V. History, Alternative Approaches, and Comparisons, P. Baran, RM-3097-PR. (This is must reading for anyone who wants to understand what work was going on at the time. Each new idea is almost always based to some degree on previous work.)

Vol. VI. Mini-Cost Microwave, P. Baran, RM-3762-PR.

Vol. VII. Tentative Engineering Specifications and Preliminary Design for a High-Data-Rate Distributed Network Switching Node, P. Baran, RM-3763-PR.

Vol. VIII. The Multiplexing Station, P. Baran, RM-3764-PR.

Vol. IX. Security, Secrecy and Tamper-Free Considerations, P. Baran, RM-3765-PR.

Vol. X. Cost Estimate, P. Baran, RM-3766-PR.

Vol. XI. Summary Overview, P. Baran, RM-3767-PR.

NOTICE that there were only 11 -- not 12 -- of them; and moreover, everything cited above is now and always has been unclassified.

d. There were two collateral documents:

RM-4236-PR by P. Baran and Rein Turn: Cryptophone: An All-digital Telephone Privacy Subsystem for the Distributed Adaptive Message Block Network (U) (Confidential) and RM-3247-PR by Rein Turn, Computer Simulation of the Cryptophone (U) (Confidential)

Since each of these could stand alone, we decided not to put them into the series. While classified at the time, the declassification interval has long since run out.

e. Finally, numbers 12 and 13 appeared and were included in the series which implies that the titles started out with "On Distributed ...":

RM-5067-PR by P. Baran, July 1966. Vol. XII On Distributed Communications: Weak Spots and Patches (For Official Use Only); and Vol XIII by P. Baran and R. Heirschfeldt, RM-5174-PR, On Distributed Communications: User Locations for the Digital Distributed Communications System (U). (Confidential).

These last four RM's were either "for official use only" or CONFIDENTIAL because 1) we discussed specific vulnerabilities, 2) we dealt with cryptography and 3) we dealt with real world geometry and physical vulnerability. Depending upon how one counts, the "dozen series" had either 11, 13, or 15 documents in it. As I mentioned above, however, the declassification interval has run out.

I cannot know of course who read what or who, out of our earshot, might have talked to whom. What I can certify is that ARPA was on the distribution list for all documents, and that the ARPA folks had security clearances in any event. Based on calendar dates that others have mentioned and provided in past postings, Paul's unclassified work -- the first 11 in the series -- predated Larry Roberts' tenure at ARPA; but we do know from various records (such as trip reports) that the work had been discussed with Lick Licklider and Bob Taylor.

The bottom line: by August 1964, full and extensive engineering details were in the public domain because we had an extensive distribution list for this work, and we know from the records that ARPA [DARPA] was included. All essential key points were discussed in unclassified volumes.

At that time, RAND document distribution always included a lengthy list of deposit campus and urban libraries; so these documents would have also been in such places. Hence, my phrase: ...in the public domain. RAND's policy also was to distribute P's (papers prepared for publication) as well as RM's (Research Memoranda) to clients.

The record is clear; Paul Baran's work on Distributed Communications, so far as all essential engineering and system details are concerned, was never classified and it was widely distributed and available.

3. Motivation -- and here semantics becomes important. The USAF and national policy at the time was mutual assured destruction which meant that if the USSR were to launch a nuclear strike, the US would have to be able to launch its nuclear forces in spite of damage inflicted by a USSR first strike. In the jargon of the time, the emphasis was on getting out "the go code" which was a fairly brief highly encrypted message specifying what nuclear attack plan was to be executed and its time table. It would be sent to all nuclear forces, land-air-sea based. The communications infrastructure to support such a last-ditch force deployment of course functioned as a command-control system of sorts but not in the usual sense of the phrase; for example, there was no return path for communications from the forces to the command structure; there was no intent to use the arrangement to prosecute a lengthy war.

I personally discussed such issues with the USAF in that interval and would ask: how do you expect to reconstitute any surviving forces for subsequent strikes? The attitude was (and with some justification since no one could really know what might survive): "...we'll make do with whatever we have left....we'll cobble things together."

Given such a posture in the national policy and given the brief nature of the go code, Paul's first proposal to the USAF was for in fact a single teletypewriter channel using the AM network in a distributed communications arrangement. It could be thought of as a minimal command control system, but certainly not an all-up C-C system with which to manage a long-term war.

The USAF asserted that it needed more bandwidth and the final proposal did in fact provide it.

So the motivation for Paul's work was to provide a minimal but highly survivable one-way communications arrangement to get out the go-code; it was NOT motivated by a requirement for a survivable command-control system that could support the forces fully in both peace and in war. Later on, of course, packet technology became involved as a component of contemporary C-C systems, and along the way, a part of the ARPANET was folded into Defense Data Net, the MILNET, etc.

Without knowing in detail how the nuclear forces were intended to be used in the 60s, it is easy to understand how things would get confused. The usage of "command control network" is not unique, is sometimes ambiguous, and often context dependent.

The Computer as a Communication Device

In a few years, men will be able to communicate more effectively through a machine than face to face.

That is a rather startling thing to say, but it is our conclusion. As if in confirmation of it, we participated a few weeks ago in a technical meeting held through a computer. In two days, the group accomplished with the aid of a computer what normally might have taken a week.

We shall talk more about the mechanics of the meeting later; it is sufficient to note here that we were all in the same room. But for all the communicating we did directly across that room, we could have been thousands of miles apart and communicated just as effectively—as people—over the distance.

Our emphasis on people is deliberate. A communications engineer thinks of communicating as transferring information from one point to another in codes and signals.

But to communicate is more than to send and to receive. Do two tape recorders communicate when they play to each other and record from each other? Not really—not in our sense. We believe that communicators have to do something nontrivial with the information they send and receive. And we believe that we are entering a technological age in which we will be able to interact with the richness of living information—not merely in the passive way that we have become accustomed to using books and libraries, but as active participants in an ongoing process, bringing something to it through our interaction with it, and not simply receiving something from it by our connection to it.

To the people who telephone an airline flight operations information service, the tape recorder that answers seems more than a passive depository. It is an often-updated model of a changing situation—a synthesis of information collected, analyzed, evaluated, and assembled to represent a situation or process in an organized way.

Still there is not much direct interaction with the airline information service; the tape recording is not changed by the customer's call. We want to emphasize something beyond its one-way transfer: the increasing significance of the jointly constructive, the mutually reinforcing aspect of communication—the part that transcends "now we both know a fact that only one of us knew before." When minds interact, new ideas emerge. We want to talk about the creative aspect of communication.

21

Creative, interactive communication requires a plastic or moldable medium that can be modeled, a dynamic medium in which premises will flow into consequences, and above all a common medium that can be contributed to and experimented with by all.

Such a medium is at hand—the programmed digital computer. Its presence can change the nature and value of communication even more profoundly than did the printing press and the picture tube, for, as we shall show, a well-programmed computer can provide direct access both to informational resources and to the *processes* for making use of the resources.

Communication: a comparison of models

To understand how and why the computer can have such an effect on communication, we must examine the idea of modeling—in a computer and with the aid of a computer. For modeling, we believe, is basic and central to communication. Any communication between people about the same thing is a common revelatory experience about informational models of that thing. Each model is a conceptual structure of abstractions formulated initially in the mind of one of the persons who would communicate, and if the concepts in the mind of one would-be communicator are very different from those in the mind of another, there is no common model and no communication.

By far the most numerous, most sophisticated, and most important models are those that reside in men's minds. In richness, plasticity, facility, and economy, the mental model has no peer, but, in other respects, it has shortcomings. It will not stand still for careful study. It cannot be made to repeat a run. No one knows just how it works. It serves its owner's hopes more faithfully than it serves reason. It has access only to the information stored in one man's head. It can be observed and manipulated only by one person.

Society rightly distrusts the modeling done by a single mind. Society demands consensus, agreement, at least majority. Fundamentally, this amounts to the requirement that individual models be compared and brought into some degree of accord. The requirement is for communication, which we now define concisely as "cooperative modeling"—cooperation in the construction, maintenance, and use of a model.

How can we be sure that we *are* modeling cooperatively, that we are communicating, unless we can compare models?

When people communicate face to face, they externalize their models so they can be sure they are talking about the same thing. Even such a simple externalized model as a flow diagram or an outline—because it can be seen by all the communicators—serves as a focus for discussion. It changes the nature of communication: When communicators have no such common framework, they merely make speeches *at* each other; but when they have a manipulable model before them, they utter a few words, point, sketch, nod, or object.

The dynamics of such communication are so model-centered as to suggest an important conclusion: Perhaps the reason present-day two-way *tele*communication falls so far short of face-to-face communication is simply that it fails to provide facilities for externalizing models. Is it really seeing the expression in the other's eye that makes the face-to-face conference so much more productive than the telephone conference call, or is it being able to create and modify external models?

The project meeting as a model

In a technical project meeting, one can see going on, in fairly clear relief, the modeling process that we contend constitutes communication. Nearly every reader can recall a meeting held during the formulative phase of a project. Each member of the project brings to such a meeting a somewhat different mental model of the common undertaking—its purposes, its goals, its plans, its progress, and its status. Each of these models interrelates the past, present, and future states of affairs of: (1) himself; (2) the group he represents; (3) his boss; (4) the project.

Many of the primary data the participants bring to the meeting are in undigested and uncorrelated form. To each participant, his own collections of data are interesting and important in and of themselves. And they are more than files of facts and recurring reports. They are strongly influenced by insight, subjective feelings, and educated guesses. Thus, each individual's data are reflected in his mental model. Getting his colleagues to incorporate his data into their models is the essence of the communications task.

Suppose you could see the models in the minds of two would-be communicators at this meeting. You could tell, by observing their models, whether or not communication was taking place. If, at the outset, their two models were similar in structure but different simply in the values of certain parameters, then communication would cause convergence toward a common pattern. That is the easiest and most frequent kind of communication.

23

When mental models are dissimilar, the achievement of communication might be signaled by changes in the structure of one of the models, or both of them.

If the two mental models were structurally dissimilar, then the achievement of communication would be signaled by structural changes in one of the models or in both of them. We might conclude that one of the communicating parties was having insights or trying out new hypotheses in order to begin to understand the other—or that both were restructuring their mental models to achieve commonality.

The meeting of many interacting minds is a more complicated process. Suggestions and recommendations may be elicited from all sides. The interplay may produce, not just a solution to a problem, but a new set of rules for solving problems. That, of course, is the essence of creative interaction. The process of maintaining a current model has within it a set of changing or changeable rules for the processing and disposition of information.

The project meeting we have just described is representative of a broad class of human endeavor which may be described as creative informational activity. Let us differentiate this from another class which we will call informational housekeeping. The latter is what computers today are used for in the main; they process payroll checks, keep track of bank balances, calculate

24

orbits of space vehicles, control repetitive machine processes, and maintain varieties of debit and credit lists. Mostly they have *not* been used to make coherent pictures of not well understood situations.

We referred earlier to a meeting in which the participants interacted with each other through a computer. That meeting was organized by Doug Engelbart of Stanford Research Institute and was actually a progress-review conference for a specific project. The subject under discussion was rich in detail and broad enough in scope that no one of the attendees, not even the host, could know all the information pertaining to this particular project.

Face to face through a computer

Tables were arranged to form a square work area with five on a side. The center of the area contained six television monitors which displayed the alphanumeric output of a computer located elsewhere in the building but remotely controlled from a keyboard and a set of electronic pointer controllers called "mice." Any participant in the meeting could move a near-by mouse, and thus control the movements of a tracking pointer on the TV screen for all other participants to see.

Each person working on the project had prepared a topical outline of his particular presentation for the meeting, and his outline appeared on the screens as he talked—providing a broad view of his own model. Many of the outline statements contained the names of particular reference files which the speaker could recall from the computer to appear in detail on the screens, for, from the beginning of the project, its participants had put their work into the computer system's files.

So the meeting began much like any other meeting in the sense that there was an overall list of agenda and that each speaker had brought with him (figuratively in his briefcase but really within the computer) the material he would be talking about.

The computer system was a significant aid in exploring the depth and breadth of the material. More detailed information could be displayed when facts had to be pinpointed; more global information could be displayed to answer questions of relevance and interrelationship. A future version of this system will make it possible for each participant, on his own TV screen, to thumb through the speaker's files as the speaker talks—and thus check out incidental questions without interrupting the presentation for substantiation.

25

At a project meeting held through a computer, you can thumb through the speaker's primary data without interrupting him to substantiate or explain.

A communication system should make a positive contribution to the discovery and arousal of interests.

Obviously, collections of primary data can get too large to digest. There comes a time when the complexity of a communications process exceeds the available resources and the capability to cope with it; and at that point one has to simplify and draw conclusions.

It is frightening to realize how early and drastically one does simplify, how prematurely one does conclude, even when the stakes are high and when the transmission facilities and information resources are extraordinary. Deep modeling to communicate—to understand—requires a huge investment. Perhaps even governments cannot afford it yet.

But someday governments may not be able *not* to afford it. For, while we have been talking about the communication process as a cooperative modeling effort in a mutual environment, there is also an aspect of communication with or about an uncooperative opponent. As nearly as we can judge from reports of recent international crises, out of the hundreds of alternatives that confronted the decision makers at each decision point or ply in the "game," on the average only a few, and never more than a few dozen could be considered, and only a few branches of the game could be explored deeper than two or three such plies before action had to be taken. Each side was busy trying to model what the other side might be up to—but modeling takes time, and the pressure of events forces simplification even when it is dangerous.

Whether we attempt to communicate across a division of interests, or whether we engage in a cooperative effort, it is clear that we need to be able to model faster and to greater depth. The importance of improving decision-making processes—not only in government, but throughout business and the professions—is so great as to warrant every effort.

The computer—switch or interactor?

As we see it, group decision-making is simply the active, executive, effect-producing aspect of the kind of communication we are discussing. We have commented that one must oversimplify. We have tried to say why one must oversimplify. But we should not oversimplify the main point of this article. We can say with genuine and strong conviction that a particular form of digital computer organization, with its programs and its data, constitutes the dynamic, moldable medium that can revolutionize the art of modeling and that in so doing can improve the effectiveness of communication among people so much as perhaps to revolutionize that also.

But we must associate with that statement at once the qualification that the computer alone can make no contribution that will help us, and that the computer with the programs and the data that it has today can do little more than suggest a direction and provide a few germinal examples. Emphatically we do *not* say: "Buy a computer and your communication problems will be solved."

What we do say is that we, together with many colleagues who have had the experience of working on-line and interactively with computers, have already sensed more responsiveness and facilitation and "power" than we had hoped for, considering the inappropriateness of present machines and the primitiveness of their software. Many of us are therefore confident (some of us to the point of religious zeal) that truly significant achievements, which will markedly improve our effectiveness in communication, now are on the horizon.

Many communications engineers, too, are presently excited about the application of digital computers to communication. However, the function they want computers to implement is the switching function. Computers will either switch the communication lines, connecting them together in required configurations, or switch (the technical term is "store and forward") messages.

The switching function is important but it is not the one we have in mind when we say that the computer can revolutionize communication. We are stressing the modeling function, not the switching function. Until now, the communications engineer has not felt it within his province to facilitate the modeling function, to make an interactive, cooperative modeling facility. Information transmission and information processing have always been carried out separately and have become separately institutionalized. There are strong intellectual and social benefits to be realized by the melding of these two technologies. There are also, however, powerful legal and administrative obstacles in the way of any such melding.

Distributed intellectual resources

We have seen the beginnings of communication through a computer—communication among people at consoles located in the same room or on the same university campus or even at distantly separated laboratories of the same research and development organization. This kind of communication—through a single multiaccess computer with the aid of telephone lines—is beginning to foster cooperation and promote coherence more effectively than do present arrangements for sharing computer programs by exchanging magnetic tapes by messenger or mail. Computer programs are very important because they transcend mere "data"—they include procedures and processes for structuring and manipulating data. These are the main resources we can now concentrate and share with the aid of the tools and techniques of computers and communication, but they are only a part of the whole that we can learn to concentrate and share. The whole includes raw data, digested data, data about the location of data—and documents—and most especially models.

To appreciate the importance the new computer-aided communication can have, one must consider the dynamics of "critical mass," as it applies to cooperation in creative endeavor. Take any problem worthy of the name, and you find only a few people who can contribute effectively to its solution. Those people must be brought into close intellectual partnership so that their ideas can come into contact with one another. But bring these people together physically in one place to form a team, and you have trouble, for the most creative people are often not the best team players, and there are not enough top positions in a single organization to keep them all happy. Let them go their separate ways, and each creates his own empire, large or small, and devotes more time to the role of emperor than to the role of problem solver. The principals still get together at meetings. They still visit one another. But the time scale of their communication stretches out, and the correlations among mental models degenerate between meetings so that it may take a year to do a week's communicating. There has to be some way of facilitating communication among people without bringing them together in one place.

A single multiaccess computer would fill the bill if expense were no object, but there is no way, with a single computer and individual communication lines to several geographically separated consoles, to avoid paying an unwarrantedly large bill for transmission. Part of the economic difficulty lies in our present communications system. When a computer is used interactively from a typewriter console, the signals transmitted between the console and the computer are intermittent and not very frequent. They do not require continuous access to a telephone channel; a good part of the time they do not even require the full information rate of such a channel. The difficulty is that the common carriers do not provide the kind of service one would like to have—a service that would let one have ad lib access to a channel for short intervals and not be charged when one is not using the channel.

It seems likely that a store-and-forward (i.e., store-for-just-a-moment-

and-forward-right-away) message service would be best for this purpose, whereas the common carriers offer, instead, service that sets up a channel for one's individual use for a period not shorter than one minute.

The problem is further complicated because interaction with a computer via a fast and flexible graphic display, which is for most purposes far superior to interaction through a slow-printing typewriter, requires markedly higher information rates. Not necessarily more information, but the same amount in faster bursts—more difficult to handle efficiently with the conventional common-carrier facilities.

It is perhaps not surprising that there are incompatibilities between the requirements of computer systems and the services supplied by the common carriers, for most of the common-carrier services were developed in support of voice rather than digital communication. Nevertheless, the incompatibilities are frustrating. It appears that the best and quickest way to overcome them—and to move forward the development of interactive *communities* of geographically separated people—is to set up an experimental network of multiaccess computers. Computers would concentrate and interleave the concurrent, intermittent messages of many users and their programs so as to utilize wide-band transmission channels continuously and efficiently, with marked reduction in overall cost.

Computer and information networks

The concept of computers connected to computers is not new. Computer manufacturers have successfully installed and maintained interconnected computers for some years now. But the computers in most instances are from families of machines compatible in both software and hardware, and they are in the same location. More important, the interconnected computers are not interactive, general-purpose, multiaccess machines of the type described by David [1] and Licklider [2]. Although more interactive multiaccess computer systems are being delivered now, and although more groups plan to be using these systems within the next year, there are at present perhaps only as few as half a dozen interactive multiaccess computer *communities*.

These communities are socio-technical pioneers, in several ways out ahead of the rest of the computer world: What makes them so? First, some of their members are computer scientists and engineers who understand the concept of man-computer interaction and the technology of interactive multiaccess systems. Second, others of their members are creative people in other fields and disciplines who recognize the usefulness and who sense the impact of interactive multiaccess computing upon their work. Third, the communities have large multiaccess computers and have learned to use them. And, fourth, their efforts are regenerative.

In the half-dozen communities, the computer systems research and development and the development of substantive applications mutually support each other. They are producing large and growing resources of programs, data, and know-how. But we have seen only the beginning. There is much more programming and data collection—and much more learning how to cooperate—to be done before the full potential of the concept can be realized.

Obviously, multiaccess systems must be developed interactively. The systems being built must remain flexible and open-ended throughout the process of development, which is evolutionary.

Such systems cannot be developed in small ways on small machines. They require large, multiaccess computers, which are necessarily complex. Indeed, the sonic barrier in the development of such systems is complexity.

These new computer systems we are describing differ from other computer systems advertised with the same labels: interactive, time-sharing, multiaccess. They differ by having a greater degree of open-endedness, by rendering more services, and above all by providing facilities that foster a working sense of community among their users. The commercially available time-sharing services do not yet offer the power and flexibility of software resources—the "general purposeness"—of the interactive multiaccess systems of the System Development Corporation in Santa Monica, the University of California at Berkeley, Massachusetts Institute of Technology in Cambridge and Lexington, Mass.—which have been collectively serving about a thousand people for several years.

The thousand people include many of the leaders of the ongoing revolution in the computer world. For over a year they have been preparing for the transition to a radically new organization of hardware and software, designed to support many more simultaneous users than the current systems, and to offer them—through new languages, new file-handling systems, and new graphic displays—the fast, smooth interaction required for truly effective man-computer partnership.

Experience has shown the importance of making the response time short and the conversation free and easy. We think those attributes will be almost as important for a network of computers as for a single computer.

Today the on-line communities are separated from one another functionally as well as geographically. Each member can look only to the processing, storage and software capability of the facility upon which his community is centered. But now the move is on to interconnect the separate communities and thereby transform them into, let us call it, a supercommunity. The hope is that interconnection will make available to all the members of all the communities the programs and data resources of the entire supercommunity. First, let us indicate how these communities can be interconnected; then we shall describe one hypothetical person's interaction with this network, of interconnected computers.

Message processing

The hardware of a multiaccess computer system includes one or more central processors, several kinds of memory—core, disks, drums, and tapes—and many consoles for the simultaneous on-line users. Different users can work simultaneously on diverse tasks. The software of such a system includes supervisory programs (which control the whole operation), system programs for interpretation of the user's commands, the handling of his files, and graphical or alphanumeric display of information to him (which permit people not skilled in the machine's language to use the system effectively), and programs and data created by the users themselves. The collection of people, hardware, and software—the multiaccess computer together with its local community of users—will become a node in a geographically distributed computer network. Let us assume for a moment that such a network has been formed.

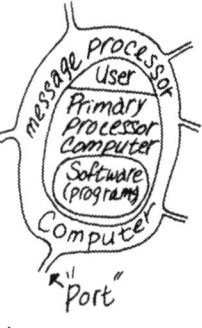

What's in a Node?

* Operating System
Graphic display
Interpreter
User Programs
Files, etc.

All nodes can be interconnected via their message processors

For each node there is a small, general-purpose computer which we shall call a "message processor." The message processors of all the nodes are interconnected to form a fast store-and-forward network. The large multiaccess computer at each node is connected directly to the message processor there. Through the network of message processors, therefore, all the large computers can communicate with one another. And through them, all the members of the supercommunity can communicate—with other people, with programs, with data, or with selected combinations of those resources. The message processors, being all alike, introduce an element of uniformity into an otherwise grossly nonuniform situation, for they facilitate both hardware and software compatibility among diverse and poorly compatible computers. The links among the message processors are transmission and high-speed *digital* switching facilities provided by common carrier. This allows the linking of the message processors to be reconfigured in response to demand.

32

A message can be thought of as a short sequence of "bits" flowing through the network from one multiaccess computer to another. It consists of two types of information: control and data. Control information guides the transmission of data from source to destination. In present transmission systems, errors are too frequent for many computer applications. However, through the use of error detection and correction or retransmission procedures in the message processors, messages can be delivered to their destinations intact even though many of their "bits" were mutilated at one point or another along the way. In short, the message processors function in the system as traffic directors, controllers, and correctors.

Today, programs created at one installation on a given manufacturer's computer are generally not of much value to users of a different manufacturer's computer at another installation. After learning (with difficulty) of a distant program's existence, one has to get it, understand it, and recode it for his own computer. The cost is comparable to the cost of preparing a new program from scratch, which is, in fact, what most programmers usually do. On a national scale, the annual cost is enormous. Within a network of interactive, multiaccess computer systems, on the other hand, a person at one node will have access to programs running at other nodes, even though those programs were written in different languages for different computers.

The feasibility of using programs at remote locations has been shown by the successful linking of the AN/FSQ-32 computer at Systems Development Corporation in Santa Monica, Calif., with the TX-2 computer across the continent at the Lincoln Laboratory in Lexington, Mass. A person at a TX-2 graphic console can make use of a unique list-processing program at SDC, which would be prohibitively expensive to translate for use on the TX-2. A network of 14 such diverse computers, all of which will be capable of sharing one another's resources, is now being planned by the Defense Department's Advanced Research Projects Agency, and its contractors.

The system's way of managing data is crucial to the user who works in interaction with many other people. It should put generally useful data, if not subject to control of access, into public files. Each user, however, should have complete control over his personal files. He should define and distribute the "keys" to each such file, exercising his option to exclude all others from any kind of access to it; or to permit anyone to "read" but not modify or execute it; or to permit selected individuals or groups to execute but not read it; and so on—with as much detailed specification or as much aggregation as he likes. The system should provide for group and organizational files within its overall information base.

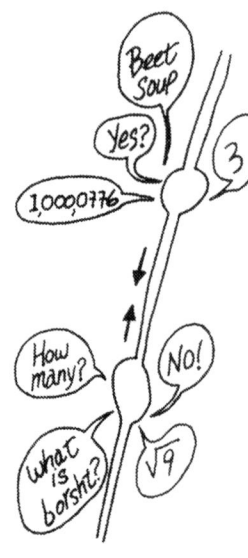

One message processor can be the messenger between two other message processors

A given pair of nodes may exchange several independent messages for simultaneous users with different interests

33

Interactive communication consists of short spurts of dialog.....

At least one of the new multiaccess systems will exhibit such features. In several of the research centers we have mentioned, security and privacy of information are subjects of active concern; they are beginning to get the attention they deserve.

In a multiaccess system, the number of consoles permitted to use the computer simultaneously depends upon the load placed on the computer by the users' jobs, and may be varied automatically as the load changes. Large general-purpose multiaccess systems operating today can typically support 20 to 30 simultaneous users. Some of these users may work with low-level "assembly" languages while others use higher-level "compiler" or "interpreter" languages. Concurrently, others may use data management and graphical systems. And so on.

But back to our hypothetical user. He seats himself at his console, which may be a terminal keyboard plus a relatively slow printer, a sophisticated graphical console, or any one of several intermediate devices. He dials his local computer and "logs in" by presenting his name, problem number, and password to the monitor program. He calls for either a public program, one of his own programs, or a colleague's program that he has permission to use. The monitor links him to it, and he then communicates with that program.

When the user (or the program) needs service from a program at another

34

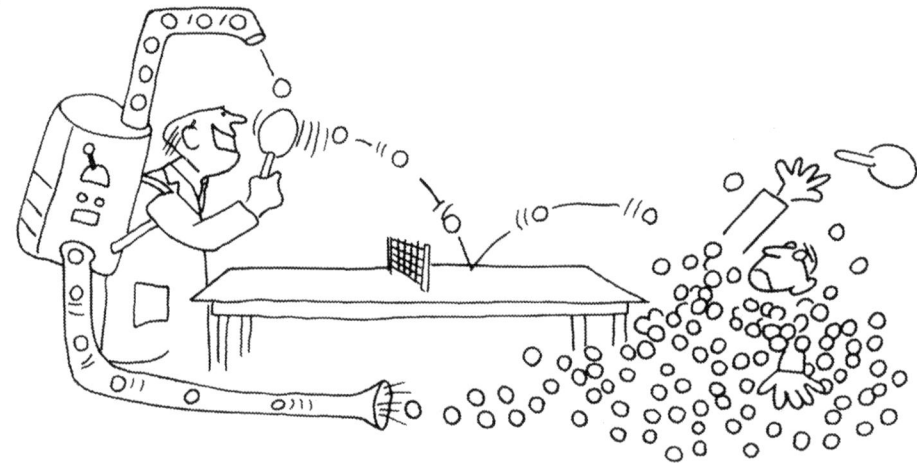

....filibustering destroys communication.

node in the network, he (or it) requests the service by specifying the location of the appropriate computer and the identity of the program required. If necessary, he uses computerized directories to determine those data. The request is translated by one or more of the message processors into the precise language required by the remote computer's monitor. Now the user (or his local program) and the remote program can interchange information. When the information transfer is complete, the user (or his local program) dismisses the remote computer, again with the aid of the message processors. In a commercial system, the remote processor would at this point record cost information for use in billing.

Who can afford it?

The mention of billing brings up an important matter. Computers and long-distance calls have "expensive" images. One of the standard reactions to the idea of "on-line communities" is: "It sounds great, but who can afford it?"

In considering that question, let us do a little arithmetic. The main elements of the cost of computer-facilitated communication, over and above the salaries of the communicators, are the cost of the consoles, processing, storage, transmission, and supporting software. In each category, there is a

35

wide range of possible costs, depending in part upon the sophistication of the equipment, programs, or services employed and in part upon whether they are custom-made or mass-produced.

Making rough estimates of the hourly component costs per user, we arrived at the following: $1 for a console, $5 for one man's share of the services of a processor, 70 cents for storage, $3 for transmission via line leased from a common carrier, and $1 for software support—a total cost of just less than $11 per communicator hour.

The only obviously untenable assumption underlying that result, we believe, is the assumption that one's console and the personal files would be used 160 hours per month. All the other items are assumed to be shared with others, and experience indicates that time-sharing leads on the average to somewhat greater utilization than the 160 hours per month that we assumed. Note, however, that the console and the personal files are items used also in individual problem solving and decision making. Surely those activities, taken together with communication, would occupy at least 25% of the working hours of the on-line executive, scientist or engineer. If we cut the duty factor of the console and files to one quarter of 160 hours per month, the estimated total cost comes to $16 per hour.

Let us assume that our $16/hr interactive computer link is set up between Boston, Mass., and Washington, D.C. Is $16/hr affordable? Compare it first with the cost of ordinary telephone communication: Even if you take advantage of the lower charge per minute for long calls, it is less than the daytime direct-dial station-to-station toll. Compare it with the cost of travel: If one flies from Boston to Washington in the morning and back in the evening, he can have eight working hours in the capital city in return for about $64 in air and taxi fares plus the spending of four of his early morning and evening hours en route. If those four hours are worth $16 each, then the bill for the eight hours in Washington is $128—again $16 per hour. Or look at it still another way: If computer-aided communication doubled the effectiveness of a man paid $16 per hour then, according to our estimate, it would be worth what it cost if it could be bought right now. Thus we have some basis for arguing that computer-aided communication is economically feasible. But we must admit that the figure of $16 per hour sounds high, and we do not want to let our discussion depend upon it.

Fortunately, we do not have to, for the system we envision cannot be bought at this moment. The time scale provides a basis for genuine optimism about the cost picture. It will take two years, at least, to bring the first interactive computer networks up to a significant level of experimental activity. Operational systems might reach critical size in as little as six years if everyone got onto the bandwagon, but there is little point in making cost estimates for a nearer date. So let us take six years as the target.

In the computer field, the cost of a unit of processing and the cost of a unit of storage have been dropping for two decades at the rate of 50% or more every two years. In six years, there is time for at least three such drops, which cut a dollar down to 12 1/2 cents. Three halvings would take the cost of processing, now $5 per hour on our assumptions, down to less than 65 cents per hour.

Such advances in capability, accompanied by reduction in cost, lead us to expect that computer facilitation will be affordable before many people are ready to take advantage of it. The only areas that cause us concern are consoles and transmission.

In the console field, there is plenty of competition; many firms have entered the console sweepstakes, and more are entering every month. Lack of competition is not the problem. The problem is the problem of the chicken and the egg—in the factory and in the market. If a few companies would take the plunge into mass manufacture, then the cost of a satisfactory console would drop enough to open up a mass market. If large on-line communities were already in being, their mass market would attract mass manufacture. But at present there is neither mass manufacture nor a mass market, and consequently there is no low-cost console suitable for interactive on-line communication.

In the field of transmission, the difficulty may be lack of competition. At any rate, the cost of transmission is not falling nearly as fast as the cost of processing and storage. Nor is it falling nearly as fast as we think it should fall. Even the advent of satellites has affected the cost picture by less than a factor of two. That fact does not cause immediate distress because (unless the distance is very great) transmission cost is not now the dominant cost. But, at the rate things are going, in six years it will be the dominant cost. That prospect concerns us greatly and is the strongest damper to our hopes for near-term realization of operationally significant interactive networks and significant on-line communities.

On-line interactive communities

But let us be optimistic. What will on-line interactive communities be like? In most fields they will consist of geographically separated members, sometimes grouped in small clusters and sometimes working individually. They

37

will be communities not of common location, but of *common interest*. In each field, the overall community of interest will be large enough to support a comprehensive system of field-oriented programs and data.

In each geographical sector, the total number of users—summed over all the fields of interest—will be large enough to support extensive general-purpose information processing and storage facilities. All of these will be interconnected by telecommunications channels. The whole will constitute a labile network of networks—ever-changing in both content and configuration.

What will go on inside? Eventually, every informational transaction of sufficient consequence to warrant the cost. Each secretary's typewriter, each data-gathering instrument, conceivably each dictation microphone, will feed into the network.

You will not send a letter or a telegram; you will simply identify the people whose files should be linked to yours and the parts to which they should be linked—and perhaps specify a coefficient of urgency. You will seldom make a telephone call; you will ask the network to link your consoles together.

You will seldom make a purely business trip, because linking consoles will be so much more efficient. When you *do* visit another person with the object of intellectual communication, you and he will sit at a two-place console and interact as much through it as face to face. If our extrapolation from Doug Engelbart's meeting proves correct, you will spend much more time in computer-facilitated teleconferences and much less en route to meetings.

A very important part of each man's interaction with his on-line community will be mediated by his OLIVER. The acronym OLIVER honors Oliver Selfridge, originator of the concept. An OLIVER is, or will be when there is one, an "on-line interactive vicarious expediter and responder," a complex of computer programs and data that resides within the network and acts on behalf of its principal, taking care of many minor matters that do not require his personal attention and buffering him from the demanding world. "You are describing a secretary," you will say. But no! Secretaries will have OLIVERS.

At your command, your OLIVER will take notes (or refrain from taking notes) on what you do, what you read, what you buy and where you buy it. It will know who your friends are, your mere acquaintances. It will know your value structure, who is prestigious in your eyes, for whom you will do what

Your computer will know who is prestigious in your eyes and buffer you from a demanding world.

with what priority, and who can have access to which of your personal files. It will know your organization's rules pertaining to proprietary information and the government's rules relating to security classification.

Some parts of your OLIVER program will be common with parts of other people's OLIVERS; other parts will be custom-made for you, or by you, or will have developed idiosyncrasies through "learning" based on its experience in your service.

Available within the network will be functions and services to which you subscribe on a regular basis and others that you call for when you need them. In the former group will be investment guidance, tax counseling, selective dissemination of information in your field of specialization, announcement of cultural, sport, and entertainment events that fit your interests, etc. In the latter group will be dictionaries, encyclopedias, indexes, catalogues, editing programs, teaching programs, testing programs, programming systems, data bases, and—most important—communication, display, and modeling programs.

All these will be—at some late date in the history of networking—systematized and coherent; you will be able to get along in one basic language up to the point at which you choose a specialized language for its power or terseness.

When people do their informational work "at the console" and "through the network," telecommunication will be as natural an extension of individual work as face-to-face communication is now. The impact of that fact, and of the marked facilitation of the communicative process, will be very great—both on the individual and on society.

First, life will be happier for the on-line individual because the people with whom one interacts most strongly will be selected more by commonality of interests and goals than by accidents of proximity. Second, communication will be more effective and productive, and therefore more enjoyable. Third, much communication and interaction will be with programs and programmed models, which will be (a) highly responsive, (b) supplementary to one's own capabilities, rather than competitive, and (c) capable of representing progressively more complex ideas without necessarily displaying all the levels of their structure at the same time—and which will therefore be both challenging and rewarding. And, fourth, there will be plenty of opportunity for everyone (who can afford a console) to find his calling, for the whole world of information, with all its fields and disciplines, will be open to him—with programs ready to guide him or to help him explore.

For the society, the impact will be good or bad, depending mainly on the question: Will "to be on line" be a privilege or a right? If only a favored segment of the population gets a chance to enjoy the advantage of "intelligence amplification," the network may exaggerate the discontinuity in the spectrum of intellectual opportunity.

On the other hand, if the network idea should prove to do for education what a few have envisioned in hope, if not in concrete detailed plan, and if all minds should prove to be responsive, surely the boon to humankind would be beyond measure.

Unemployment would disappear from the face of the earth forever, for consider the magnitude of the task of adapting the network's software to all the new generations of computer, coming closer and closer upon the heels of their predecessors until the entire population of the world is caught up in an infinite crescendo of on-line interactive debugging.

40

Acknowledgements

Evan Herbert edited the article and acted as intermediary during its writing between Licklider in Boston and Taylor in Washington.
Roland B. Wilson drew the cartoons to accompany the original article.

References

[1] Edward E. David, Jr., "Sharing a Computer," *International Science and Technology*, June, 1966.

[2] J. C. R. Licklider, "Man–Computer Partnership," *International Science and Technology*, May, 1965.

PART B
Planning the ARPANET

Memoirs of the Sixties

Leonard Kleinrock

I was one of the first on the scene as a pioneer of data networks (and am often referred to as the Father of Modern Data Networking). My research dates back to 1959 while a Ph.D. student in Electrical Engineering at MIT.

At MIT, I found that the vast majority of my classmates were doing their Ph.D. research in the overpopulated area of Information Theory. This was not for me since I wanted to have more impact than I could by refining this well-researched area. Consequently, I chose to break new ground in the virtually unknown area of data networks. Indeed, in 1959, I submitted a Ph.D. proposal to study data networks, thus launching the technology which eventually led to the Internet. I published the first paper on packet switching in July 1961. I completed my doctoral research in 1962, and the dissertation was later published (1964) by McGraw-Hill as an MIT book entitled *Communication Nets [This was the first book on packet networks. In this work, Kleinrock developed the basic principles of packet switching, thus providing the fundamental underpinnings for that technology. These principles (along with his subsequent research) continue to provide a basis for today's Internet technology. Kleinrock is arguably the world's leading authority and researcher in the field of computer network modeling, analysis and design and a father of the Internet —PHS].*

But the commercial world was not ready for data networks and my work lay dormant for most of the 1960s as I continued to publish results on networking technology while at the same time rising through the professorial ranks at UCLA where I had joined the faculty in 1963. In the mid-1960s, the Advanced Research Projects Agency (ARPA—which was created in 1958 as the United States' response to Sputnik—became interested in networks. Under the direction of [J.C.R.] Lick Licklider, ARPA had been supporting a number of computer scientists around the country and, as new researchers were brought in, they naturally asked ARPA to provide powerful computers (each endowed with all the advances that had been achieved at the other ARPA-sponsored research sites) on which they could do their research; however, ARPA reasoned that this community of scientists would be able to share the power of their colleagues' machines, rather than replicating that power on everyone's machines, if these computers were connected together by means of a data network.

Dr. Larry Roberts, an MIT classmate of mine, was recruited by Robert Taylor (who was Director of ARPA's Information Processing Techniques Office) to join his group at ARPA to manage and direct the development of this network, which was to be called the ARPANET. Because of my unique expertise in data networking, Roberts called on me to play a key role in a group that would prepare a functional specification for the ARPANET—a government-supported data network that would use the technology which by then had come to be known as "packet switching." This group consisted of about a half-dozen researchers interested in networking, including Taylor, Roberts, Tom Cheatham, Herb Baskins, and me as well as several others.

Baskins, who had spent considerable time developing time-sharing systems, insisted that the response time of the network be no greater than one second for short messages, or it would not be useful for interactive work; so the specification was set at one second. I insisted that adequate measurement and test software be included in the network since this was to be an experimental network and such software was required to measure the outcome of the experiment; so the specification of sophisticated measurement and test software was included.

The specification for the ARPANET was prepared in 1968, and in December 1968, a Cambridge-based computer company, Bolt, Beranek and Newman (BBN) won the contract to design, implement and deploy the ARPANET; the team that BBN fielded for this purpose was headed by Frank Heart, and included designers such as Robert Kahn, Dave Walden, Bill Crowther, Alex McKenzie, John McQuillan, Severo Ornstein, and others. It was their job to take the specification and develop a computer that could act as the router for the packet-switched ARPANET. BBN selected a Honeywell minicomputer as the base on which they would build the router.

Due to my role in establishing data networking technology over the preceding decade, ARPA decided that UCLA, under my leadership, would become the first node to join the ARPANET. This meant that the first router (known as an Interface Message Processor—IMP) would arrive on the Labor Day weekend, 1969, and the UCLA team of 40 people (including, Steve Crocker, Jon Postel, Charlie Kline, Vint Cerf and others) that I organized would have to provide the ability to connect the first (host) computer to the first IMP. This was a challenging task since no such connection had ever been attempted. (This minicomputer had been released in 1968 and Honeywell displayed it at the 1968 Spring Joint Computer Conference where I saw the machine suspended by its hooks at the conference; while running, there was this muscle-bound brute whacking it with a sledge hammer just to show it was robust. *[Kleinrock suspects that that particular machine is the one that was delivered by BBN to UCLA. —PHS])* As it turned out, BBN was running two weeks late (much to my delight, as we badly needed the extra development time); BBN, however, shipped the IMP on an airplane instead of on a truck, and it arrived on time. Aware of the pending arrival date, my team and I worked around the clock to meet the schedule.

The IMP arrived on the Labor Day weekend, and on the Tuesday after Labor Day (September 2, 1969), the circus began—everyone who had any imaginable excuse to be there, was there to witness the inauguration of the network. My team and I were there; BBN was there; Honeywell was there (the IMP was built out of a Honeywell minicomputer); Scientific Data Systems was there (the UCLA host machine was an SDS machine); AT&T long lines was there (we were attaching to their network); GTE was there (they were the local telephone company); ARPA was there; the UCLA Computer Science Dept. administration was there; the UCLA campus administration was there; plus an army of Computer Science graduate students. Expectations and anxieties were high because, everyone was concerned that their piece might fail. Fortunately, the team had done its job well and bits began moving between the UCLA computer and the IMP that same day. By the next day we had messages moving between the machines. THUS WAS BORN THE ARPANET, AND THE COMMUNITY WHICH HAS NOW BECOME THE INTERNET!

A month later the second node was added (at Englebart's lab at the Stanford Research Institute) and the first Host-to-Host message ever to be sent on the Internet was launched from UCLA. This occurred in late October when one of my programmers, Charlie Kline, and I proceeded to "login" to the SRI Host from the UCLA Host. The procedure was to type "log" and the system at SRI was set up to be clever enough to fill out the rest of the command, namely to add "in," thus creating the word "login." A telephone headset was available to the programmers at both ends so they could communicate by voice as the message was transmitted. At the UCLA end, we typed in the "l" and Charlie asked

SRI if they received it; "got the l" came the voice reply. UCLA typed in the "o," asked if they got it; back came the reply, "got the o." UCLA then typed in the "g" and the darned system CRASHED! It was not the IMPs that crashed, it was not the long-haul line that crashed, it was not our UCLA Host that crashed; it was the SRI Host. Quite a beginning. And so the very first message ever sent over the Internet was "Lo!" as in "Lo and behold!" Quite a prophetic message indeed.

Little did we realize what we had created. However, I was quoted in a July 1969 press release in which I predicted much of what we have in today's Internet. Most of the ARPA-supported researchers at that time were opposed to joining the network for fear that it would enable outsiders to load down their "private" computers. I had to convince them that joining would be a win-win situation for all concerned, and managed to get reluctant agreement in the community. By December 1969, four sites were connected (UCLA, Stanford Research Institute, UC Santa Barbara, and the University of Utah) and UCLA was already conducting a series of extensive tests to debug the network. Indeed, under my supervision, UCLA served for many years as the ARPANET Network Measurement Center (in one interesting experiment in the mid-1970s, UCLA managed to control a geosynchronous satellite hovering over the Atlantic Ocean by sending messages through the ARPANET from California to an East Coast satellite dish). As head of the Center, it was my mission to stress the network to its limits and, if possible, expose its faults by "crashing" the net; in those early days, we could bring the net down at will, each time identifying and repairing a serious network fault. Some of the faults we uncovered were given descriptive names like Christmas Lockup and Piggyback Lockup.

By mid-1970, ten nodes were connected, spanning the USA. BBN had designed the IMP to accommodate no more than 64 Host computers and only one network (today, the Internet has many millions of computers and hundreds of thousands of networks!). In 1976, I published the first book describing the ARPANET and its performance [Queueing Systems, Volume II: Computer Applications —PHS].

Electronic mail (email) was an ad-hoc add-on to the network in those early days and it immediately began to dominate network traffic; indeed, the network was already demonstrating its most attractive characteristic, namely, its ability to promote "people-to-people" interaction. The ARPANET evolved into the Internet in the 1980s and was discovered by the commercial world in the late 80s; today, the majority of the traffic on the Internet is from the commercial and consumer sectors, whereas it was earlier dominated by the scientific research community. Indeed, few of us in those early days predicted how enormously successful data networking would become.

Retrospective on the Arpanet Protocols and RFCs

Steve Crocker

This collection of Arpanet documents and related material vividly brings back the early period of the development of the Arpanet protocols starting in 1968. I'm often asked today how much of the present shape and scope of the Internet we envisioned and understood "way back then." The answer is a qualified, "yes." We didn't have a grand plan or perfect vision as we worked on the Arpanet, but we did understand this was important technology that would open the door for broad connection of computers across the country and eventually around the world.

The ARPA computer science research environment

The Arpanet was conceived, designed and implemented within the ARPA research community. "ARPA"—now "DARPA"—is the Advanced Research Projects Agency. ARPA is a part of the Department of Defense. It supports research ideas that will make a large difference in the technology available for future systems. One portion of ARPA, the Information Processing Techniques Office (IPTO), focused on new ideas in computer science.* From its inception in the early 1960s, it spent heavily on computer architecture, computer graphics, artificial intelligence and time-sharing systems. By 1968 there was a significant community of a couple dozen ARPA-supported groups. Most of these groups were within universities but a few were at prominent non-profit or commercial laboratories. MIT, Carnegie Mellon University, Stanford University, three campuses of the University of California (UCB, UCLA and UCSB), the University of Illinois, the University of Utah, and Harvard University were among the academic institutions. SRI in Menlo Park, CA, Bolt, Beranek and Newman and Computer Corporation of America in Cambridge, MA, Systems Development Corporation and The Rand Corporation in Santa Monica, CA were among the non-university group.

It was an exciting time for computer science research. Hot new ideas were being pursued actively at all of these sites, and breakthroughs were coming each year. For the most part, each group was self-sufficient, although the heads of the projects met in a three day workshop with the director of IPTO each year, and those working on similar topics would get to know each other at conferences and symposia.

The 1968–69 computing environment

It's useful to paint a bit of the picture of the computing environment in those days. Computers were quite expensive. It was typical to have one or only a few computers for the entire organization. Minicomputers were not yet prevalent, and personal computers had only been dreamed of. In the commercial world, IBM dominated the marketplace and the majority the machines in use were batch processors. Programs were prepared on either

---

* In the three and half decades since the initial work on the Arpanet, the Information Processing Techniques Office within (D)ARPA was split into two offices, folded down, and re-created. One effect of the success of the Internet is that virtually all Offices within DARPA now depend on Internet technology and many of their programs extend and advance Internet technology. Thus, as the technology transformed the world, it also transformed the Agency that created the technology.

punched cards or magnetic tape and submitted for compilation and execution. The staff of operators in the computer center then scheduled time to run each program. The results of a program consisted of printed output and/or tapes of additional data. It was not uncommon for the user to wait a few hours for the output from even the shortest job, and hence the user was lucky to get more than a few iterations of a program during in the course of a day.

The situation was different in most of the better computer science research groups. "Time-sharing" had been invented a few years earlier, which meant that several users could share the same computer concurrently. Each user would sit at a terminal, usually a Teletype or similar typewriter-like device, and interact with his program. The computer would run each user's program for a short period of time, usually a fraction of a second, and then switch its attention to the next user's program. In this way, the total power of the computer was split among the several users, so each user was given the effect of having a computer all to himself, albeit one which ran a great deal slower than the real computer actually did. A great portion of the time, the user's program would be waiting for him to enter input, so during these periods the computer would spend its time servicing the other users.

The computers were extraordinarily diverse. Each vendor supplied its own, quite distinct operating system with its hardware. (Unix had not yet been invented.) The operating system was almost invariably written in assembly language. Users programmed in Fortran except in the artificial intelligence groups, which made extensive use of Lisp. Invention and experimentation with new programming languages was a fertile area. C and object oriented programming were still in the future. Even mundane issues like the representation of character sets had not settled down. Most of the vendors had adopted the ASCII character set, but IBM, the dominant vendor, used EBCDIC.

Since it was uncommon for computers of different vendors to interact, this schism persisted for a fairly long time. Similarly, word sizes had not settled down. Typical word sizes were 8-bits, 16-bits, 18-bits, 32-bits, 36-bits and 48-bits, with smaller numbers of computers with 18-, 30- or 60-bit word lengths. Each system used a different strategy for packing characters into words. On the 36-bit IBM 7094, characters were 6 bits wide and packed six to the word. On IBM's 360 series, characters were 8 bits wide. In contrast, Digital Equipment Corporation's popular PDP-10 had 36-bit words, like the IBM 7094, but the characters were usually 7 bits wide and packed five to the word. Meanwhile, on the experimental Multics system built by Honeywell, Bell Labs and MIT, the word length was also 36-bits but the characters were 8-bits wide. Interconnection of these systems was not destined to be a simple task! And these were just the beginning of the technical troubles.

The Birth of the Arpanet

In the period 1964 through 1967, a handful of experiments were conducted linking computers together in small networks. One experiment involved Lincoln Laboratories and the ARPA office. Another involved System Development Corporation. A larger but unsuccessful project involved several computers at UCLA. Finally, in 1967–68, ARPA embarked on the ambitious course of creating a large-scale experimental packet-switched network that would use 50,000 bit/second data lines across country to connect the ARPA-sponsored research sites.

Considerable attention was given to the design of the Interface Message Processors (IMPs), which are what we now call "routers," and to the topology of the data lines connecting the sites. Contrary to ARPA's usual practice of selecting contractors based on unsolicited proposals or other criteria, a formal request for proposals (RFP) was written. Competitive bids arrived and were evaluated. Bolt, Beranek and Newman in Cambridge, MA, already an ARPA contractor doing work on artificial intelligence and programming languages, won the bidding and set about to build the Arpanet.

Early on, it had been decided to grow the network from the west. The ARPA research groups were not thrilled when they were notified that ARPA was going to build a network that would connect them to each other. They viewed themselves as self-sufficient. They did not need access to other sites, and they did not want outsiders intruding into their sites and consuming their resources. This resistance was stronger in the east than in the west. Some of the western sites actually looked forward to the idea of interconnection. For example, UCLA, with a research group headed by Len Kleinrock, was developing sophisticated models of queuing behavior in networks.

One of SRI's research groups headed by Doug Engelbart had developed a sophisticated interactive system which featured a mouse for one hand and a five-fingered keyboard for the other hand. It also had structured documents with variable depth of display and hyperlinks that connected documents together, thus anticipating modern URLs. These two sites, and UCSB and the University of Utah were chosen as the initial test bed for the Arpanet.

In contrast to the high level of attention to the design of routers, selection of routes for the data lines, and all of the attendant technical and management problems inherent in such activities, almost no attention was focused on what the user community would do with the network once it was built. It was just blandly expected that the community would figure out useful ways to use this network. One modest exception to this benign neglect was a meeting in the latter part of the summer of 1968. Elmer Shapiro of SRI, responding to a request from ARPA to organize interaction among the four test sites, chaired a meeting at UCSB with representatives from those sites. Each site sent one or two people. All were graduate students or staff members; none of the heads of the research projects came.

That first meeting was both ordinary and special. Vint Cerf and I were the lucky ones representing UCLA. Like others coming from SRI, UCSB and Utah, we arrived expecting to hear a reasonably organized plan and discovered there wasn't any. However, we all found ourselves asking similar questions, and it was immediately clear that we were all thinking along similar lines and had similar questions and intuitions. The only decision made at that meeting was to have more meetings, thus setting the most important precedent for network meetings that persists today! We agreed to hold a few more meetings, rotating among the four sites. Over the next several months, we met at SRI, UCLA, Utah and again at UCSB. Later during the fall, BBN was announced as the winner of the competitive procurement for the IMPs, with their contract to start in January 1969. Their schedule called for the delivery of the first IMP to UCLA on September 1, 1969, with monthly delivery to the other three sites. It was also understood that the network would almost certainly grow beyond four nodes and become a nationwide system of fifteen nodes over the next year or so.

The first months of our nascent network working group were terribly exciting. We were unrestrained by any specific near term deadline, so we focused on grand, "compleat" thoughts. We didn't have our first contact with BBN until February 1969, and we didn't have to focus on anything as mundane as the interface between IMPs and hosts until BBN published its specification, 1822, in the spring of 1969. The period from late summer 1968 until late spring 1969 was devoted to the larger questions of what we would do with this new medium.

Because we each represented a research group whose very essence was the creation of something unique and special, we took it as an implicit ground rule that whatever protocols we designed should allow—or even facilitate—remote interactive use of the varied and evolving special capabilities of each lab. These included large multiprocessors, i.e. the "supercomputers" of the day, elaborate graphics workstations, very large database computers, and artificial intelligence systems. Of course, we recognized that remote use of a system could not be identical to local use in every situation, but we wanted to leave as many doors open as possible. We also kept in mind that the lines connecting the sites ran at 50,000 bits per second. This was considered enormously fast compared to ordinary dial up lines that ran at 110 baud or 300 baud, but we considered them slow compared to the speed of communication between a mainframe and a local graphics workstation.

These intuitions led toward thinking in terms of what is now called client-server style of computing. We focused first on an open, layered system of protocols, and second on moving specialized programs from the server site to the client site to facilitate the interaction. More on this in a bit.

Layered protocols

In thinking about how the Arpanet would be used, I think all of us held two thoughts in mind. We could easily see how to use the network for relatively simple, straightforward activities such as moving a file from one machine to another or logging in remotely for an interactive session. At the same time, we also knew there were surely more interesting and important applications yet to be designed, but no clear picture of exactly what these would turn out to be. It was therefore fundamental in our thinking that whatever we designed would only be a starting point for future work and not a finished and complete system in its own right. It was thus natural for us to think about the protocols we were designing as a set of tools for other developers to use in designing their systems. Our audience was other researchers and developers, like ourselves, not end-users. This is the essentially the credo of the open systems movement today, but we didn't conceptualize this as a political agenda; it was simply the sensible way to think in a research environment.

In thinking about the design of protocols, we looked for ideas which were likely to be useful building blocks for others. It was therefore natural to think in terms of layers. The lower layers of the design should provide simple and generally useful functions which would be the basis for more complex functions to be built above. The key example of this was the decision to build a stream-based protocol and then use that to provide similar but distinct protocols for moving files and for supporting interactive sessions.

The idea of using multiple layers in designing the protocols was not just a way of packaging our own work. We viewed each layer as important and accessible on its own. This is a key point. Many systems are designed in layers, but only the top layer is accessible outside the development group. In the Arpanet protocol environment, we viewed each layer as a possible entry point for others to work from. Higher layer protocols were provided as a convenience and added value, not as a requirement.

The Host-Host Protocol, Telnet and FTP

The basic network delivered individual messages from one host to another. Each message was no longer than about 8,000 bits (1,000 bytes today). We could see that many of the likely applications in the future would all need to send an arbitrarily long sequence of bits, and they would all need for those bits to arrive in the same order they were sent. Further, we could see the need for some way for the receiving side to slow down or shut off the sending process if it had trouble keeping up with the flow of data or couldn't move it from the network into memory or from memory onto the disk quickly enough. These two features, ordering an indefinitely long stream of bits and providing a feedback path from the receiver to the sender to control the flow, were the basic attributes of the first layer we designed. At the time, we viewed this layer as so fundamental that it hardly had a distinguishing name. We called it the "Host-Host protocol." We envisioned each operating system would have some additional software to interact with the Arpanet, and we gave that software the generic name of Network Control Program or NCP. In short order, the term "NCP" became the handle for the protocol itself and came to mean Network Control Protocol.

The first protocols which were built on top of the Host-Host protocol were Telnet and FTP. Telnet is the protocol for interactive terminal sessions, and FTP is the file transfer protocol. These were similar but different. In the file transfer protocol, once the transfer is started, it should continue until the file is completely copied from the sending site to the receiving site. In the case of Telnet, the session is indefinitely long and the transfer takes place incrementally. The Telnet protocol also needed to provide a way for the user to gain the attention of the remote system and interrupt the computation that was in progress.

As we gained experience with these initial protocols, the Host-Host protocol was seen as needing important changes, but the Telnet and FTP protocols remained relatively stable with only modest embellishments and changes over three decades. The two biggest changes needed at the Host-Host level were the transition from bits to bytes as the unit of transmission, and the need for checksums and retransmissions to compensate for unreliability in the underlying network.

The issue of checksums had actually been considered from the beginning. Jeff Rulifson from SRI urged us to include checksums and retransmissions in the original design, and we were inclined to do so. However, at the first meeting we had with BBN in February 1969, Frank Heart argued against this because it would add overhead and reduce the efficiency of the overall network. I asked him how reliable the network would be, and he replied, "as reliable as your accumulator." In those days, the accumulator was the key part of the central processing unit of each computer. If it was not working or if it was even slightly dysfunctional, the entire computer was completely unusable. Frank was in charge of the network project at BBN and except for Larry Roberts at ARPA was the most official authority there was. He also had the advantage of seniority and was vociferous and unrelenting when he felt strongly about something. We acceded and removed the checksums from our design. The network itself was indeed highly reliable. Strong checksums were included in the transmissions between each IMP, and it was rare for messages to arrive garbled. Rare but not impossible. The weakest link turned out to be the interfaces between the Host and IMP. Lincoln Laboratory was one of the early sites on the Arpanet. They were having a terrible time debugging their software, and they finally tracked the problem down to the interface hardware. It turned out that if there was a data transfer in progress with the drum at the same time as with the network, the network interface sometimes lost or garbled some bits. This was only the harbinger. As the network transformed from the tightly engineered Arpanet built by the small, disciplined team at BBN into the broad-based Internet of multiple networks and an unending array of products and technologies, Rulifson's admonition to have each layer operate with a sensible degree of caution and suspicion become obviously good advice.

Mobile code

Part of our thinking about an open framework for protocols was to leave as much room as possible for using the medium efficiently. We wanted to avoid constraining the design and thus imposing obstacles for others. In addition to the notion of defining multiple, shallow protocol layers and making all layers accessible, we also speculated on other ways to provide highly flexible and general interactions. Since we were all programmers and experienced with modern programming languages, it was natural to think in terms of designing a new programming language to facilitate interactions. We had in mind that when an interactive session was started, the remote side would send across a small program which would handle the local interaction and speed up some of the simpler actions. In the language of today, we had in mind the remote system would control the look and feel of the interaction by forwarding a small program for execution on the local side.

Part of the technical debate focused on how hard it would be for each site to implement an interpreter for this yet-to-be designed language and how general the language should be. Should it be a fully general programming language, or should it be a more restrictive language, perhaps based on finite state machines, which could be analyzed by the recipient and understood to be completely safe? We opted for generality.

Jeff Rulifson took the first crack and created the Decode-Encode Language (DEL), RFC 5 in June 1969. Michel Elie took another crack at this idea and wrote the Network Interchange Language (NIL), RFC 51 in May 1970. I believe there was a trial implementation of Rulifson's language but no real usage or experimentation.

These early efforts at mobile code didn't have any immediate effect, but the general idea remained in the mindset of many networkers and finally emerged as a major force with the invention of Java from Sun Microsystems and the promulgation of

ActiveX programs in Microsoft systems. To my mind, the emergence of Java completes the original vision we had in the early network working group meetings

The RFCs and the Network Working Group

The first set of protocol meetings included people from the University of Utah, SRI, University of California, Santa Barbara (UCSB) and University of California, Los Angeles (UCLA). C. Stephen Carr from Utah, Jeff Rulifson and Bill Duvall from SRI, Ron Stoughton from UCSB and Vint Cerf and I from UCLA were heavily involved, and I've undoubtedly left out others who participated in some of the first meetings. ARPA soon designated other sites to join the network, and representatives from those sites started coming to the meetings. Very quickly the meetings transformed from a casual group of six to eight people into a full scale operation involving thirty to fifty people at a time. We needed formal meeting places and scheduled meetings to coincide with the major professional meetings such as the AFIPS Spring Joint Computer Conference in Atlantic City in Spring 1970.

We called this group the Network Working Group or NWG. There was no formal organization. I found myself nominally in charge and handled the logistics, but we didn't spend any time on formal machinery such as a charter or designated roles. There was no membership, per se. Everyone was welcome, and no one had any titular authority.

These early meetings laid the foundation for successive versions of the same idea, culminating in the formation of today's Internet Engineering Task Force (IETF). Today, the IETF meets thrice yearly at locations all over the world. Over 1,000 people attend each meeting, and the work is carried out in scores of working groups within the IETF. The IETF remains open to anyone, and although its primary activity is the development and evolution of the protocols in the Internet and is thus a meeting ground for professional peers, the openness of its operation makes it easy for new people, young and old, to enter the arena, learn the fundamentals and test their ideas. This openness is sometimes viewed as a burden, but I believe its one of the things that makes the Internet standards process qualitatively different from the more formal processes of ANSI and the ITU.

The first set of meetings from late summer 1968 through spring 1969 were mostly discussion sessions. In the spring 1969, while we were meeting in Utah, we agreed we needed to document our thoughts, and we assigned writing tasks to ourselves. I took on the administrative chore of organizing the notes. I was deeply conscious of our informal status. None of us had been appointed to a specific role or given formal authority. I was nervous that the mere act of writing down our thoughts might be viewed as attempt to assert authority, and perhaps there was someone already appointed—or about to be appointed—whom we hadn't yet heard from. As it turned out, there wasn't a plan to have protocols developed more formally and Larry Roberts at IPTO was delighted our group had organized itself.

In releasing the first set of notes, I jotted down some basic ground rules, emphasizing the informal and unofficial nature of these notes. To emphasize that each was intended to advance and not close off discussion, I named each note a "Request for Comments." I expected these would be a temporary set of notes which would be replaced by formal specifications, and that the entire mechanism would fade away as we built the network. I did not imagine the series would persist for decades and be distributed through the medium we hadn't yet built.

In 1971, I took a job at ARPA and Jon Postel took over the stewardship of the RFCs. He continued in this role until his untimely death in the fall of 1998. His able leadership, technical wisdom, dedication and selflessness were central to making the series the all important corpus it has become. All over the world, engineers learn about the Internet protocols, develop new applications and contribute new ideas through this medium.

Steve Crocker
Bethesda, Maryland
November 16, 2006

STANFORD RESEARCH INSTITUTE
MENLO PARK, CALIFORNIA

December 1968

Final Report

A STUDY OF COMPUTER NETWORK DESIGN PARAMETERS

By: E. B. SHAPIRO

Prepared for:

ADVANCED RESEARCH PROJECTS AGENCY
WASHINGTON, D.C. 20301

CONTRACT DAHC04-68-C-0017

SRI Project 7016

Approved: D. R. BROWN, DIRECTOR
Information Science Laboratory

TORBEN MEISLING, EXECUTIVE DIRECTOR
Information Science and Engineering

This research was supported by the Advanced Research Projects Agency and was monitored by the U.S. Army Research Office-Durham under Contract DAHC04-68-C-0017.

Copy No. ......9...

ABSTRACT

This report examines the nature of information that would be exchanged among computers of a large network. Attention is specifically directed to communication between the host computers of the ARPA computer network. Topics discussed here include control information, fault and recovery procedures, file movement, and standards.

Note: page iv in the original document was blank.

CONTENTS

I	INTRODUCTION	1
II	THE NATURE OF INFORMATION FLOW	5
III	THE WORKING ENVIRONMENT	7
IV	ASPECTS OF INTERHOST CONTROL	11
V	USER INTERACTION	17
VI	THE USE OF STANDARDS	31
	REFERENCES	35
	APPENDIX A – Proposed ARPA Network Standards For Some Executive Functions	37
	APPENDIX B – Control of User Access	53
	APPENDIX C – The Control of Remotely Located Programs	59
	APPENDIX D – File Management	69

ILLUSTRATIONS

Fig. 1 -- The Network Model 2

SECTION I: INTRODUCTION

This report describes work conducted under Contract DAHC04-68-C-0017.

This work examined the nature of communications that would be exchanged among the computers of a large network. The proposed ARPA computer network is an example of such a collection of machines; much of the study effort assumed this network as a model. The ARPA network has been described by ARPA (see Ref. DSSW) and in concept by Marill and Roberts (see Ref. MARIL).

The model network shown in Fig. 1 consisted of a communication subsystem that served to interconnect the computers of primary interest -- these computers are called "hosts". The communication subsystem consisted of transmission facilities and computers that could provide such services as store-and-forward switching of host messages. These communication computers are called Interface Message Processors or "IMPs."

Information may be exchanged between various sets of elements within such a complex network. There exist three combinations of source-receiver pairings: IMP-IMP, host-IMP, and host-host. It is not necessary that the the elements of a pair be topologically adjacent: thus one IMP may communicate with another IMP that is accessible only through one or more intermediate IMPs.

The particular interest here is in the host-host pairing. We observe, however, that several other communication exchanges may be necessary to effect host-host communication, as evidenced by this possible path of message flow: host to IMP to IMP to IMP to host. Considerable attention has been devoted to the matters of line disciplines, codes, and communication control that would apply to IMP-IMP

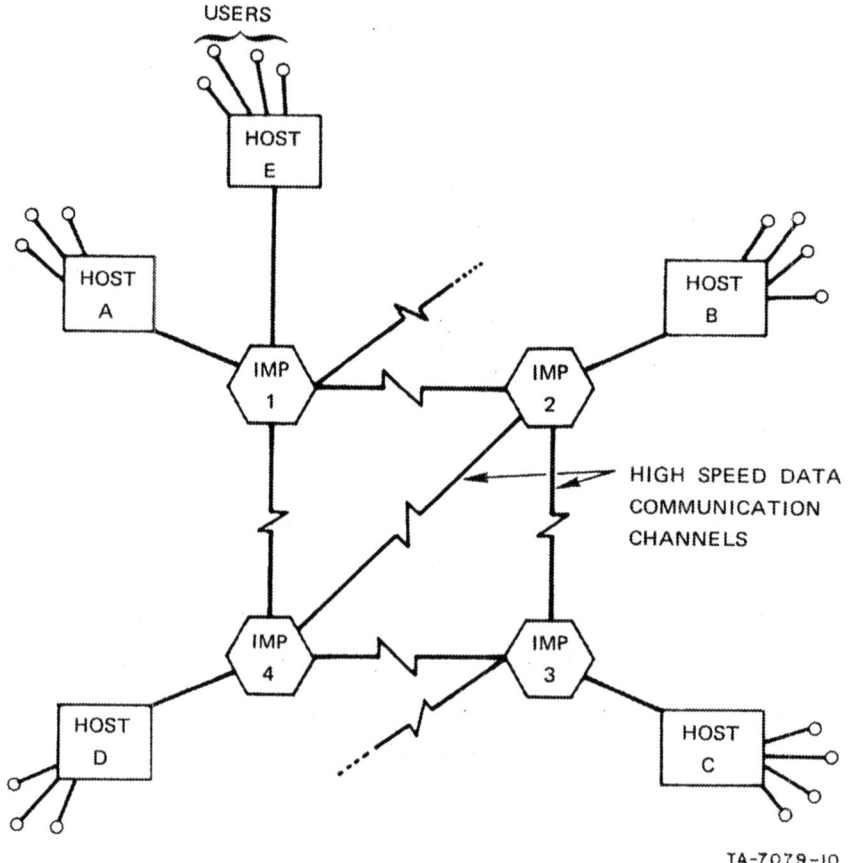

FIG. 1 THE NETWORK MODEL

communication. This work has been reported by the United States of America Standards Institute (see Refs. USASI1, USASI2, and USASI3), by Eisenbies (see Ref. EISEN), and by Bhushan and Stotz (see Ref. BHUS).

We see the opportunity for several forms of codes, languages, messages, and protocols to exist simultaneously within the network. The attention here is only upon the codes, languages, messages, and protocols that could serve all host-host communication.

Ideally the communication subsystem should represent a "transparent pipe" between hosts, in that a message from host A for host B would arrive at B as an identical copy of the source message. It is known that a realistic communication subsystem cannot attain this ideal at all times, for there will be occasions when messages will be delivered containing errors, messages will be lost or misdirected, and deliveries will be delayed. These failings will be noted in the ensuing analyses, but will not assume a dominant role.

Section II of this report discusses the broad types of information that would flow between hosts. Section III describes the working environment of the network. Great significance is accorded to the needs of the interactive user. The typical host computer is characterized as a "time-sharing" machine. Section IV focuses attention upon the control aspects of the network and the unusual requirements that they present. Section V studies the interactive user's role as he makes use of the network's resources, such as executing a remotely located program. Finally, Section VI discusses the need for standards and protocols in host-host communication. Some standards are proposed by way of example.

Note: page 4 in the original document was blank.

SECTION II: THE NATURE OF INFORMATION FLOW

The resources that a host has to offer to other hosts of the network are as follows:

Its collection of programs

The data in its files

Its capacity to do computing

Its capacity to store information.

Clearly only programs and files can be transported among hosts.

The potential of the network is such that a program may be stored in one host and files in another, and they may be brought together at still a third host for actual processing, at which time the program, input file, and output files can be once again distributed throughout the network. In such an environment various techniques of resource optimization can be exercised, and various degrees of decentralization can be realized.

The network model used here does not anticipate the use of such extreme decentralization a described above for several years. The network model postulates significant differences between hosts with respect to their programming languages, compilers, operating systems, and hardware. Because of these differences there is likely to be little actual movement of programs among hosts: rather, a host will be called upon to execute programs already in its own inventory, or programs will be constructed (via the network) within a host for eventual execution there.

A typical use of the network would be to move data to a host, have it processed there by a resident program, and have the resultant data returned to the source host. Included in the scope of this typical use is the opportunity for an interacting user at one host to employ an interactive program at a remote host.

We have seen that programs and files represent two types of information that can flow between hosts. These are not the only types, however, for "control" information represents still another. Much of the remainder of this report will be concerned with control information. At this point control information will be broadly defined to be that information exchanged between hosts for purposes of administering the flow and use of files and programs. Such administration is concerned with control of access to these resources, with reporting of abnormal conditions, and with recovery from abnormal conditions.

SECTION III: THE WORKING ENVIRONMENT

Let us now describe some of the salient features of the network that affect the nature of its control, namely mechanisms of use and forms of standardization. The model network will be characterized as large, capable of performing many parallel tasks, heterogeneous, supporting interactive applications, and rugged.

Size and Parallelism

Some tens of hosts will be assumed as members of the model network in which the communication subsystem permits any host to communicate with any other host. The typical host will use an operating system that provides a multiprogramming service, of which a major aspect is service to interactive users. The ability of all hosts to intercommunicate, plus the multiprogramming feature, permits many simultaneous "conversations" to occur. It is assumed that the communication subsystem and the hosts can provide for such parallelism.

A simple example should demonstrate the potential extensiveness of the parallelism. Consider first a pair of hosts, A and B. Several programs or users at A should be able to simultaneously and independently make use of the various resources of B. At the same time, the same possibility should exist for programs and users at B with respect to A. Now let a third host, C, be added. In addition to the existing communications between A and B, new, independent, simultaneous communications should be possible between A and C and between B and C. The expansion to the entire network is obvious.

As a practical matter, congestion in the communication subsystem and at the hosts might well restrict the number of parallel communications that could be processed. However, it is assumed that there are no logical restrictions within the communication subsystem or the hosts to prevent such communication.

Heterogeneity

As mentioned in Section II, the hosts are seen as being heterogeneous, differing in programs and hardware. (Homogeneous networks have been previously proposed but not constructed; see Lichtenberger's report, Ref. LICHT.) These differences are such that two hosts with identical hardware will be unlike because of differing operating systems. These differences hinder interchangeability of programs, interpretation of contents of files, and interpretation of control information.

If these differences are not overcome, the potential benefits of the network cannot be attained. The establishment of standards or of metalanguages to describe the nature of the information are but two approaches to the general network problem. Creation of specially tailored translation programs represents a solution to specific problems of incompatibility. Section VI discusses several alternative methods of resolving these host differences.

Interactive Applications

The interactive user obtains access to his own host via an on-line terminal such as a teletype or a cathode-ray tube (CRT) device. Such a user requires a rapid response to some of his actions. For example, after a key is struck on his keyboard a new line of text may be presented to him. The elapsed time between the end of the keystroke and the start of the response to him should not exceed an average of 1/2 second. The rate at which the message is presented to him should be at least several tens of characters per second.

The time between user executions of such an activity may vary from seconds to tens of seconds.

These characteristics have a substantial impact upon the network. In particular, they make speed essential; thus the elapsed time will need to be the order of 1/4 second for a character to arrive at a remote host after the user has struck a key. The response should be similarly fast. Also, the volume of information sent from an interactive user to a remote host may be significantly lower than the volume returned to him. Messages from him may be as small as one character each; replies for him may be tens to hundreds of characters, though single-character responses are not excluded.

Economy dictates the use among all network users of a high degree of time sharing of the communication subsystem and of the host-IMP links. Attendant to this form of time sharing (multiplexing) is once again the need for control information.

Ruggedness

It is an objective that the network should be rugged in the following respects:

It should be highly immune to faults;

If faults do occur they should be restricted in their impact;

The effects of faults should be handily overcome.

The potential sources of faults are numerous. The communication subsystem and the hosts will be the foci of software and hardware faults. Because of the complexity and research activity associated with the hosts, they should be a far larger source of faults than the communication subsystem. Another factor is the user, who will be a source of procedural faults, and must be reckoned with.

Alternate routing capability, error control features, and self-recovery features in the communication subsystem should contribute its ruggedness. The redeeming features of the users and the hosts will be considered in Section IV and in Section V.

SECTION IV: ASPECTS OF INTERHOST CONTROL

Functions of Control

We now examine the nature of the control information that could flow between hosts, being primarily concerned with the functions being performed. Details of protocol and message structure are treated in Section VI.

We identify four network needs for control:

  Time multiplexing of the information exchanged between hosts

  Synchronization of host activities

  Control of access to resources

  Program control.

Information Multiplexing

The need for information multiplexing in host-host transfers has been previously described. The effect of the multiplexing is to intermix in time, on a common host-IMP link, in a somewhat random manner, messages to and from many independent users. The communication subsystem should typically deliver messages to a given destination, from a given source, in the order of output by that source.

The impact upon the control feature is to necessitate relating each message with a user. This relationship should be bilateral in the sense that messages from a user to a remote host, and all messages from that remote host resulting from their input, should relate to the same user.

Synchronization of Activities

Within limits, most host computers can be treated as infinite sinks for messages addressed to them. Within more restrictive limits, most host computers can be treated as perfectly responsive to these received messages. An example will illustrate the matter. Consider a user who intends to use a remote host, and for that reason causes a LOGIN message to be sent. If the remote host is an infinite sink, then it will accept the message. If it is perfectly responsive it will effect the LOGIN in a timely manner, i.e. before the next message from that particular user arrives.

If all hosts were completely ideal, then interhost communication could be effected on an open-loop basis, with the receiving host never needing to return a response unless specifically directed. However, no host is expected to be completely ideal. A deviation from idealness can result when the remote host is out of service or severely congested so that it cannot or will not accept incoming messages, such as the LOGIN message; thus it is not an infinite sink. Other deviations occur when the receiving host has no available computing or storage capacity to serve the user within the time required. Thus the receiving host may accept the user's mesage but not be able to act on it. Such a host is not totally responsive.

Control of Access

Each host has a dual responsibility with respect to the network, in that it must protect its users from various aspects of network operation and likewise protect the network from its own users. What is the degree and nature of the required protection? This is essentially a philosophical question to be answered and dealt with at various levels: network-wide, between pairs of hosts, and at the individual host. We will observe that protection might be afforded by various techniques used in various combinations. One dominant technique is to limit a user's access to a system. Appendix B discusses in detail the problems of user access.

Categories of Protection

Protection at Home

A host should protect the integrity of its files, where typically guarantees must be provided against unauthorized file loss or file modification. In other instances file privacy should be ensured, in that unauthorized reading of a file must be avoided. Programs are also held as files and must be protected as such.

The distribution of the host's computing and storage capacity must be restrained such that the network does not usurp excessive amounts, to the detriment of its own users. Most multiprogrammed systems allocate a system's resources on a short-term basis (e.g., time interavls in the millisecond range). Network operation will require long-term allocation processes (time intervals measured in hours and in fractions of days).

Protection of the Network

One of the prime tasks of a host is to screen the users desiring to make use of the network. The ARPA network, for instance, will be limited to use only by those engaged in ARPA business. The user's host is in the best position to determine the validity of the user's request for network access.

The user's host should also provide its IMP only with valid traffic, that is, message formats should conform to established protocols and message destination validity should be checked. The IMPs and other hosts should provide for the handling of abnormal messages in such a way that the network's integrity is not jeopardized. The processing of such messages will use network capacity, and for this reason the introduction of such messages should be minimized by each host.

Program Control

A remote user should be able to exercise some control over a remotely executing program. The program should also be able to report information as to its state of progress. If the remote program is operating from an interactive environment and the user is an on-line user, then the executive systems serving them should already have available such program control features. Thus a user could initiate a program, stop it, restart it, open various registers for purposes of examination or change, etc. Likewise the appearance of abnormal conditions during program execution would be reported to the user for correction to be effected by him.

Other forms of user-program arrangements may not already have these convenient features. Consider situations where the user is a program, and not a human, or the remote program is not designed for interactive execution. Some simple problem situations immediately become evident. A noninteractive program, for instance, must be able to report to the other host whenever a normal or abnormal termination condition has been reached.

As another example, an interactive user may initiate a remote, batch-processed program. If he obtains no response within a "reasonable" time, his concern will be aroused and need to be satisfied so that he can determine whether all is well or not. Thus he should be able to inquire of the remote host whether the job has started and if so, whether it is still in progress, and if it is in progress, how much CPU time has been used. The user may consider that things are amiss, and should be able to terminate the remote job and perhaps get a dump. Appendix C discusses in more detail the control of remote programs, while Appendix D considers the control of file movement and storage.

Degree of Automaticity

The presence of a human user in a processing loop simplifies, in many ways, the problem of effecting control over remote operations. Such a user can be very aware of deviations in response times from previous norms. Deviations in message sequences are apparent to him. He is a good detector of system states. His intelligence permits him to view many alternative courses of action to cope with unusual conditions. He can profitably conduct "gedanken" experiments upon these remote systems.

In a highly automatic environment programs will be the major interpreters of control information and the effectors of control processes. Thus a system at one host may routinely call for the execution of a remote program as if it were a subroutine. LOGIN and LOGOUT at the remote host could take place automatically, as could the transfer of files and the reporting of terminations.

Programs could call upon remote programs which in turn could call upon other remote programs. Complex tree and loop control structures could be automatically established.

In such a world the human user may still be present but know little of the network resources involved in his name on his behalf. Troubles in that world may be difficult for him to cope with.

SECTION V: USER INTERACTION

Introduction

We now consider a hypothetical sequence of interactions among various elements of the ARPA network. Let us define the terms "using host" and "serving host." They apply to the roles that a given pair of hosts play with respect to a given user. The using host is the first computer to receive signals from the user's terminal and the last to process signals sent to that terminal. The serving host is the machine that executes the subsystem that led the user to employ the services of the network. Let us not be concerned here with whether a host really consists of one or more computers, such as a main processor and an I/O processor -- the entire collection constitutes a "host."

The network should be able to accomodate several users at once, so that it is possible for a given host to play a serving role at one time, a using role at another time, or indeed both roles at once. The role of using or serving host, then, has meaning only with respect to a specified pair of hosts and a specific user associated with that pair.

The Notion of the Communication Executive Program

This report uses the notion of a "communication executive program." This program supports all the additional features required to enable a host to participate in the network -- features the host would not otherwise need to possess. It is convenient to call all of these features by the name "communication executive" or "comm exec." The actual realization of the features may, of course, be distributed over many different programs, so that a communication executive may not exist, as such.

The comm exec supports one set of functions in its using host role and another set of functions in its serving host role. As a using comm exec it serves to couple many users with the common link to the network, by time sharing the link. The using comm exec also screens the requests of users for network access. As a serving comm exec, it serves to couple many remote users, as represented by messages on the common link to the network, to the many subsystems of the serving host.

A Scenario

Let us now consider a scenario involving, as major "players," the user, the using host, the serving host, their respective comm execs, and a subsystem belonging to the serving host. The "acts" are then as follows:

LOGIN

The user has already logged in at the using host and may have been busy with its various subsystems. Our interest begins with the first move the user takes to gain access to the network. We follow events until he is logged in as a bona fide user at the serving host he desires.

Transfer of Files from the Using to the Serving Host

File transfers are an optional activity. We will deal with the following:

Files whose point of creation was the using host (considered to be an unlikely event here)

Files that were previously created at the serving host, but

retained at the using host because of storage-allocation problems at the serving host. The action deals with initiation and execution of the transfer, and the assignment of proper identifiers to the files.

User Interaction with the Serving Host

This activity is our main concern. Information from the user's terminal is passed to the serving host. Replies from that host, some of them spontaneously generated there, are returned to the user's terminal.

Transfer of Files to the Using Host from the Serving Host

The previous comments on file transfers apply here.

LOGOUT

The user has no further need of the services of the serving host. We follow him as he logs out of the serving host and, finally, at the using host, he terminates his use of the network.

Faults and Recovery

At any time the user can encounter a fault that interferes with the execution of his work. Such faults may arise in the serving host, the network's facilities, or the using host. Our interest is in the user's actions and the network's actions as recovery is attempted. In some cases the user will be able to resume his previous work; in other cases he will not.

LOGIN Activity

19

Initial Activity at the Using Host

The using host executive recognizes the user's command to connect him to the comm exec. This connection is executed.

The comm exec confirms its presence.

The user commands the comm exec to execute a LOGIN at the host specified by the user.

The comm exec checks the following:

The status of the user: is he entitled to network access?

The working relationship with the named host: have they agreed to communicate?

The believed availability of the named host: is it operational? Can it be reached by the network?

If the command is rejected the comm exec appropriately notifies the user.

If the command is accepted, then a message is created for the comm exec of the named host and offered to the network. The message indicates that it is for the purpose of requesting a LOGIN, and it contains parameters describing the user's terminal. Note that the user's identity is not mentioned.

Activity at the Serving Host

The comm exec receives the LOGIN request message, noting the name of the using host, and accepts the user terminal parameters.

The comm exec checks the following:

   The status of the serving host: is it available for network access?

   Its account with the using host: has the using host used its allotment of CPU time or storage space at the serving host?

   If the request is rejected, an appropriate message is sent to the using comm exec, and the serving comm exec clears all items pertaining to the request.

   If the request is accepted, a code table (relating symbols and their coded representations) is sent to the using comm exec. A "link" is then established for the using host, as a user, to a user's executive program at the serving host. This latter program then sends an initial LOGIN message to the user.

   Activity Back at the Using Host

   If a rejection message is received, then an appropriate message is passed to the user. The using comm exec resets itself and awaits the next user command.

   Receipt of the code table causes the information to be stored for the comm exec. The using comm exec then connects the user to the serving comm exec via the code table. The initial LOGIN message from the serving host's user executive is passed through the code table to the user. Henceforth, all user-serving host communication is via the code table.

   User and serving host exchange messages as the user executes the serving host's LOGIN ceremony.

21

Transfer of Files from Using to Serving Host

Activity at the Using Host

The user generates a special "escape" signal.

This signal is not passed to the serving host but is intercepted by the using comm exec. Until a special subsequent action, all further user communication is with the using comm exec. The user is not logged out of the serving host as a result of the use of the "escape" signal.

The user commands the using comm exec to transfer a file to the serving host. The command implies output to the network (the using comm exec interprets this as meaning to the serving host), and specifies the identifier of the file as it is known at the using host.

The comm exec causes the file to be fetched and transferred as binary messages. As necessary, the file is disassembled into a series of "network" messages, with a maximum length of about 8192 bits each.

The comm exec notifies the user, after the transfer has taken place, as to whether it was successful or not.

The user can retry the transfer if a failure has occurred. Otherwise he will direct the comm exec to "return" him to the serving host; once again the comm exec connects the user to the serving host.

The user commands the user's exec at the serving host to call the file just received from the using host by a name that he specifies. That name will have meaning at the serving host only.

Activity at the Serving Host

The serving comm exec is unaware that the user has escaped to his own comm exec. Without prior notice, the serving host comm exec begins to receive a binary file from the using host.

The comm exec assembles the many messages into a single file that is put away for later use; the user's exec is told of the file's receipt.

The comm exec does not know when the user once again becomes linked to the serving host. The comm exec only sees the user's message on its way to the user's exec; that message is the one requesting the renaming of the file.

User Interaction with the Serving Host

Activity at the Using Host

Each user's keystroke or button push (except that for "escape") is translated through the code table and sent as a separate message to the serving host.

The comm exec tracks the user's manipulations of his pointing device, and provides direct feedback to the user.

Upon user "execution" of the pointing device the comm exec computes the following:

The "hit" within the logical display list

The logical coordinates of the pointer.

Both parameters are sent in the same message to the serving host.

The comm exec accepts entire logical display lists from the serving host. The elements are translated and reformatted, and a physical display list is generated. This latter list is used to drive the user's terminal.

Activity at the Serving Host

The comm exec receives each keystroke, button push, or pointer message, and passes it along to the subsystem, or exec program, etc., in use at that time by the user.

These programs pass entire logical display lists to the comm exec. A new display list will usually (but not always) be generated in response to each keystroke, button push, or pointer action of the user. In some instances the subsystem may generate a new display list independent of user activity -- such might be the case when an abnormal situation arises.

The comm exec passes the logical display list to the using host.

Transfer of Files to Using Host from Serving Host

Activity at the Serving Host

The user's executive program at the serving host accepts the command of the remote user to transfer a specific file to the network. As part of the command, the user specifies the name of the file as it is known at the serving host.

The comm exec causes the file to be fetched and proceeds to transfer it to the using host as a series of binary messages. The comm exec disassembles the file into several messages of up to 8192 bits each, as necessary.

During the execution of the file transfer the user is sent no messages. After the transfer is complete the user is notified by the serving host as to the disposition of the transfer.

If the transfer has encountered trouble, then the user can reinitiate the process. Otherwise he may proceed as he wishes. Typically, he might proceed as follows.

Activity at the Using Host

The using comm exec assembles the received messages into a file.

After notification of proper execution of the transfer, the user gives the "escape" signal to the using comm exec.

The comm exec acknowledges the signal to the user and temporarily breaks the link between user and the serving host.

The user commands the comm exec to dispose of the file it received from the net. This should result in the file being safely put away, under a name just assigned by the user.

After that command has been executed, an acknowledgement is sent to the user.

The user commands the comm exec to "return" his link to the serving system. The serving host has received no messages from the user up to this time.

LOGOUT

Activity at the Serving Host

The user executes all of the necessary protocol to LOGOUT from the serving host. After the final acknowledgement has been sent to the user, the serving host regards the link to the using host as broken. To reestablish the link, either the serving or the using host will need to send a LOGIN request to the other.

Activity at the Using Host

The using comm exec is not aware of the fact that the user has logged out of the serving host, and regards the user and serving host as still linked.

The user sends the "escape" signal to the comm exec.

The user then directs the comm exec to terminate the link between the user and the serving host.

The comm exec does not send any messages to this effect to the serving host, but updates its tables to indicate that the link to that serving host is once more available.

The user still has the attention of the comm exec. He can request a new LOGIN to any host (including the one he has just used), or he can command an escape from the comm exec back to his own user exec, thus ending his activity with the network until the next time.

Faults and Recovery

Some Assumptions and Precepts

It is assumed that automatic recovery processes will be difficult to incorporate as a feature of the initial network. The concern here is with the following:

The difficulty of developing useful techniques to suit an unknown environment

The difficulty of implementing such techniques.

The need for recovery processes, even in the beginning, is unquestioned. Therefore if automatic processes are ruled out, then manual processes are indicated. Envisioned here are processes initiated and directed by a user through his terminal, and as a last resort, other modes of access (e.g., via other machine terminals, machine consoles, or telephone communication).

An essential element to the initial form of the recovery process is that the comm exec does not spontaneously communicate to any host element on behalf of the user. Thus the comm exec at the serving host does not proceed to LOGOUT a remote user when it is established at the serving host that communication is not possible with the using host. Such an approach tends to leave the user with a better notion of the state of the hosts.

We postulate a special feature of the using host comm exec -- a "recover" command -- that requests the following things from the serving host:

Retransmission of its code table

Transmission of the latest version of the logical display list.

The following four subsections examine the user's behavior when a few "typical" faults are encountered.

Fault in Serving Subsystem but Not in Serving Comm Exec

Here the user has as much recovery capability as a local user of the serving host. He can still issue commands to the serving host and observe its responses.

Fault in Serving Comm Exec

The user may need to resort to issuing a new request to LOGIN. If that is effective, he is somewhat in the state described in Section B, above. If he is unable to effect recovery in this manner, then he must use the telephone to request help.

Fault in Network

If a network fault is cleared in a timely manner, the user can simply resume his work. Otherwise he will need to telephone the serving host and ask to be logged out. The network link is easily broken at the using host through the use of normal comm exec commands.

Fault in Using Comm Exec

If timely recovery is not possible the user must telephone the serving host and request to be logged out.

If the recovery is timely and nothing has been lost, he can simply resume. Loss of display buffers, code tables, etc. may force the user to reenter his comm exec and issue a recover command to the serving host he names. If the serving host is still in order it will note that the using host is still logged in. The response will be to send the code tables (so as to establish the using comm exec) and the logical display list (so as to give the user a view of his work at the serving host).

The using host, if not logged in at serving host, will find that the latter rejects the recover command. Then the user must start from scratch.

Note: page 30 in the original document was blank.

SECTION VI: THE USE OF STANDARDS

Introduction

Within the network, agreements will need to be established between a sender of information and its recipient. The agreements can range from the assignment of the value 1 to a particular binary state, to the interpretation of ordered sets of bits as characters, to the interpretation of ordered sets of characters as messages, etc.

We observe that within the network there will be users, subsystems, other host programs, host hardware, IMP hardware and programs, and communication facilities. Each of these elements may be a sender or a receiver, so that a large number of potential sender-receiver pairs can exist within a multimode network. If a given agreement encompasses many like pairs of senders and receivers, then such an agreement can be referred to as a "standard."

The breadth and depth of potential standards is of concern to all members of the network. To the researcher a standard may present a constraint upon his efforts. To the subsystem programmer it may represent a need to provide additional code in order to "conform". To the network implementers it may represent a convenient way to effect growth, as new agreements need not always be developed. Finally, to the casual user it may represent a "one-time" learning process that can serve him well in many different computing environments.

Escaping from Standards

The significance of an element of information will vary as that element moves through the network. Thus the striking of an "A" key by a user may give rise to a multibit message to a remote subsystem. The identity of the "A" key may well be buried in a message that also contains such auxiliary information as the user's name, his host's name, his present location, the name of the remote host providing the subsystem, and various check bits.

It is likely that only the subsystem is concerned with the "A" of the message; it is likely that the IMP is concerned only with the name of the remote host and the check bits. Finally, only the user himself may be concerned with the exact sequence of his own operations.

For this reason it is not necessary that a particular standard have effect everywhere. The IMP need be concerned only with the grossest characteristics of the message being processed, for instance. The host need never see any network traffic control messages and hence need not be directly concerned with their format and the protocols in which they are used.

To some extent, then, standards might be decoupled and separately developed. In the remainder of this section this partitioned approach is taken. In particular, only host-host communications are studied, thus ignoring host-IMP and IMP-IMP exchanges. The host tends to not to see these exchanges, and regards that aspect of the network as transparent.

Some Proposed Standards

Appendix A is a proposal for standardization of some executive subsystem functions in the host. This portion of the network was chosen for examination for a variety of reasons. First, the necessity for standards in IMP-IMP communication is quite evident and can be readily implemented by the supplier of the IMPs. (See refs. USASI1, USASI2, USASI3, and EISEN). Such standards need not interact strongly with the hosts. Second, the host-IMP interface is a poor candidate for standardization because of the widely differing characteristics of the host input-output channels. Furthermore, at each site the "agreement" used to communicate across that interface need affect only a very small portion of the site's facilities and staff.

This leaves the information exchanged between host subsystems, executive subsystems, and users. This area is also under study by others in the ARPA community. These other studies are concerned with standards for communication with graphic output terminals and a variety of user terminals. The present study concerns itself with the remainder, that is, the control functions. Studies by Mooers (see Refs. MOOERS1, MOOERS2, MOOERS3, and MOOERS4) and by Little (see Ref. LITTL) addressed themselves to the teletype-oriented user and to the formats of data. They may be of interest to the user.

Host-host communication standards will affect all hosts, all users, and most programmers. They will have an impact upon existing and future systems and programs.

The standards proposed in Appendix A support the control functions described in Section IV and the on-line user activities described in Section V, and offer room for expansion to highly automatic network operation of the future.

It would appear that the handling of abnormal conditions represents a highly unstructured area within the network, and is therefore less amenable to standardization at this time. Abnormalities may be reported by hosts and IMPs. They represent a place where standards with wide scope may be required.

Note: page 34 in the original document was blank.

REFERENCES

(DSSW) Defense Supply Service-Washington, "Specifications of Interface Message Processors For the ARPA Computer Network," RFQ No. DAHC15 69 Q 0002 (29 July 1968).

(MARIL) T. Marill and L. G. Roberts, "Toward A Cooperative Network of Time-Shared Computers," AFIPS Conf. Proc., Vol. 29, pp. 425-31 (1966).

(USASI1) USASA, "Transparent-Mode Control Procedures for DAta Communication, Using the American Standard Code for Information Interchange -- A Tutorial," Comm. ACM, Vol. 8, No. 4, pp. 203-6 (April 1965).

(USASI2) USASA, "Code Extension in ASCII (An ASA Tutorial)," Comm. ACM, Vol. 9, No. 10, pp. 758-62 (October 1966).

(USASI3) USASI, "Heading Format for Data Transmission (A USASI Tutorial)," Comm. ACM, Vol. 11, No. 6, pp. 441-8 (June 1968).

(EISEN) J. L. Eisenbies, "Conventions for Digital Data Communcation Link Design," IBM Systems Journal, Vol. 6, No. 4 (1967).

(BHUS) Ashay K. Bhushan and Robert H. Stotz, "Procedures and Standards for Inter-Computer Communicatons," AFIPS Conf. Proc. Vol. 32, pp. 95-104 (1968).

(LICHT) W. Lichtenberger (editor), "Tentative Specification for a Network of Time-Shared Computers," ARPA Doc. No. 40.10.130 (9 September 1966).

(MOOERS1) C. N. Mooers, "Standards for User Procedures and Data Formats in Automated Information Systems and Networks, Part I: The Need for Standardization and the Manner in Which Standardization Can Be Accomplished," U.S. Govt. Clearinghouse for FSTI, No. PB 177 550 (5 July 1967).

(MOOERS2) C. N. Mooers, "Standards for User Procedures and Data Formats in Automated Information Systems and Networks, Part II: The Standardizable Elements of User Control Procedures and a Unified System Model," U.S. Govt. Clearinghouse for FSTI, No. PB 177 551 (10 August 1967).

(MOOERS3) C. N. Mooers, "Standards for User Procedures and Data Formats in Automated Information Systems and Networks, Part III: A Suggested Standard Keyboard Assignment for the Elemental User Control Actions," U.S. Govt. Clearinghouse for FSTI, No. PB 177 552 (1 August 1967).

(MOOERS4) C. N. Mooers, "Standards for User Procedures and Data Formats in Automated Information Systems and Networks, Part IV: A Standard Method for the Description of Extended Data Formats," U.S. Govt. Clearinghouse for FSTI, No. 177 553 (28 August 1967).

(LITTL) John l. Little and C. N. Mooers, "Standards for User Procedures and Data Formats in Automated Information Systems and Networks," AFIPS Conf. Proc., Vol. 32, pp. 89-94 (1968).

APPENDIX A: PROPOSED ARPA NETWORK STANDARDS FOR SOME EXECUTIVE FUNCTIONS

Section AI: Introduction

Several activities of the network are candidates for standardization. This appendix examines three such activities--LOGIN and LOGOUT, fault reporting and recovery, and file transfers. These activities will be associated with a host's executive subsystem. Other topics such as display format and text characteristics and input-terminal features are under investigation elsewhere.

The benefits to be derived from standardization of these areas of executive subsystems will vary from user to user. In particular, the casual user with limited needs will benefit greatly in that he need only learn a restricted set of rules in order to make use of the network's facilities. The heavy user or the sophisticated user, on the other hand, will make use of many subsystems, exploiting some to their utmost. Learning to use executive subsystems may well be only a small additional burden to him.

In the next section of this appendix we explore the possible depth of a user's involvement with remote executive systems and then in the two following sections we examine those areas where standardization might be effected. In the final section a set of standards is proposed.

Section AII: Assumed Features of the Executive Subsystem

We shall treat executive programs as one more form of subsystem. They may have their own languages, commands, and responses. Special features of the executive subsystems, as compared to the other subsystems, are as follows:

APPENDIX A: PROPOSED STANDARDS

They represent the initial entry point and final departure point in any user-host session.

They can provide the user with status information regarding the host's system, and in particular the status of the user with respect to the host.

They can execute a powerful set of file and program management functions.

They can report the occurrence of abnormal conditions affecting the user.

Typically, a network user will be dealing with an executive program in his own host and with other executive programs in one or more remote hosts. It will be necessary for the user to be able to selectively communicate with each executive program.

If no other program intervenes, an interactive dialogue will transpire directly between a user and an executive program. The user will issue commands and parameters, while the executive program executes commands, generates queries, or offers advisory messages. The nature of the executive program responses may be more sensitive to the state of the user and of the system than those of other subsystems. Likewise, the time of occurrence of such responses may be less predictable than for other subsystems -- the appearance of a fault could be one cause for such behavior.

In the simplest of situations a user of a remote host need only

APPENDIX A: PROPOSED STANDARDS

deal with that host's executive subsystem to LOGIN, to call the subsystem he desires to use, and then to LOGOUT. Superimposed upon these interactions are, of course, the user's interactions with his own executive subsystem, which has controlled his entry into his own host and likely processed his call to his own host's subsystem for effecting his linkage to the remote host.

In less simple situations the user will be subjected to the effects of faults arising in the remote host as a result of his own actions, or of that host's actions. The result of such a fault will likely be an unexpected message from the executive subsystem at the remote host to the user's host. disposition of this message at the user's host may be to pass it directly to the concerned user, or attempt to process it without user intervention. The likelihood of this latter form of processing is estimated to be quite small for several years to come because of the complexity of the required responses.

When a user receives a message of a fault condition he must make some form of response — giving up in disgust is one such response, though an extreme one. More moderate responses might call for one of the following:

    Reexecution of an action after a minor error has been corrected

    Backing up to some more distant starting point

    Execution of a different process.

APPENDIX A: PROPOSED STANDARDS

Another extreme is to delay action until some major difficulty has been rectified.

The particular choice of response will be dictated by such factors as the following:

The amount of work that might be lost

The amount of work needed to execute the response

The probability that the response will be effective.

In order to select a response, the user should have various items of information regarding the remote host's system and the user's status in that system. Some of the folowing questions might need answering:

Is the fault local to the user or system-wide?

Is the cause a user error, a software bug, or a hardware fault?

What user process was under way at the time of the occurrence?

What is the present state of that process?

A reasonable executive subsystem will enable the user to answer such questions and will enable him to execute a reasonable course of action to effect recovery.

APPENDIX A: PROPOSED STANDARDS

Section AIII: Opportunities to Use Standards

Let us restrict ourselves, for the moment, to matters associated with LOGIN, LOGOUT, fault messages, and status requests. Matters of file movement are treated in the next section.

We will take the view that standardization within the ARPA network is intended to serve the needs of the user and the needs of the network implementers (e.g., host programmers and hardware designers). In particular, the user should not be overburdened with learning a large number of rules, say one set of rules for each host, to enable him to perform the same task at each host. Similarly, the system implementer should not be overburdened with learning a similar number of rules and with the design of translators to enable host programs to communicate.

The ease with which standardization can be established also affects the opportunity to standardize. We identify stability and the presence of structure of the target subject as indicators of standardization ease. LOGIN and LOGOUT procedures are deemed to exhibit both stability and structure. The nature of the information elements in the LOGIN and LOGOUT messages are fairly identical across most systems, so that structure is present. No significant changes appear to have taken place in many years, so that stability is present.

Neither stability nor structure is particularly apparent in the area of fault handling. Here the nature of the information exchanged between system and user is greatly a function of the system's design,

APPENDIX A: PROPOSED STANDARDS

and it often changes appreciably during the lifetime of the system. Message structure and coding are highly system dependent; indeed, many messages are undecipherable without the use of an appropriate table in the system manual.

It is doubtful that messages associated with fault handling, system status, etc., can be appreciably standardized within the next few years. a simple first step to standardization will have been made if exception messages are all provided with the same unique flag. Such a flag would allow the receiving host to easily and immediately recognize a violation of protocol by the appearance of an unusual condition. The receiving host could then suspend further action on the protocol, and perhaps pass the message to a human operator (likely the user).

Another simple step in standardization would be the rationalization of message content. Messages can assume four degrees of intelligibility:

In clear text and clearly stated

In clear text and confusing

In coded text and clearly stated in the supporting table of the system manual

In coded text and confusingly stated in the supporting table of the system manual.

APPENDIX A: PROPOSED STANDARDS

In support of a standard applying to exception messages, we set as an objective that all unusual-condition messages to the user should be available in clear text and clearly stated. The matter of clarity of statement is considered to be beyong the scope of this appendix. However, the availability of clear text as a standard feature means on-line availability. This condition can be satisfied by either of the following:

Eliminating the use of coded messages

Providing the user with a means of generating a query that will respond with the clear (even verbose) text associated with the code.

This approach might be difficult to apply to all subsystems; however, the executive subsystem could be the minimum point of implementation.

Section AIV: File Movement

Let us distinguish between two forms of message exchanges that can occur between hosts. We shall call one form a "communication" and the other form a "file."

By convention the maximum size of a communication will be limited to 8000 bits; no such constraint will be placed upon a file. A communication may be spontaneously sent from one host to another; that is, the latter need not be forewarned of the arrival of a communication. All hosts should normally be equipped to handle such

APPENDIX A: PROPOSED STANDARDS

messages routinely.

A file, by virtue of its typically large size (in excess of 8000 bits), may severely tax the receiving host unless storage space is allocated there for it before its arrival. For this reason, the receiving host should be able to defer a file's arrival until the conditions are suitable.

The receiving host should then be aware of the impending arrival of a file and of the file's size, so that adequate storage space can be made available; and it should be able to delay the initiation of the transfer until such space has been found and other initializing actions taken.

The impetus for a file transfer may arise at the sending host or at the receiving host, where by definition the sending host has the file before the transfer and the receiving host has a copy after the transfer. At the sending host there may be a user with a file which he desires to have processed at the remote host; such a file may have been created at the sending host, or it may have been stored there merely because of storage problems elsewhere in the network. In other cases the user may want a file from a remote host in order to process it further on his own machine, or to relieve storage problems at the remote host.

Two protocols might be established with regard to file movement — one for movement initiation by the sending host, and the other for initiation by the receiving host. As we shall see later, it might only be necessary to have a receiving host initiation protocol.

APPENDIX A: PROPOSED STANDARDS

Sending Host Initiation Protocol

Sending host to receiving host communication: "May I send to a file named #K in my system, of size #Y, and to be named #Z in your system?"

Receiving host to sending host communication: "Send me your file named #K."

Sending host to receiving host file: "This is my file named #K."

Receiving Host Initiation Protocol

Receiving host to sending host communication: "May I have the file named #X in your system?"

Sending host to receiving host communication: "The file named #X in my system is available to you and is of size #Y."

Receiving host to sending host communication: "Send me your file named #X."

Sending host to receiving host file: "This is my file named #X."

Alternative to Sending Host Initiation

It is possible to effect all file transfers by invoking only

APPENDIX A: PROPOSED STANDARDS

the "receiving host initiation" protocol. Consider that a user (or a program) at the sending host wishes to cause such a file transfer. That user could LOGIN to the receiving host, becoming a user on that system. Via a user communication from the sending to the receiving host, the user could then place a request upon the receiving host to acquire a file from the sending host. Contained in this communication would be the name of the file, as known at the sending host, and the name by which it would be known at the receiving host. At this point the receiving host can use the protocol for "receiving host initiation."

Section AV: Proposed Standards

Some Assumptions

It will be assumed that the identity of the host originating a message need not be incorporated in the message by that host. Such identification should have been provided by the IMPs.

It will also be assumed that the user associated with a message need not be associated with the host originating that message.

It will be assumed that message headings and control elements are organized by characters, though the remainder of the message may be binary-oriented. Also, the IMPs should provide necessary codes to mark the beginning and end of each message.

Proposed General Message Structure

APPENDIX A: PROPOSED STANDARDS

It is proposed that all messages have the same general field structure.

The first field would consist of a single 8-bit character (indicated here in hexadecimal notion) representing its type. if the character is 00, then the message is a communication to a user or the subsystem being employed by the user. Any other character in field 1 indicates that the message is likely for some destination other than the user.

The second field begins immediately after field 1 and identifies the user associated with the message. This field is variable in length from 0 to 22 characters, and may be subdivided into two subfields. If it is so subdivided, the first subfield represents the name of the user's host. This subfield may vary in length from 0 to 5 characters, and is separated from the other subfield by a group separator (GS) character. This character is not included in the count of either subfield but is in the count of field 2. the second subfield is the user's name. It may vary in size from 0 to 16 characters.

Fields 2 and 3 are separated by a field separator (FS) character, if there is a field 3. the FS character is not included in the count of fields 2 or 3.

Special interpretations may be put upon the absence of fields, or the existence of null fields (i.e., fields with no characters between separator characters.)

APPENDIX A: PROPOSED STANDARDS

In field 2 the absence of a GS character should be interpreted to mean that the entire field is the user's name as it has been reassigned by the pair of communicating hosts. Once a new user has logged in to a host the reassignment could be made; the new name could well be a single character. That character would always refer to that same user until he executed a LOGOUT.

Null user-host subfields and null user-name subfields might be used to effect special host-host or host-IMP message transfers.

As we shall see, not all messages need have a field 3, in which event no FS character is needed to terminate field 2. Where additional fields are used the FS character serves to separate them; however, no FS character is required to terminate the last field.

In the following sections we shall use the following asssignments for the field 1 character:

00 - normal

01 - LOGIN

02 - LOGOUT

03 - exceptional condition

04 - file transfer request (by receiving host)

APPENDIX A: PROPOSED STANDARDS

      05 - file descriptor

      06 - file transfer initiation

      07 - file

      08 - file transfer request (by sending host)

      09 - ff are unassigned

Normal Message

This is a communication. Only field 3 is added to the basic message. Field 3 may vary in length from 0 to a maximum such that the total IMP message size of 8000 bits is not exceeded.

LOGIN Message

This is a communication. If no fields are used in addition to fields 1 and 2, a link is established between the user and an executive subsystem where the user may be required to execute the LOGIN ritual. Otherwise fields 3, 4, and 5 will be provided; all fields are variable in length, each with a maximum limit of 16 characters. Any and all fields may be null.

Field 3 is the job number, or its equivalent; field 4 is a password; field 5 is the name of the first subsystem to be called.

LOGOUT Message

APPENDIX A: PROPOSED STANDARDS

This communication consists of fields 1 and 2. Some other message type might prove necessary to serve to acknowledge the LOGOUT. Such an acknowledgement might be necessary if the host reciving the LOGOUT message wished to send a reply message to the user before the LOGOUT was really completed.

Exceptional Condition

This communication has the "error" message in field 3. Field 3 should have a character format so that it can be examined by a user's terminal.

File Transfer Request (by receiving host)

This communication uses two variable-length fields for fields 3 and 4. Field 3 is the name of the user owning the file. The field's characteristic is the same as for field 2. Field 4 is the file's name, as it is known at the sending host, and may have a maximum of 16 characters. Note that the user indicated in field 2 is the requestor and need not be the same as the user indicated in field 3.

This message is used by a receiving host to request a file from the sending host.

File Description

This communication contains fields 3, 4, and 5, where field 2 is the identity of the user requesting the file and fields 3 and 4

50

APPENDIX A: PROPOSED STANDARDS

are the identity of the file's owner and the file's name as it is known at the sending host. Field 5 is the number of 8-bit characters in the file. We estimate that a maximum of 8 characters will suffice for this variable field, though the coding of the size is not specified. The coding might well be decimal in 8-bit ASCII to aid in interpretation and to avoid the generation of ASCII control characters if straight binary coding is used.

This message is from the sending host in reply to file transfer request communication from the receiving host.

File Transfer Initiation

This communication is identical in format to the "file transfer request communication from the receiving host".

This message from the receiving host is the "go ahead" to the sending host.

File

This file message has, for the first 4 fields, the same format as the "file transfer request communication from the receiving host." Field 5 is a variable field of up to 5 characters indicating the sequence number of the message (not the packet) where multiple messages must be sent to move a large file. A special character, perhaps 0, indicates the last message. Field 6 is the file, which may be in binary or characte

51

APPENDIX A: PROPOSED STANDARDS

File Transfer Request (by the sending host)

Field 2 of this communication is the identity of the user initiating the request. fields 3 and 4 are the identity of the file's owner at the sending host and the name of the file at the sending host. Fields 5 and 6 are the identity of the file's owner and the file's name, both as they should be known at the receiving host. Field 7 is the file's size in bits.

Note that the names contained in fields 2, 3, and 5 may all be different. Likewise, the file's name may be different in fields 4 and 6.

APPENDIX B: CONTROL OF USER ACCESS

Section BI: Introduction

This appendix examines several aspects of control of user access to the resources of the many host computers of the ARPA network. A user may be a person; a user may be a nonhuman entity such as an operating system. It will be assumed that a user has an identity and an affiliation, where his identity distinguishes him from all other users and his affiliation is the host held responsible for his actions.

The needs of a user may require that some network resources be allocated on his behalf. These resources include processing capacity, storage capacity, and stored information. These resources may have restricted availability; the restrictions may depend upon the nature of the user and upon the demands of all the other users. In the former case we have privacy and other applications of privilege at work. In the latter case there is the need to allocate shared resources in the face of conflicting demands.

It will be assumed that each host computer will be responsible for control of its own resources, and that this control is absolute and need not be shared with any other host. In the execution of its responsibility each host will set its own standards of security and of allocation efficiency.

This appendix examines certain basic capabilities that must be present in all hosts if reasonable network operation and performance are to be achieved. It discusses user identifiers, logging actions, lines of control, and user affiliations.

Section BII: Logging Actions

APPENDIX B: CONTROL OF USER ACCESS

The use of a LOGIN and a LOGOUT procedure at each host for network users appears advisable from many viewpoints. LOGIN actions permit a host to do the following:

Validate a user's identity

Verify the resource allocation available to that user (that is, that he has an account in good standing)

Manage its load

Form a link between successive actions of a user.

In network operation, in particular, it is desirable to reduce communication and processing overhead and avoid repeating these processes with each user action, if these actions are all related. Such an application is clearly needed when the user is causing single-character messages (e.g., keystrokes) to be moved between hosts. An adjunct to the LOGIN process might be the assignment of a special, minimal-size identifier to the user for use in messages, to further reduce the communication overhead.

A LOGIN message may consist of a minimum amount of information -- the user's name, the name of the user's home host, and a job number. Each user has only one home host and that host is the one to be debited with all charges incurred by that user, and is that host to which will be referred all questions of the user's identity. It is clear that each host must possess a network name uniquely assigned to it. The name of a user is assumed to be unique only among the set of

APPENDIX B: CONTROL OF USER ACCESS

all the users sharing a common home host. Maintaining the uniqueness of the job number, among all the numbers of that user, is the responsibility of the home host. This arrangement serves to decouple all hosts with regard to identifier generation and checking, yet identifiers can be created having network-wide uniqueness. A central directory of user identifiers is clearly not mandatory.

Conceptually any host could initiate a LOGIN message to any other host on behalf of any network user -- its own or otherwise. Long chains of "indirect" LOGIN actions could be developed if that concept is applied. Thus a user Y, with A as his home host, may require the execution of a program at host B that in turn requires access to a file stored at host C. Host B, knowing the LOGIN message has originated with A, need not question the validity of Y's identification nor the validity of Y's use of the network for which A will be charged. Host C, however, can properly question Y's identity and network use, since the LOGIN message received by C was originated by B; user Y, after all, has A as his home host. If C finds itself unable to trust B it may be necessary for C to contact A to resolve all doubts regarding Y.

An alternative approach would have B request A to LOGIN Y at C for the purpose of effecting interactions between hosts B and C on Y's behalf.

Another approach requires that host A know in advance the names of all hosts to be used by Y during the upcoming LOGIN interval. Host A would proceed to LOGIN Y at these hosts indicating to each the anticipated processing links to the other hosts on behalf of Y. The

55

APPENDIX B: CONTROL OF USER ACCESS

approach fails only in exceedingly complex processes, where host A cannot anticipate the full use to be made of the network by Y.

This latter approach has much to recommend it when it when LOGOUT is to be effected. Conditions affecting the initiation of LOGOUT are the following:

Departure of the user from the network

The appearance of an exception condition in the execution of any process

The appearance of a fault in a host or the network.

The administration of the LOGOUT process is simpler in a star control configuration (i.e., host A at the center, with B and C at ray ends) than in some linear configuration (i.e., host A linked to B linked to C).

Section BIII: The Itinerant User

The itinerant user is one operating at the console of another host that is not his home host. Thus, user Y, with home host A, is visiting host B and desires to use the facilities of the network, in particular, his own programs and files at A, but via a console attached to B. Clearly Y should not attempt to LOGIN at B using only his name. There exists the possibility that his name is already assigned to another user at B and he may falsely be identified as that user. There also exists the possibility that his name is not

APPENDIX B: CONTROL OF USER ACCESS

recognized at B, Y will be rejected and all efforts to enter the network will be rebuffed.

These difficulties can be avoided if such a user includes his home host's name in his identifier. Upon detecting the home host's name in the identifier, host B would provide user Y extremely limited access to the network, without further ado, provided that:

The name of the home host is a valid host name in the network

The home host's name is not that of B

The home host has an outstanding "credit" with host B.

If no home host name is included in the user's identifier then host B can assume user Y to be a user with home host B.

The network access provided by B is limited to establishing communication with A for purposes of executing the LOGIN operation. Upon satisfactory execution of the LOGIN at A, host B can be so notified, so that user Y can proceed to make use of the resources of A and B only. The volume and nature of the communication between B and A for LOGIN purposes will depend upon the ritual followed, e.g., password transfers, checks, etc.

It was proposed in Section BII that only the home host of the user should initiate the LOGIN act with other network hosts. If this approach is to be followed then information must be passed from B to A to enable the latter to act on behalf of Y in executing LOGIN

57

APPENDIX B: CONTROL OF USER ACCESS

elsewhere. A feature of the Section 3 proposal was that the LOGIN action should indicate the processing links each host will have with other hosts in service of the given user. The application of this feature to the itinerant user may result in host A redefining the LOGIN at B to accommodate those processing links not necessarily known to exist at the time of the initial B and A contact.

For the itinerant user the LOGOUT process is more complex than for the nonitinerant user. In the latter case the user can directly LOGOUT of his home host and that host will LOGOUT that user on all other concerned hosts. Likewise, if any concerned host loses contact with another host then the concerned host has just and sufficient cause to LOGOUT, at its own site, all users of that home host.

With the itinerant user these lines of control become more tenuous. In particular, if user Y logs out at host B this fact must be transmitted to host A so that A can execute the LOGOUT procedures at all other concerned hosts, except, perhaps B. It would also appear that host A must be able to force Y out of the network, even at host B, by initiation of its own LOGOUT action. Finally, loss of communication between A and B, whether due to the crash of either host or to the failure of the communication facilities, should result in a LOGOUT action at all concerned hosts. If A has become inoperable then all the concerned hosts, including B, can effect the LOGOUT, oblivious of the fact that Y is at B. If B has become inoperable, then it is the responsibility of A to execute these LOGOUTs on behalf of Y.

APPENDIX C: THE CONTROL OF REMOTELY LOCATED PROGRAMS

Introduction

This Appendix explores one aspect of host-to-host communication within the ARPA network. It considers the information exchanges required to enable a program at one host to control the execution of a program at another host. For the most part the entire IMP-communication complex of the network will be regarded as a transparent transmission mechanism linking these two hosts. The network mechanism will make its presence known by contributing delays to the information transport process, or by exhibiting an inability to transport information. It will be convenient throughout this discussion to ignore matters of host-IMP protocols and IMP-IMP protocols.

The Characterization of the Remote Program

Let a program, remote or otherwise, be characterized in the following terms:

    An identifier

    Input files

    Output files

    Input control signals

    Output control signals.

The identifier serves to uniquely distinguish the subject program from all other programs in the network that are within the total

59

APPENDIX C: CONTROL OF REMOTE PROGRAMS

inventory of "network" programs. The input files and input control signals represent all the information elements communicated from the network to the program, while the output files and output control signals represent all the information elements communicated to the network from the program. Files will be distinguished from control signals, in that the files form a strong bond between the subject program and the storage facilities of the network, whereas the control signals form a strong bond between the subject program and the supervisory systems of the network.

In the execution of a local program, the linkages with other elements of the host may be afforded by the local hosts operating system, perhaps by implication. With a remote program these linkages must be explicitly established, for the operating system of the remote host is not privy to all of the information available to the local host.

When the call is made upon the remote program the following course of events can be expected.

The program must be identified precisely by name, user affiliation (in a time-share system), and the remote host storing the program.

The input files, or their identifiers, must be provided that program (any initialization parameters are regarded as input files).

If only input file identifiers are provided, the actual files

APPENDIX C: CONTROL OF REMOTE PROGRAMS

need to be fetched, at some point.

Directions must be provided for the disposition of all outputs to be generated by the program. These outputs consist of files, exception messages, status reports, interrupts.

The program must be controlled, i.e., started, stopped, interrupted, and tested.

The outputs must be disposed of.

File Operations

Input Files

The transfer of input files may involve a one-step or a two-step process. In the one-step process, a list of the actual input files can be passed to the remote program. Position within the list may be used to relate a particular file to a particular program input. The two-step process involves the transfer to the remote program of an input list consisting of file identifiers. At times dictated by the remote program, or by the operating system of remote host, these files need to be fetched. Such files might be located at any host in the network, including the remote host. It is clear that a mixed process could be used, wherein some elements of a input list could be files while the remaining elements of the same list could be file identifiers.

Several factors enter into the choice of the particular input

APPENDIX C: CONTROL OF REMOTE PROGRAMS

process to use, where it is anticipated that many different processes will be in use throughout the network. The network factors include communication delay, communication overhead, and file security; the remote host may itself need be considered in terms of available storage capacity.

This matter can be examined in a qualitative manner. Applications involving very small input files representing the keystrokes of a console user might best be handled by the direct transfer of the file to the remote program. here it is easier to achieve fast response; communication overhead need not be excessive; the remote host should encounter little difficulty in providing storage for a small amount of information; no loss in communication processing occurs as the file is certain to be used.

If the program is sufficiently complex it may be difficult, if not impossible, to determine beforehand those input files that will actually be used from all the input files that the remote program might use. Working from a list of input file identifiers the remote program can selectively fetch, at execution time, only those input files actually required. Also, the remote host's operating system can administer these input-file requests in accordance with the availability of storage space.

In executing these file fetches the remote host needs to ascertain the location of the desired file. A first-order decision is concerned with whether or not the file is already at the remote host, and if not, where it is. This matter of file location and movement within the network is a topic for analysis in a subsequent

APPENDIX C: CONTROL OF REMOTE PROGRAMS

memorandum. Here we will simply suggest that the file identifier should directly contribute to the resolution of the question of file location. As a start we might consider a file identifier consisting of three elements: the file name, the name of the user owning the file, and the name of the home host. The home host is defined as the host that always lists this file in its directory. This directory listing indicates the actual location of the file, its psuedonyms, etc. Typically the file will reside in the home host.

If file privacy is a matter of concern a file will not be released unless the "need to know" is established by the requesting host. We will proceed here on the basis of the name of the user related to the request. (Let us ignore in this appendix the problem of validating the user's identity.) It would appear that the user of concern here is initiating the execution of the remote program. If this is so, then it is necessary that the user's identity be provided to the remote program, perhaps as an element of the input list. In turn this identity is passed to each host from which a fetch is to occur.

Output Files

Let us begin by examining the ways of disposing of an output file. It will be assumed that output files are non-trivial so that purging is an unacceptable sole means of disposition. Furthermore, it will be assumed that output files may continue to exist after the program responsible for its creation has ceased all execution. An output file, then, can only be disposed of by placing it in

APPENDIX C: CONTROL OF REMOTE PROGRAMS

storage in one of the network hosts, including the remote host. Regardless of the storage site it must be assigned an identifier to facilitate its subsequent retrieval. This identifier is, of course, identical to that of an input file, in that it contains the elements of file name, user name, and home host name.

Two mechanisms can be used to transfer an output file out of the remote host. One mechanism depends upon the remote host to initiate the transfer. In this case the remote host needs to determine when the file is available for transfer. If a given output file is repeatedly overwritten by the remote program, the transfer must be delayed until after the last writing operation. Also the remote host must associate an identifier with the file so that the receiving host can determine the proper mode of disposition. The receiving host may change the file identifier or retain the one assigned by the remote host. It is possible, of course, for the identifier to have been specified as an element of list of output files.

In the second case, the output file is retained in the remote host until fetched by the concerned host. The remote host has a somewhat more complex role now. Somehow the remote host must indicate to the concerned host, perhaps through one or more intermediaries, that the file is ready to be fetched. This indication may be a control signal generated by the remote host. The remote host must be able to associate the fetch request it receives with the particular output file of interest. If the file identifier is specified in the output file list and the fetch uses this identifier then the association is readily accomplished. The

APPENDIX C: CONTROL OF REMOTE PROGRAMS

remote host must protect the privacy of the file while it exists in that host.

Once again we shall defer to a subsequent memorandum the problems at the remote host of temporary storage of "foreign" files and the use of foreign or temporary identifiers.

Program Control

Input Signals

A limited set of input signals should provide adequate control by a host of a remote program. These signals should be able to "start", "stop", "interrupt", and "status check" the remote program. It is not clear that additional features such as "suspend", "reactivate", and "set new parameter" are required as separate actions.

The "start" signal may not be needed in many instances. Initiation of processing might commence automatically, for instance, after the complete program call has been received (input lists, output lists, etc.) The start signal might be used to repeatedly activate a program that is part of an interactive process. It might also be used to delay the initiation until some later time, in which case, processing should not automatically begin after the call has been received.

Typically a program would halt when its processing is complete, so a "stop" signal would not be needed then. In other

65

APPENDIX C: CONTROL OF REMOTE PROGRAMS

instances, however, the stop must be forced, as in the case of a looping process.

The "interrupt" signal might well consist of a large set of signals. A feature common to all of these signals is the randomness of their time of generation. Some are spontaneously generated by the remote program, the others are responses to inquiries resulting from receipt of input "status check" signals. It is anticipated that the interrupt signals would contain a small number of bits, perhaps 16 or less. Some of these signals are intended to interrupt or redirect the processing of the remote program. Other signals indicate exception conditions that have occurred elsewhere, including normal termination of a program. Still others are the replies to status check output signals of the remote program.

When exception conditions arise an exception message may be generated. When such messages are short they may be incorporated in the output signal. Long messages might be placed in an exception message output file of the remote program, either to be fetched by the receiving program, after the latter has received an exception type interrupt signal, or automatically forwarded by the remote program.

It is clear that the disposition of the received interrupt signal rests with the program or host receiving the signal. Thus an interrupt signal need not cause an interrupt; it may be forwarded to another program or host; it may be ignored, etc.

APPENDIX C: CONTROL OF REMOTE PROGRAMS

The "status check" signal is anticipated for use in status checking. This signal might also consist of a set of signals, each representing a different check to be performed. In concept the subject program should always respond to a status check, and should proceed unaffected.

Output Signals

The output signals are for use by the program to exercise control over or report its status to other network programs. The set of output signals is identical to the set of input signals. The management of the output signals encompasses the generation and the disposition of these signals. Clearly the coding and decoding of these signals by the remote and receiving programs, requires the use of prearranged definitions, or by specification prior to execution time.

The identification of the receiving program might well be by implication, that is, all output signals could be directed to the user associated with the remote program. If the signals are destined for elsewhere they could be relayed by that receiving program. A far more complex mechanism would involve transmittal, with the remote program call, of an identifier list for use by the remote program in addressing its output signals.

Note: page 68 in the original document was blank.

APPENDIX D: FILE MANAGEMENT

Introduction

File management within the network is concerned with the following:

    Assigning identifiers to files

    Relating files to users

    Determining a file's location

    Moving files

    Purging unneeded files.

The existence of multiple copies of the same file is still another problem to be faced, as the possibility exists for several copies of the same file to be known by the same identifier, or by differing identifier. The possibility exists for two files with identical identifiers to differ in content.

It is assumed in this appendix that there exist file directories listing pertinent information of the network files. The notion of single, combined network file directory is rejected, as is the notion of any form of combined directory.

Who Has The File?

Consider a program that is being executed at host A. At some point that program requires the contents of a file W, where the identifier of W is known to A. In its quest for W host A would

APPENDIX D: FILE MANAGEMENT

examine its own directory to determine if W is already at A. If W is present then the fetch can be readily executed by A. If W is not present, then A must determine if it is located elsewhere in the network, if it exists at all. It is judged that an undirected search of the network by A for W would be undesirable in view of the network size, potential traffic, and unpredictable (is it up or not) hosts.

Let there be a unique host, called the file's home host, for each file. For W let its home host be B. The inclusion of the file's home host's name in the file's identifier would greatly aid in the execution of a directed search. Here it would be possible for host A to direct an inquiry to B regarding W. An examination by B of its directory would establish the location, availability, indeed, the existence or non-existence, of W. If W is at B, then a transfer to A could be effected. If W is elsewhere, then a transfer to A would need to be arranged.

If the identifier of A contained no home host name, or that of A, then the home host of W would be established as A.

Let the course of events be such that W was indeed at B and was transferred to A, so that two copies of W exist. It is likely that the program at A will make several references to W; each reference might well employ the same identifier as used in the original fetch. If the copy at A remains identical to the copy at B then repeated fetches from B to A are undesirable. For each subsequent reference to be satisfied by A's copy it is necessary that A be aware of the presence of W within its system. This awareness implies that W is entered in the overall directory maintained at A. The file W now is a

APPENDIX D: FILE MANAGEMENT

form of foreign body within the stored files of A, for its identifier shows the name of B as its home host rather than A.

We note that there are no constraints to prevent A from altering its copy, independent of B's actions, or to prevent B from altering its copy, independent of A's actions. The result in either case is the existence of two files, differing in contents but each bearing the same identifier. Such file differences can produce onerous effects if, for example, the program at A must make use of the most up-to-date version of W. Various techniques can be used to avoid these difficulties. For instance, the directory at A can be caused to purge the listing of W immediately after the first reading of W at A. Alternatively, some form of renaming can be employed at A enabling the program to distinguish between the version of W held at A and the version retained at B.

Finally, we can examine still another aspect of file complexity by purging the copy of W at B once the transfer to A has been satisfactorily accomplished. If the purging process also deletes the entry of W from the file directory at B, then W ceases to exist as far as any host is concerned other than A. If the entry at B is still present it should point to host A as the repository for W.

Now let the program at A modify W and return the new W, with its original identifier, to B. If the directory at B still has W listed then it must be updated to indicate W is now at B and not at A. If W was dropped from A's directory then it needs to be reentered. Upon reentry the file, for all practical purposes, again takes on an existence with respect to the remainder of the network. This file

APPENDIX D: FILE MANAGEMENT

creation process, it is clear, need not have depended upon the previous existence of W; the file might well have been created by the program at A.

Creation of Remote Files

The creation of a file by a host (A) that is not the file's home host (B) presents the network with several special situations. If such a file is created without B's knowledge then it will not be entered in B's directory, nor can it be fetched by B. A transfer of control information from A to B might be used to update B to the situation at A. Such control information might include the identifier of the file. If the file is to be known at A by an identifier indicating the home host as B, then the identifier must be unique within B's directory. Such uniqueness is most readily achieved by the preassignment of the identifier by B. That identifier could be passed to A as an element of the input and output specification list associated with the program that will create the file.

In certain situations it may not be desirable to specify the identifier in advance, as when an "exception message or condition" file is created. Consideration should be given to reserving a limited number of names, network-wide, for such exceptional files.

Purging of Files

Present computing system practice requires user programs to effect the removal of a permanent file. Temporary files are automatically removed when the user leaves the system. Such a

APPENDIX D: FILE MANAGEMENT

practice can be extended to network operation, except that it may be desirable to expand the definition of temporary files. Such an expansion would cause all foreign files at a host to be treated as temporary, where we recall that a foreign file is one whose identifier contains a home host name other than that of the host of concern. Thus, when a user logged out of the concerned host all foreign files related to him would be purged. Clearly there will be situations where it will be desirable to retain the contents of a foreign file as a permanent file. Assignment of a new identifier, listing the concerned host as the home host, could provide this ability.

Files with multiple copies and listings can become a headache as purging is exercised. In particular, the directory of the home host must be updated if a remote host purges a file pointed to by the home host directory. The housekeeping associated with the purging process may become cumbersome; it is also certain that in time, because of various faults, the network directories will contain a significant number of entries pointing to nonexistent files in remote hosts.

This difficulty can also be overcome by a further expansion of the definition of a temporary file. In particular, a file in a remote host, but listed in its home host's directory, would be treated as a temporary file by the home host until a copy of the file is delivered to the home host. If such a file is not delivered to the home host at the time the user logs out, the file's listing will be removed from the home host's directory.

This complete set of notions guarantees the following:

APPENDIX D: FILE MANAGEMENT

Whenever no network users are present, all hosts retain only their own files

The "crash" of any host will not cause spurious files or directory listings to appear or remain in other hosts

The responsibility for this file management process can be assigned to an executive-level program in each host and need not burden the user program.

Title: Host Software

Author: Steve Crocker

Installation: UCLA

Date: 7 April 1969

Network Working Group Request for Comment: 1

CONTENTS

INTRODUCTION

I. A Summary of the IMP Software
   Messages
   Links
   IMP Transmission and Error Checking
   Open Questions on the IMP Software

II. Some Requirements Upon the Host-to-Host Software
    Simple Use
    Deep Use
    Error Checking

III. The Host Software
     Establishment of a Connection
     High Volume Transmission
     A Summary of Primitives
     Error Checking
     Closer Interaction
     Open Questions

IV. Initial Experiments
    Experiment One
    Experiment Two

Introduction

The software for the ARPA Network exists partly in the IMPs and partly in the respective HOSTs. BB&N has specified the software of the IMPs and it is the responsibility of the HOST groups to agree on HOST software.

During the summer of 1968, representatives from the initial four sites met several times to discuss the HOST software and initial experiments on the network. There emerged from these meetings a working group of three, Steve Carr from Utah, Jeff Rulifson from SRI, and Steve Crocker of UCLA, who met during the fall and winter. The most recent meeting was in the last week of March in Utah. Also present was Bill Duvall of SRI who has recently started working with Jeff Rulifson.

Somewhat independently, Gerard DeLoche of UCLA has been working on the HOST-IMP interface.

I present here some of the tentative agreements reached and some of the open questions encountered. Very little of what is here is firm and reactions are expected.

I. A Summary of the IMP Software

Messages

Information is transmitted from HOST to HOST in bundles called messages. A message is any stream of not more than 8080 bits, together with its header. The header is 16 bits and contains the following information:

```
Destination     5 bits
Link            8 bits
Trace           1 bit
Spare           2 bits
```

The destination is the numerical code for the HOST to which the message should be sent. The trace bit signals the IMPs to record status information about the message and send the information back to the NMC (Network Measurement Center, i.e., UCLA). The spare bits are unused.

Links

The link field is a special device used by the IMPs to limit certain kinds of congestion. They function as follows. Between every pair of HOSTs there are 32 logical full-duplex connections over which messages may be passed in either direction. The IMPs place the restriction on these links that no HOST can send two successive messages over the same link before the IMP at the destination has sent back a special message called an RFNM (Request for Next Message). This arrangement limits the congestion one HOST can cause another if the sending HOST is attempting to send too much over one link. We note, however, that since the IMP at the destination does not have enough capacity to handle all 32 links simultaneously, the links serve their purpose only if the overload is coming from one or two links. It is necessary for the HOSTs to cooperate in this respect.

PAGE 1

The links have the following primitive characteristics. They are always functioning and there are always 32 of them.

By "always functioning," we mean that the IMPs are always prepared to transmit another message over them. No notion of beginning or ending a conversation is contained in the IMP software. It is thus not possible to query an IMP about the state of a link (although it might be possible to query an IMP about the recent history of a link -- quite a different matter!).

The other primitive characteristic of the links is that there are always 32 of them, whether they are in use or not. This means that each IMP must maintain 18 tables, each with 32 entries, regardless of the actual traffic.

The objections to the link structure notwithstanding, the links are easily programmed within the IMPs and are probably a better alternative to more complex arrangements just because of their simplicity.

IMP Transmission and Error Checking

After receiving a message from a HOST, an IMP partitions the message into one or more packets. Packets are not more than 1010 bits long and are the unit of data transmission from IMP to IMP. A 24 bit cyclic checksum is computed by the transmission hardware and is appended to an outgoing packet. The checksum is recomputed by the receiving hardware and is checked against the transmitted checksum. Packets are reassembled into messages at the destination IMP.

Open Questions on the IMP Software

1. An 8 bit field is provided for link specification, but only 32 links are provided, why?
2. The HOST is supposed to be able to send messages to its IMP. How does it do this?
3. Can a HOST, as opposed to its IMP, control RFNMs?
4. Will the IMPs perform code conversion? How is it to be controlled?

II. Some Requirements Upon the Host-to-Host Software

Simple Use

As with any new facility, there will be a period of very light usage until the community of users experiments with the network and begins to depend upon it. One of our goals must be to stimulate the immediate and easy use by a wide class of users. With this goal, it seems natural to provide the ability to use any remote HOST as if it had been dialed up from a TTY (teletype) terminal. Additionally, we would like some ability to transmit a file in a somewhat different manner perhaps than simulating a teletype.

Deep Use

One of the inherent problems in the network is the fact that all responses from a remote HOST will require on the order of a half-second or so, no matter how simple. For teletype use, we could shift to a half-duplex local-echo arrangement, but this would destroy some of the usefulness of the network. The 940 Systems, for example, have a very specialized echo.

When we consider using graphics stations or other sophisticated terminals under the control of a remote HOST, the problem becomes more severe. We must look for some method which allows us to use our most sophisticated equipment as much as possible as if we were connected directly to the remote computer.

Error Checking

The point is made by Jeff Rulifson at SRI that error checking at major software interfaces is always a good thing. He points to some experience at SRI where it has saved much dispute and wasted effort. On these grounds, we would like to see some HOST to HOST checking. Besides checking the software interface, it would also check the HOST-IMP transmission hardware. (BB&N claims the HOST-IMP hardware will be as reliable as the internal registers of the HOST. We believe them, but we still want the error checking.)

III. The Host Software

Establishment of a Connection

The simplest connection we can imagine is where the local HOST acts as if it is a TTY and has dialed up the remote HOST. After some consideration of the problems of initiating and terminating such a connection, it has been decided to reserve link 0 for communication between HOST operating systems. The remaining 31 links are thus to be used as dial-up lines.

Each HOST operating system must provide to its user level programs a primitive to establish a connection with a remote HOST and a primitive to break the connection. When these primitives are invoked, the operating system must select a free link and send a message over link 0 to the remote HOST requesting a connection on the selected link. The operating system in the remote HOST must agree and send back an accepting message over link 0. In the event both HOSTs select the same link to initiate a connection and both send request messages at essentially the same time, a simple priority scheme will be invoked in which the HOST of lower priority gives way and selects another free link. One usable priority scheme is simply the ranking of HOSTs by their identification numbers. Note that both HOSTs are aware that simultaneous requests have been made, but they take complementary actions: The higher priority HOST disregards the request while the lower priority HOST sends both an acceptance and another request.

The connection so established is a TTY-like connection in the pre-log-in state. This means the remote HOST operating system will initially treat the link as if a TTY had just called up. The remote HOST will generate the same echos, expect the same log-in sequence and look for the same interrupt characters.

High Volume Transmission

Teletypes acting as terminals have two special drawbacks when we consider the transmission of a large file. The first is that some characters are special interrupt characters. The second is that special buffering techniques are often employed, and these are appropriate only for low-speed character at time transmission.

We therefore define another class of connection to be used for the transmission of files or other large volumes of data. To initiate this class of link, user level programs at both ends of an established TTY-like link must request the establishment of a file-like connection parallel to the TTY-like link. Again the priority scheme comes into play, for the higher priority HOST sends a message over link 0 while the lower priority HOST waits for it. The user level programs are, of course, not concerned with this. Selection of the free link is done by the higher priority HOST.

File-like links are distinguished by the fact that no searching for interrupt characters takes place and buffering techniques appropriate for the higher data rates takes place.

A Summary of Primitives

Each HOST operating system must provide at least the following primitives to its users. This list knows not to be necessary but not sufficient.

a) Initiate TTY-like connection with HOST x.

b) Terminate connection.

c) Send/Receive character(s) over TTY-like connection.

d) Initiate file-like connection parallel to TTY-like connection.

e) Terminate file-like connection.

f) Send/Receive over file-like connection.

Error Checking

We propose that each message carry a message number, bit count, and a checksum in its body, that is transparent to the IMP. For a checksum we suggest a 16-bit end-around-carry sum computed on 1152 bits and then circularly shifted right one bit. The right circular shift every 1152 bits is designed to catch errors in message reassembly by the IMPs.

Closer Interaction

The above described primitives suggest how a user can make simple use of a remote facility. They shed no light on how much more intricate use of the network is to be carried out. Specifically, we are concerned with the fact that at some sites a great deal of work has gone into making the computer highly responsive to a sophisticated console. Culler's consoles at UCSB and Englebart's at SRI are at least two examples. It is clear that delays of a half-second or so for trivial echo-like responses degrade the interaction to the point of making the sophistication of the console irrelevant.

We believe that most console interaction can be divided into two parts, an essentially local, immediate and trivial part and a remote, more lengthy and significant part. As a simple example, consider a user at a console consisting of a keyboard and refreshing display screen. The program the user is talking typing into accumulates a string of characters until a carriage return is encountered and then it processes the string. While characters are being typed, it displays the characters on the screen. When a rubout character is typed, it deletes the previous non-rubout character. If the user types H E L L O ← ← P CR where ← is rubout and CR is carriage-return, he has made nine keystrokes. If each of these keystrokes causes a message to be sent which in return invokes instructions to our display station we will quickly become bored.

A better solution would be to have the front-end of the remote program -- that is the part scanning for ← and CR -- be resident in our computer. In that case, only one five character message would be sent, i.e., H E L P CR, and the screen would be managed locally.

We propose to implement this solution by creating a language for console control. This language, current named DEL, would be used by subsystem designers to specify what components are needed in a terminal and how the terminal is to respond to inputs from its keyboard, Lincoln Wand, etc. Then, as a part of the initial protocol, the remote HOST would send to the local HOST, the source language text of the program which controls the console. This program would have been by the subsystem designer in DEL, but will be compiled locally.

The specifications of DEL are under discussion. The following diagrams show the sequence of actions.

A. Before Link Establishment

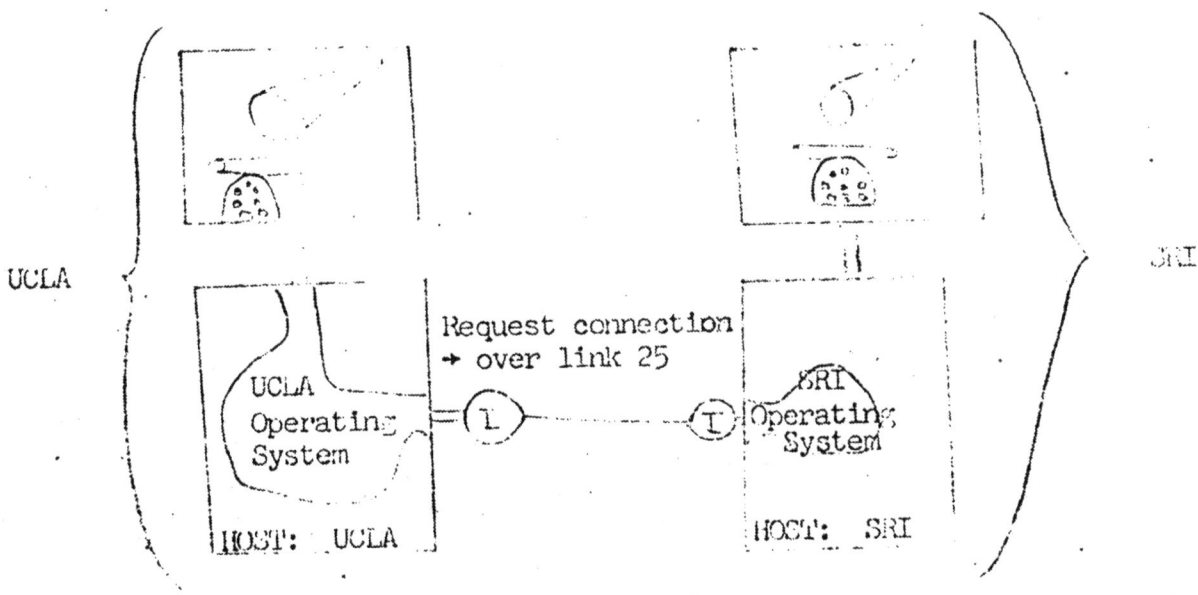

b. After Link Establishment and Log-in

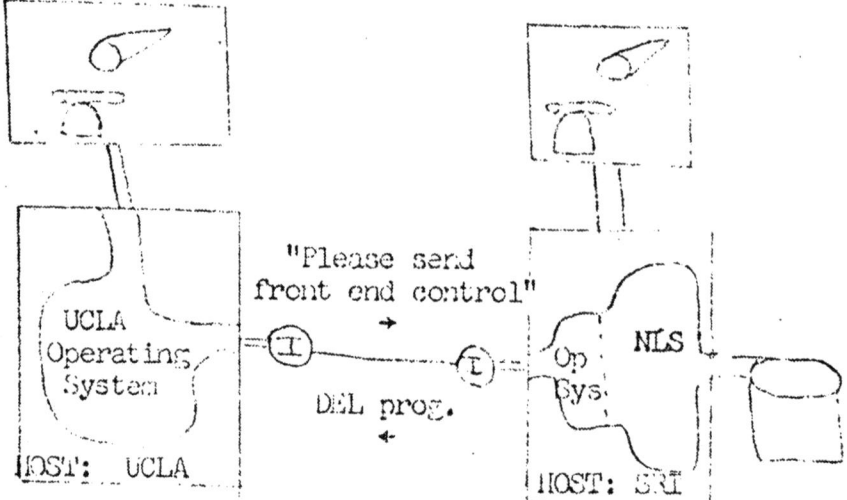

c. After Receipt and Compilation of the DEL program

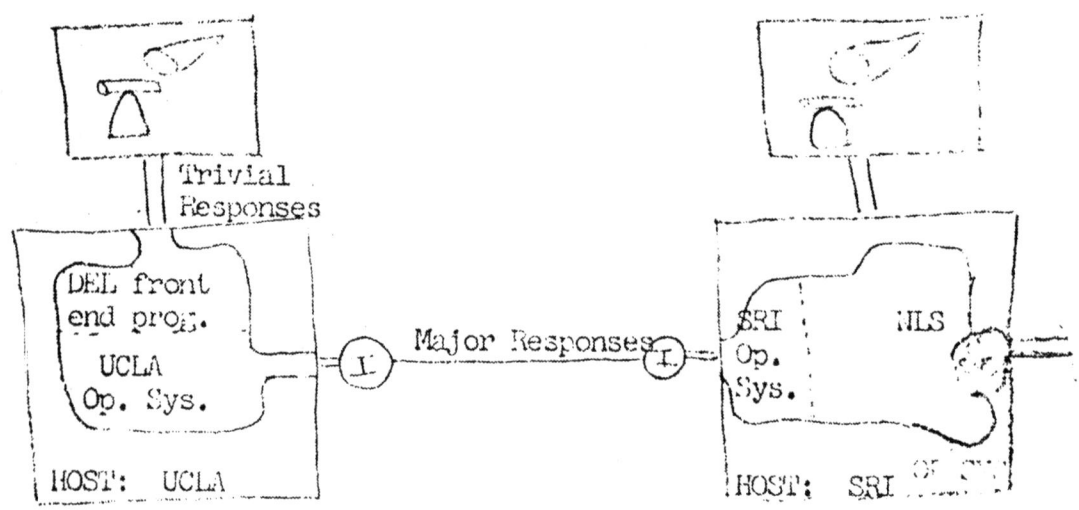

Open Questions

1. If the IMPs do code conversion, the checksum will not be correct.
2. The procedure for requesting the DEL front end is not yet specified.

IV. Initial Experiments

Experiment One

SRI is currently modifying their on-line retrieval system which will be the major software component of the Network Documentation Center so that it can be operated with model 35 teletypes. The control of the teletypes will be written in DEL. All sites will write DEL compilers and use NLS through the DEL program.

PAGE 6

Experiment Two

SRI will write a DEL front end for full NLS, graphics included. UCLA and UTAH will use NLS with graphics.

1 LINKS

1a Control Links

1a1 Logical link 0 will be a control link between any two HOSTs on the network

    1a1a Only one control link may exist between any two HOSTs on the network. Thus, if there are n HOSTs on the network, there are n-1 control links from each HOST.

1a2 It will be primarily used for communication between HOSTs for the purposes of:

    1a2a Establishing user links

    1a2b Breaking user links

    1a2c Passing interrupts regarding the status of links and/or programs using the links

    1a2d Monitor communication

1a3 Imps in the network may automatically trace all messages sent on link 0.

1b Primary Links

1b1 A user at a given HOST may have exactly 1 primary link to each of the other HOSTs on the network.

    1b1a The primary link must be the first link established between a HOST user and another HOST.

    1b1b Primary links are global to a user, i.e. a user program may open a primary link, and that link remains open until it is specifically closed.

    1b1c The primary link is treated like a teletype connected over a normal data-phone or direct line by the remote HOST, i.e. the remote HOST considers a primary link to be a normal teletype user.

    1b1d The primary link is used for passing (user) control information to the remote HOST. e.g. it will be used for logging in to the remote host (using the remote hosts standard login procedure).

1c Auxilliary Links

1c1 A user program may establish any number of auxilliary links between itself and a user program in a connected HOST.

1c1a These links may be used for either binary or character transmission.

1c1b Auxilliary links are local to the sub-system which establishes them, and therefore are closed when that subsystem is left.

2 MANIPULATION OF LINKS

2a Control Links

2a1 The control link is established at system load time.

2a2 The status of a control link may be active or inactive

2a2a The status of the control lnk should reflect the relationship between the HOSTs.

2b Primary Links

2b1 Primary links are established by a user or executive call to the monitor

2b1a The network identification number of the HOST to be linked to must be included in the call

2b1b An attempt to establish more than one primary link to a particular HOST will be regarded as an error, and the request will be defaulted

2b1c Standard Transmission Character Set

2b1c1 There will be a standard character set for transmission of data over the primary links and control links.

2b1c1a. This will be full (8 bit) ASCII.

2b1d (getlink) The protocol for establishing a link to HOST B from HOST A is as follows

2b1d1 A selects a currently unused link to HOST B from its allocation tables

2b1d2 A transmits a link-connect message to B over link 0.

2b1d3 A then waits for:

2b1d3a. A communication regarding that link from B

2b1d3b. A certain amount of time to elapse

2b1d4 If a communication regarding the link is recieved from

B. It is examined to see if it is:

2b1d4a A verification of the link from B.

2b1d4a1 This results in a successful return from the monitor to the requestor. The link number is returned to the requestor, and the link is established.

2b1d4b A request from B to establish the link. this means: that B is trying to establish the same link as A independently of A.

2b1d4b1 If the network ID number of A(Na) is greater than that of B(Nb), then A ignores the request, and continues to await confirmation of the link from B.

2b1d4b2 If, on the other hand, Na<Nb, A:

2b1d4b2a Honors the request from B to establish the link.

2b1d4b2b Sends verification as required.

2b1d4b2c Aborts its own request, and repeats the allocation process.

2b1d4c Some other communication from B regarding the link.

2b1d4c1 This is an error condition, meaning that either:

2b1d4c1a A has faulted by selecting a previously allocated link for allocation.

2b1d4c1b B is transmitting information over an un-allocated link.

2b1d4c1c Or a message regarding allocation from B to A has been garbled in transmission.

2b1d4c2 In this case, A's action is to:

2b1d4c2a Send a link disconnect message to B concerning the attempted connection

2b1d4c2b Consider the state of HOST B to be in error and initiate entry to a panic routine(error).

2b1d5 If no communication regarding the link is recieved from B in the prescribed amount of time, HOST B is considered to be in an error state.

2b1d5a. A link disconnect message is sent to B from A.

2b1d5b. A panic routine is called(error).

2c Auxilliary Links

2c1 Auxilliary links are established by a call to the monitor from a user program.

2c1a The request must specify pertinent data about the desired link to the monitor

2c1a1 The number of the primary link to B.

2c1b The request for an auxilliary link must be made by a user program in each of the HOSTs (A and B).

2c1c If Na > Nb, then HOST A proceeds to establish a link to HOST B in the manner outlined above (get link).

2c1d If Na<Nb, then A waits:

2c1d1 For HOST B to establish the link (after looking to see if B has already established the corresponding link).

2c1d2 For a specified amount of time to elapse.

2c1d2a This means that HOST B did not respond to the request of HOST A.

2c1d2b The program in HOST A and B should be able to specify the amount of time to wait for the timeout.

3 ERROR CHECKING

3a All messages sent over the network will be error checked initially so as to help isolate software and hardware bugs.

3b A checksum will be associated with each message, which is order dependent.

3b1 The following algorithm is one which might be used:

3b1a A checksum of length 1 may be formed by adding successive fields in the string to be checked serially, and adding the carry bit into the lowest bit position of the sum.

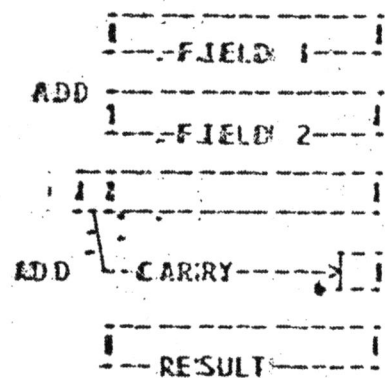

3b1a1 This process is known as folding.

3b1a2 Several fields may be added and folded in parallel, if they are folded appropriately after the addition.

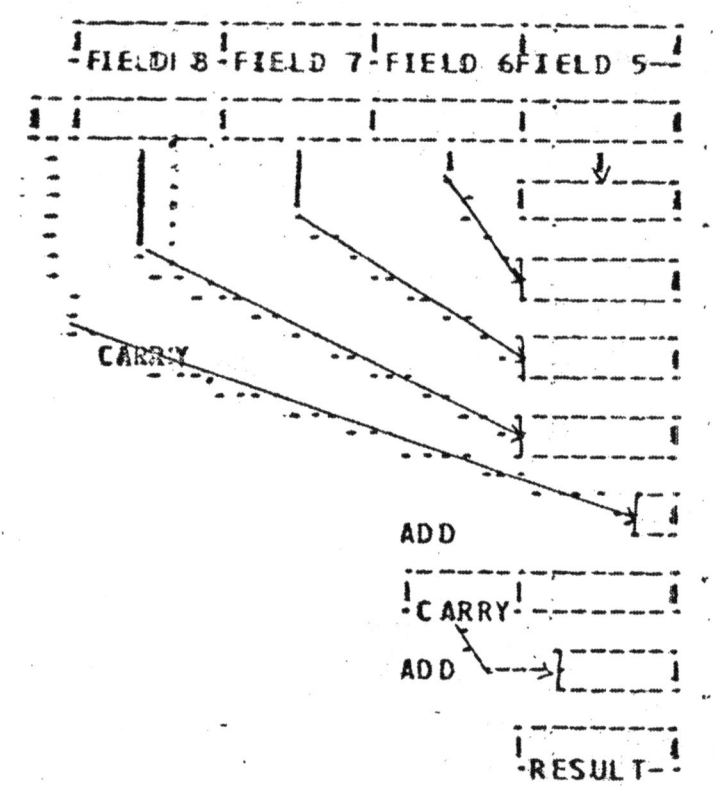

3b1a2a Using this scheme, it is assumed that, if there are n fields, the carries from the first n-1 fields are automatically added into the low order position of the next higher field, so that in folding, one need only add the n result fields to the carry from the nth field, and then add in an appropiately sized carry from that addition (and repeat the desired number of times) to achieve the result.

3b1a3 A checksum computed in this manner has the advantage that the word lengths of different machines may each be used optimally.

3b1a3a If a string of suitable length is chosen for computing the checksum, and a suitable checksum field length is selected, the checksum technique for each of the machines will be relatively optimal.

3b1a3a1 Field length: 288 bits (lowest common denomenator of (24,32,36)

3b1a3a2 Checksum length: 8 bits (convenient field size for all machines)

3b1b If a message is divided into groups of fields, and each group is checksummed in this manner, an order dependent checksum may be got by shifting the checksum for each group, and adding it in (successively) to the checksum of the next group

3c A facility will be provided where two HOSTs may enter a mode which requires positive verification of all messages. This verification is sent over the control link.

4 MONITOR FUNCTIONS

4a Network I/O drivers

4a1 Input

4a1a Input message from IMP.

4a1b Do error checking on message.

4a1b1 Verify checksum

4a1b2 Send "message recieved" aknowledgement over control link if aknowledge mode is in effect.

4a1c (transd character translation.

4a1c1 There is a strong possibility that the character translation may be done in the IMP.

4a1c2 This needs to be explored further with BBN.

4a1c3 There are two main considerations

> 4a1c3a Should the transltaion be done by table or algorithm?
>
>> 4a1c3a1 Initially it seems as though the best way to go is table.
>
> 4a1c3b How should we decide which messages should be translated, i.e. is it desirable to not translate everything (YES!!) and by what means can we use to differentiate?

4a1d Decode header, and pass message to correct recipient as identified by source, and link.

4a2 Output

4a2a Build header

4a2b Character translation

> 4a2b1 See remarks under the section on output translation (trans).

4a2c Create checksum

4a2d Check status of link

> 4a2d1 If there has not been a RFNM since the last message transmitted out the link, wait for it.

4a2e Transmit message to IMP

4a2f If aknowledge mode is in effect, wait for

> 4a2f1 RFNM from destination IMP.
>
> 4a2f2 Response from destination HOST over control line 0.

4b Network status

4b1 Maintain status of other HOSTs on network

> 4b1a If an IMP is down, then his HOST is considered to be down.

4b2 Maintain status of control lines.

4b3 Answer status queries from other HOSTs.

4b4 Inform other HOSTs as to status of primary and auxilliary links on an interrupt basis.

4b5 Inform other HOSTs as to status of programs using primary and secondary links

5 EXECUTIVE PRIMITIVES

5a Primary Links

5a1 These require the HOST number as a parameter.

5a1a Establish primary link

5a1b Connect controlling teletype to primary link

5a1c INPUT/OUTPUT over primary link

5a1d Interrogate status of primary link

5a1d1 don't know what, exactly, this should do, but it seems as though it might be useful.

5a1e Disconnect controlling teletype from primary link

5a1f Kill primary link

5b Auxiliary Links.

5b1 Establish auxilliary link.

5b1a requires the HOST number as a parameter

5b1b It returns a logical link number which is similar to a file index. It is this number which is passed to all of the other Auxilliary routines as a parameter.

5b2 INPUT/OUTPUT over auxilliary link

5b3 Interrogate status auxilliary link.

5b3a don't know what, exactly, this should do, but it seems as though it might be useful.

5b4 Kill auxilliary link.

5c Special executive functions

5c1 Transparent INPUT/OUTPUT over link

5c1a This may be used to do block I/O transfers over a link

5c1b The function of the monitor in this instance is to transfer a buffer directly to its IMP

5c1c It does not modify it in any way

5c1c1 This means that the header and other control information must be in the buffer.

5c1d The intended use of this is for network debugging.

6 INITIAL CHECKOUT

6a The network will be initially checked out using the links in a simulated data-phone mode.

6a1 All messages will be one character in length.

6a2 Links will be transparent to the monitor, and controlled by user program via a special executive primitive.

6a2a The initial test will be run from two user programs in different HOSTs, e.g. DDT to DDT.

6a2b It will be paralleled by a telephone link or similar.

Network Working Group
Request for Comments: 3

Steve Crocker
UCLA
9 April 1969

DOCUMENTATION CONVENTIONS

The Network Working Group seems to consist of Steve Carr at Utah, Jeff Rulifson and Bill Duvall at SRI, and Steve Crocker and Gerard Deloche at UCLA. Membership is not closed.

The Network Working Group (NWG) is concerned with the HOST software, the strategies for using the network, and initial experients with the network.

Documentation of the NWG's effort is through notes such as this. Notes may be produced at any site by anybody and included in this series.

Content

The content of a NWG note may be any thought, suggestion, etc. related to the HOST software or other aspect of the network. Notes are encouraged to be timely rather than polished. Philosophical positions without examples or other specifics, Specific suggestions or implementation techniques without introductory or background explication, and explicit questions without any attempted answers are all acceptable. The minimum length for a NWG note is one sentence.

These standards (or lack of them) are stated explicitly for two reasons. First, there is a tendency to view a written statement as _ipso facto_ authoritative, and we hope to promote the exchange and discussion of considerably less than authoritative ideans. Second, there is a natural hestancy to publish something unpolished, and we hope to ease this inhibition.

Form

Every NWG note should bear the following information:

1. "Network Working Group"
   "Request for Comments:" x
   where x is a serial number.
   Serial numbers are assigned by Bill Duvall at SRI.
2. Author and affiliation
3. Date
4. Title. The title need not be unique.

Distribution

One copy only will be sent from the author's site to:

1. Bob Kahn, BB & N
2. Larry Roberts, ARPA
3. Steve Carr, UCLA
4. Jeff Rulifson, UTAH
5. Ron Stoughton, UCSB
6. Steve Crocker, UCLA

Documentation Conventions
Page 2

Reproduction if desired may be handled locally.

<u>Other Notes</u>

Two notes (1 & 2) have been written so far. These are both titled <u>HOST Software</u> and are by Steve Crocker and Bill Duvall, separately.

Other notes planned are on
1. Network Timetable
2. The Philosophy of NIL
3. Specifications for NIL
4. Deeper Documentation of HOST Software.

Title: Network Timetable

Author: Elmer B. Shapiro

Installation: Stanford Research Institute

Date: 24 March 1969

Network Working Group Request for Comment: 4

;N10, 03/24/69 1342:42 EBS ;

1   (n10) network checkout

2   Installation of communication gear 8/1/69

    2a From AT&T and/or BBN need dimensional, power and cabling specifications

    2b Need to establish SRI desired alternate locations, so as to determine maximum telco cable lengths

    2c Need to establish location and drops on voice coordination circuits

    2d Need circuit information on voice drops for tie to intercom system

    2e Need to order and instal a.c. power (coordinate with 4b)

    2f See 16

3   Design and construct host-Imp interface 9/1/69

    3a Need specifications from BBN

    3b Develop trial design

    3c Review with system programmers

    3d Establish final design

    3e Biuld and design hardware

    3f Debug trial software with hardware loop test

4   Imp installation 9/15/69

    4a From BBN get dimensional, power and cabling specifications

    4b SRI orders and installs a.c. power (coordinate with 2e)

5   Debug host-Imp interface 10/1/69

    5a Get debug specifications and procedures from BBN

    5b Write programs to debug with BBN

        5b1 Transfers of test messages

        5b2 Test procedures for crash and recovery

        5b3 Check message fil and stripping procedures

1

5c   Try own transfer tests

    5c1   Verify transfers to Imp

    5c2   Verify transfers from Imp

    5c3   Verify transfers looped with Imp

5d   Work out Imp reload and restart procedures

Test messages between UCLA-SRI 10/15/69

6a   Network configuration

```
      SRI |
          |
          |
          |
     UCLA |
```

6b   Agree with UCLA on nature of test messages

    6b1   Formats

    6b2   Sequences

    6b3   Checks

    6b4   Test procedures

    6b5   Fault reporting

6c   Test integrity of messages

6d   Test sequence of delivery

6e   Measure delays

6f   Loop with UCLA

6g   System response to invalid and abnormal conditions

6h   Lose and restore facilities

    6h1   Communication link

    6h2   Imps

    6h3   Hosts

6i Develop net trouble reporting scheme

7 Test messages between UCSB-SRI 11/15/69

   7a Network configuration

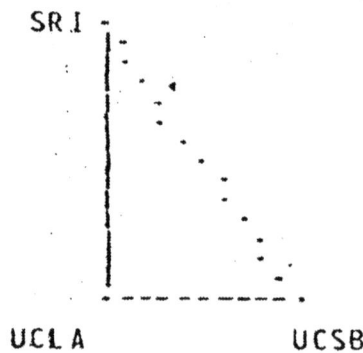

   7b All of 6

   7c Load network for alternate routing to be effective

   7d Develop voice coordination scheme

      7d1 Three way conference

      7d2 Design and build conference gear

      7d3 Deliver conference gear to UCLA and UCSB

   7e Route messages around ring

      7e1 Via Imps

      7e2 Via hosts

      7e3 Six tests

         7e3a UCLA-I, UCSB-I

         7e3b UCLA-H, UCSB-I

         7e3c UCLA-H, UCSB-H

         7e3d UCSB-I, UCLA-I

         7e3e UCSB-H, UCLA-I

         7e3f UCSB-H, UCLA-H

8 Test messages between UTAH-SRI 12/15/69

8a Network configuration

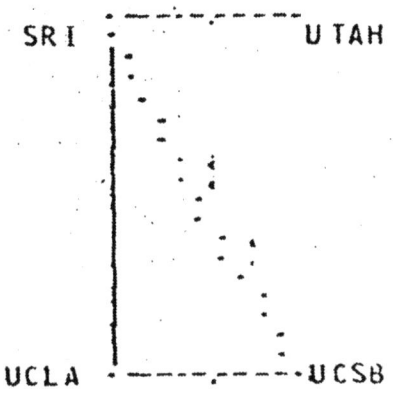

8b Selected groups of previous tests

   8b1 All of 6

   8b2 7b

8c Expand voice coordination scheme

   8c1 UTAH has access to UCLA and UCSB via SRI

   8c2 with BBN, and ARPA

9 Run sample TTY systems

9a Single user access

   9a1 On a serving host

      9a1a A to B

   9a2 From a using host

      9a2a A to B

9b Multiple user access

   9b1 On a serving host

      9b1a A,C to B

   9b2 From a using host

      9b2a A,A to B

   9b3 Various combinations

9c Login, logout, in and out of subsystems

- 9d Handling of error messages, crashes, recoveries
- 9e Establish message formats
- 9f Establish protocols
- 9g File storage and retrieval
- 9h Need user's guides for each site
- 9i Need to establish usage schedules
- 9j Need to set user names
- 9k Design and build comm exec or its equivalent

10 Run simple typewriter systems
- 10a Same as 9c - 9g
- 10b How define when in half or full duplex mode
- 10c How to set "break" characters

11 Run arbitrary terminals without local feedback

12 Run arbitrary terminals

13 Move files

14 Develop debugging techniques
- 14a Fault detection
    - 14a1 Conformance to manual
    - 14a2 "REasonableness" of result
    - 14a3 Comparison with alternate form of use
- 14b Cause localization
    - 14b1 Comm-imp complex
    - 14b2 Serving host
    - 14b3 Using host
    - 14b4 Try other programs
    - 14b5 Monitor subsystem via "link" procedures, where possible
        - 14b5a Use dialup Dataphone

            14b5b   Use voice coordination channel

        14b6   Move canned messages

    14c Cause determination

    14d Cause correction

Title: DEL

Author: Jeff Rulifson

Installation: Stanford Research Institute

Date: 2 June 1969

Network Working Group Request for Comment: 5

;DEL, 02/06/69 1010:58 JFR ; .DSN=1; .LSP=0; [*=] AND NOT SP ; [*?];
dual transmission?

Abstract.

The Decode-Encode Language (DEL) is a machine incependent language tailored to two specific computer network tasks:

accepting input codes from interactive consoles, giving immediate feedback, and packing the resulting information into message packets for network transmission.

and accepting message packets from another computer, unpacking them, building trees of display information, and sending other information to the user at his interactive station.

This is a working document for the evolution of the DEL langauge. Comments should be made through Jeff Rulifson at SRI.

Foreword.

The initial ARPA network working group met at SRI on October 25-26, 1968.

It was generally agreed beforehand that the running of interactive programs across the network was the first problem that would be faced.

This group, already in aggrement about the underlaying notions of a DEL-like approach, set down some terminology, expectations for DEL programs, and lists of proposed semantic capability.

At the meeting were Andrews, Baray, Carr, Crocker, Rulifson, and Stoughton.

A second round of meetings was then held in a piecemeal way.

Crocker meet with Rulifson at SRI on November 18, 1968. This resulted in the incorporation of formal co-routines.

and Stoughton meet with Rulifson at SRI on December 12, 1968. It was deceided to meet again, as a group, probably at UTAH, in late Janurary, 1969.

The first public release of this paper was at the BBN NET meeting in Cambridge on February 13, 1969.

NET Standard Translators.

NST The NST library is the set of programs necessary to mesh efficiently with the code compiled at the user sites from the DEL programs it receives. The NST-DEL approach to NET interactive system communication is intended to operate over a broad spectrum.

The lowest level of NST-DEL useage is merely transmits to the server-host, information is the same to that the user would receive at the user-host.

In this mode, the NST defaults to inaction. The DEL program does not receive universal hardware representation input but input in the normal fashion for for the user-host.

And the DEL program becomes merely a message builder and sender.

A more intermediate use of NST-DEL is to have echo tables for a TTY at the user-host.

In this mode, the DEL program would run a full duplex TTY for the user.

It would echo characters, translate them to the character set of the server-host, pack the translated characters in messages, and on appropiate break characters send the messages.

When messages come from the server-host, the DEL progam would translate them to the user-host character set and print them on his TTY.

A more ambitous task for DEL is the operation of large, display-oriented systems from remote consoles over the NET.

Large interactive systems usually offer a lot of feedback to the user. The unusual nature of the feedback make it impossible to model with echo table, and thus a user program must be activated in a TSS each time a button state is changed.

This puts an unnecessarily large load on a TSS, and if the system is begin run through the NET it could easily load two systems.

To avoid this double overloading of TSS, a DEL program will run on the user-host. It will handel all the immediate feedback, much like a complicated echo table. At appropiate button pushes, message will be sent to the server-host and display updates received in return.

One of the more difficult, and often neglected, problems is the effective simulation of one non-standard console on another non-standard console.

We attempt to offer a means of solving this problem through the co-routine structure of DEL programs. For the complicated interactive systems, part of the DEL programs will be constructed by the server-host programmers. Interfaces between this program and the input stream may easily be inserted by programmers at the user-host site.

2

Universal Hardware Representation

    To minimize the number of translators needed to map any facility's user codes to any other facility, there is a universal hardware representation.

    This is simply a way of talking, in general terms, about all the hardware devices at all the interactive display stations in the initial network.

    For example, a display is thought of as being a square, the mid-point has coordinates (0,0), the range is -1 to 1 on both axes. A point may now be specified to any accuracy, regardless of the particular number or density of rastor points on a display.

    The representation is discussed in the semantic explanitations accompaning the formal description of DEL.

Introduction to the Network Standard Translatore (NST).

    Suppose that a user at a remote site, say Utah, is entered in the AHI system and wants to run NLS.

    The first step is to enter NLS in the normal way. At that time the Utah system will request a symbolic program from NLS.

        REP This program is written in DEL. It is called the NLS Remote Encode Program (REP).

        The program accepts input in the Universal Hardware Representation and translates it to a form usable by NLS.

        It may pack characters in a buffer, also do some local feedback.

    When the program is first received at Utah it is compiled and loaded to be run in conjunction with a standard library.

    All input from the Utah console first goes to the NLS NEP. It is processed, parsed, blocked, translated, etc. When NEP receives a character appropriate to its state it may finally initiate transfers to the 940. The bits transferred are in a form acceptable to the 940, and maybe in a standard form so that the NLS need not differentiate between Utah and other NET users.

Advantages of NST :

    After each node has implemented the library part of the NST, it need only write one program for each subsystem, namely the symbolic file it sends to each user that maps the NET hardware represenataion into its own special bit formats.

        This is the minimum programming that can be expected if each console is used to its fullest extent.

Since the NST which runs the encode translation is coded at the user site, it can take advantage of hardware at its consoles to the fullest extent. It can also add or remove hardware features without requiring new or different translation tables from the host.

Local users are also kept up to date on any changes in the system offered at the host site. As new features are added, the host programmers change the symbolic encode program. When this new program is compiled and used at the user site, the new features are automatically included.

The advantages of having the encode translation programs transferred symbolically should be obvious.

Each site can translate any way it sees fit. Thus machine code for each site can be produced to fit that site; faster run times and greater code density will be the result.

Moreover, extra symbolic programs, coded at the user site, may be easily interfaced between the user's monitor system and the DEL program from the host machine. This should ease the problem of console extension (e.g. accmodating unusual keys and buttons) without loss of the flexibility needed for man-machine interaction.

It is expected that when there is matching hardware, the symbolic programs will take this into account and avoid any unnecessary computing. This is immediaely possible through the code translation constructs of DEL. It may someday be possible through program composition (when Crocker tells us how??).

AH1 NLS — User Console Communication — An Example.

Block Diagram

The right side of the picture represents functions done at the user's main computer; the left side represents those done at the host computer.

Each label in the picture corresponds to a statement with the same name.

There are four trails associated with this picture. The first links (in a forward direction) the labels which are concerned only with network information. The second links the total information flow (again in a forward direction). The last two are equivalent to the first two but in a backward direction. They may be set with pointers t1 through t4 respectively.

4

["">tif"] OR ["">nif"];   ["<tif"] OR ["<nif"];

User-to-Host Transmission

keyboard is the set of input devices at the user's console. Input bits from stations, after drifting through levels of monitor and interrupt handlers, eventually come to the encode translator. [>nif(encode)]

encode maps the semi-raw input bits into an input stream in a form suited to the serving-host subsystem which will process the input. [>nif(hrt)]<nif(keyboard)]

> The Encode program was supplied by the server-host subsystem when the subsystem was first requested. It is sent to the user machine in symbolic form and is compiled at the user machine into code particularly suited to that machine.
>
> It may pack to break characters, map multiple characters to single characters and vice versa, do character translation, and give immediate feedback to the user.

ldm Immediate feedback from the encode translator first goes to local display management, where it is mapped from the NET standard to the local display hardware.

> A wide range of echo output may come from the encode translator. Simple character echoes would be a minimum, while command and machine-state feedback will be common.
>
> It is reasonable to expect control and feedback functions not even done at the server-host user stations to be done in local display control. For example, people with high-speed displays may want to selectively clear curves on a Culler display, a function which is impossible on a storage tube.

Output from the encode translator for the server-host goes to the invisible IMP, is broken into appropriate sizes and labeled by the encode translator, and then goes to the NET-to-host translator.

> Output from the user may be more than on-line input. It may be larger items, such as computer-generated data, or files generated and used exclusively at the server-host site but stored at the user-host site.
>
> Information of this kind may avoid translation, if it is already in server-host format, or it may undergo yet another kind of translation if it is a block of data.

hrp It finally gets to the host, and must then go through the host reception program. This maps and reorders the standard transmission-style packets of bits sent by the encode programs into messages acceptable to the host. This program may well be part of the monitor of the host machine.[>tif(net mode)<nif(encode)]

Host-to-User Transmission

decode Output from the server-host initially goes through decode, a translation map similar to, and perhaps more complicated than, the encode map. [>nif(urt)>tif(imp ctrl)<tif(net mode)]

> This map at least formats display output into a simplified logical-entity output stream, of which meaningful pieces may be dealt with in various ways at the user site.

>> The Decode program was sent to the host machine at the same time that the Encode program was sent to the user machine. The program is initially in symbolic form and is compiled for efficient running at the host machine.

>> Lines of characters should be logically identified so that different line widths can be handled at the user site.

>> Some form of logical line identification must also me made. For example, if a straight line is to be drawn across the display this fact should be transmitted, rather than a series of 500 short vectors.

>> As things firm up, more and more complicated structural display information (in the manner of LEAP) should be sent and accomodated at user sites so that the responsibility for real-time display manipulation may shift closer to the user.

> imp ctrl The server-host may also want to send control information to IMPs. Formatting of this information is done by the host decoder. [>tif(urt) <tif(decode)]

> The other control information supplied by the host decoder is message break up and identification so that proper assembly and sorting can be done at the user site.

From the host decoder, information goes to the invisible IMP, and directly to the NET-to-user translator. The only operation done on the messages is that they may be shuffled.

urt The user reception translator accepts messages from the user-site IMP and fixes them up for user-site display. [>nif(d ctrl)>tif(prgm ctrl)<tif(imp ctrl)<nif(decode)]

> The minimal action is a reordering of the message pieces.

>> dctrl For display output, however, more needs be done. The NET logical display information must be put in the format of the user site. Dispay control does this job. Since it coordinates between (encode) and (decode) it is able to offer

6

features of display management local to the user site.[>nif(display)<nif(urt)]

prgmctrl Another action may be the selective translation and routing of information to particular user-site subsystems. [>tif(d ctrl)<tif(urt)]

> For example, blocks of floating-point information may be converted to user-style words and sent, in block form, to a subsystem for processing or storage.

> The styles and translation of this information may well be a compact binary format suitable for quick translation, rather than a print-image-oriented format.

(display) is the output to the user. [<nif(d ctrl)]

User-to-Host Indirect Transmission

(net mode) This is the mode where a remote user can link to a node indirectly through another node.[>tif(decode)<tif(hrt)]

DEL Syntax.

Notes for NLS Users.

All statements in this branch which are not part of the compiler must end with a period.

To compile the DEL compiler:

> Set this pattern for the content aalyzer (+PI SE(PI) < -"_i). The pointer "del" is on the first character of pattern.

> Jump to the first statement of the compiler. The pointer "c" is on this statement.,

> And output the compiler to file("/A-DEL"). The pointer "f" is on the name of the file for the compiler output.

Programs.

Syntax.

.meta file (k=100, m=300, n=20, s=900)

file = mesdecl $declaration $procedure "FINISH";

procedure =
    ∩
    procname (
        {

```
                type "FUNCTION" /
                              ?
                "PROCEDURE" ) .id $(type .id / .empty)) /
            "CO-ROUTINE") ';  /
        $declaration labeledst $(labeledst ";) "endp." ;

    labeledst = (+.id ': / .empty) statement;

    type = "INTEGER" / "REAL" ;

    procname = .id;
```

Functions are differentiated from procedures to aid compilers in better code production and run time checks.

Functions return values.

Procedures do not return values.

Co-routines do not have names or arguments. Their initial envocation points are given the pipe declaration.

It is not clear just how global declarations are to be??

Declarations.

Syntax.

```
    declaration = numbertype / structuredtype / label / lcl2uhr /
    uhr2rmt / pipetype;

    numbertype = ("REAL" / "INTEGER") ("CONSTANT" conlist /
    varlist);

    conlist =
        .id '+ constant
        $(', .id '+ constant);

    varlist =
        .id ('+ constant / .empty)
        $(', .id ('+ constant / .empty));

    idlist = .id $(', .id);

    structuredtype = ("tree" / "pointer" / "buffer" ) idlist;

    label = "LABEL" idlist;
```

```
    pipetype = "PIPE" pairedids $(', pairedids);

.   pairedids = .id .id;

    procname = .id;

    integerv = .id;

    pipename = .id;

    labelv = .id;
```

Variables which are declared to be constant, may be put in read-only memory at run time.

The label declaration is to declare cells which may contain the machine addresses of labels in the program as their values. This is not the B5500 label declaration.

In the pipe declaration the first .ID of each pair is the name of the pipe, the second is the initial starting point for the pipe.

Arithmetic.

  Syntax.

```
    exp = ("IF" conjunct "THEN" exp "ELSE" exp;

    sum = term (

        "+ sum /

        "- sum /

        .empty);

    term = factor (

        "* term /

        "/ term /

        "* term /

        .empty);

    factor = "- factor / bitop;

    bitop = compliment (

        "\"/ bitop /

        "/"\ bitop /
```

```
        "& bitop / (
        _empty);

    compliment = "—" primary / primary;
```

* means mod, and /\ means exclusive or.

Notice that the unary minus is allowable, and parsed so you can write x*-y.

Since there is no standard convention with bitwise operators, they all have the same precedence, and parentheses must be used for grouping.

Compliment is the 1's compliment.

It is assumed that all arithmetic and bit operations take place in the mode and style of the machine running the code. Anyone who takes advantage of word lengths, two's compliment arithmetic, etc. will eventually have problems.

Primary.

Syntax.

```
    primary =
        constant / (
        builtin /
        variable / (
        block /
        "( exp ");
    variable = _id (
        "= exp /
        "( block ") /
        _empty);
    constant = integer / real / string;
    builtin =
        mesinfo /
        contnin /
```

```
("MIN" / "MAX") exp $("," exp) "\" ;
```

parenthesised expressions may be a series of expressions. The value of a series is the value of the last one executed at run time.

Subroutines may have one call by name argument. ?

Expressions may be mixed. Strings are a big problem?? Rulifson also wants to get rid of real numbers!!

Conjunctive Expression.

Syntax.

```
conjunct = disjunct ("AND" conjunct / .empty);

disjunct = negation ("OR" negation / .empty);

negation = "NOT" relation / relation;

relation =
    "(" conjunct ")" /
    sum (
        "<=" sum /
        ">=" sum /
        "<" sum /
        ">" sum /
        "=" sum /
        "#" sum /
        .empty);
```

The conjunct construct is rigged in such a way that a conjunct which is not a sum need not have a value, and may be evaluated using jumps in the code. Reference to the conjunct is made only in places where a logical decision is called for (e.g. if and while statements).

We hope that most compilers will be smart enough to skip unnecessary evaluations at run time. I.e. a conjunct in which the left part is false or a disjunct with the left part true need not have the corresponding right part evaluated.

Arithmetic Expression.

Syntax.

```
statement = conditional / unconditional;

unconditional = loopst / casest / controlst / iost / treest /
   block / null / exp;

conditional = "IF" conjunct "THEN" unconditional (

   "ELSE" conditional /

   empty);

block = "begin" exp $(";" exp) "end";
```

An expressions may be a statement. In conditional statements the else part is optional while in expressions is is mandatory. This is a side effect of the way the left part of the syntax rules are ordered.

Semi-Tree Manipulation and Testing.

Syntax.

```
treest = setpntr / insertpntr / deletepntr;

setpntr = "set" "pointer" pntrname "to" pntrexp;

pntrexp = direction pntrexp / pntrname;

insertpntr = "insert" pntrexp "as"

   (("left" / "right") "brother") /

   (("first" / "last") "daughter") "of" pntrexp;

direction =

   "up" /

   "down" /

   "forward" /

   "backward" /

   "head" /

   "tail";

planttree = "plant" tree "in" treename;

replacepntr = "replace" pntrname "with" pntrexp;
```

12

```
deletepntr = "delete" pntrname;
tree = '(' tree1 ')' ;
tree1 = nodename $ nodename ;
nodename = terminal / '(' tree1 ')' ;
terminal = treename / buffername / pointername;
treename = .id;
treedecl = "pointer" .id / "tree" .id;
```

Extra parentheses in tree building results in linear subcategorization, just as in LISP.

Flow and Control.

```
controlst = gost / subst / loopst / casest;
```

Go To Statements.

```
gost = "GO" "TO" (labelv / .id);
    assignlabel = "ASSIGN" .id "TO" labelv;
```

Subroutines.

```
subst = callst / returnst / cortnout;
    callst = "CALL" procname (exp / .empty);
    returnst = "RETURN" (exp / .empty);
    cortnout = "STUFF" exp "IN" pipename;
cortnin = "FETCH" pipename;
```

FETCH is a builtin function whose value is computed by envoking the named co-routine.

Loop Statements.

Syntax.

```
loopst = whilest / untilst / forst;
whilest = "WHILE" conjunct "DO" statement;
untilst = "UNTIL" conjunct "DO" statement;
forst = "FOR" integerv '←' exp ("BY" exp / .empty) "TO" exp
```

13

"DO" statement;

The value of while and until statements is defined to be false and true (or, 0 and non-zero) respectively.

For statements evaluate their initial exp, by part, and to part once, at initialization time. The running index of for statements is not available for change within the loop, it may only be read. If some compilers can take advantage of this (say put it in a register) all the better. The increment and the to bound will both be rounded to integers during the initialization.

Case statements.

  Syntax.

    casest = ithcasest / condcasest;

    ithcasest = "ITHCASE" exp "OF" "BEGIN" statement $(';' statement) "END";

    condcasest = "CASE" exp "OF" "BEGIN" condcs $(';' condcs) "OTHERWISE": statement "END";

    condcs = conjunct ':' statement;

  The value of a case statement is the value of the last case executed.

Extra statements.

  null = "NULL";

I/O Statements.

  iost = messagest / dspyst ;

  Messages.

    Syntax.

      messagest = buildmes / demand;
        buildmes = startmes / appendmes / sendmes;
          startmes = "start" "message";
          appendmes = "append" "message" "byte" exp ;
          sendmes = "send" "message";
          demandmes = "demand" "message";

```
mesinfo =
    "get" "message" "byte" /
    "message" "length" /
    "message" "empty" ? ;

mesdcl = "message" "bytes" "are" _num "bits" "long" ; ;
```

Display Buffers..

Syntax.

```
dspyst = startbuffer / bufappend / estab;
startbuffer = "start" "buffer" clear(b);
bufappend = "append" bufstuff $("& bufstuff);
                           be
bufstuff =
    "parameters" dspyparm $("," dspyparm) /
    "character" exp /
    "string" string /
    "vector" ("from" exp ":" exp / _empty) "to" exp "," exp /
    "position" (onoff / _empty) "beam" "to" exp ":" exp /
    "curve" ;
dspyparm =
    "intensity" "to" exp /
    "character" "width" "to" exp /
    "blink" onoff /
    "italics" onoff;
onoff = "on" / "off";
estab = "establish" buffername;
```

Logical Screen.

The screen is taken to be a square. The coordinates are normalized from -1 to +1 on both axes.

Associated with the screen is a position register, called PREG. The register is a triple <x,y,r>, where x and y specify a point on the screen and r is a rotation in radians, counter clockwise, from the x-axis.

The intensity, called INTENSITY, is a real number in the range from 0 to 1. 0 is black, 1 is as light as your display can go, and numbers in between specify the relative log of the intensity difference.

Character frame size.

Blink bit.

Buffer Building.

The terminal nodes of semi-trees are either semi-tree names or display buffers. A display buffers is a series of logical entities, called bufstuff.

When the buffer is initilized, it is empty. If no parameters are initially appended, those in effect at the end of the display of the last node in the semi-tree will be in effect for the display of this node.

As the buffer is built, the logical entites are added to it. When it is established as a buffername, the buffer is closed, and further appends are prohibited. It is only a buffername has been established that it may be used in a tree building statement.

Logical Input Devices.

   Wand.

   Joy Stick.

   Keyboard.

   Buttons.

   Light Pens.

   Mice.

Audio Output Devices.

.end

Sample Programs

Program to run display and keyboard as tty.

```
to run NLS.
    input part
    display part
        DEMAND MESSAGE;
        while LENGTH # 0 DO
            ITHCASE GETBYTE OF Begin
                IHCASE IGETBYTE OF %file area iupdate% BEGIN
                    %literal area%
                    %message area%
                    %name area%
                    %bug%
                    %sequence specs%
                    %filter specs%
                    %format specs%
                    %command feedback line%
                    %file area%
                    %date time%
                    %echo register%
                BEGIN %DEL control%
```

Distribution List

   Steve Carr

      Department of Computer Science

      University of Utah

      Salt Lake City, Utah 84112

      Phone 801-322-7211 X8224

   Steve Crocker

   3?? Boelter Hall

University of California

Los Angeles, California 90024

Phone 213-825-6864

Jeff Rulifson

Stanford Research Institute

333 Ravenswood

Menlo Park, California 94305

Phone 415-326-6200 X4116

Ron Stoughton

Computer Research Laboratory

University of California

Santa Barbara, California 93106

Phone 805-961-3221

Mehmet Baray

Corey Hall

University of California

Berekely, California 94720

Phone 415-843-2621

Network Working Note
Request for Comments: 6

Steve Crocker, UCLA
10 April 1969

CONVERSATION WITH BOB KAHN

I talked with Bob Kahn at BB&N yesterday. We talked about code conversion in the IMP's, IMP-HOST communication, and HOST software.

BB&N is prepared to convert 6, 7, 8, or 9 bit character codes into 8-bit ASCII for transmission and convert again upon assembly at the destination IMP. BB&N plans a one for one conversion scheme with tables unique to the HOST. I suggested that places with 6-bit codes may also want case shifting. Bob said this may result in overflow if too many case shifts are necessary. I suggested that this is rare and we could probably live with an overflow indication instead of a guarantee.

With respect to HOST-IMP communication, we now have a five bit link field and a bit to indicate conversion. Also possible is a 2-bit conversion indicator, one for converting before sending and one for converting after. This would allow another handle for checking or controlling the system.

The HOST can send messages or portions of a message to its IMP specifying

1. Tracing
2. Conversion
3. Whether message is for destination IMP or HOST
4. Send RFNM
5. HOST up or down
6. Synchronization
7. Format Error Messages
8. Master Link Clear
9. Status Requested

The IMP can send to its HOST information on

1. Conversion
2. RFNM Arrived
3. IMP up or down
4. Synchronization
5. Called HOST not Responding
6. Format Error
7. Status in IMP

I also summarized for Bob the contents of Network Notes 1, 2, and 3.

Title: Host-Imp Interface

Author: G. Deloche

Installation: University of California at Los Angeles

Date: May 1969

Network Working Group Request for Comment: 7

G. Deloche → Prof. J. Estrin
Prof. L. Kleinrock
Prof. B. Bussel
D. Mandell
S. Crocker
L. Bonamy

Object : Arpa Network - Specification outlines :
Host-IMP (HI) interface programs.

I. Introduction

II. Scope of the software organization
    II-1 Network program
    II-2 Handler program

III. Questions

I. Introduction

This paper is concerned with the proposed software design of the HOST-IMP interface. Its main purpose is on the one hand to state functions that will be implemented, and on the other hand to provide a base for discussion.

This study is based upon a study of report no. 762.

II Scope of the software organization.

The system is based upon two main programs: the <u>Handler</u> program that drives the channel hardware unit, and the <u>Network</u> program which carries out the user's transmission requests.

As the communication is full duplex, each of these programs can be viewed as divided into two parts: one concerned with the output data, the other with the input. (See fig. 1)

These two programs exchange data through a <u>pool of buffers</u>, and logical information through an <u>interface table</u>.

In the following we only focus on the <u>output part of each program</u>. (See fig 2). The input part would be very similar.

II-1 Network program.

II-1-1. Multiplex function

This program multiplexes the outgoing messages (and distributes the incoming messages). The multiplexing consists in stacking up all the user's (or caller, or party) requests and filling up the pool of buffers so as to keep the handler busy emitting.

Multiplexing (and distribution) is based on the link identification numbers. (Link = logical connection between two users). The multiplexing problem is closely related to the interface between an user's and the the network program, that is in fact operating system (see below: Questions).

II-1-2 Output messages processing.

When an user's program wants to send out text it should indicate the following information (through a macro, or as call parameters): text location, text lenght in bytes, and destination.

Using these data the Network program:

* **prepares** a 16 bits Host heading (1 bit: trace, 2 bits: spares, 8 bits: link identification n°, 5 bits: dest host)

* **inserts** a 16 bits marking between the heading and the text so as to start the text at a word boundary. This marking consists of a one preceding the first bit of the text and, in turn, preceded by fifteen zeros to fill up the gap.

* **checks** the lenght of the user's text. If it exceeds 1006 bytes $\left[\dfrac{8080(\text{max Host message lenght}) - 32(\text{heading + marking})}{8 \,(\text{byte} = 8 \text{bits})}\right]$ the program **breaks down** the text into a sequence of messages whose maximum lenght is 1006 bytes. Each of these mes-

is preceded by a heading as explained above.

Remark: in that case one of the heading space bits ca be used for indicating that several messages belong t the same texte.

* transcodes the EBCDIC characters constituting the messages into ASCII characters.

* fills the buffers of the pool with the content of the messages.

* updates the content of the interface table and move the filling pointer (see below)

II-2   Handler program.

This program is initiated either by the network program, or by the I/O interrupt.

This program will be very short. It will be code in master mode (privileged instructions) and should be integrated in the I/O supervisor of the operating sy

This program:

* controls the channel hardware unit. It init the emission, eventually provides data chaining between the buffer tests the different device states upon receiving an interrup

* empties the buffers that are filled up by

[The following text appears to be from a page missing in all the photocopy collections I've had access to. It is taken from the online transcription of RFC 07 made by SRI-ARC, which apparently had a more complete copy. I cannot corroborate this text, and the RFC's outline does not list a Section II-3, but Section II-2 does cut off abruptly and this makes sense in context. —PHS]

the network program.
  * _explores_ and _updates_ the interface table (see below).
  * can eventually insure a control transmission procedure with the IMP (See Questions).

II-3 Buffers and Interface Table.

II-3-1 Buffers.

They should be large enough for containing the maximum host message text + heading and marking (1006 + 4 = 1010 bytes).

Consequently the buffer size could be chosen equal to 256 words (1024 bytes). As for the buffer number it will determine the link utilization frequency -

II-3-2 Interface table.

It is through this table that the network program informs the handler with the location and length of the emitting data.

This table could be a ring table with 2 pointers, one for filling, the other for extracting. They are respectively updated by the network and the handler program.

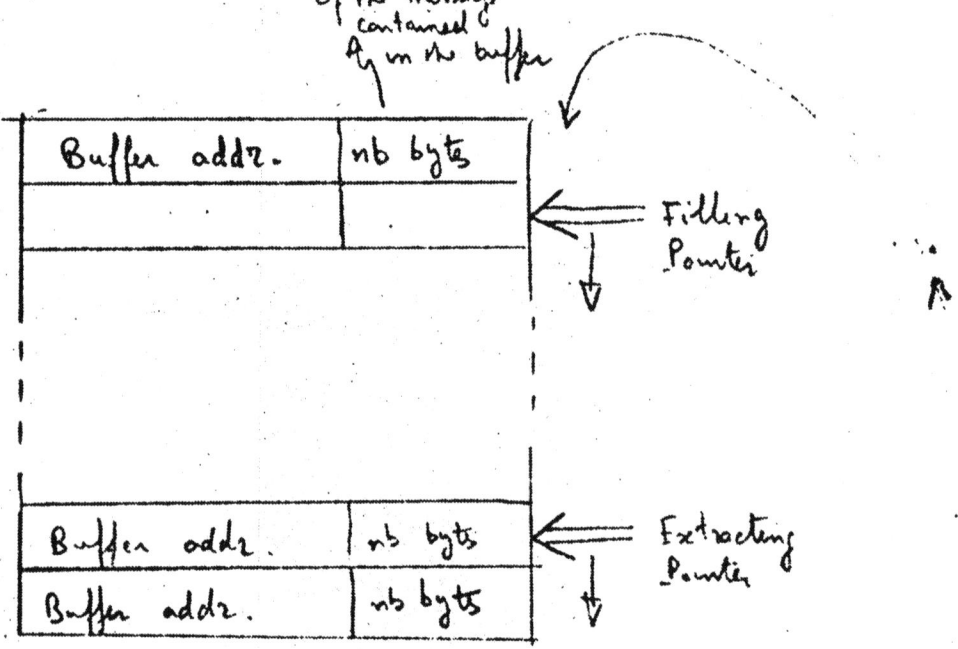

III   Questions

III-1.   Why is there not a simple control procedure between the HOST and the IMP? What happens if a message, issued from the HOST, reach the IMP with an error due to the transmission? From the BBN specifications it appears that this error will be transmitted as far the receiving HOST. In that case must an HOST-HOST control procedure be provided?

III-2.   Where will the special channel hardware unit be connected (MIOP/SIOP)?

How will this device be notified of an outgoing message end in order to start the padding?

(The program will provide to the MIOP SIOP the number of bytes of the outgoing message, and will receive back an interrupt when the last byte is sent out. Is it that signal which will be also sent to the special device?)

Vice versa how does the Handler know the lenght of the incoming message? From the content of the previous or should this program always ready to receive a mes of maximum lenght? (then an interrupt should be trigge when the real end is detected by the hardware)

III-3   When does the Gordo documentation will be available in order to design the user-network program interface. What are the mechanisms for program initiations, transferring parameters from one program to another etc...

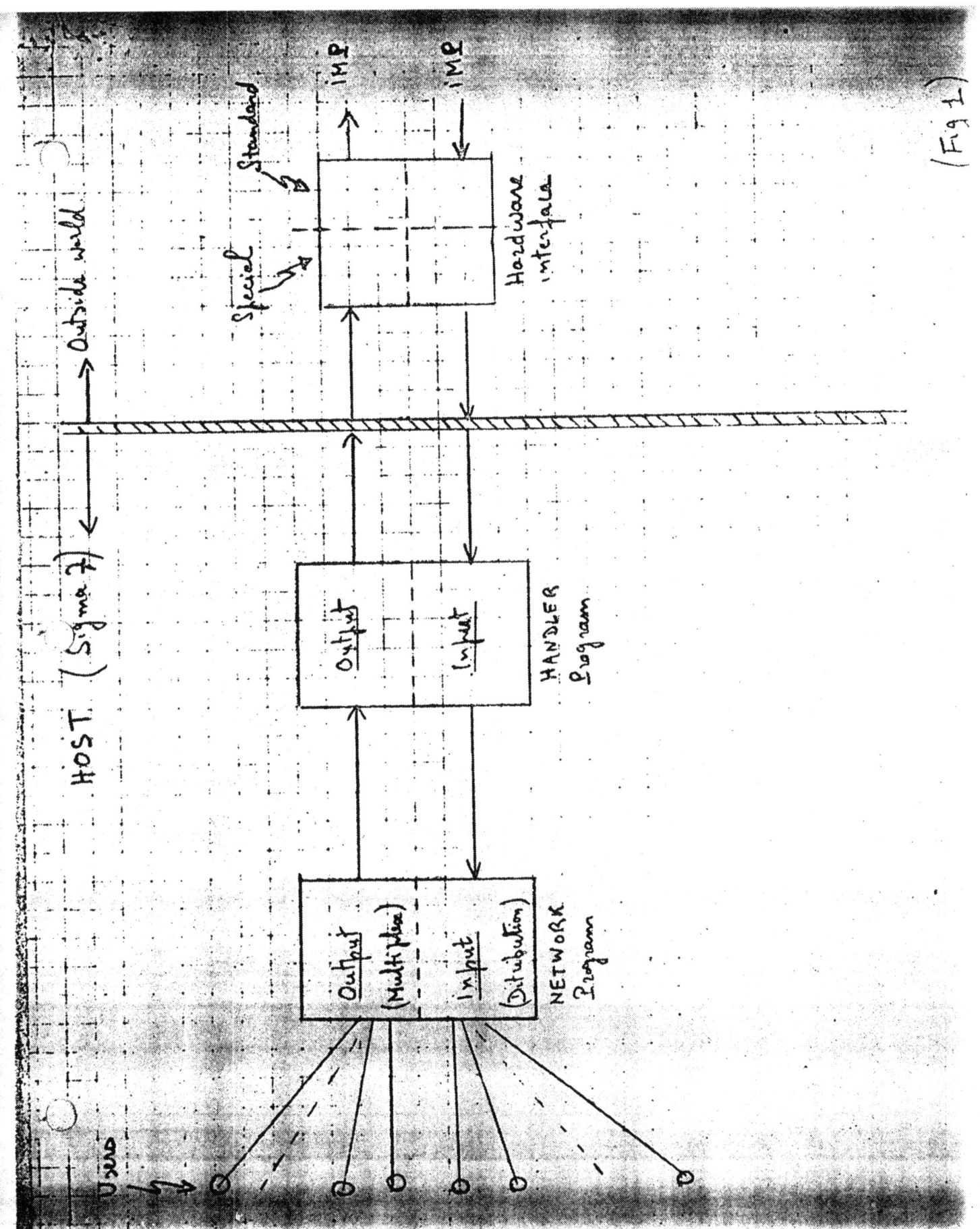

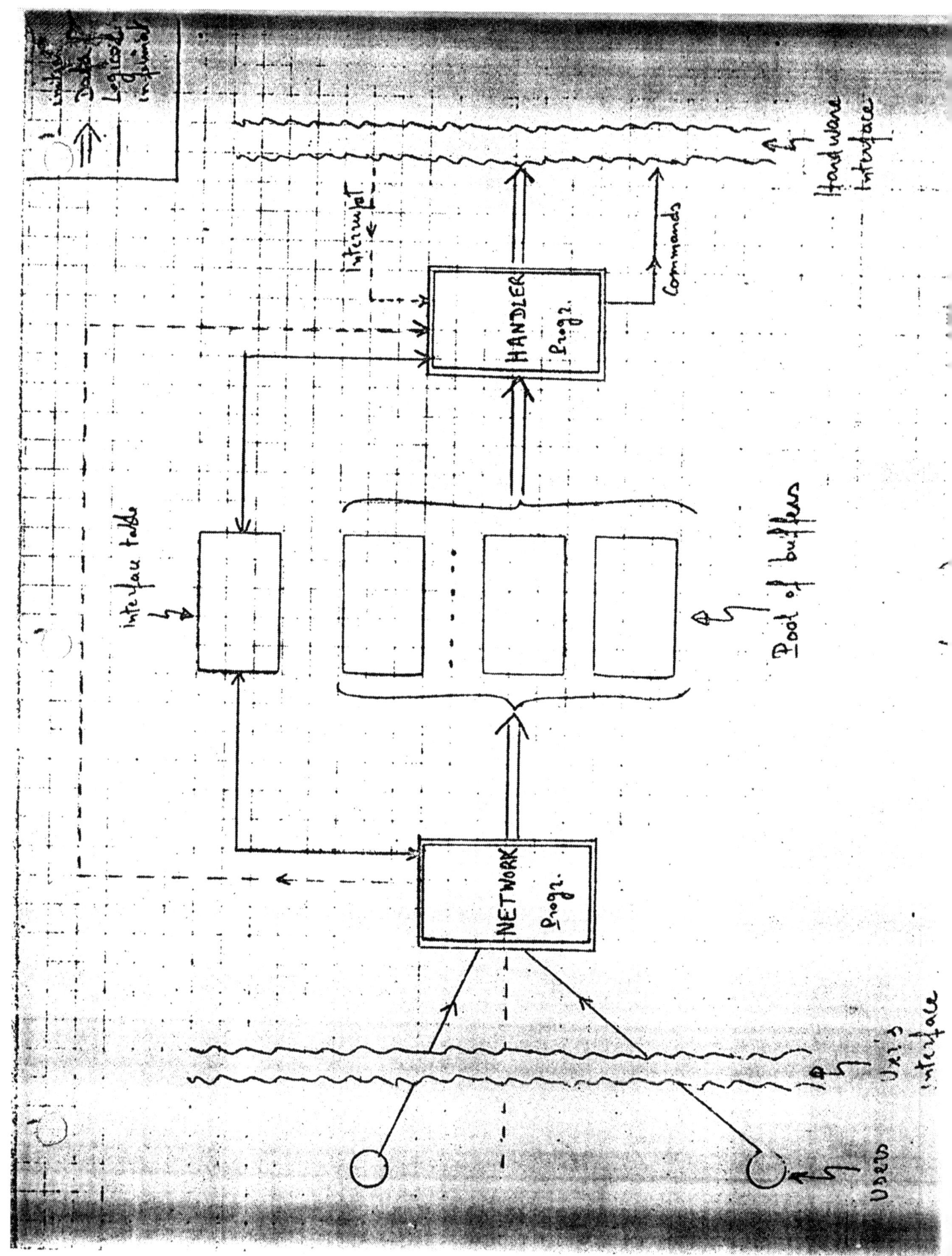

Title: ARPA Network Functional Specifications

Author: G. Deloche

Installation: University of California at Los Angeles

Date: 5 May 1969

Network Working Group Request for Comment: 8

ARPA network: Functional spec!

TABLE OF CONTENTS.

I. Transmission features
  1. Transmission checking
  2. HOST(A) to HOST(B) links.

II. Functional software specifications.
  1. User program – DEL language
  2. Network program
  3. Transmission Handler

III. Link establishment procedure.
  1. General procedure
  2. Example

I Transmission features

I-1 Transmission checking

There exists two kind of transmission checking:

* IMP to IMP

It is a cyclic checksum computed and checked by the BBN hardware.

* HOST to HOST

It is a special 16 bits checksum computed and checked by the HOST programs.

For this purpose a HOST message is divided into 1152 bits pieces A, B, C ... (1152 = 2·2·... # of bits)

For each piece, we calculate an odd-numbered sum and form the checksum as follows:

Checksum = Sum of A + 2 × Sum of B + 4 × Sum of C + ...

This 16 bits checksum is located just after the marking of the HOST heading, that is at the beginning of a message itself (see fig 1).

This checking procedure allows the verification of the right IMP to IMP procedure. It also protects against HOST to IMP (or IMP to HOST) bad transmission, and against IMP packet number inversion.

Remark: Example of an end-around carry sum:

```
   101
 + 101       Checksum = 011
  ────
  1 010
    ↺
```

I-2   HOST(A) to HOST(B) links.

32 links are possible between two HOSTS. Each of those links are viewed as full duplex.

Link 0 is considered as a control link (require connection, status of any kind ....)

The 31 others are used either for "teletype like" connections or for file transmission connections.

A "TTY like" connection is one where:
- ASCII characters are sent or received
- Echos are generated by the remote HOST
- The remote HOST looks for specific characters (break or interrupt control characters).
- The transmission is slow.

II Functional software specifications.

- See fig 2 -

II-1 User program. DEL language

It's an application program that exists within a HOST. For example the NLS program at SRI. For network purposes this program should be viewed as parted in two: The local part and the hard p[art] (the body).

- The hard part represents the user application.
- The local control part is the user interfa[ce]. It exerts immediate control of the terminal and prov[ides] specific responses to the man's inputs.

In order to facilitate and speed up remote inter[action] the 'local control' program can be transmitted to another H[OST]. Thanks to that capability an UCLA user, for example, will u[se] its terminal exactly like the SRI user uses [his] own. Also only 'the program data are transmit[ted] over the link (versus the user 'terminal dialogue') - See [fig]

DEL language. (Decode Encode Language)

The 'local control' program should be written in DEL language. When it is transmitted over to a user [HOST]...

II-2 Network Program

- This program should provide:
  - The outgoing messages multiplexing (and incoming messages distribution)
  - The link initiation procedure: see below.
  - The HOST message Heading.
  - The "HOST-HOST" checksum computation/checking
  - The receiving of the RFNM control messages.
  - The supervisory control of the Handler program.

II-3 Transmission Handler Program

This program is initiated either by the Network program, or by the I/O interrupt. Its purpose is to control the channel hardware unit.

This program is very short and basely called in the Network program.

Remark. As the communication is full duplex, the Network and Handler programs can be viewed as divided into 2 parts: one is concerned with the outgoing messages, the other with the incoming messages.

III Link establishment procedure

III-1 General procedure

* Establish link to HOST (x).
  A "TTY like" connection is established to HOST(x). Connection is in a pre-log-in state. Standard TTY are expected. The remote HOST provides the echo.

* Send/Receive characters over "TTY like" link

* Establish file transmission link parallel to existing "TTY like" link. This must be executed by both HOST user programs.

* Send/Receive over "file like" link.

III-2 Example

Suppose that we, at UCLA, want to use NLS at SRI

a) Local arrangements
  * Log in on local TTY to Sigma 7. We are now talking to the command level of the Sigma operating system.
  * Select an user program to put in execution

We start up a program we presumably write on ITY and the transmission with SRI.

* O₂ select the standard UCLA communical program. This is the standard option for any control of a remote HOST.

b) Connection to SRI

* Initiate link to remote HOST

The previously selected program asks the UCLA the program to initiate a link to SRI. The Network program:

- Selects an open link e.g. 25
- Sends a message to SRI over link 0 v connection on link 25.
- Waits for an acceptance from the SRI network program. This acceptance is in the form of another message on link 0.
- If it should happen that both SRI & UCLA try to initiate a connection over 25, the one with the higher priority prevail. (This is extremely rare.) We suggest that the priority be according the HOST identification number.
- This connection is teletype-like since only a standard subset of ASCII is accepted or accepted.
- The connection is a "pre-login" as the remote HOST expects its standard log-in sequence.

* Log-in at SRI.

This may be done either by the UCLA main program if it knows how, or by the man at UCLA by typing the required sequence. We are now talking [to] the command level of the SRI operating system.

(c) Request 'local control' program for SRI

* The UCLA selected program sends over the link to the SRI user program. The [program] requests that SRI transmit to UCLA the [local] program which is written in the DEL language.

* We compile this program through a compiler.

* We turn control of the TTY link & terminal over [to] the just compiled DEL program

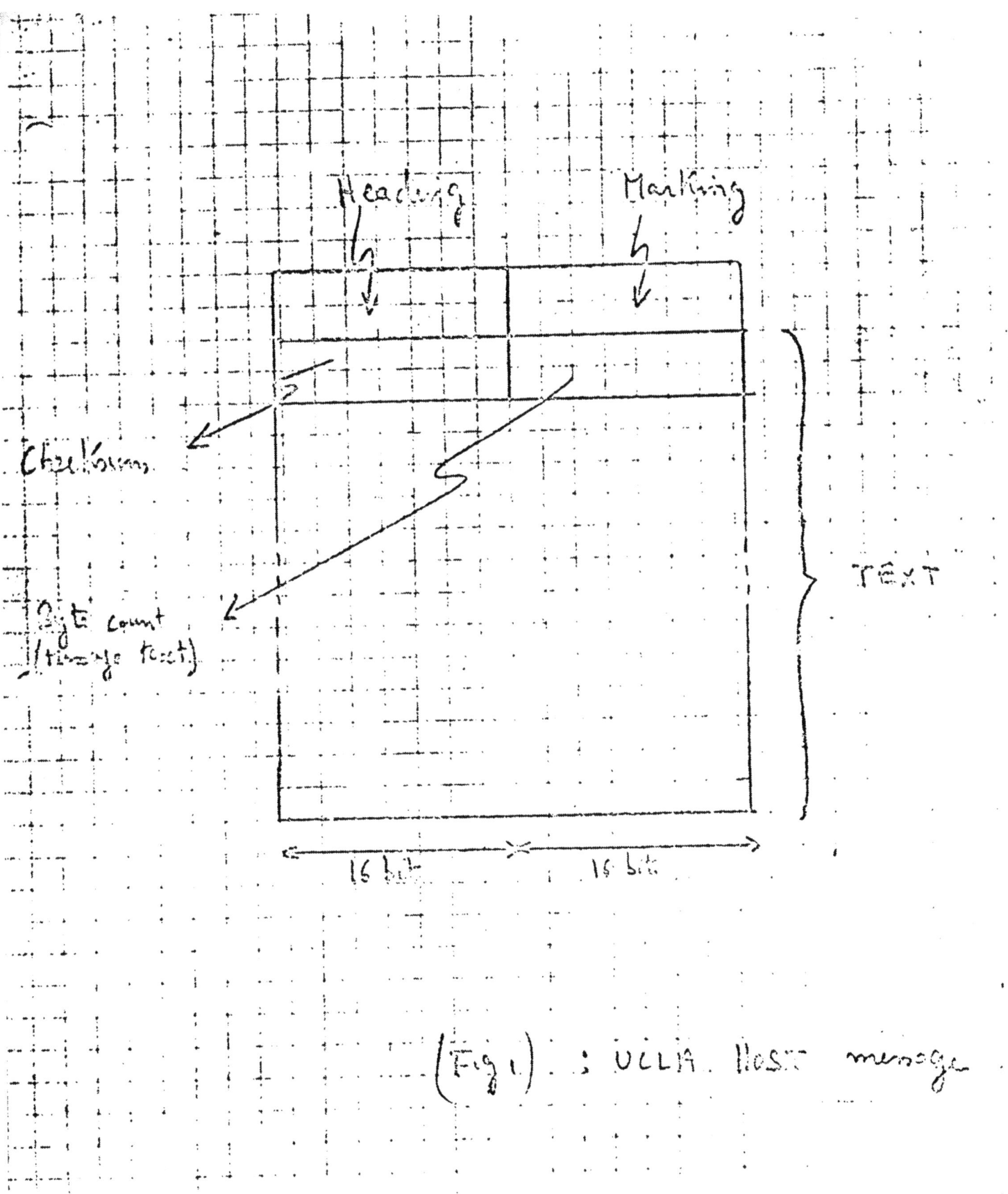

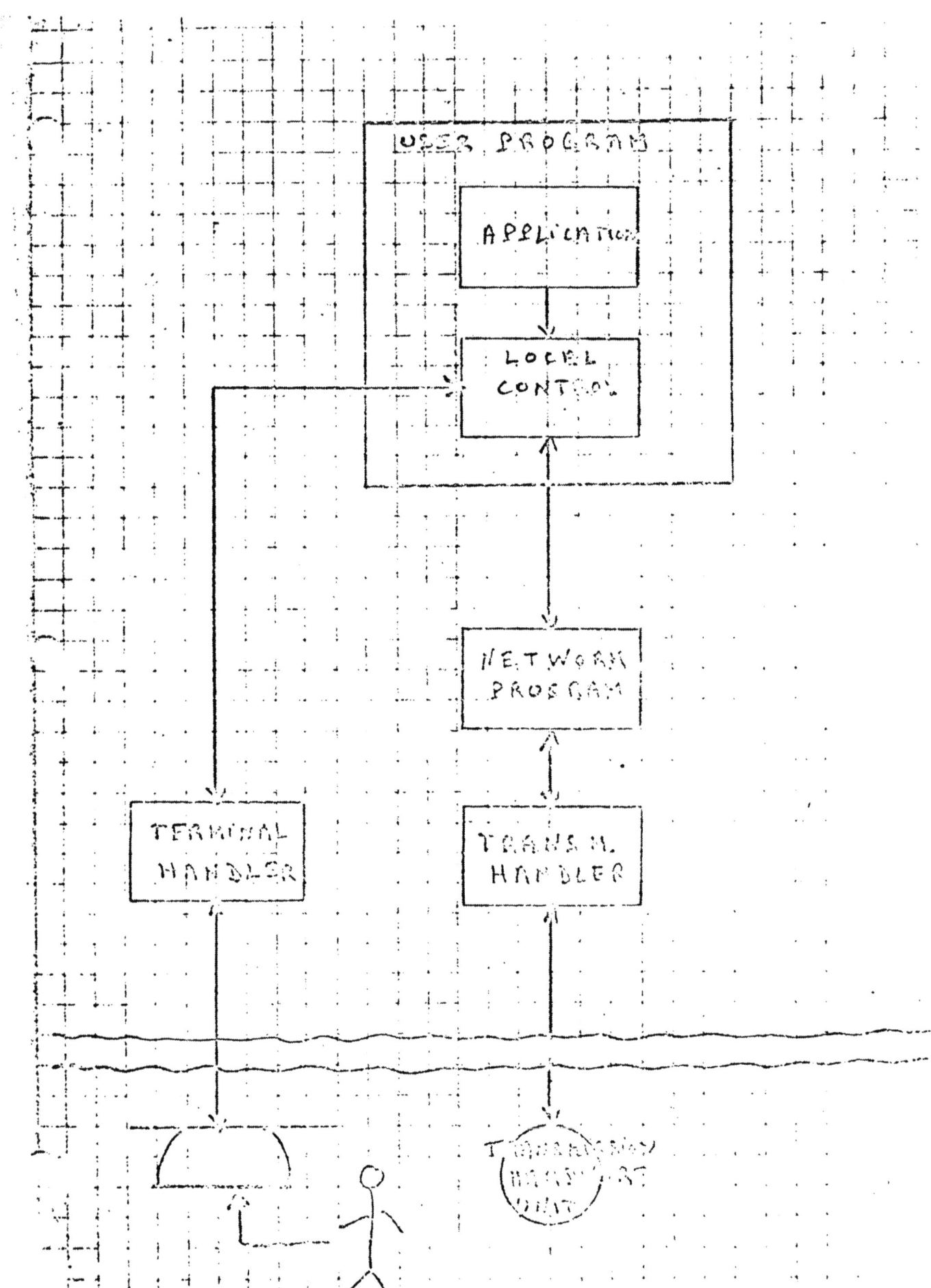

Network Working Group
Requests for Comments: 9

HOST SOFTWARE

G. Deloche, U.C.L.A.
1 May 1969

TABLE OF CONTENTS

1. Introduction

2. HOST-HOST Protocol
    - 2.1 Logical Links
        - 2.1.1 Primary
        - 2.1.2 Auxiliary
    - 2.2 Link Establishment
        - 2.2.1 General Procedures
        - 2.2.2 Example

3. Network Service Calls
    - 3.1 List of Service Calls

4. Data Structure
    - 4.1 "HOST" Table
    - 4.2 "LINK" Table
    - 4.3 "USER" Table

5. Network Program

1. Introduction

This paper concentrates upon the HOST-HOST dialogue procedure.

Chapter 2 describes the logical links connecting the HOST, and the way data are exchanged over these links.

The emphasis of Chapters 3, 4, and 5 is on software organization and data structure.

Figure 1 highlights the different programs involved in a HOST.

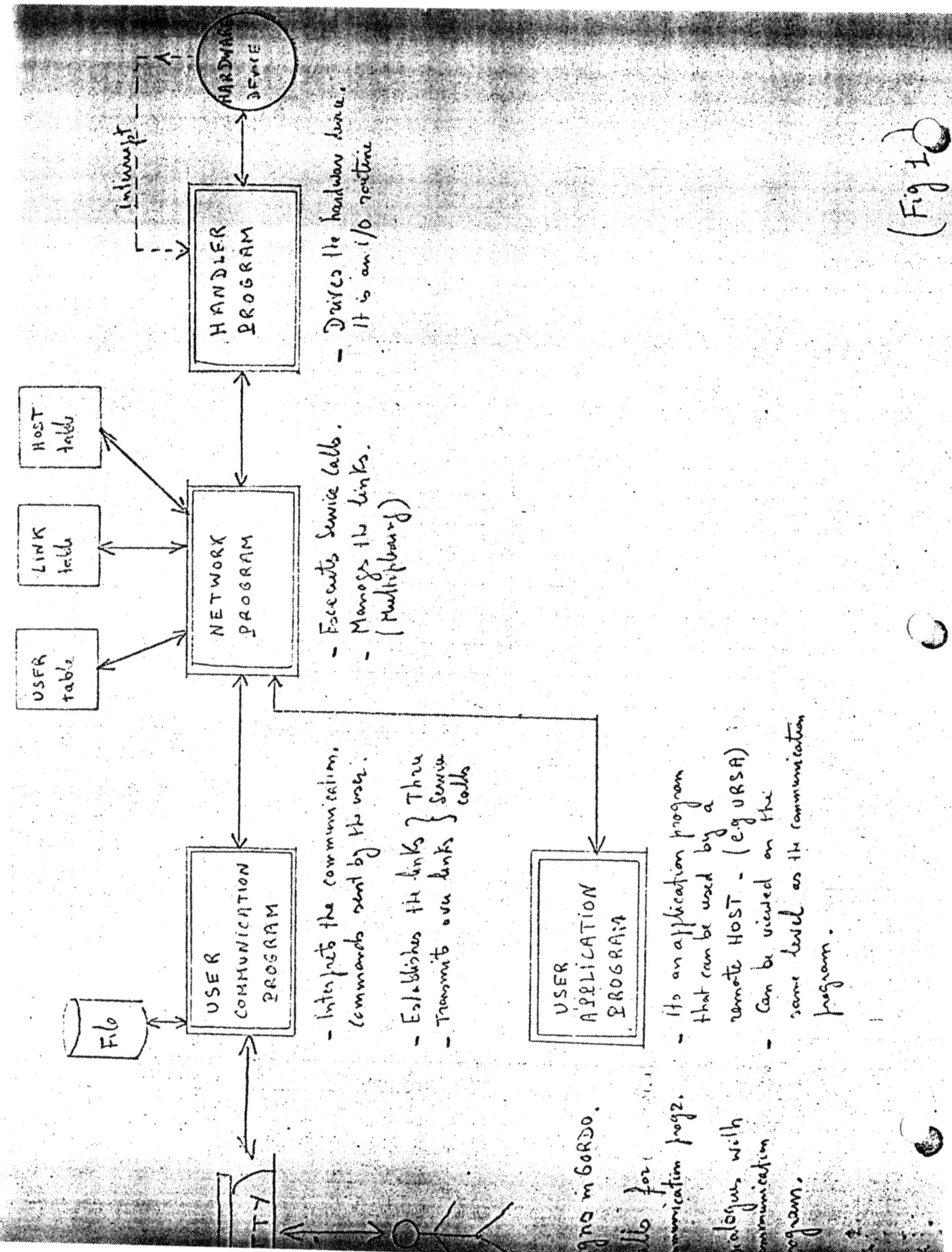

2. HOST-HOST Protocol

2.1 Logical Links (Figure 2)

Any IMP can be viewed as an interface between a local center and the trunk network. Locally, an IMP may serve up to four HOSTs; for each of them it provides 256 logical links to any remote HOST.

However, between an IMP and all the other IMPs no more than 64 links may be in use simultaneously. In other words, a HOST dialoguing with a remote HOST can consider its local IMP as a switching center offering 256 lines to the remote HOST, but only 64 can be activated at a time. (If a local center includes η HOSTs, 64 should be shared amount the η HOSTs).

The 256 logical links connecting two HOSTs can be distinguished as follows:

Link 0 has a special status. It is the control link (connection requests, status report of any kind...).

The 255 others can be used either as <u>primary</u> links, i.e., "teletype like" connections, or as <u>auxiliary</u> links for file transmission.

2.1.1 Primary Links Features

A primary link
* is the first link established for a HOST-HOST transmission.
* is a "TTY-like" connection that is:
  - ASCII characters are transmitted.
  - Echos are generated by the remote HOST.
  - The remote HOST scans for break character.
  - The transmission is slow (less than 20 characters per second).
* is mainly used for transmitting control commands, i.e., for log-in to the remote HOST operating system.
* provides special buffering techniques for slow, short transmission.

2.1.2 Auxiliary Links Features

An auxiliary link
* is used for transmission of large volumes of data.
* is established in parallel to the primary link
* can be established only if the following conditions are fulfilled:
  user programs, at the two extremities, must both require its opening.
* is used for either binary or character transmission.

2.2 Link Establishment

2.2.1 General Procedures

Each HOST(X) user will respect the following procedure for communicating with HOST(Y).

(a) Establish a primary link to HOST(Y).
   A primary link is established to HOST(Y) through the control link 0. The connection is then in a pre-log-in state, i.e., the remote HOST expects its standard log-in procedures.

(b) Log-in Sequence
   Standard ASCII characters are sent/received over the primary link. In that way, the HOST(X) user signs in to remote HOST(Y) by using its standard log-in procedures.

(c) Establish an auxiliary link to HOST(Y)
   This establishment must be executed by both extremities. As in (a), this is done by using the control link 0.

(d) Send/Receive Text over Auxiliary link

2.2.2 Example

Figure 3 focuses on the data exchanged over the links during a HOST(X)-HOST(Y) dialogue.
HOST(X) has the network identification 8.
HOST(Y) has the network identification 5.

Notations Used:
* Circled stuffs represent characters, e.g. (ENQ)
* Parenthesised numbers are used for cross referencing with further explanations, e.g. (2)

Explanations

* (1) and (2) constitute the primary link establishment
   -HOST(X) sends the following message over link 0:
   " (ENQ)(PRIM)(0)(1)(2)(OPT) "

   (ENQ): Enquiry for link establishment (ASCII character)
   (PRIM): Link type: primary (Special Character)
   (0)(1)(2): Logical link identification number in decimal (3 ASCII characters)
   (OPT): Options: it is an alphanumerical character, e.g.(9). Possible options could be: Full Echo, data type...

   -HOST(Y) acknowledges by sending back:
   " (ACK)(ENQ)(PRIM)(0)(1)(2)(OPT) "

   (ACK): postive acknowledgement (ASCII character)-Link 12 is now established.
   (ENQ)(PRIM)(0)(1)(2)(OPT): The previous message is returned to the requestor for security purpose.

* (3) and (4) constitute a trivial example of a log-in procedure. -See remark 2 below-

*(5): HOST(X), talking to the operating system of HOST(Y), requests for URSA. URSA is supposed to be a user application program in HOST(Y).

*(6) and (7) constitute the auxiliary link establishment. After (5) an auxiliary link should be established. This is done by HOST(X) since it has the higher identification number in network. e.g., 8 against 5.
The procedure is very much like (1) and (2)

*(8): HOST(X) transmits a "file" to URSA. The transmission is done over link 25 which has just been established.

*(9): HOST(Y) answers back with a "file" over link 25. And the dialogue goes on...

*(10): HOST(X) frees the links he has established
(EOT): End of transmission (ASCII character).
(0)(0)(2): Number of links wanted to be closed (3 ASCII character)
(0)(1)(2)(0)(2)(5): Link identification number (ASCII characters)

*(11) HOST(Y) acknowledges back as in (2), (7).

Remark 1: The figure 3 doesn't show the heading of each message which are of course transmitted over these links. The characters represented on each line should be viewed inserted in the text zone of a message.

Remark 2: These characters -see (3) and (4)- can either be transmitted one at a time over the line (each character constitutes the text of a message) or be packed before transmission by the user communication program.

In either case, the remote HOST can consider the link as a normal teletype (Searchs breaking characters, provides echos...).

Remark 3: In (2), (7), or (11), HOST(Y) can answer back a negative acknowledgement character (NAK) instead of (ACK). This, for many various reasons such as bad transmission, HOST(X) wants to open a link already established, and so forth. The message could be (NAK) (IND) where (IND) is a character indicating why the previous block has been refused. Upon receiving back such negative acknowledgements, HOST(X) will repeat its message until HOST(Y) accepts it. An emergency procedure will take place if too many successive NAK occur.

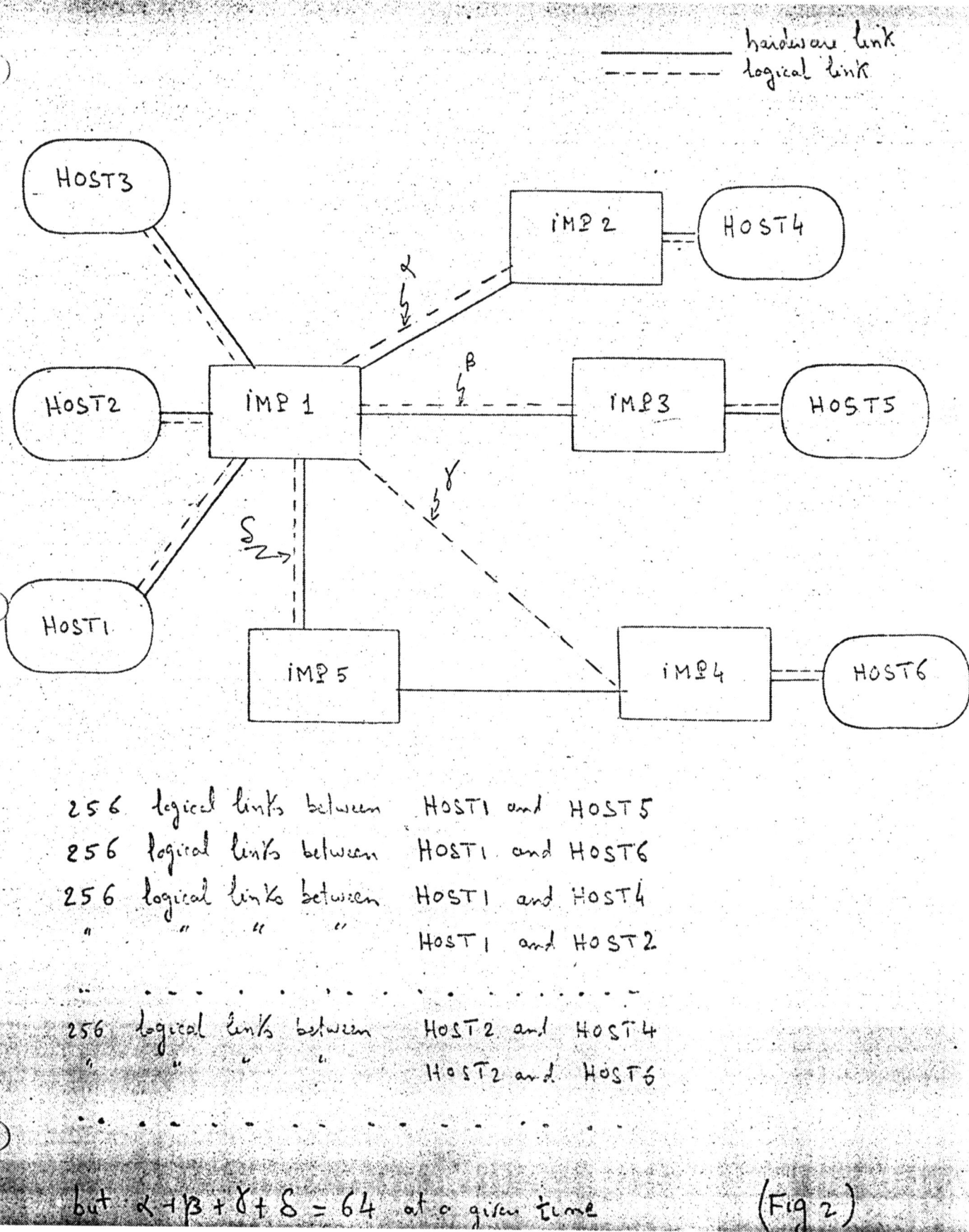

(Fig 2)

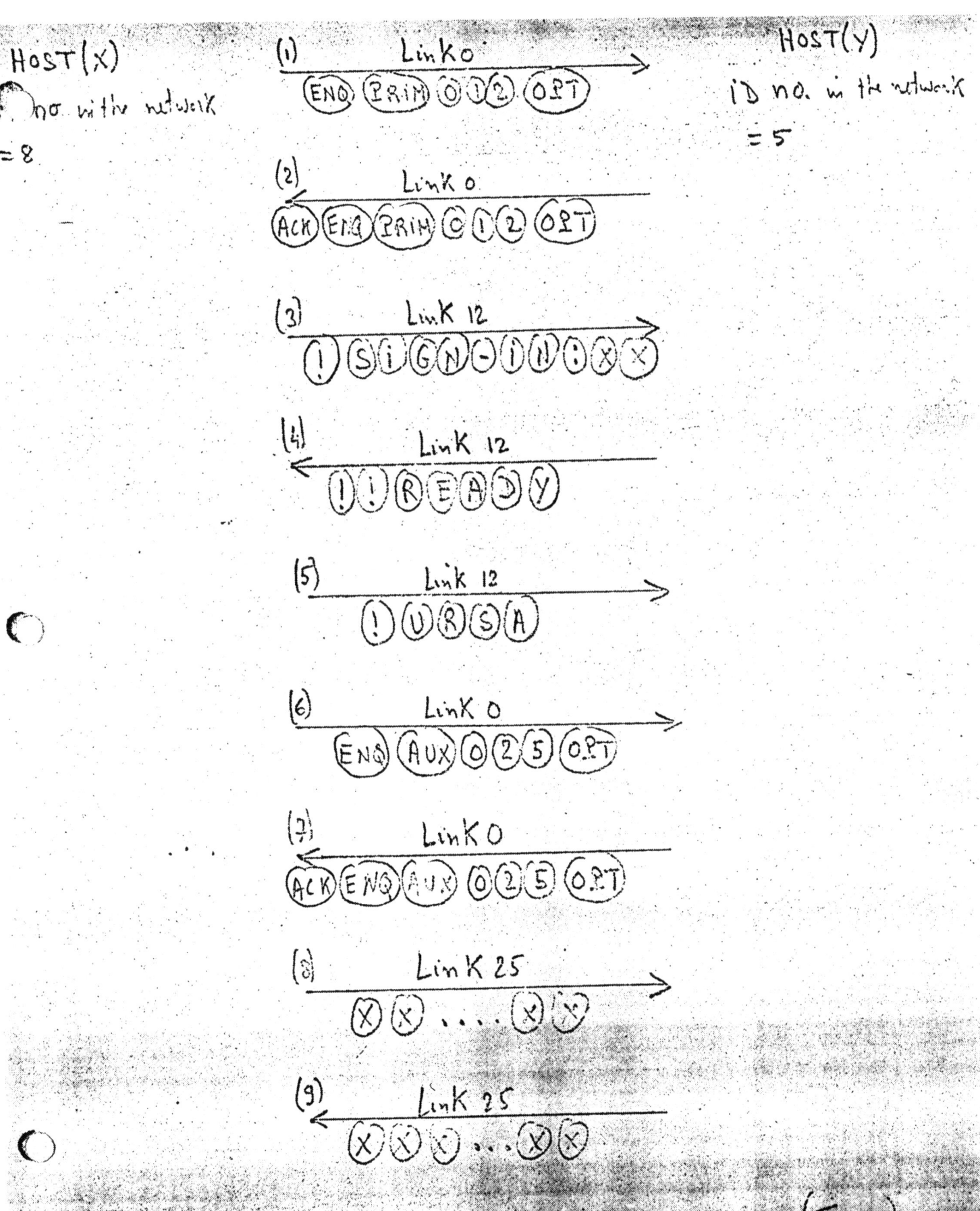

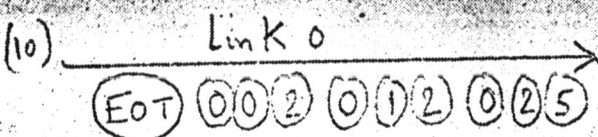

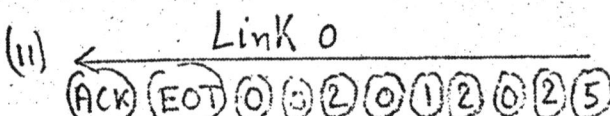

(Fig 3)

3. Network Service Calls

A user program accesses the network facilities (link establishment, data transmission...) through service calls. Under execution, a service call traps to a monitor service routine that interprets and executes the service. Control is then routed back to the user program.

3.1 List of service calls at user's disposal.

(a) **Open Primary Link**

OPENPRIM(PRIMID, HOSTID, BUFFADDR, INTRPT-CODE, [OPT])

PRIMID: User identification of the primary link.
HOSTID: Remote HOST identification.
BUFFADDR: Buffer address for the incoming messages.
INTRPT-CODE: Code that the network program should give to the user program when he is interrupted because a message has come back.
OPT: Options such as "full echo" (for testing purpose), message required after successful link establishment, etc....

Remark: [ ]: not required.

(b) **Open auxiliary link**

OPENAUX(AUXID, PRIMID, BUFFADDR, INTRPT-CODE, [OPT])

AUXID: User identification of the auxiliary link.
PRIMID: User identification of a primary link. Refers to an already established primary link.
BUFFADDR, INTRPT-CODE, OPT same meaning as above.

(c) **Transmission over link**

TRANSLINK (ID, BUFFADDR, N, [OPT])

ID: User link identification. Depending on which type of links we want to transmit, this identification number will be equal to a previously defined AUXID/PRIMID.
BUFFADDR: Data location address for transmission.
N: Data bytes number for transmission.
OPT: Options such as data type (character vs. binary), acknowledgements required (utilization of the auxiliary links in a half duplex mode), trace bit, etc....

(d) **Modify link parameters**

MODIFLINK (ID, OPT)

ID: User link identification (Equal to either AUXID/PRIMID)

(e) **Close link**

CLOSE LINK (ID, [OPT])

ID: Same meaning as above.
OPT: Can be used to close all the links in use by the user.

4. Data Structure

The allocation and the management of the links are carried out by means of three tables:
- A Table Sorted By HOST.
- A Table Sorted By LINK.
- A Table Sorted by USER.

4.1 HOST Table (See Figure 4)

It is a bit-table indicating, for a given remote HOST, which links are free. (bit-0 means free link)

This table should provide 256 bits per HOST (256 logical links possible). At a given time no more than 64 bits can be set to 1 in the whole table.

4.2 LINK Table (See Figures 4 and 5)

This table contains as many sections as links in use. Figure 5 describes the structure of a section.
Starting and retrieval are carried out dynamically upon using a hashing technique based on the network link identifications.

4.3 USER Table (See Figure 4)

The table structure is given on Figure 4. These are as many sections as active users. Each section contains the user identification (given by the operating system) and the identifications of the links in use by this user. Notice that a link has two identifications: that of the user (given as a parameter in the OPEN service call) and that of the network (that is attributed by the network program).

This table is hashed by users.

Network Program

The emission functions of the network programs are fulfilled by monitor service routines. In that sense, this program can be viewed as belonging to the operating system.

These functions are concerned with the link establishments and data transmission; they are started by the service calls previously described.

Let's explain how these routines allocate and manage the links by describing the operations involved during the execution of the OPENPRIM routine.

Suppose that the value of the parameter HOSTID is equal to j.

(a) j is used as an index for the "HOST" table to reach the "HOST j"

(b) In "HOST j" section, we select the first free link (First bit=0) e.g., i^{th} bit.

(c) j and i determine respectively the HOST-IMP destination and the network link number.

(d) This j-i value is used as a hashing code to open a new section in the <u>link table</u>. e.g. section ℓ.

(e) In this section ℓ, the link ID zone is filled up with j-i, the "link opened by us" and "primary" bits are set to 1. (See Figure 5.)

(Remark: It is only when we receive back the acknowledgement message from the remote HOST — See Figure 3: (2)—that the link is considered completely established. Then we set to 1 the bit "link established".). Also in this section ℓ, we store the parameter BUFFADD Value in the "buffer address zone", and the user identification number, implicitly given, in "the user ID zone".

(f) Using the user identification number, we hash the USER Table to open (or find) the right m section.

We update this m section by storing the user link ID number (PRIMID) and the network link ID number (i).

(g) We prepare the message text:
(ENQ) (PRIM) (0) (0) (1) (OPT)

(h) We prepare a heading according to BBN specifications (in order to send the message over link 0).

(i) We calculate the HOST checksum.

(j) We put together the heading, checksum, text by providing marking.

(k) We queue up this message for the handler.

The receiving functions will use these tables in a very similar way.

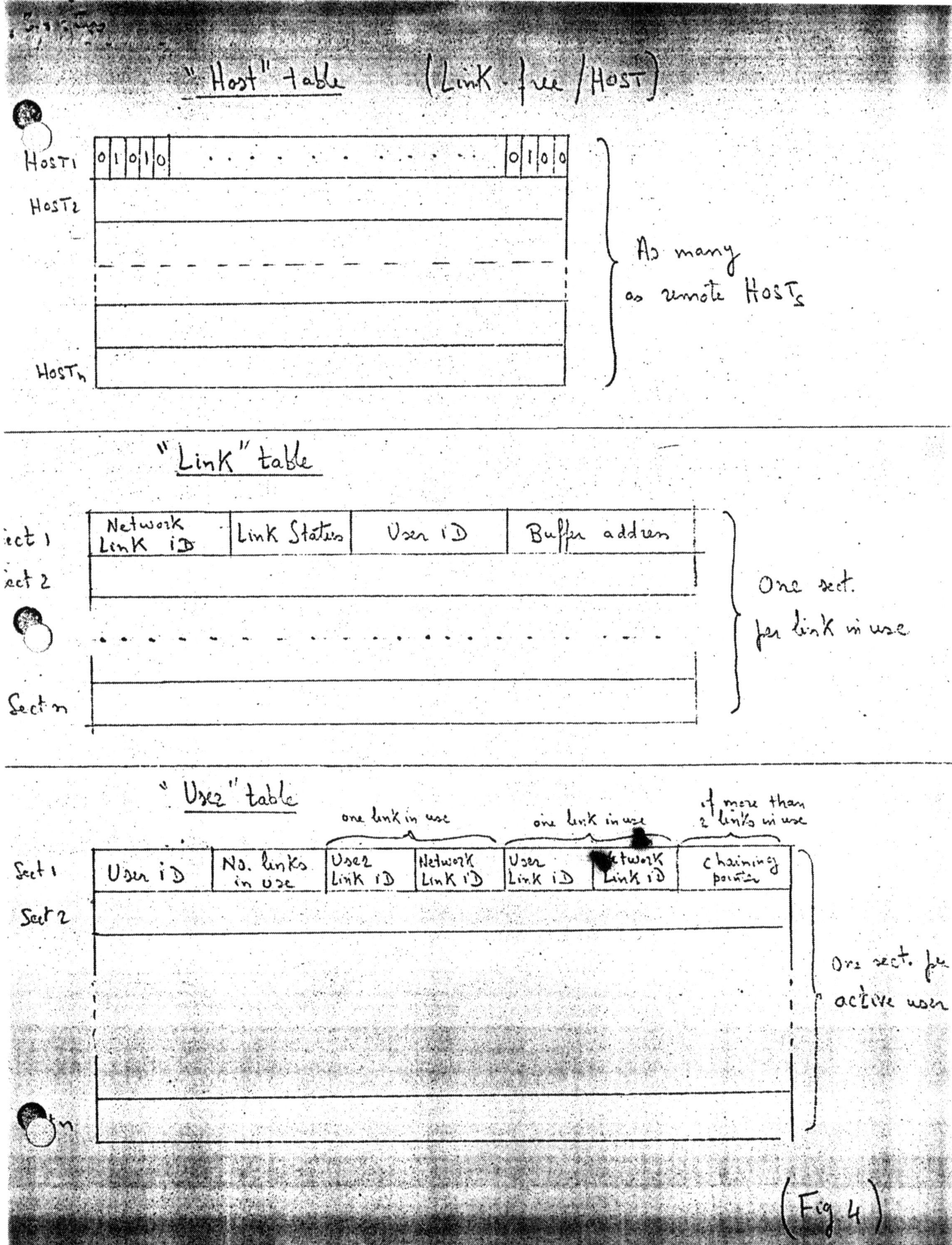

(Fig 4)

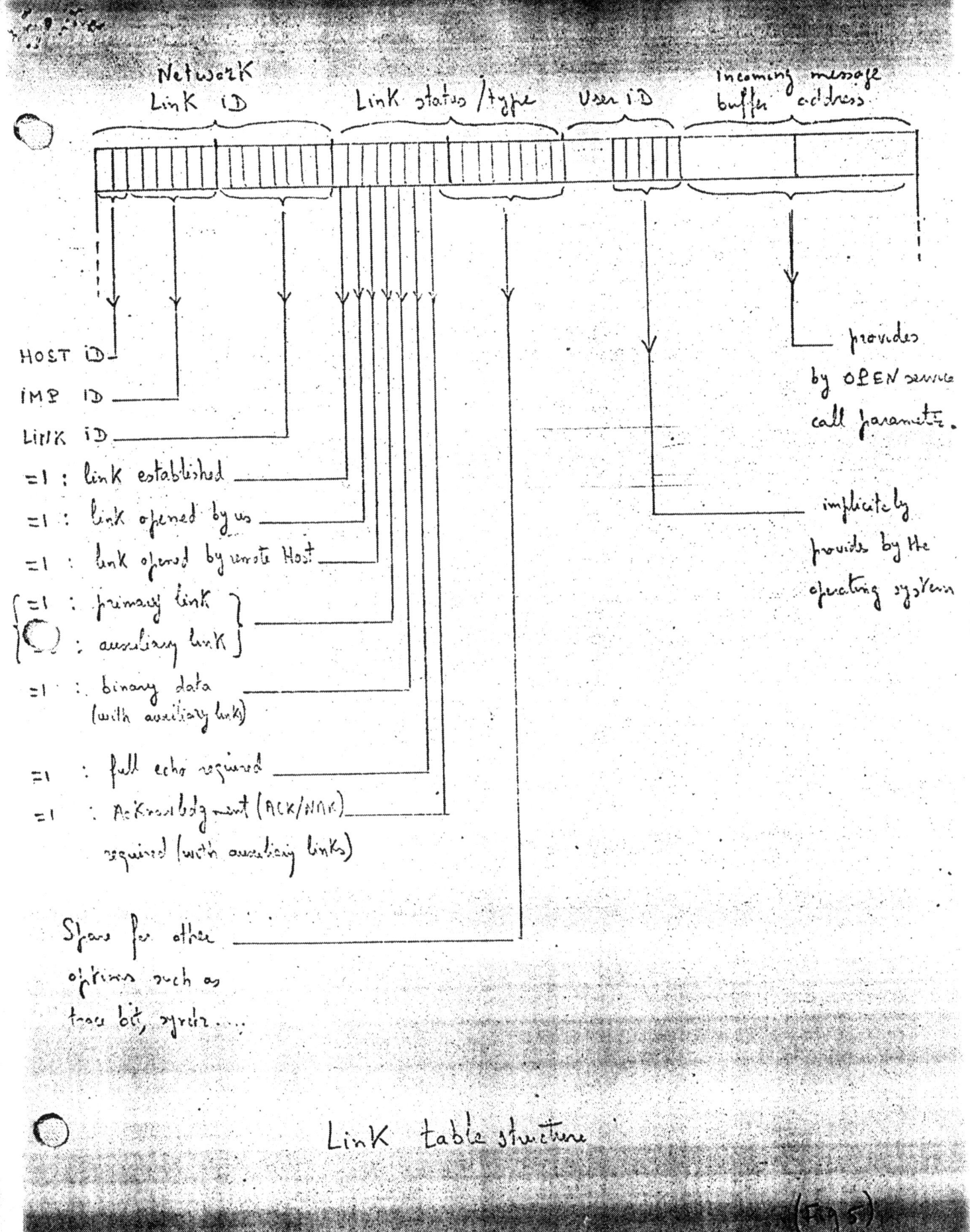

Link table structure

Network Working Group   S. Crocker
Request for Comments: 10   UCLA
                                                29 July 1969

DOCUMENTATION CONVENTIONS

This note is a revision of NWG/RFC #3

The Network Working Group seems to consist of Steve Carr at Utah, Elmer Shapiro and Bill English SRI, Steve Crocker at UCLA, John Haefner at RAND, Paul Rovner and Jim Curry at Lincoln Labs. Membership is not closed.

The Network Working Group (NWG) is concerned with the HOST software, the strategies for using the network, and initial experience with the network.

Documentation of the NWG's effort is through notes such as this. Notes may be produced at any site by anybody and included in this series.

Content

The content of a NWG note may be any thought, suggestion, etc. related to the HOST software or other aspect of the network. Notes are encouraged to be timely rather than polished. Philosophical positions without examples or other specifics, specific suggestions or implementation techniques without introductory or background explication, and explicit questions without any attempted answers are all acceptable. The minimum length for a NWG note is one sentence.

These standards (or lack of them) are stated explicitly for two reasons. First, there is a tendency to view a written statement as _ipso facto_ authoritative, and we hope to promote the exchange and discussion of considerably less than authoritative ideas. Second, there is a natural hesitancy to publish something unpolished, and we hope to ease this inhibition.

Form

Every NWG note should bear the following information:

1. "Network Working Group"
   "Request for Comments: X"
       where X is a serial number. Serial numbers are assigned by Steve Crocker at UCLA

2. Author and affilitation

3. Date

Documentation Conventions
Page Two

    4. Title
       The title need not be unique

Distribution

One copy only will be sent from the author's site to:

1. Steve Crocker, UCLA
2. Ron Stoughton, UCSB
3. Elmer Shapiro, SRI
4. Steve Carr, Utah
5. John Haefner, RAND
6. Paul Rovner, LL
7. Bob Kahn, BB and N
8. Larry Roberts, ARPA
9. Jerry Cole, SDC

Reproduction if desired may be handled locally.

Addresses

Below are the most current addresses I have. Please correct as necessary:

Steve Crocker
3732 Boelter Hall
UCLA
Los Angeles, California 90024
   UCLA
   (213) 825-4864
   825-2543 (Sec'y)

Ron Stoughton
Computer Research Lab
UCSB
Santa Barbara, Calif. 93102
   UCSB
   (805) 961-3221

Elmer Shapiro
Stanford Research Institute
333 Ravenswood
Menlo Park, Calif. 94025
   SRI
   (451) 326-6200

Steve Carr
Computer Science Dept.
University of Utah
Salt Lake City, Utah 84112
   Utah
   (801) 322-8224

John Haefner
The Rand Corporation
1700 Main Street
Santa Monica, Calif. 90406
   RAND
   (213) 393-0411

Paul D. Rovner
Mass. Inst. of Tech.
Lincoln Laboratory B-115
P. O. Box 73
Lexington, Mass. 02173
   LL
   (617) 562-5500
   X7211

Documentation Conventions
Page Three

```
Robert Kahn                          BBN
Bolt, Beranek and Newman             (617) 491-1850
50 Moulton St.                             491-1868
Cambridge, Mass. 02138

Larry Roberts                        ARPA
ODS/ARPA                             (202) OX7-8663
3D167 Pentagon                             OX7-8654
Washington, D.C. 20301

Jerry Cole                           SDC
7842 Croyden                         2500 Colorado
Los Angeles, Calif. 90045            Santa Monica, Calif. 90406
                                     (213) 393-9411, X438
                                                 X6019 (Sec'y)
```

Network Working Group
Request for Comments: 11

Implementation of the HOST - HOST

Software Procedures in GORDO

G. Deloche, UCLA
1 August 1969

TABLE OF CONTENTS

Chapter			Page
1.	Introduction		3
2.	HOST-HOST Procedures		4
	2.1 Generalities		4
	2.2 Connections and Links		5
		2.2.1 Definitions	5
		2.2.2 Connection types	6
	2.3 Message Structure		9
	2.4 User Transactions		12
		2.4.1 List of transactions	12
		2.4.2 HOST-HOST protocol and control messages	14
3.	Implementation in GORDO		19
	3.1 Introduction to GORDO		19
		3.1.1 GORDO file system	19
		3.1.2 GORDO process	19
	3.2 Software Organization Overview		22
	3.3 Software Description		24
		3.3.1 Data structures	24
		3.3.1.1 Allocation tables	24
		3.3.1.2 Buffer pages	20
		3.3.2 Programs	36
		3.3.2.1 Handler	36
		3.3.2.2 Network	37

	Page
3.4 Software Procedures	40
3.4.1 Description of some typical sequences	40
Appendix A: Flowcharts	44

1. INTRODUCTION

This technical note concentrates upon (1) the HOST-HOST procedures and (2) the implementation of the corresponding programs in GORDO (Operating System of the UCLA HOST).

The first section is closely related to the BBN reports No. 1822 and 1763[1] and specifies the HOST functions for exchanging messages. It mostly deals with links and connections, message structure, transactions, and control messages.

The second section is software oriented; it explains how the HOST functions are implemented and integrated into GORDO. It is involved with data structures, programs, buffers, interrupt processing, etc.

[1] Parts of this section are taken from or referred to those reports.

2. HOST-HOST PROCEDURES

2.1 Generalities

The basic idea is that several users, at a given HOST, should simultaneously be able to utilize the network by time-sharing its physical facilites.

This implies that within each HOST operating system, there must exist a special program that multiplexes outgoing messages from the users into the network and distributes incoming messages to the appropriate users. We will call this special program the Network program.

2.2 Links and Connections   (See figure 1)

2.2.1 Definitions

It is convenient to consider the Network as a black box – a system whose behavior is known but whose mechanisms are not – for communicating messages between remote users rather than between pairs of HOST computers.

(a) Logical connections

We define a logical connection as being a communication path linking two users at remote $HOST_s$.

With that concept, a user (user program) in a HOST computer can (1) establish several logical connections to any remote HOST users, and (2) send or receive messages over those connections.

Connections appear to users as full duplex.

One of the purposes of the Network program is to serve the users in establishing, identifying, and maintaining these connections.

(b) Logical links

Each logical connection is made of a pair of directional links: one for transmitting, the other for receiving.

Those links, called logical links, are established by the Network programs and used by them.

Note here that users are only interested in connections and are completely unaware of links. Relationships between links and connections are carried out by the Network program.

One of the advantages to define a connection as a pair of directional links is that a HOST will have the capability to loop himself through its IMP (it opens a connection to himself). This feature can be useful for debugging purposes.

Further on through this paper we will not use any more the attribute logical when referring either to links or connections.

2.2.2 Connection types

In order to reach a high flexibility in utilizing the Network there is advantage to classify the connections.

Three types of connections are distinguished: (a) control connection, (b) primary connection, and (c) auxiliary connection.

(a) Control connection

This connection has a special status and is unique between a pair of $HOST_s$, e.g., if the Network includes x $HOST_s$, there are at most $x - 1$ control connections issued from one HOST.

This connection is used by remote Network programs for passing control messages back and forth. Control messages are basic to the establishment/deletion of standard connections. (See 2.4.2)

Note here that this control connection is the only connection which is ignored [not used] by the HOST users.

Let us describe now the standard connections.

(b) Primary connection

These connections connect remote users.

A primary connection:

* Is unique between a pair of users and is the first to be

established.

* Is "teletype-like", i.e.:
    - ASCII characters are transmitted;
    - Echos are generated by the remote HOST;
    - The receiving $HOST_s$ scan for break characters;
    - The transmission rate is slow (less than 20 characters/sec).
* Is mainly used for transmitting control commands, e.g., for log-in into a remote HOST operating system.

(c) <u>Auxiliary connection</u>

These connections also connect remote users:

An auxiliary connection:

* Is opened in parallel to a primary connection and is not unique, i.e., several auxiliary connections can be established between users.
* Is used for transmitting large volumes of data (file oriented).
* Is used either for binary or character tranmission.

7

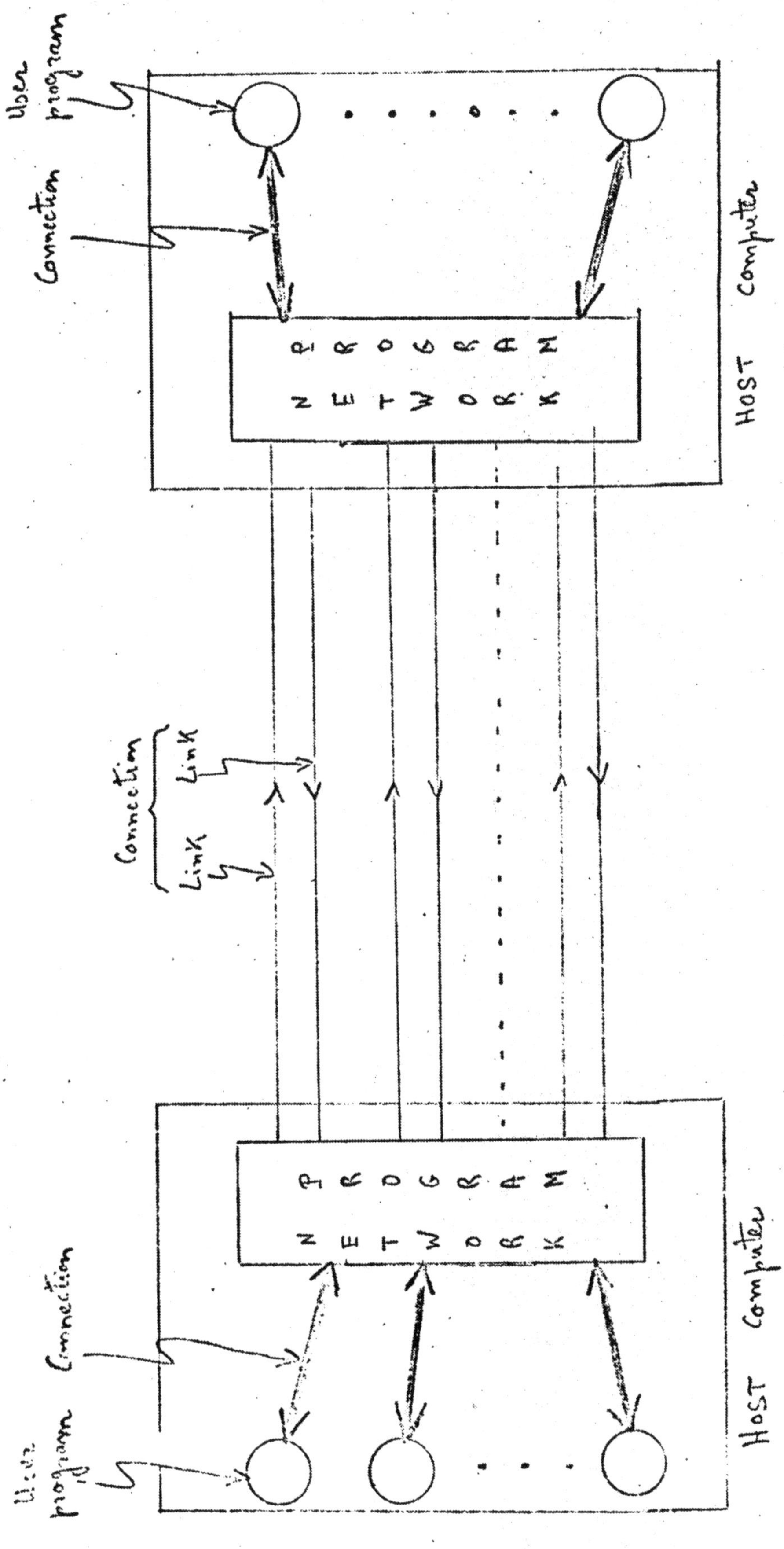

Figure 1. Links and Connections

2.3 Message Structure

The HOSTs communicate with each other via messages. A message may vary in length up to 8095 bits (See down below the structure). Larger transmission must therefore be broken up by HOST users into a sequence of such messages.

A message structure is identified on figure 2.

It includes the following:

(1) A leader (32 bits): Message type, Source/Destination HOST, link number. (See BBN report No. 1822, pp 13, 17)

(2) A marking (32 bits when sent by the Sigma 7) for starting a message text on a word boundary. (See BBN report No. 1822, pp. 17, 19)

(3) The message text (Max: 8015 bits for the Sigma 7). It mostly consists of user's text. However, it may represent information for use by the Network programs. (Control messages, see 2.4.2)

(4) A checksum (16 bits). Its purpose is to check, at the HOST level, the right transmission of a message. (Changes in bit pattern or packet transposition; packets are defined in BBN report No. 1763, p. 13) See down below for checksum calculation.

(5) A padding for solving word length mismatch problems. (See BBN report No. 1822, p. 17, 19.) As far as software is concerned, padding is only involved at message reception for delineating message ends. (At transmission the hardware takes care of the padding.)

Remark:

Checksum calculation:

The last 16 bits of every message sent by a HOST is a checksum. This checksum is computed on the whole message including any marking, but excluding the 32 bit leader and any padding. To compute the checksum:

1. Consider the message to be padded with zeroes to a length of 8640 bits.

2. Section the 8640 bits into six 1440-bit segments, $S_0, S_1 \ldots S_5$.

3. Section each 1440-bit segment S into 90 16-bit elements, $t_0, t_1 \ldots t_{89}$.

4. Define a function $\oplus$, which takes two 16-bit elements as inputs and outputs a 16-bit element. This function is defined by

$$t_m \oplus t_n = t_m \oplus t_n, \text{ if } t_m + t_n < 2^{16}$$

$$t_m \oplus t_n = t_m \oplus t_n - 2^{16} + 1, \text{ if } t_m + t_n \geq 2^{16}$$

5. For each 1440-bit segment S_i compute $C_i = K(S_i)$, where

$$K(S) = t_0 \oplus t_1 \oplus \ldots \ldots t_{89}$$

6. Compute $C = C_0 \oplus C_1 \oplus C_1 \oplus C_2 \oplus C_2 \oplus C_2 \oplus C_2 \ldots \oplus C_5$

(Notice that $C_i \oplus C_i$ is just C_i rotated left one bit)

The number C is the checksum. The reason the C_i are rotated by i bits is to detect packet transposition.

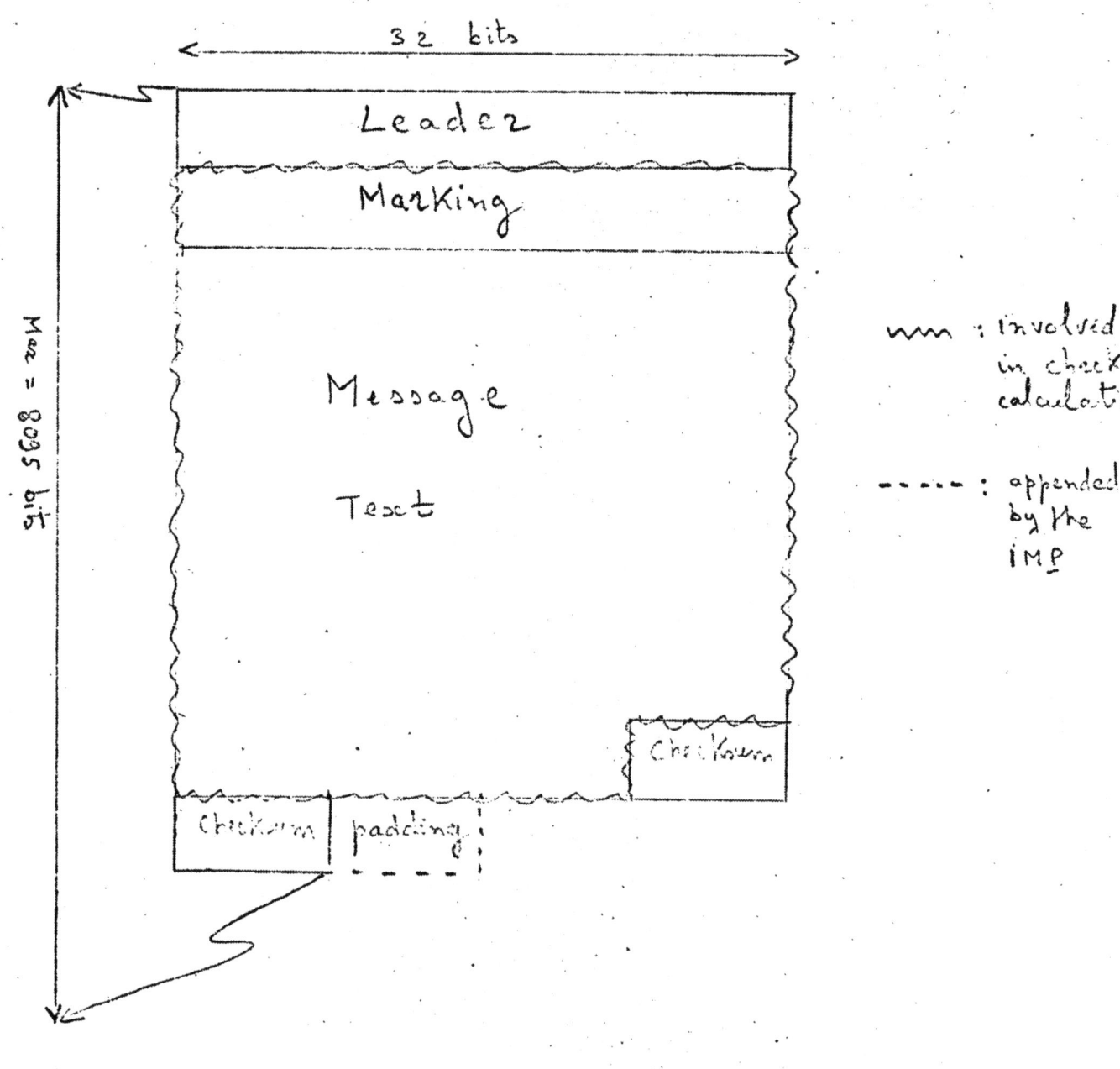

Format of a message sent by the Sigma 7

Figure 2

2.4 User Transactions

From what has been discussed until here, the Network appears to a user as a bunch of connections. Let us now explain how one can make use of these connections.

First, we are going to describe the set of transactions that a user should be able to access for utilizing the connection facilities.

Then, we are going to explain the role of the Network program for the execution of these transactions. This will cover a HOST-HOST protocol in which control messages are exchanged between network programs.

For explanation purposes those transactions are represented, at the user level, in the form of subroutine calls and parameters. However, this does not imply at all that the implementation will closely follow this pattern. (We are more involved here with the description than the implementation aspect, see chapter 3.)

2.4.1 List of transactions

Listed below are the descriptions of subroutines that could be at user's disposal for creating/breaking connections and transmitting/receiving data over them. This set of subroutines can be considered as a kind of interface between the user level and the network program level.

(a) Open primary connection:

OPENPRIM (CONNECTID, HOSTID, BUFFADDR, [OPT])

CONNECTID: Connection identification #

HOSTID: Remote HOST identification #

BUFFADDR: Buffer address for incoming messages.

OPT: Options such as message required after successful connection establishment, "full echo" (each message is transmitted back by the remote HOST for checking purpose), etc.

Remark: [ ] means optional

   (b) Open auxiliary connection

OPENAUX (CONNECTID, BUFFADDR, N, [OPT])

CONNECTID: Connection identification #, i.e., the identification of the corresponding primary connection (First a user has to open a primary connection).

BUFFADDR: Same meaning as above.

N: Number of auxiliary connections that should be opend.

OPT: Same meaning as above.

   (c) Transmission over connection

TRANSM (CONNECTID, NO, BUFFADDR, N, [OPT])

CONNECTID: Connection identification #

NO: Connection #. The primary connection is always referred to as being NO = 0. An auxiliary connection number corresponds to the order in which it has been established. (The first auxiliary opened is referred to by NO = 1, the second by NO = 2, etc.)

BUFFADDR: Buffer address of the message to be transmitted.

N: Message size (byte number)

OPT: Options such as data type (characters vs. binary), trace bit, etc.

(d) Close connection

CLOSE (CONNECTID, [N], [NO])

CONNECTID: Connection indentification #.

N: Number of connections to be closed. If omitted all connections in use by the user, included the primary link, are closed.

NO: In case of N different from zero this number indicates the auxiliary connection # to be closed.

2.4.2 HOST-HOST protocol and control messages

The HOST-HOST protocol is carried out by the Network programs. It mainly involves the execution of the previous transactions (initiated by users) and covers a HOST-HOST dialogue.

This dialogue fulfills control procedures for opening or breaking connections and consists in exchanging control messages over the control link. A control message has a structure identical to that of a regular message; it only differs from it by the text which is for use by Network programs instead of users.

Let us insist that this control procedure is completely unrelated to transmission control procedures implemented in the IMP computers. We are here at the HOST level (Network programs), and therefore control messages, that are going to be described below, are transmitted over the IMP_s like regular messages.

Consider now the previous transactions and describe for each of them which messages are exchanged over which links. Each case will be explained by means of trivial examples.

We suppose that a HOST(x) user wants to talk to a remote HOST(y) program called URSA.

(a) <u>Open a primary connection: (OPENPRIM)</u>

The HOST (x)'s Network program, waken up (See 3.3) by a use for opening a primary connection, starts a dialogue with the HOST (y)'s Network program.

(i) HOST(x) sends the following control message:

HOST(x) $\xrightarrow{\text{Control link}}$ HOST(y)
ENQ PRIM 0 1 2

ENQ: Enquiry for connection establishment (one ASCII character)

PRIM: Connection type: primary (one special character)

0 1 2 : Outgoing link #. It is a decimal number (3 ASCII characters), e.g., link #12.

This link # has been determined by the HOST(x) Network program (See implementation: 3.3)

(ii) HOST(y) acknowledges by sending back the following control message:

HOST(x) $\xleftarrow{\text{Control link}}$ HOST(y)
ACK ENQ PRIM 0 1 2 0 1 5

ACK: Positive acknowledgment (one ASCII character)

ENQ PRIM 0 1 2 : Same meaning as above. This part of the message is returned for checking purposes.

0 1 5 : Incoming link #. It follows the same pattern as the outgoing link #. This link # has been determined by the HOST(y) Network

program.

Now the connection is established; it will use links #12 and 15 for exchanging user messages. The connection is said to be in a pre-log-in state, i.e., the remote HOST(y) expects its standard log-in procedures.

(b) <u>Transmission over primary connection: (TRANSM)</u>

By means of TRANSM subroutines referring to the primary connection, the HOST(x) user is able to sign-in into the HOST(y) operating system and then to call for the URSA program (HOST(y) user program).

The Network programs at both ends will use the link #12 and #15 for passing along messages. These messages are standard messages whose contents serve for log in sequence.

A trivial example could be:

```
HOST(x)   ─── Prim. Link #12 ───────►   HOST(y)
              ! S I G N - I N : X X

HOST(x)   ◄─── Prim. Link #15 ───────   HOST(y)
              ! ! R E A D Y

HOST(x)   ─── Prim. Link #12 ───────►   HOST(y)
              ! U R S A
```

(c) <u>Open an auxiliary connection: (OPENAUXI)</u>

In a very similar manner as (a) an auxiliary connection is established between HOST(x) and HOST(y). For so doing control messages are exchanged over the control link.

```
HOST(x)   ─── Control link ──────────►   HOST(y)
              ENQ AUX 0 2 5

HOST(x)   ◄─── Control link ──────────   HOST(y)
              ACK ENQ AUX 0 2 5 0 2 1
```

16

Now the auxiliary connection is established, it will use links #25 and 21 for exchanging standard messages.

(d) Transmission over auxiliary connection: (TRANSM)

By means of TRANSM subroutines referring to the auxiliary connection, the users at both ends can exchange data:

```
HOST(x)         Aux. Link #25              HOST(y)
             ─────────────────────>
                X X ...... X X

HOST(x)         Aux. Link #21              HOST(y)
             <─────────────────────
                X ............. X
```

etc...............

(e) Close connections: (CLOSE)

This is carried out in a similar manner as (a). The user calls a CLOSE subroutine and then the Network programs at both ends exchange control messages.

```
HOST(x)          Control Link              HOST(y)
             ─────────────────────>
              EOT  0 0 1  0 1 2
```

EOT: End of transmission (one ASCII character)

0 0 1 : No. of connections to be closed (3 decimal ASCII characters)

0 1 2 : Outgoing link # to be closed.

Then HOST(y) acknowledges back as in (a).

```
HOST(x)          Control Link              HOST(y)
             <─────────────────────
           ACK EOT 0 0 1 0 1 2 0 1 5
```

Remark 1 - In (a), (c), and (e) HOST(y) may answer back a message including a negative acknowledgment character NAK instead of ACK. This for

17

many various reasons such as: wrong sequence, connection already opened, and so forth. The message could be NAK IND, where IND is an alphanumerical character indicating, in a coded form, why the previous block has been refused. Upon receiving back such acknowledgments HOST(x) will repeat its message until HOST(y) accepts it. An emergency procedure will take place if too many successive "NAK messages" occur.

Remark 2 — On each of the above illustrations (arrows) only the message text is represented. In fact, complete messages (with leader, marking, padding...) are exchanged over these links.

3. IMPLEMENTATION IN GORDO

3.1 Introduction to GORDO

GORDO is a time-sharing system implemented on SDS Sigma 7. We outline below some of the characteristics relevant to our paper.

3.1.1 GORDO file system

The file system is page oriented. It is composed of files and directories. A file consists of a heading and a number of pages which compose the body of the file. A directory consists of a number of entries that point to either files or other directories.

3.1.2 GORDO process

* A process is a program (procedures and data) plus its logical environment. In other words a process is a program which is known and controlled by the GORDO scheduler.

* A user (a job) may have several processes as different as compiler, loader, editor, application program, etc. A process is created through a system call (FORK).

* The space a process can refer to is the Virtual Space of 128k word length. A part (8k) of it is reserved for the operating system, the other part (120k) is directly accessed by the user. This later may fill or modify its part of the virtual space upon 'coupling'. (See below:

service calls) pages taken from different files. Figure 3 illustrates this coupling.

* A process can request for services by means of system calls. The system calls relevant to our paper are:

    WAKE   for awaking (set active) a sleeping process

    SLEEP   for putting asleep another process (or itself)

    COUPLE   for coupling a page from the file space to the virtual space.

* A process ordinarily runs in slave mode. However if it is set up as an I/O process it can access privileged instructions.

* Processes can share data through files attached to "mail box" directories.

Remark: Through this note the words process and program are used interchangeably.

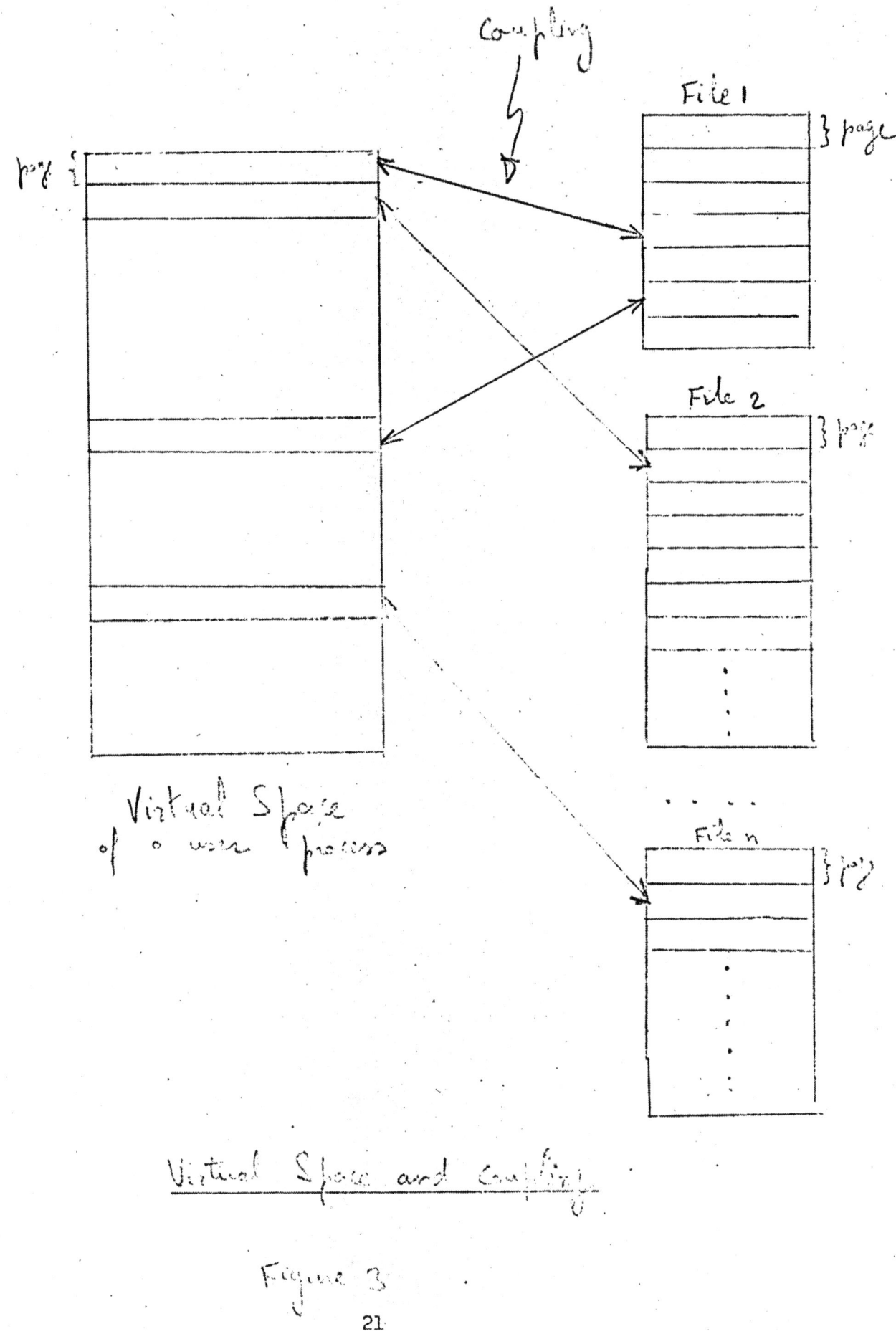

Virtual Space and Coupling

Figure 3

3.2 Software Organization Overview

Figure 4 illustrates the overall organization.

The system is based upon two main programs: the "Network" and the "Handler".

The Handler is an I/O interrupt routine closely related to the IMP-HOST hardware interface. It serves the Network process in transmitting and receiving network messages.

The Network process carries out most of the work.

Its main function is to satisfy the users' requests for opening/closing connections and transmitting/receiving network messages. For so doing,

* it establishes, identifies and breaks the links upon using the allocation tables (HOST, CONNECT, INPUT LINK; see 3.3.1.1)
* it is aware of the presence of new users upon exploring the Network mail box directory;
* it communicates with active users by means of shared pages through which messages and requests are exchanged (connection shared pages);
* it formats incoming/outgoing messages in a working page. This working page has an extension (emergency ring);
* it communicates with the Handler by means of a shared page (I/O communication page) which contains the I/O communication buffers.

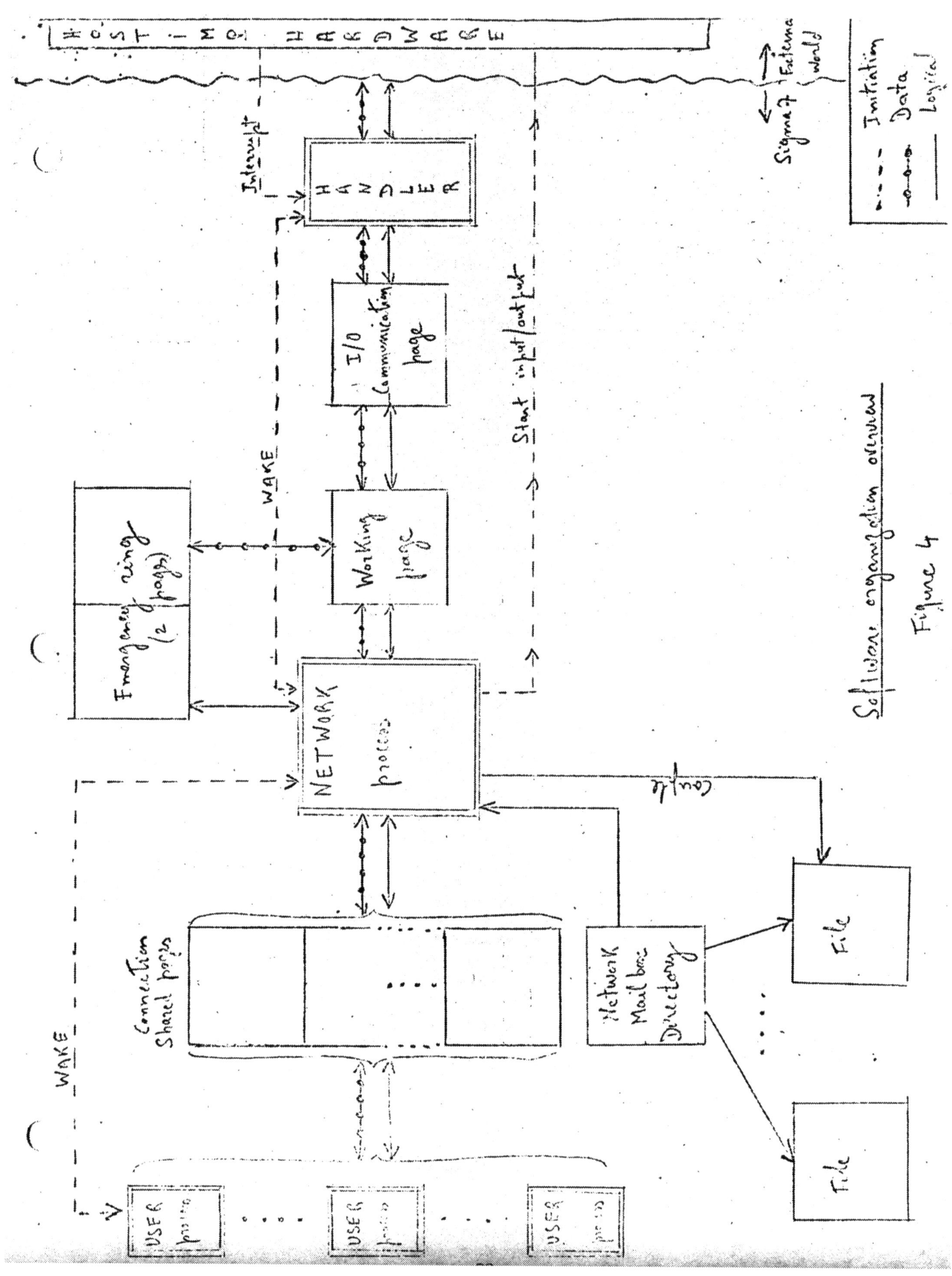

Software organization overview

Figure 4

3.3 Software Description

3.3.1 Data Structures

3.3.1.1 Allocation tables: HOST, CONNECT, INPUT LINK

The Network program establishes, identifies, and breaks links and connections upon using 3 tables:

A table sorted by remote HOST #.

A table sorted by connection #

A table sorted by input link #.

(a) HOST table   (See figure 5)

It is a bit table indicating the free outgoing links. It has the following characteristics:

* Location: Disc resident
* Coupling: Coupled to the Network process virtual space.
* Size: As many slots as remote $HOST_s$.
* Slot structure: As many bits as possible outgoing links to a remote HOST, i.e., 256.
* Access: Indexing. Each slot is accessed through a remote HOST #.
* Specific feature: Throughout the whole table no more than 64 bits can be turned on. This figure corresponds to the maximum number of outgoing links that can be activated at one time (No matter what is the number of remote $HOST_s$).

(b) CONNECT table

This table keeps track of all the connections' environment. It has the following characteristics:

* Location: Disc resident
* Coupling: Coupled to the Network process virtual space
* Size: As many slots as connections in use.
* Slot structure: See figure 6. Each slot is 2 word length
* Access: Indexing. Each slot is accessed through a connection #. See 3.4 the way it is handled.
* Specific feature 1: The slot structure corresponding to a primary connection is not identical to that of an auxiliary connection (See figure 7). This because user identifications and requests are done through primary shared pages.
* Specific feature 2: This table is handled in parallel with the connection pages (See 3.3.2 (b))
* Specific feature 3: This table is mainly used for transmitting messages. (For each connection it contains the outgoing link # and remote HOST #, i.e., all the information required for transmitting a message.)

(c) INPUT LINK table

This table keeps track of all the incoming (input) links and so is closely related to the CONNECT table.

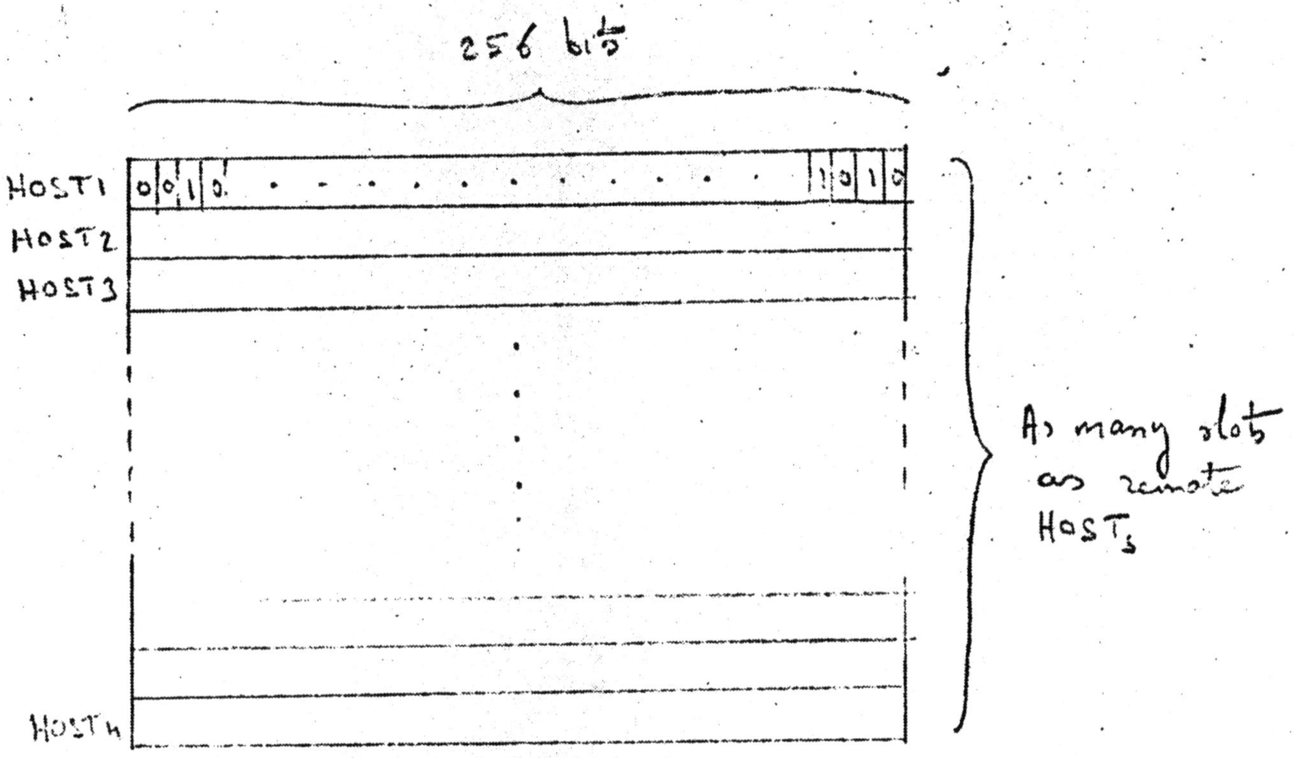

```
          256 bits
       ┌─────────────────────┐
HOST1  │0│0│1│0│. . . . . .│1│0│1│0│  ⎫
HOST2  │                          │   │
HOST3  │                          │   │
       │         ·                │   ⎬ As many slots
       │         ·                │   │   as remote
       │         ·                │   │   HOSTs
       │                          │   │
HOSTn  │                          │   ⎭
       └─────────────────────┘
```

Link-free / HOST

HOST table

Figure 5

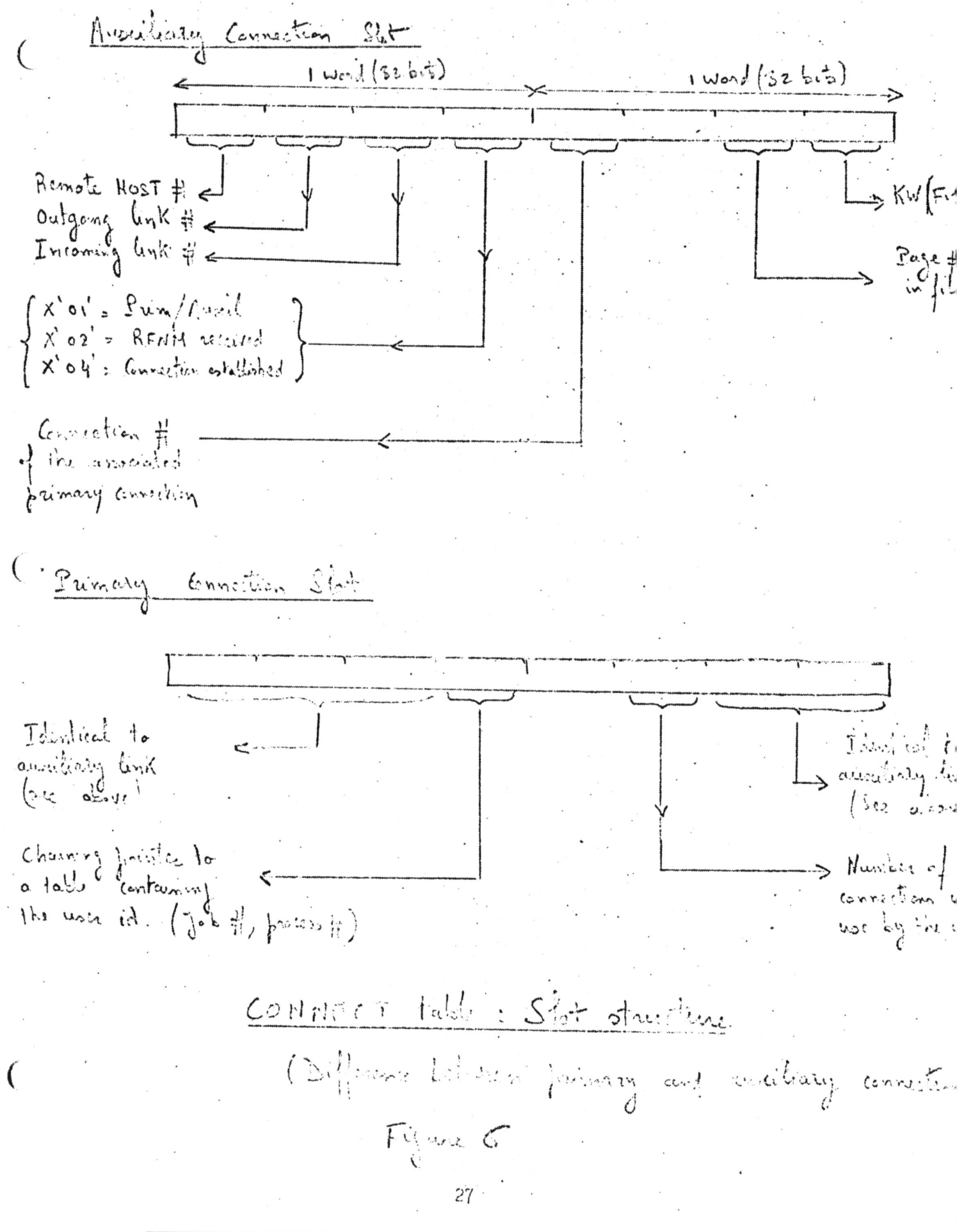

Figure 6

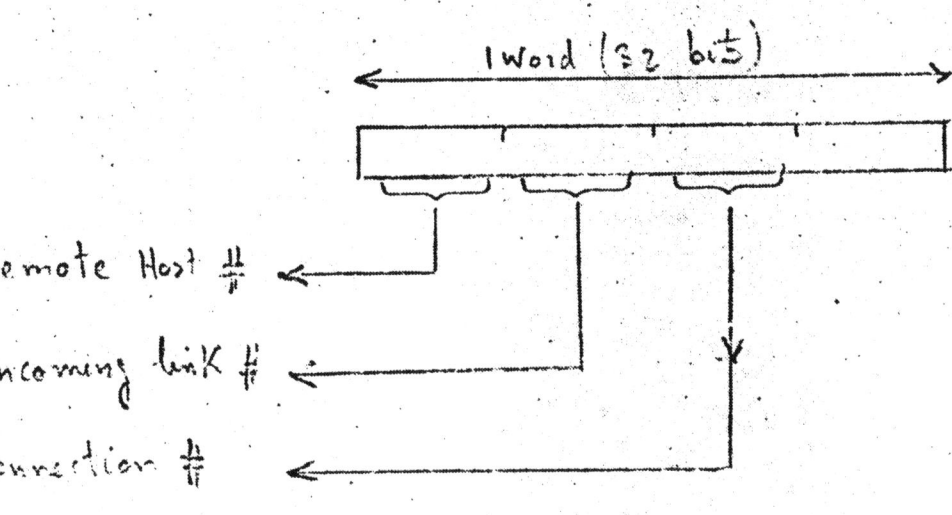

Remark: During a link establishment the outgoing link # is momentarily stored instead of the incoming link #.

INPUT LINK table : Slot structure

Figure 7

It has the following characteristics:

* Location: Disc resident.
* Coupling: Coupled to the Network process virtual space
* Size: As many slots as incoming links, i.e., as connections
* Slot structure: See figure 7. Each slot is 1 word length
* Access: Hashing. The hashed key value is mainly based upon the incoming link # and the remote HOST #.
* Specific feature 1: This table is also used for momentarily memorizing the connection number while establishing the next connection. See 3.4 the way it is handled.
* Specific feature 2: This table is primarily used upon receiving messages. (For each incoming link it contains the corresponding connection #, i.e., indirectly the user identification to which the message should be passed along)

3.3.1.2 Buffer pages

All the pages that are now to be described contain two buffers (input and output). These buffers are used for either passing along or processing messages.

The size of each of these buffers should at least be equal to that of a message, i.e., 8095 bits. We have chosen a buffer size of 253 words (8096 bits) so that both of the buffers are included within one page (512 words). The 6 remaining words of the page are generally used for control.

A typical buffer page structure is identified on figure 8.

(a) <u>I/O communication page</u>

See figure 9.

This I/O communication page is used as an interface between the Handler and the Network program.

In the buffers of this page the messages are assembled (input) or de-assembled (output) word by word by the Handler, e.g., a "ready to go" message, sorted by the Network program in the output buffer, is shipped out word by word by the Handler.

Main characteristics:
* Location: Resident in core: Locked page
* Coupling: Coupled to the Network process virtual space
* Content:
  * Input buffer (253 words) for incoming messages
  * Output buffer (253 words) for outgoing messages
  * Input control zone (6 half words)
  * Output control zone (6 half words)
* Structure: See figure 9.
* Specific feature:
  * The input buffer is filled by the Handler (read from hardware) and emptied by the Network program
  * Vice versa for the output buffer

(b) <u>Connection shared pages</u> (User-Network shared zone)

General features:
* There are as many shared pages as connections.

* These pages shared between the network and the user processes
  constitute a communication zone for (1) passing the messages
  back and forth, and (2) exchanging control information, e.g.,
  a request for establishing new connections.

Main characteristics:

* Location: Disc resident
* Coupling: Coupled to both a user process virtual space and the
  network process virtual space.
* Content: - Input buffer (253 words) for incoming messages
  - Output buffer (253 words) for outgoing messages
  - Input control zone (6 half words)
  - Output control zone (6 half words)
* Structure: See figure 10.
* Specific feature 1: - The input buffer is filled by the Network
  and emptied by the user.
  - Vice versa for the output buffer.
* Specific feature 2: The control zone corresponding to a primary
  connection shared page differs from that
  of an auxiliary connection. This because
  it is via a "primary connection control
  zone" that auxiliary connection establishment requests are transmitted to the Network process.

(c) Working page

General feature:

* This page allows the Network and the Handler programs to work

independently on different messages and so contributes to an overlapping. For instance, when the Handler is busy transmitting a message to the hardware, the Network program can format (leader, marking, etc.) the reset message to be shipped out, so that it can reinitiate the Handler as soon as it is free.

Main characteristics:
* Location: Disc resident
* Coupling: Coupled to the Network process virtual space
* Content: — Input buffer (253 words) for incoming messages
          — Output buffer (253 words) for outgoing messages

Remark:

During reception it may happen that a user program is not ready to accept a new message. In that case, to avoid clogging up the system, the Network stores momentarily the incoming message in one of the buffer of the emergency ring. (If this ring is full a help routine will be invoked.)

During emission all operations are synchronized with the $RFNM_s$, therefore such procedures need not be provided. (The Network program allows a user to re-emit only when having received the RFNM of the previous transmitted message.)

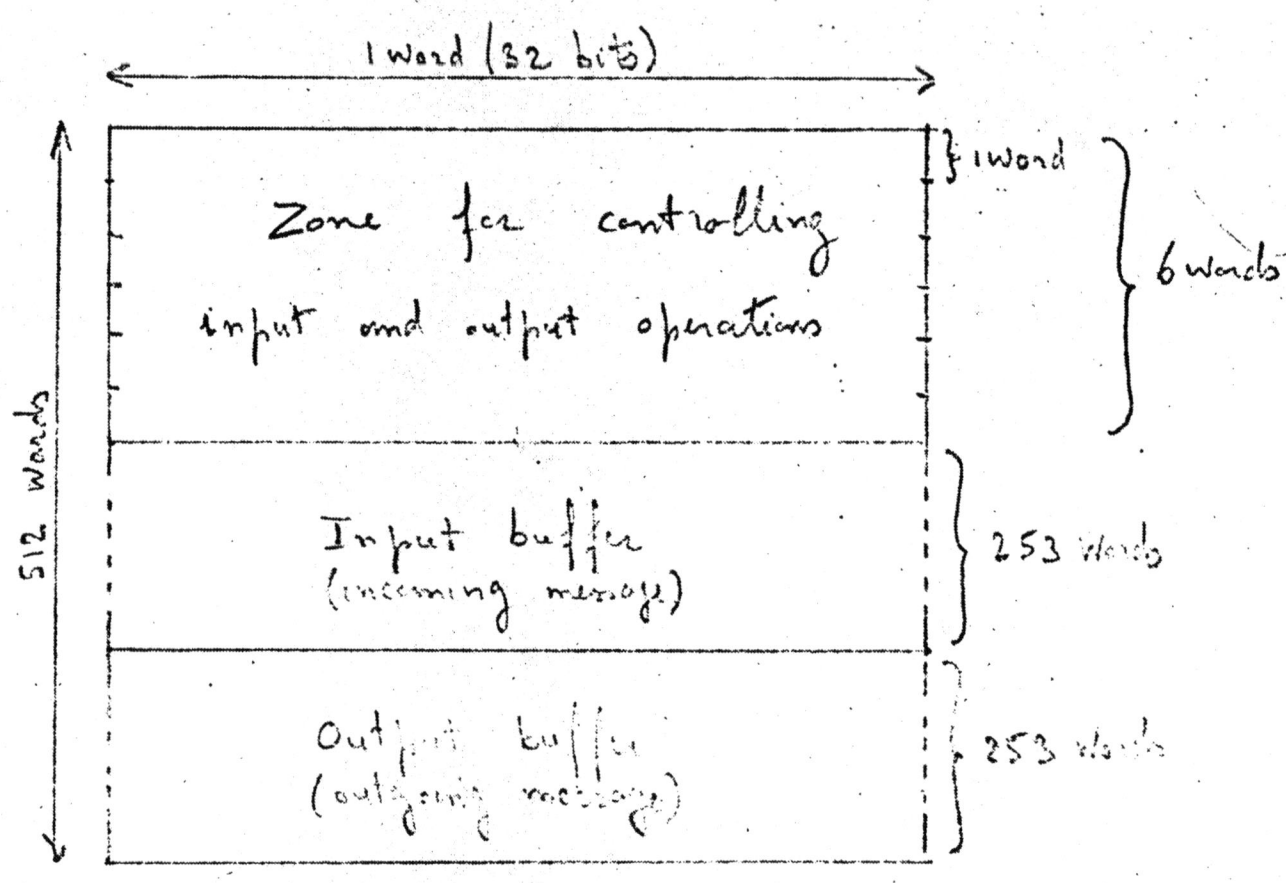

Typical buffer page

Figure 3

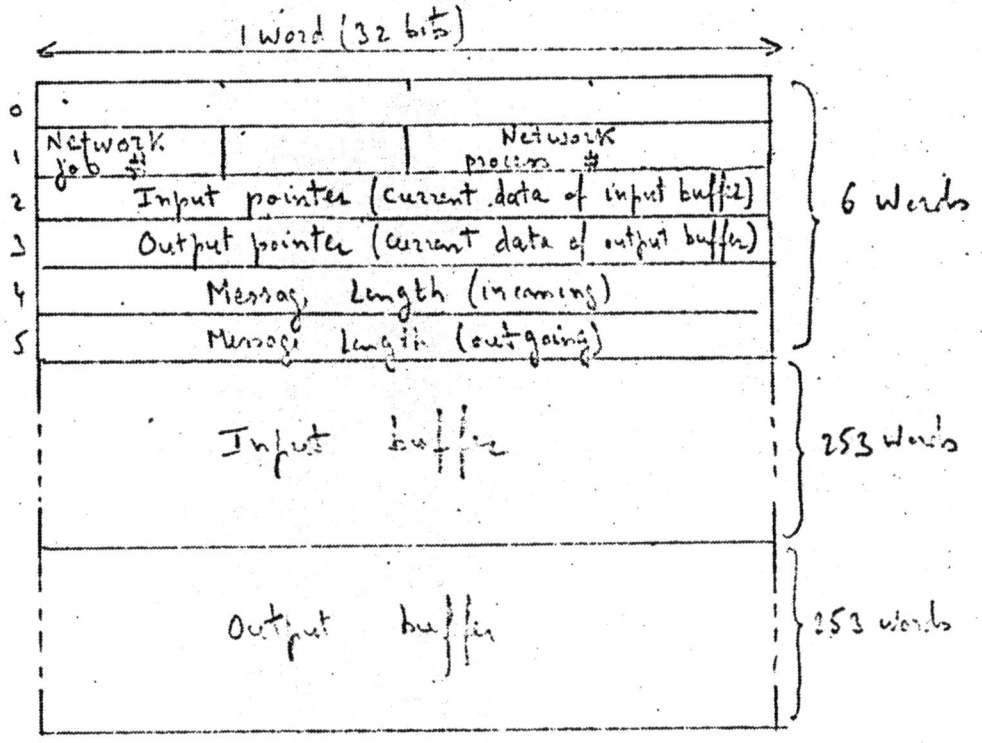

Word 0 structure: X'80000000' = "Thru recv" bit } Dialogue
                    X'00008000' = "Thru send" bit } with Network program
                    X'10000000' = "OK recv" bit   } Dialogue
                    X'00001000' = "OK send" bit   } with HOST-IMP hardware.

I/O communication page structure

(Locked page)

Figure 9

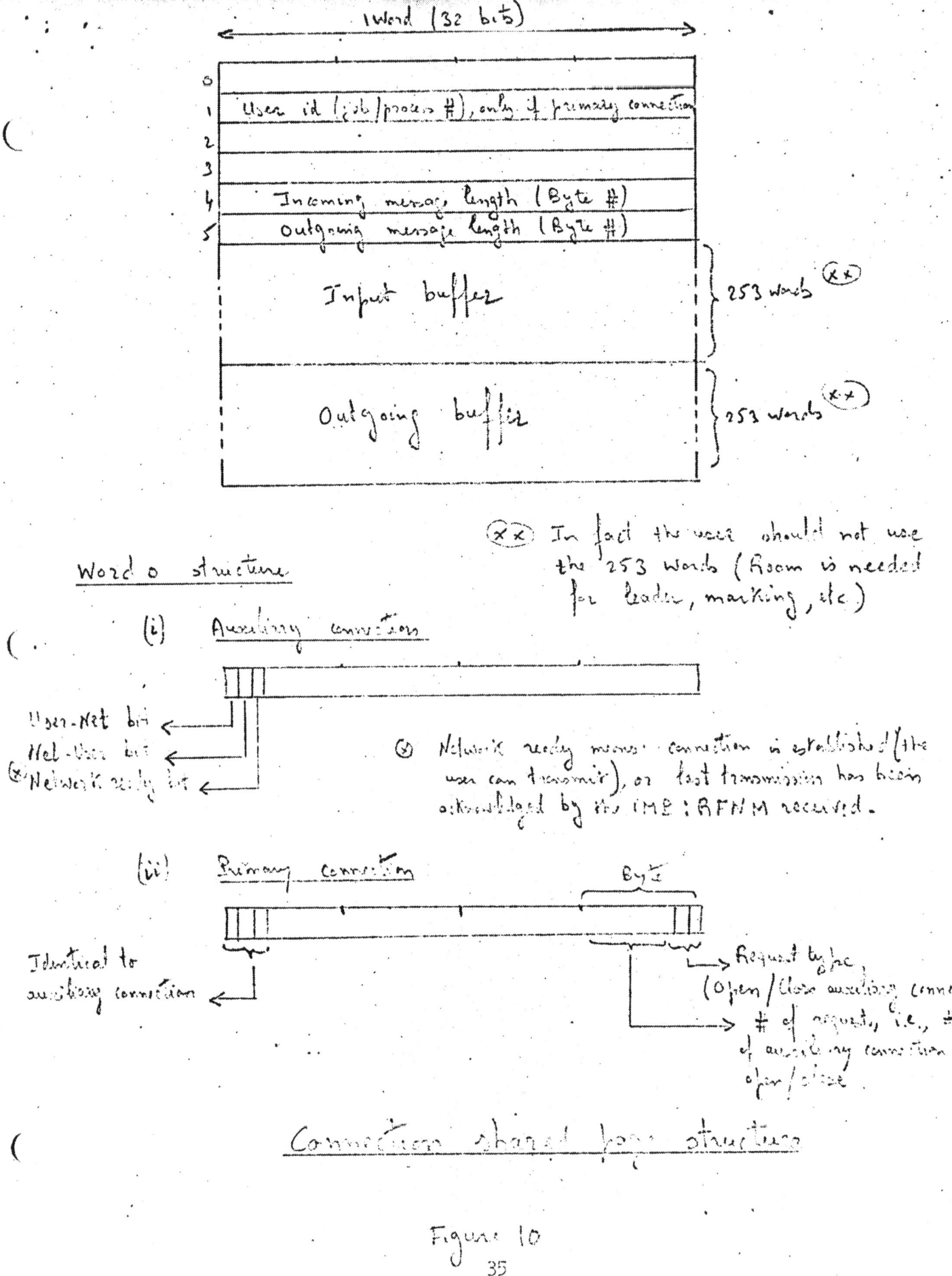

Figure 10

3.3.2 Programs

3.3.2.1 Handler program

General features:

It is an I/O interrupt routine which drives the IMP/HOST hardware interface in order to transmit or receive messages. Transmission and reception are carried out in a full duplex mode.

Main characteristics:

* Location: Core resident. The Handler is in the same memory zone as the operating system and can be considered as part of it.

* Initiation: By the IMP-HOST hardware interrupt. This interrupt is triggered either:

    * during transmission when a message word is completely sent to the IMP

    * during reception when a message word has been completely received from the IMP

    * during idle time when the hardware received either a 'start input' or 'start output' order from the Sigma 7 CPU. Those orders are issued by the Network program for provoking interrupts back (consequently for indirectly initiating the Handler).

* Main functions: * Empties the output buffer upon transmitting its content (outgoing message to the IMP. This operation is carried out word by word (32 bits) and makes use of "Write" orders for

driving the HOST-IMP hardware.

* <u>Fills the input buffer</u> with data received from HOST-IMP hardware (incoming message). This operation is also carried out word by word and makes use of "Read" orders for driving the HOST-IMP hardware.

* Wakes up the Network program when any of the previous operations is complete.

3.3.2.2 Network program

General features:

This program serves the user for opening/closing connections and transmitting/receiving messages. It uses the Handler as an aid for interfacing with the hardware.

For the GORDO point of view it is a regular process and treated as such.

Main characteristics:

* Location: Disc resident. More precisely it is on disc when asleep and called in core when awakened by a program.
* Initiation: It is initiated through 'WAKE' service calls issued either by a user process or by the Handler.
* Main functions:
  * <u>Establishes/deletes outgoing connections</u> upon users' requests. For so doing it sends control messages (see 2.4.2) to remote $HOST_s$ in order to get links established/released; it then notifies back the users.
  * <u>Insures the processing of incoming control messages</u> (transmitted over control links), e.g.,

for contributing to establishments/deletions of connections (those requested by remote HOSTS).

* <u>Prepares transmission of outgoing messages.</u> It picks up text messages from shared pages (the messages are stored there by users), formats them (adds leader, marking, checksum..), and passes them along to the Handler for transmission.

* <u>Insures delivery of incoming messages.</u> It is the opposite of the above operation. The users to which the messages should be delivered are identified through the leaders.

* Virtual space configuration: See figure 11.
* Specific feature: It is integrated as an I/O process, so that it can access privileged instruction (RD/WD for indirectly initiating the Handler).

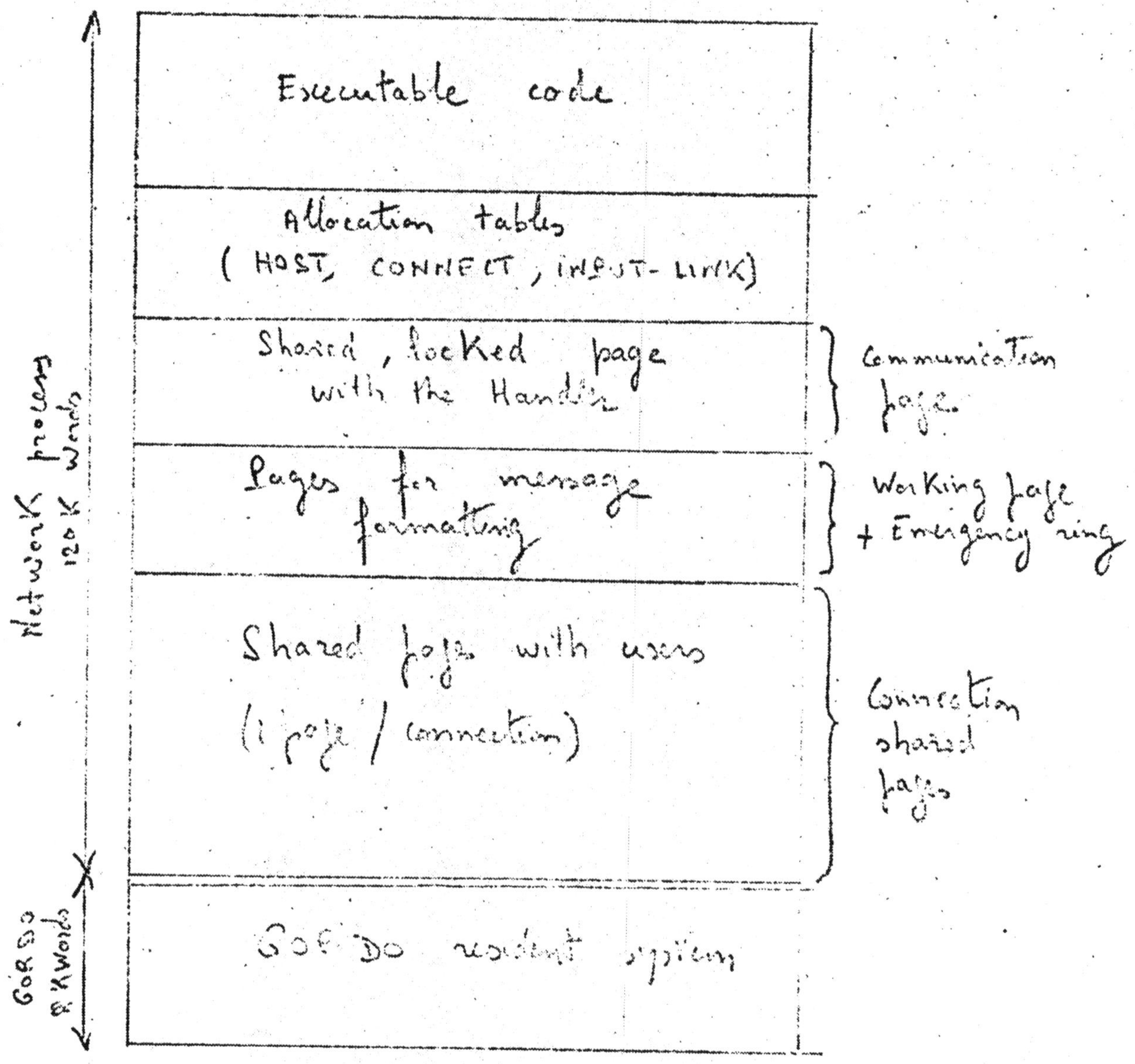

```
                ┌─────────────────────────────────┐
             ↑  │                                 │
             │  │      Executable code            │
             │  │                                 │
             │  ├─────────────────────────────────┤
             │  │   Allocation tables             │
             │  │  (HOST, CONNECT, INPUT-LINK)    │
             │  ├─────────────────────────────────┤
    Network  │  │  Shared, locked page       ⎫ Communication
    process  │  │   with the Handler         ⎭    page
    120 K    │  ├─────────────────────────────────┤
    words    │  │  Pages for message         ⎫ Working page
             │  │    formatting              ⎭ + Emergency ring
             │  ├─────────────────────────────────┤
             │  │                            ⎫
             │  │  Shared pages with users   ⎬ Connection
             │  │  (1 page / connection)     ⎪  shared
             │  │                            ⎭   pages
             ↓  ├─────────────────────────────────┤
    GORDO    ↑  │                                 │
    8 K      │  │    GORDO resident system        │
    words    ↓  │                                 │
                └─────────────────────────────────┘
```

Network process virtual space

Figure 11

3.4   Software Procedures

The detailed software procedures are given on the flowcharts attached with Appendix A.

However, to get a quick understanding of the implementation we list below some typical software procedures.

3.4.1   Description of some typical sequences

Consider some of the transactions at user's disposal (See 2.4) and point out the basic software procedures they imply. For each case we will delineate (i) what the user program does and (ii) what the Network program does.

(a)   Open a primary link   (See also 2.4.2)

  (i)   What the user program does[1]:

   * it stores in the Network mail box directory the name of a file, e.g., DATA;
   * it couples the first page of this file to its virtual space;
   * it stores information in this page (its job/process #, the remote HOST #, e.g., (i));
   * it wakes up the Network process;
   * it goes to sleep.

  (ii) What the Network program does:

   * it explores the Network mail box directory and accesses the file DATA;

* it couples the first page of this file to its virtual space (Shared Zone, see 3.3.1.2). Suppose this paget be the kth in the shared zone; k is the internal connection #;
* it explores the ith slot of thw HOST table (See 3.3.1.1 (a)) and selects the first bit = 0, e.g., the αth bit; α corresponds to the outgoing link #;
* it stores information (job/process #, remote HOST # (i), outgoing link # (α)) in the kth slot of the CONNECT table (See 3.3.1.2).
* it momentarily stores the connection # (k) in the INPUT LINK table. This is carried out upon creating an entry in this table (Hashing the key value: "outgoing link # (α) + remote HOST # (i) + outgoing flag".);
* it prepares the message text ENQ PRIM 0 0 α and formats a complete message in adding leader, marking, checksum, etc.;
* it checks the Handler state (bit in I/O locked page). <u>If</u> the Handler is free, it stores the 'ready to go' control message in the output buffer of the I/O locked page, initiates the Handler, and goes to sleep. <u>Else</u> it goes to sleep.

After a while the Handler wakes up the Network process because it has received a complete message. We suppose this message be the control message sent by the remote HOST for acknowledging the establishment of the connection. The message text should be:

ACK ENQ PRIM 0 0 α 0 0 β

where β is the incoming link #. (See 2.4.2)

Let's see now what <u>the Network program does when receiving the above control message</u>:

* it retrieves the connection # previously stored in the INPUT LINK table upon re-hashing the same key value (See above). Also it deletes this entry;
* it creates an entry in the INPUT LINK table for the incoming link. For so doing it hashes the key value: "incoming link # (β) + remote HOST # (i) + incoming flag". In this entry it stores the HOST # (i), the incoming link # (β), and connection # (k);
* it updates the kth slot of the CONNECT table in storing the incoming link # (β);
* it turns on the 'net-user' bit in k^{th} shared page (page corresponding to the primary connection that has just been opened) and wakes up the user process;
* it goes to sleep.

(b) <u>Transmit a message over primary link</u>

    (i) <u>What the user program does</u> [1].

* it stores the message text in the output buffer of the primary connection shared page (See 3.3.1.2);
* it turns on the 'user-net' bit of this page and wakes up the Network process;
* it goes to sleep.

42

(ii) <u>What the Network program does:</u>

* it looks for user request, i.e., it explores in sequence the connection shared pages and selects the one that has its 'user-net' bit turned on. Suppose k be the selected page # on the shared list, K is the connection #;

* it determines the request type in testing the "request bits' of the shared page k. It finds out that it is a request for transmitting a message.

* it takes the message text from the output buffer of the shared page k, formats it into a complete message and transmits to the Handler in a very similar way as above (See Open a primary link).

* it goes to sleep.

[1] Remark: In a first phase the user will directly write the network functions in his program. Later on subroutines will be put at user's disposal. These subroutines will be very close to those described in 2.4.

APPENDIX A

Flowcharts

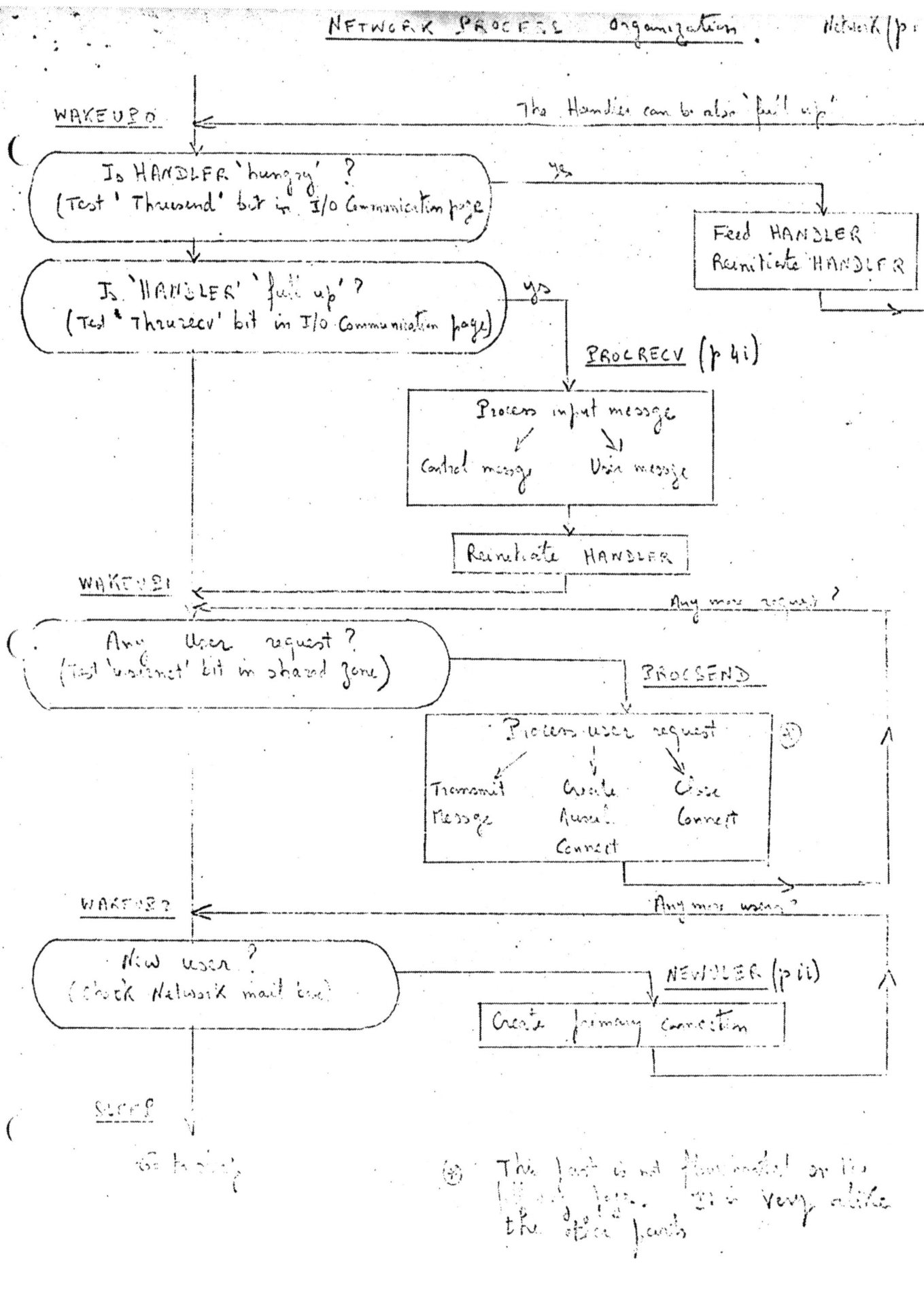

Network (p ii)

NEWUSER

Couple a new shared page
- Take the first page (will be 'primary' shared page) of the file referred to in the Network mail box & couple it to the Network virtual space (Shared list).
- Assume (α) be { the page # index } on the shared page list connection #

↓

Get information stored in this page by the user
- Remote HOST # (ℓ)
- Job/User #

↓

Select an outgoing link #
- Explore 1st entry of HOST table & select the first (α) bit = 0; outgoing link # = (α)

↓

Update CONNECT table
- Access αth entry & store:
  - Remote HOST #
  - Job/User #
  - xW (File id), Page # in f.b. (=1)
  - Outgoing link # (α)

↓

Protect CONNECT #
- Store momentarily the connection # (k) in the HOST LINK table — to bring in an entry in ordered upon having the key value "outgoing link # (α) + remote HOST # (ℓ) + outgoing (lk)"

↓

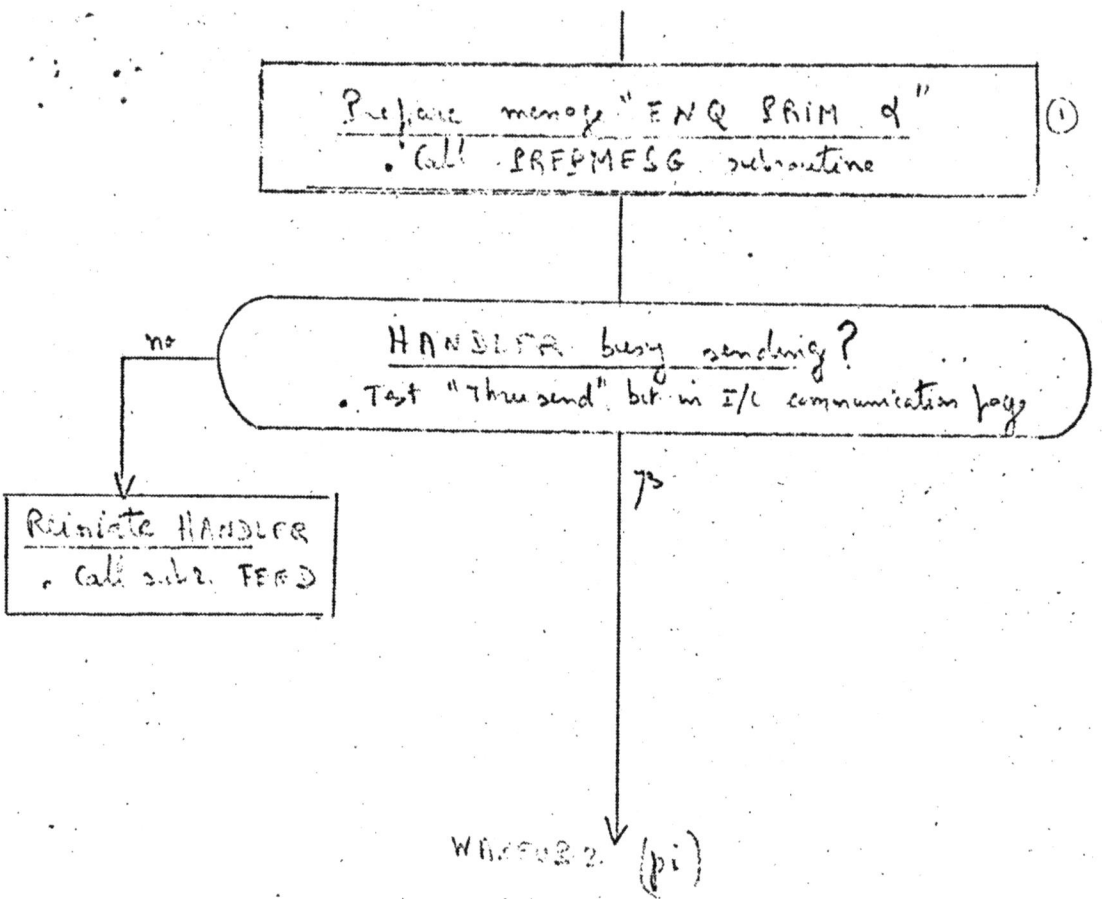

(1) PREPMESG subroutine formats the message to be shipped out (border marking, checksum, etc)

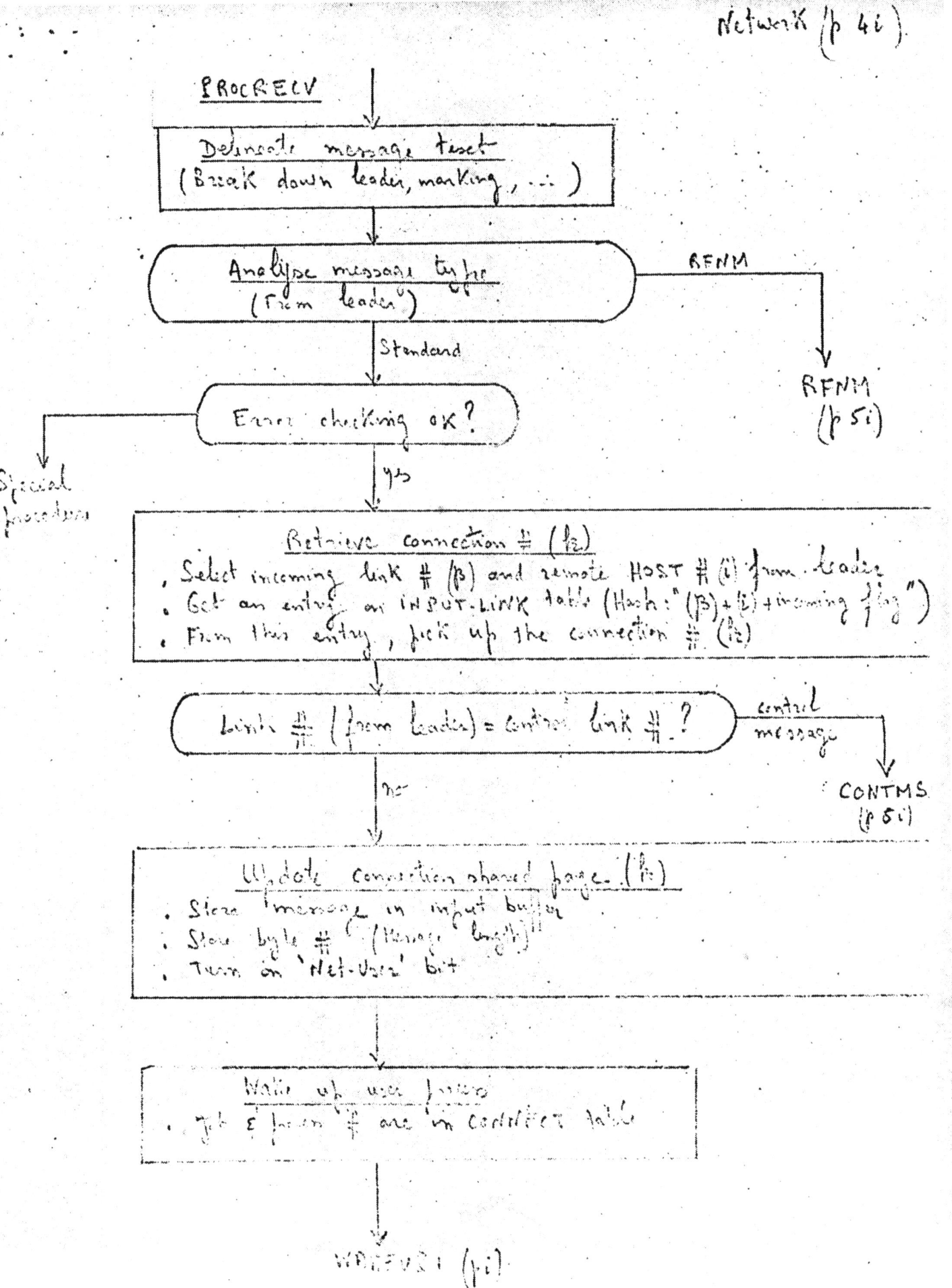

Network (p 5i)

```
              RFNM
                │
                ▼
┌──────────────────────────────────────┐
│ Update CONNECT table (entry k)       │
│ • Turn on RFNM bit                   │
└──────────────────────────────────────┘
                │
                ▼
   ╭──────────────────────────────────────────╮         We are waiting
   │ Is it a RFNM corresponding to a user     │ ──────▶ for a control
   │ message?                                 │         message (AC ?)
   │ • Test "connection established" bit in   │
   │   CONNECT (k)                            │              │
   ╰──────────────────────────────────────────╯              ▼
                │ yes                                      WAKEUE
                ▼                                           (pi)
┌──────────────────────────────────────┐
│ Update connection shared page (k)    │
│ • Turn on "Net-User" & "Network      │
│   ready" bit                         │
└──────────────────────────────────────┘
                │
                ▼
┌──────────────────────────────────────┐
│ Wake up user process                 │
│(1)• Job & process # are in CONNECT   │
│   table                              │
└──────────────────────────────────────┘
                │
                ▼
            WAKEUP (pi)
```

(1) The user can start a new transmission

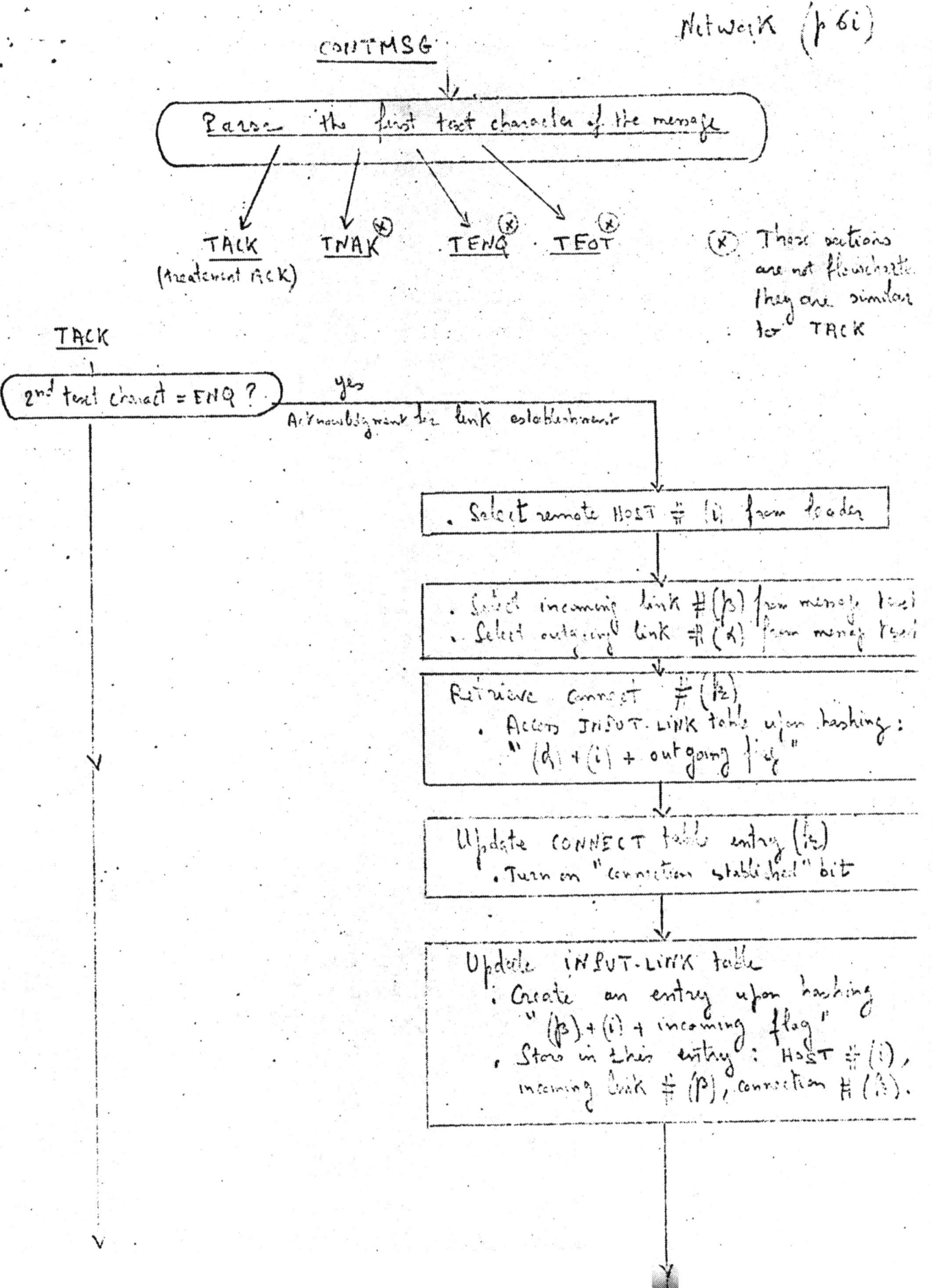

RFC 11 / Implementation of the HOST-HOST Software Procedures in GORDO

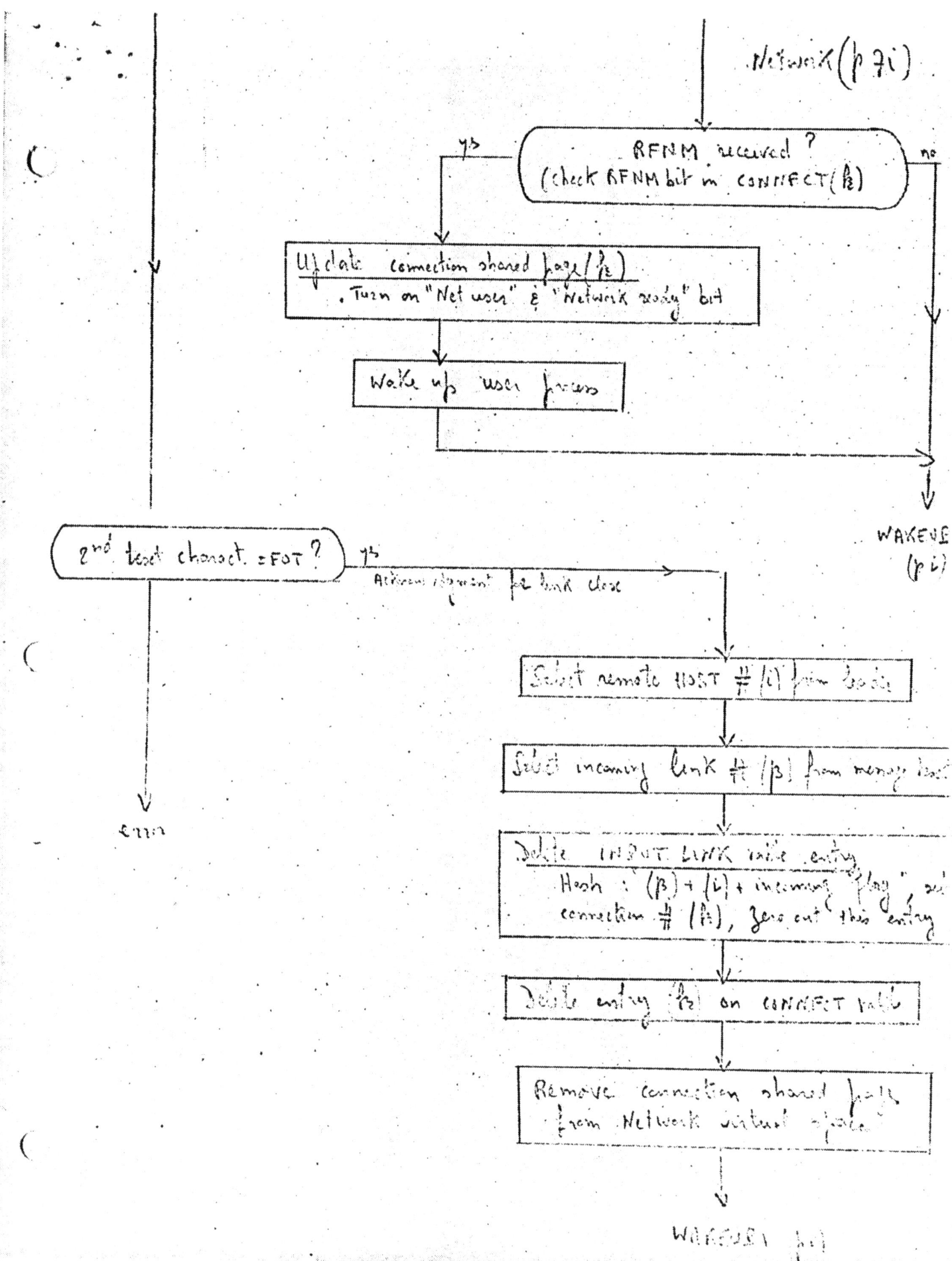

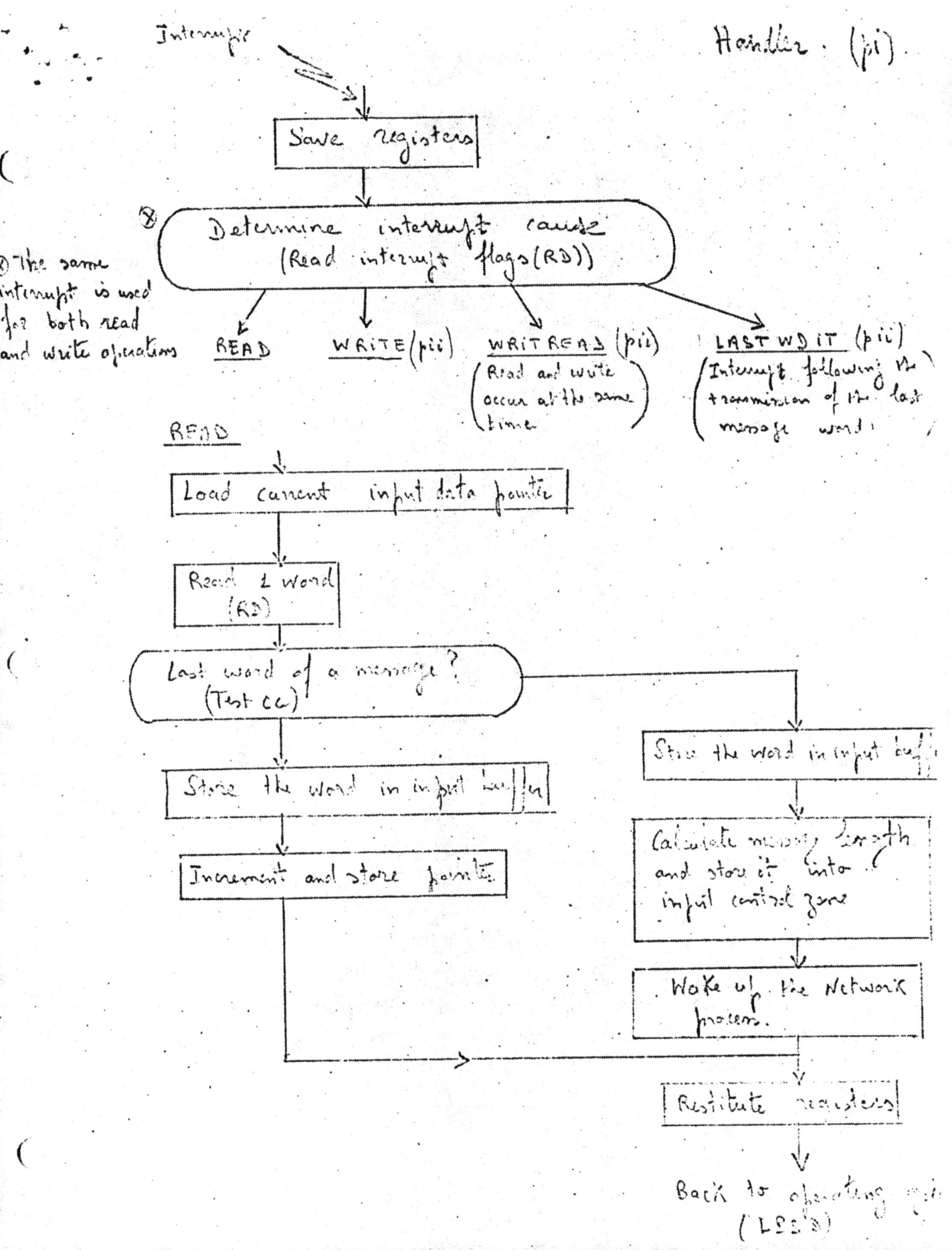

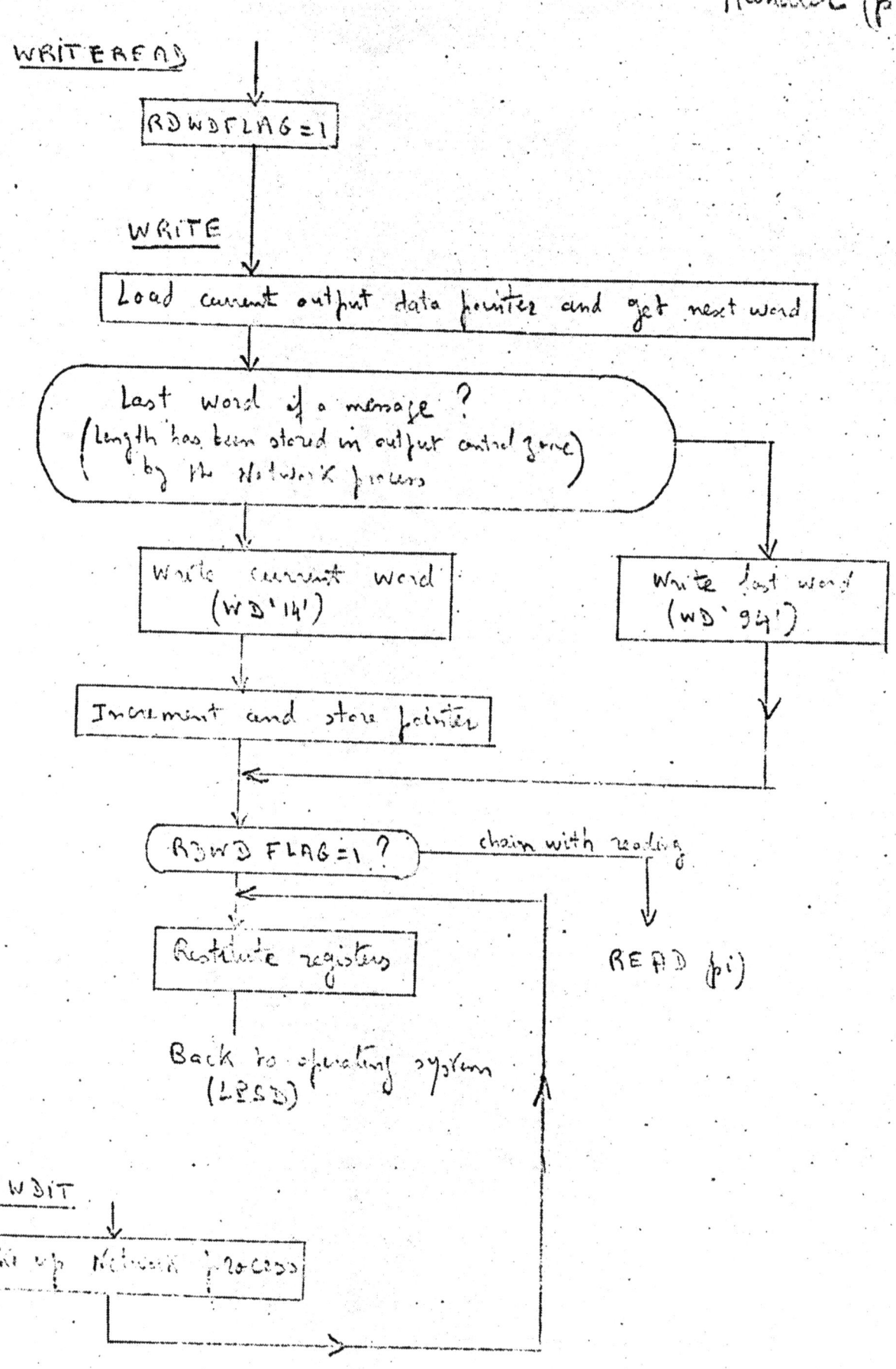

Network Working Group M. Wingfield
Request for Comments: 12 26 August 1969

IMP-HOST INTERFACE FLOW DIAGRAMS

The following flow diagrams were extracted from the logic diagrams provided in Appendix B of BBN Report No. 1822. These diagrams indicate the logical sequence of hardware operations which occur within the IMP-HOST interface. The logic names appearing in the blocks correspond to the logic elements found in Appendix B.

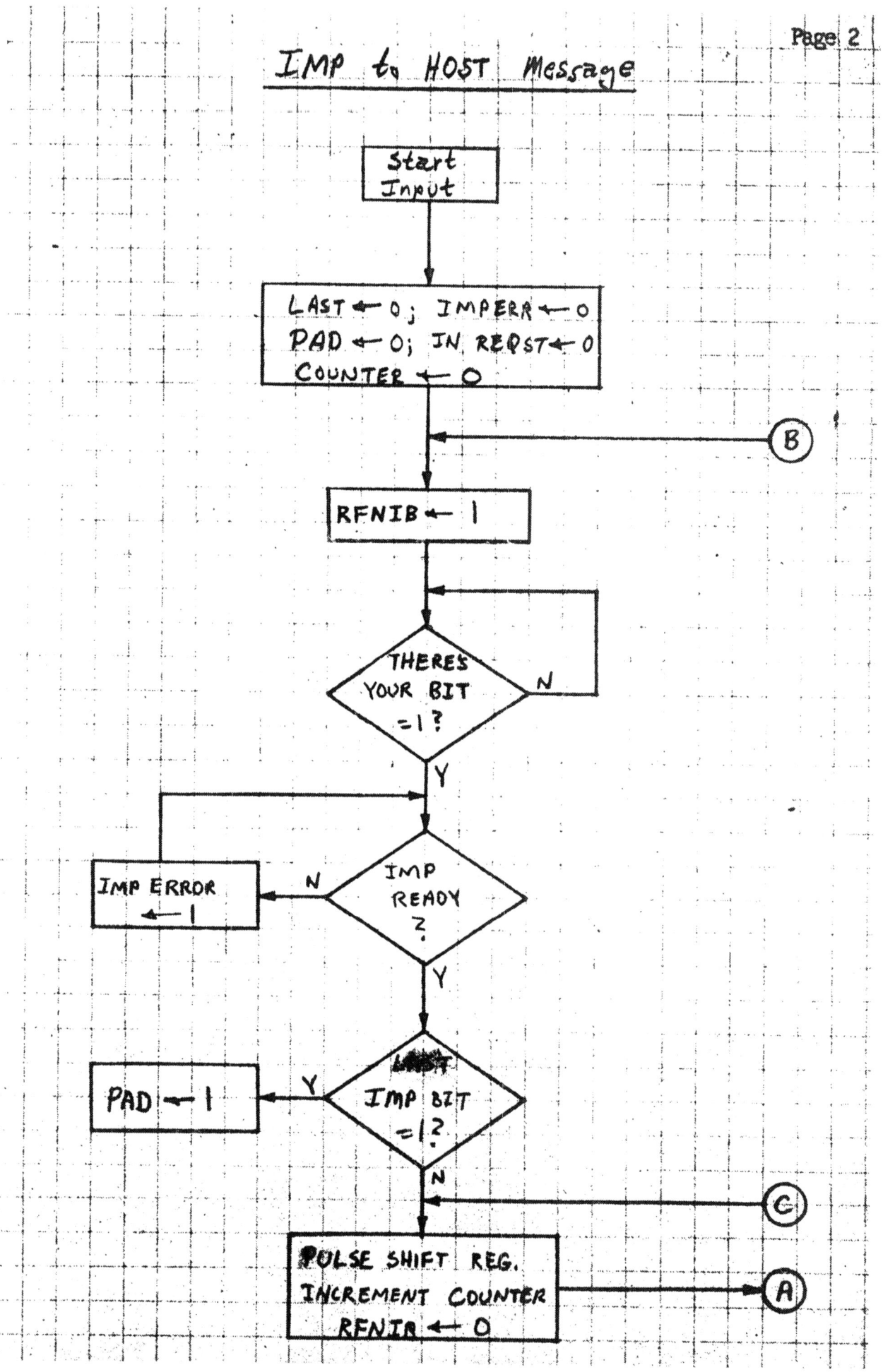

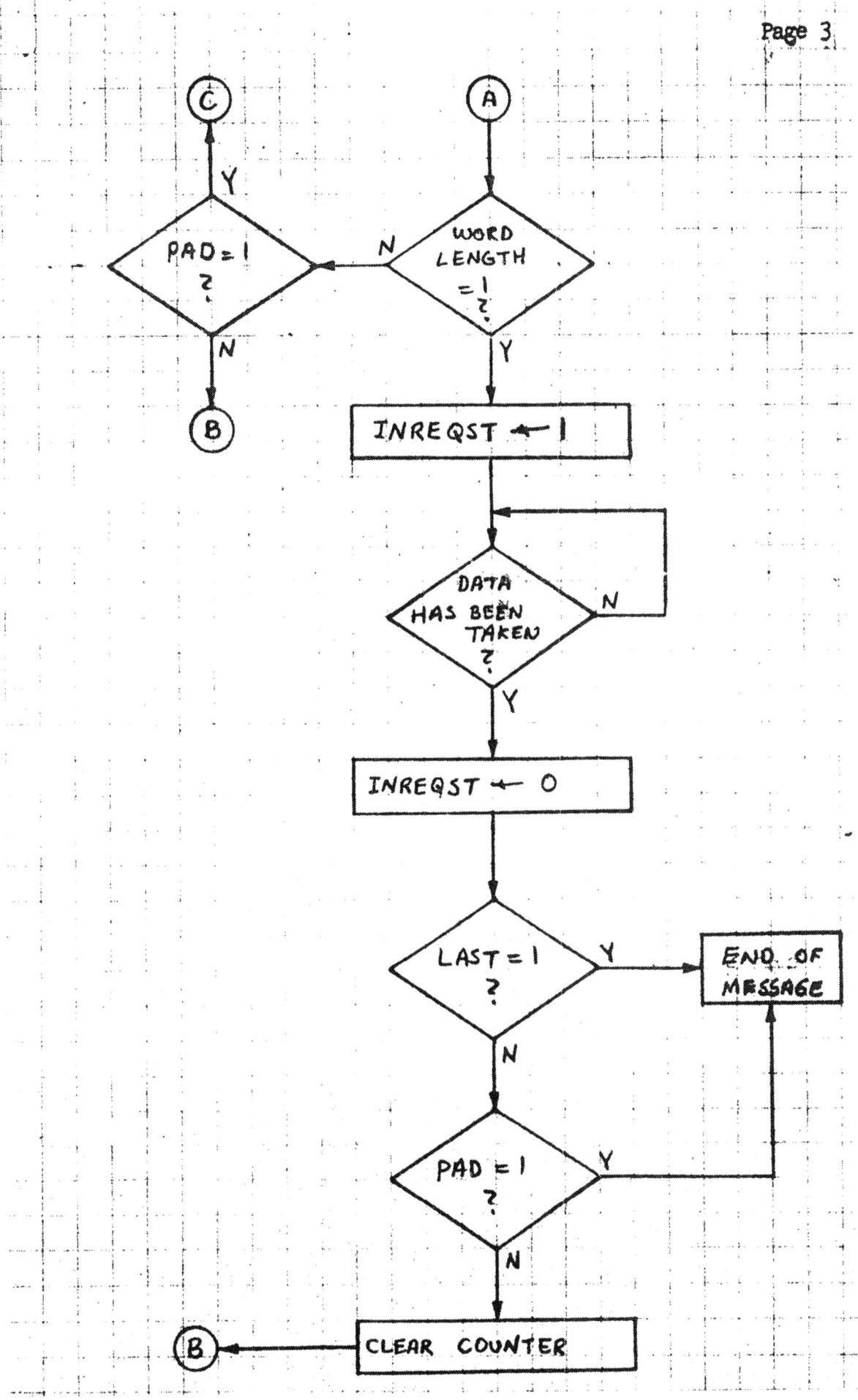

HOST TO IMP MESSAGE

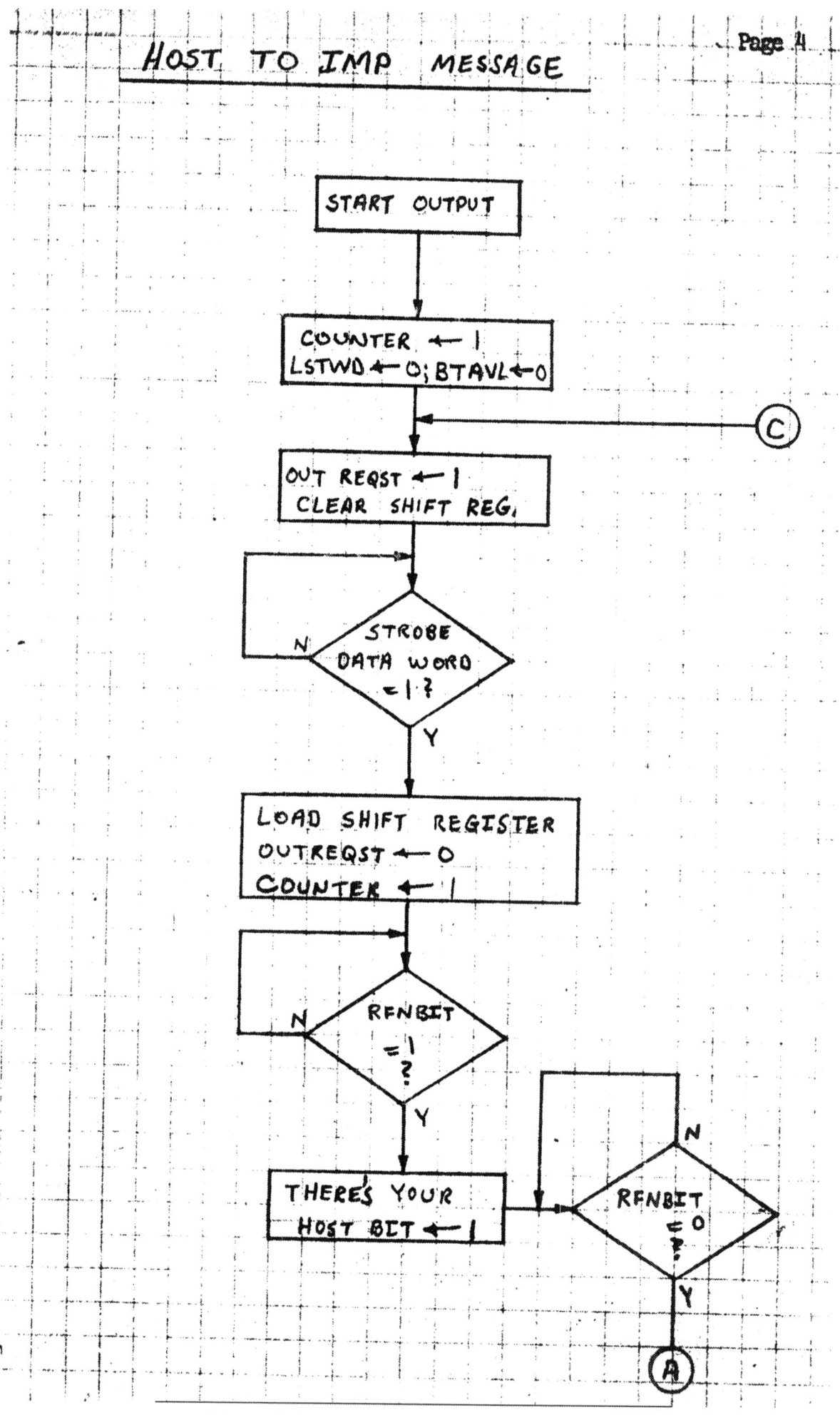

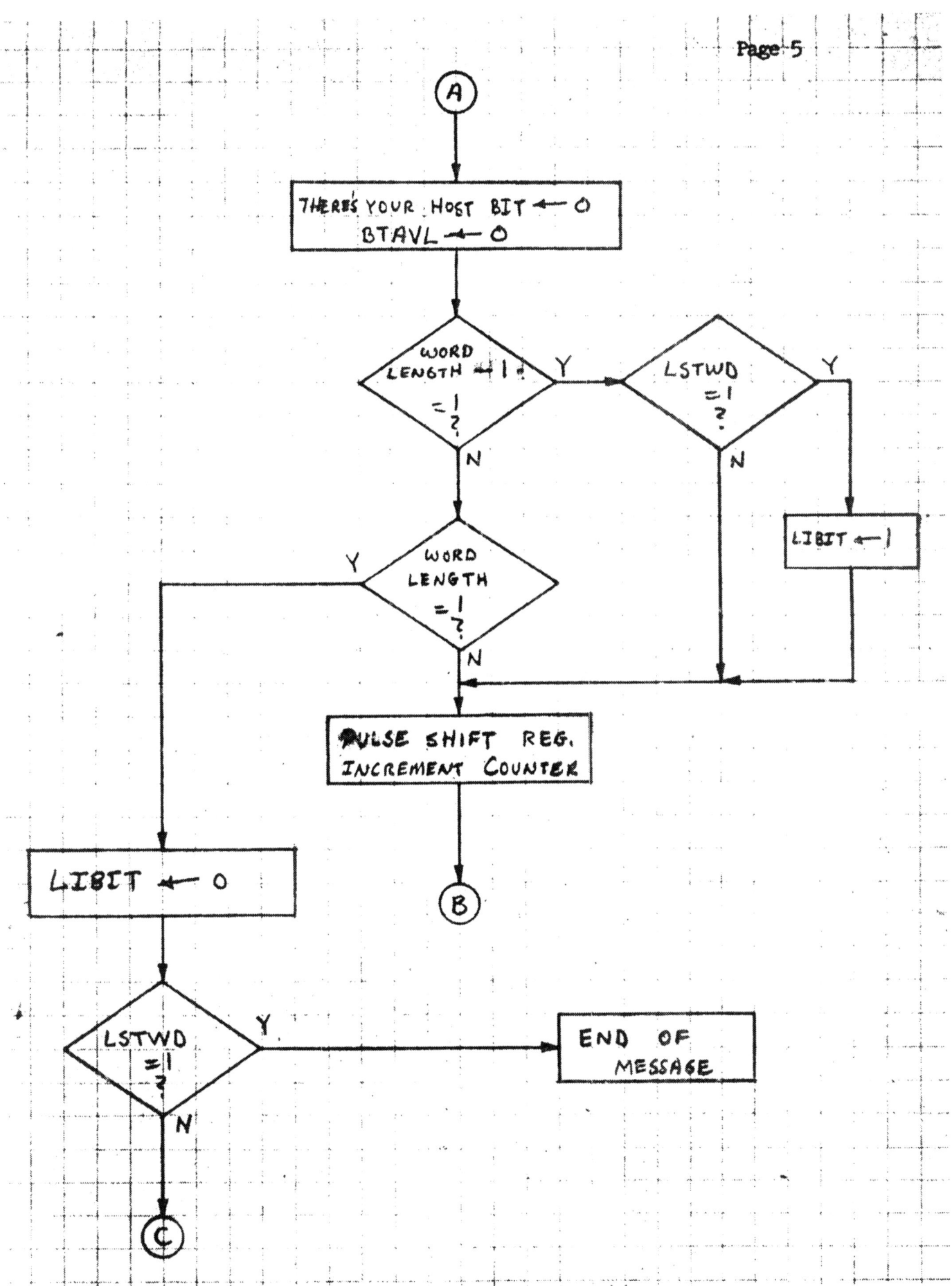

Network Working Group
Request for Comments: 13

Vint Cerf
UCLA
20 August 1969

Referring to NWG/RFC: 11, it appears that file transmissions over auxiliary connections will require some mechanism to specify "END-OF-FILE." It is proposed that a length 0 (zero) message be used for this purpose. Figure 1 shows the format:

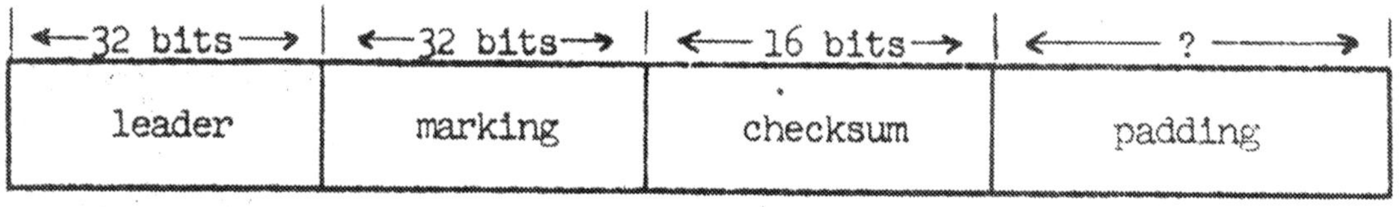

←32 bits→	←32 bits→	←16 bits→	← ? →
leader	marking	checksum	padding

Figure 1

Zero Text Length EOF Message

Network Working Group
Request for Comments: 15

Network Subsystem
for Time Sharing Hosts

C. Stephen Carr
UTAH
25 September 1969

Introduction

A set of network primitives has been defined (Network Working Group Note 11) for inclusion in the monitor systems of the respective HOSTS. These primitives are at the level of system calls: SPOP's or BRS's on the 940; UUO's on the PDP-10. Presumably these UUO's are accessible to all user programs when executing for users whose status bits allow network access.

In addition to user program access, a convenient means for direct network access from the terminal is desirable. A sub-system called "Telnet" is proposed which is a shell program around the network system primitives, allowing a teletype or similar terminal at a remote host to function as a teletype at the serving host.

System Primitives

G. Deloche of U.C.L.A. has documented a proposed set of basic network primitives for inclusion in the operating systems of the respective HOSTs (NWG Note: 11). The primitives are:

Open primary connection

Open auxiliary connection

Transmit over connection

Close connection.

The details and terminology are defined by Deloche and others in previous memos. The primitives are system calls, available to programmers, and are most likely a part of the resident monitor, rather than the swappable executive.

Basic Terminal Access

In addition to user programming access, it is desirable to have a subsystem program at each HOST which makes the network immediately accessible from the teletype without special programming. Subsystems are commonly used system components such as text editors, compilers and interpreters. The first network-related subsystem should allow users at HOST A to connect to HOST B and appear as a regular terminal user to HOST B. It is expected that more sophisticated subsystems will be developed in time, but this basic one will render the early net immediately useful.

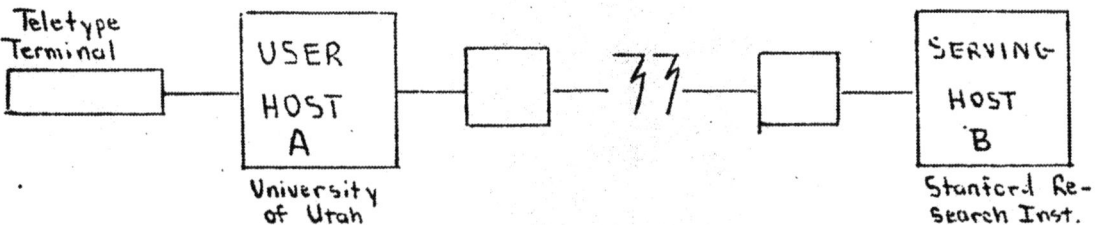

Figure 1: User accesses distant serving HOST via shunt subsystem in his own Host computer.

-3-

Simple Dialogue -- PDP-10 to 940

A user at Utah is sitting at a teletype dialed into the University's dual PDP-10's. He wishes to operate the CAL sub-system on the 940 at SRI in Menlo Park, California.

.LOGIN↓

PDP-10 login

.R TELNET↓

The PDP-10 run command is issued to call and start the TELNET sub-system.

*ESCAPE CHARACTER IS #↓

The user indicates an escape character which TELNET will watch for in subsequent input from the user.

*CONNECT TO SRI↓

The TELNET subsystem will make the appropriate system call (UUO) to establish a primary connection. The connection will be established, provided:

	1. SRI is willing to accept another foreign user;
	2. The UTAH user is cleared for network access at Utah. This is determined by a status word kept in the PDP-10 monitor for each user.
@<u>LOGIN CARR</u>.	The user logs in SRI.

Characters typed on the user's teletype are transmitted unaltered through the PDP-10 (user Host) and on to the 940 (serving HOST.) (The exception to this is a possible one-for-one code conversion required between the UCLA Sigma 7 and the PDP-10, for example).

@<u>CAL</u>.	The PDP-10 TELNET subsystem switches to full duplex, character-by-character transmission, since this is required by 940's. Characters typed by the user are underlined. Full duplex operation is allowed for by the PDP-10,

though not used by most DEC subsystems.

The user wishes to load a CAL file into 940 CAL from the file system on his local PDP-10.

CAL AT YOUR SERVICE

>READ FILE FROM NETWRK.

'NETWRK' is a predefined 940 name similar to PAPER TAPE OR TELETYPE. The 940 file opening BRS is set to expect an auxiliary connection and the file from UTAH.

#NETWRK: ← DSK:MYFILE.CAL⟩

The user types the prescribed escape character, followed by the TELNET command, to send the desired file to SRI on an auxiliary connection. The user's next statement is in CAL again.

The Telnet Subsystem

The Telnet subsystem coding should fit easily into one core page, for it does very little. It effectively establishes a shunt in the user HOST between the remote user and the serving HOST. Telnet commands are:

ESCAPE CHAR IS _____↲   Declares a character which Telnet will watch for. Subsequent strings typed between this character and a carriage return are not shunted through to the serving host, but sent instead to the Telnet program in the user's local HOST.

This escape character is not the same as the user's host rubout character.

CONNECT TO _____↲   The official site name of the desired serving HOST is typed (i.e.: SRI, UTAH, UCLA, UCSB). Telnet attempts to establish a connection. If the attempt is successful, the following characters are shunted through the user's local machine. The connection places the

LOGOUT↓   user in the pre-logged in state at the serving HOST. Telnet issues the logout command sequence to the serving HOST. If the user simply rubs out and kills his PDP-10 job, the PDP-10 will indicate to the 940 that the connection is closed. The 940 system primitives do whatever they do when a normal dataphone connection is suddenly broken.

COPY FILE   A file copying command is available in TELNET to move data along on auxiliary connections from the user's HOST file system to the serving HOST.

On the 940 this is:
<u>C</u>OPY <file name> TO <u>N</u>ETWRK.

On the PDP-10:

NETWRK ← DSK: <file name>
―――――――――――――――――――

These TELNET commands are accepted when the TELNET subsystem is first entered or following the declared escape character.

CONCLUSION

Given the basic system primitives, the TELNET subsystem at the user host and a manual for the serving host, the network can be profitably employed by a remote user. TELNET subsystem constitutes a "level 0" network program which will quickly be surpassed. It is, however, simple enough to be working fairly soon.

Network Working Group   Steve Crocker
Request for Comments: 16   27 August 1969

                              M. I. T.

M.I.T. is now to receive all Network Working Group memos. Memos should
be addressed to:

                    Abhai Bhushan
                    Room 807 - Project MAC
                    545 Technology Square
                    Cambridge, Mass. 02139

Abhai's phone is (617) 864-6900, X 5857.

Network Working Group
Request for Comments: 17

John E. Kreznar
SDC
27 August 1969

Some Questions Re: HOST-IMP Protocol

1. Automatic deletion of links, as indicated in BBN 1822, page 11, seems bad:

   a) Link use may be dependent upon human use of a time share terminal — indefinite time between messages.

   b) Program using link may be slow due to:

      i) Busy HOST (many jobs)

      ii) Much local I/O and/or CPU time between messages — is it that, if a HOST's user fails to use a link for 15 seconds, the HOST network program must generate a dummy message merely to keep the link open?

2. Steve Crocker, HOST Software, 1969 Apr 7, asks on page 2: "Can a HOST, as opposed to its IMP, control RFNM's?" BBN, Report No. 1837, 1969 Jul, says on page 2: "The principal function of the (IMP) program...includes ...generating of RFNM's..." What if an IMP generates an RFNM and then discovers it cannot, for some reason, complete timely delivery of the last received message to its HOST? This seems especially pressing since I don't recall seeing anywhere an IMP constraint upon HOSTs that they must accept incoming messages within some specified maximum time.

3. A HOST has to be prepared to repeat transmissions of a message into network (see, e.g., Page 17, BBN 1822) therefore why the special discardable NOP message (Page 12, BBN 1822).

4. "Arbitrary delays," middle paragraph, page 23, BBN 1822, seems inconsistent with automatic link deletion questioned in 1 above. Normally the times involved differ by many orders of magnitude but a high priority non-network HOST responsibility could delay next bit for a long time.

1. Abhi Bhushan, Proj. MAC
2. Steve Crocker, UCLA
3. Ron Stoughton, UCSB
4. Elmer Shapiro, SRI
5. Steve Carr, Utah
6. John Haefner, RAND
7. Paul Rovner, LL
8. Bob Kahn, BB & N
9. Larry Roberts, ARPA
10. Sal Aranda, SDC
11. Jerry Cole, "
12. John Kreznar, "
13. Dick Linde, "
14. Bob Long, "
15. Reg Martin, "
16. Hal Sackman, "
17. C. Weissman, "

Network Working Group
Request for Comments: 17a

THE FOLLOWING COMMENTS ARE IN RESPONSE TO JOHN KREZNAR'S QUESTIONS
WHICH WERE RAISED IN NWG:- 17

The deletion of a link entry from an IMP's link table will, in
general, have no effect upon a Host transmission (or reception)
at that IMP's site. Let us distinguish between non-use of a link
in-between messages and non-use of a link due to Host program delays
in the middle of transmitting or receiving a message. When the
Host transmits a message on a link for which an entry is not in the
link table, one will simply be inserted there. There is no need
for "dummy" Host messages to keep a link "open" since a link is
effectively always open. Only if the link table becomes full
immediately after an entry is deleted (a situation we do not expect
to occur) is there a possibility of resulting delay.

Arbitrary delays introduced by Host programs are also not inconsistent
with the link entry deletion procedure. A link is blocked when the
first access of the link table is made during transmission from
the source IMP and is unblocked when the RFNM returns. Only non-
blocked transmit link entries are deleted after 30 seconds of disuse.
The statement on page 23 referencing *arbitrary* delays was only
intended to have hardware implications insofar as the Host/IMP
interface is designed to transfer bits asynchronously between the
Host and the IMP.

A RFNM is returned from the destination IMP to the source IMP when
a message reaches the head of the destination IMP's output queue
to the Host (i.e. just before a message is sent to the Host). If
a destination IMP cannot then deliver that full message to the Host,
at most one more message may possibly arrive at that IMP due to
the premature release of the RFNM. The new message will subsequently
take its place at the end of the output queue to the Host thus
guaranteeing the preservation of the proper message arrival sequence.

The NOP message is a special control message which is available for
use during initiation of communication between the Host and its IMP.
The Host may, of course, decline to send NOP messages during this
period, but the first received message after IMP startup or after
the Host ready indicator has gone on, may be discarded by the IMP.
We do not require a Host to be prepared to repeat transmissions
into the network.

R.E. Kahn
BOLT BERANEK AND NEWMAN INC.

Sept, 1969
Vint Cerf
UCLA

Network Working Group/Request for Comment #18

It is suggested that link 1 be used for the HOST-HOST control link and link 0 be used for IMP-IMP control.

This will facilitate communication between Hosts and reduce delays due to interference with IMP-IMP communications.

Network Working Group
Request for Comments #51

M. Elie
4 May 70
Hostel
UCLA

Proposal for a Network Interchange Language

Introduction

In this paper an attempt is made to specify a high level programming language for computer networks, and more specifically the ARPA network. The main concept introduced is the one of an abstract Network Machine, which is consistent with the idea of a HOST asking a service from the computer network considered as an overall computing facility. The dialogue is always between a HOST and the Network Machine which language is always the same, though its configuration may vary according to the real remote HOST.

From a programming language point of view, this concept is similar to the UNCOL proposed in 1958 [STR058] but never implemented, however, the application to a computer network implies a realtime interaction between programs. Also, the possibility for the user to use NIL either in a standard mode or in an extended mode where he defines himself his own entities should give to NIL a maximum of flexibility.

1. Basic concepts introduced in NIL

1.1 Aim of NIL

The two main objectives of NIL are:

a) to describe the environment in which a program is executed (its complement); this involves the description of:

  - data formats and data structures
  - exchanges with input and output devices and characteristics expected from them
  - interface with operating system

b) to express the front end part of an interactive system:

  The data flow through an interactive system generally decreases as the data reaches the kernel of the system: it is assumed that in many interactive systems a separable module exists or can be defined which involves a great amount of data exchanged with the user, and much less exchanged with the rest of the system. This module is called Front-End. It is important that the response time of the system is affected as little as possible by additional transmission delays. Also, it is desirable to keep the data rates as low as possible on the network.

It is assumed that the transfer of a Front End does not imply to solve the whole problem of program transferability.

Network Working Group　　　　　　　　　　　　　　　　　　　M. Elie
Request for Comments #51　　　　　　　　　　　　　　　　　　4 May 70

1.2　　NIL subcategorization

As pointed out by S. Volansky [　　] it's convenient to divide languages in several sublanguages corresponding to their main functions. NIL is thus subdivided in:

- a control sublanguage
- an operation sublanguage
- a data declaration sublanguage
- an environment sublanguage

1.2.1 Control sublanguage

The control sublanguage states WHEN a computation is done: It describes the flow of control or ordering of the computations. With some information contained from the other sections of the language, it also states WHERE the computations are to be executed.

As a computer network introduces loose connections between several systems, the control language of the Network Machine should be able, in an elaborate version, of assigning computations to available processors, taking into account the time delays and resource allocation problems involved. It is not our purpose to consider this level at the moment.

1.2.2 Operation sublanguage

The operation sublanguage describes the operations to be performed on the data without indication of the sequencing between operations, it answers to the question of HOW an operation is performed. The operations are subdivided into two groups.

- a computation group
- a data manipulation group

The later is the most important part of NIL since its main purpose is the transformation of data structures and patterns.

1.2.3 Data declaration sublanguage

The data declaration sublanguage is necessary to declare the variables and data structures on which operations are performed.

The possibility is given to build structures of atomic elements called beads. NIL provides a standard set of beads used in the "standard mode"; in the "extended mode" a user may define new beads and new structures of them.

Network Working Group
Request for Comments #51

M. Elie
4 May 70

1.2.4 Environment sublanguage

The environment sublanguage expresses the context in which a program expects to operate; expected characteristics of the peripherals, semantics of the exchanges with the outside world through a particular operating system.

Thus a complete "program descriptor" will contain four distinct sections:

- environment section
- data declaration section
- control section
- operation section

The identification section is omitted because it corresponds to the log in and socket grabbing part of the initialization procedure.

1.3 The Network Machine

One fundamental concept in NIL is that of an abstract Network Machine which has the following characteristics:

- an infinite memory: there is no problem of memory allocation or garbage collection in this machine. But as an item must be accessible, it must still have an address.

- variable word length: a word may be considered as the smallest intelligible and addressable item of data. The atomic element called bead is in fact the machine word. The structure and length of each type of beads are expressed in the data definition sublanguage.

As presented on figure 1.3.1, one HOST only communicates with a Network Machine which may operate in two modes.

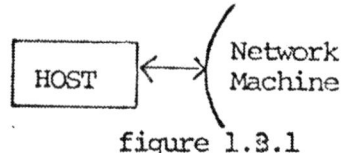

figure 1.3.1

- standard mode where the beads, their structures, and the allowed transformations on them are standard and need not to be redefined: standard beads and structures are known of every HOST

- extended mode where in addition to or instead of the standard data definitions and manipulation, a HOST may specify new beads structures and transformations. The extended mode allows the user to define his own machine as the Network Machine. This is then equivalent to the modes MY LOCAL, YOUR LOCAL proposed in RFC #42 by Ancona. If the definition of a name has not been altered the standard definition is assumed.

3

The data definition sublanguage is as well used for the purpose of documenting the set of standard beads.

The instruction set of the Network Machine stands at a high level permitting global transformations of data structures.

The environment of the Network Machine is determined by the subset of the environment of the server's HOST which is used by the program in execution; the system HOST-Network Machine can take two main configurations shown in figure 1.3.2.

a) The Network Machine stands for the user of a program provided by the HOST (server HOST)

b) The HOST machine is the user of a program provided by the Network Machine.

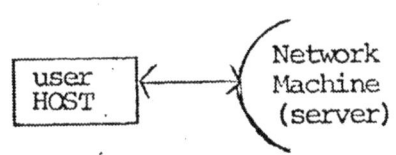

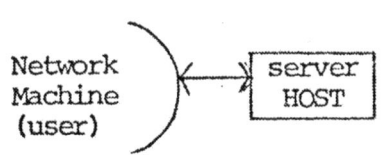

figure 1.3.2

The server machine assigns its hardware environment to the user machine. This choice is made so that programs can be remotely used without being modified; it is up to the user of a remote program to adapt himself and his own environment.

Thus, when the Network Machine is server, it defines the Data Definition and Environment sections.

Network Working Group
Request for Comments #51

M. Elie
4 May 70

1.4   Implementation

The data and environment definition sublanguages should be able to describe as well environment and data in HOSTs as data in Network Machine. At the limit it should enable two programs written in different languages to communicate,

as long as the data representation they use are expressible in the data description sublanguage.

In each HOST will be implemented a "generator" which will accept rules describing the HOST data structures and environment and will generate an adequate translator to translate them in Network Machine format, as shown in the figure 1.4.1.

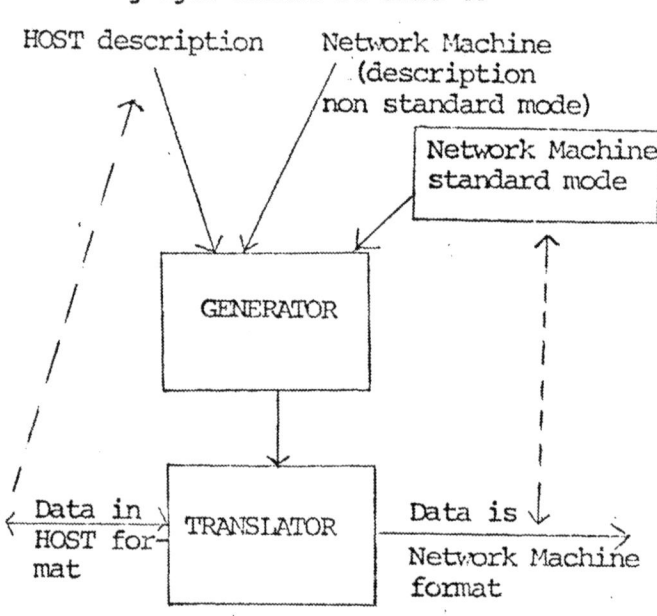

figure 1.4.1

Once the network machine standards will be settled it seems valuable to think about emulating the translator using a microprogramed unit which would be either added to the Host or rather to the IMP" thus avoiding the load of a translation which may involve lengthy operations on the bit level - (Figure 1.4.2.)

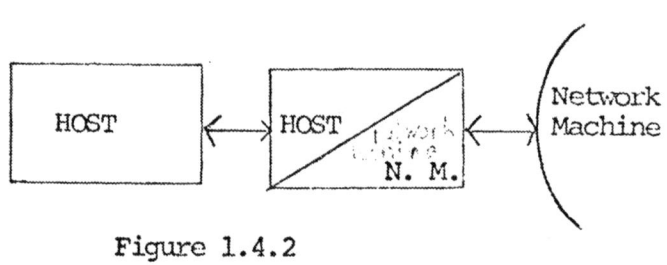

Figure 1.4.2

Network Working Group
Request for Comments #51

M. Elie
4 May 70

2. Data definition sublanguage

2.1 Fields

All communications with the Network Machine are done using strings of bits: these strings of bits, also referred to as messages are parsed by the receiving HOST to reconstruct inside its memory the data structures in its own memory and code.

Bits are grouped into significant fields: a field is a group of bits having definite contents. It may contain:

    a) an element of data (data field)
    b) some bit pattern specifying environment parameters
    c) a pointer
    d) the identification of some other fields.

The method to describe the formats of beads is derived from the method of description of a binary message suggested in RFC #31:

    a) each field is declared with its name and length in number of bits.
    b) commonly used fixed values of a field that correspond to a special meaning, may be given names.
    c) legal ways of concatenating fields are initiated by rules; when only certain fixed values of a field are allowed, they may be either specified by their value or by the corresponding name.

2.2 Data beads.

Data fields (type (a)) are concatenated to form data beads: a bead is an indivisible atomic unit of data used as building element of any data structure to be transmitted between HOSTs and Network Machine. A bead is the smallest unit of data that can be referenced.

The legal ways of forming a bead by concatenation of several fields are indicated in a construction rule. Beads have a fixed length and an unambiguous structure. In real machine beads are usually defined as an integer number of contiguous registers. This constraint does not apply here, though it may turn out to be more efficient to favor HOSTs with, for instance, 32 bit words, and 4 bytes per word, which are the most common word structure on the ARPA network.

Data beads may be considered as the operands of the language in which fields of type (b) and (c) would be operators.

2.3 Control fields

The way data beads are linked one to the other and the environment in which they operate are specified by additional control fields which cannot be referenced and are operators on or identifiers of the following string of beads, or linkage between individual beads.

The scope of a control field may as well be all the beads or substructures of a structure, if it is specified at the level of the head of the structure. To be more precise, two kinds of structures of beads must be defined: homogeneous and heterogeneous structures.

A structure is defined as homogeneous if both a unique type of bead and a fixed parameter environment for the whole structure is specified at the head of the structure.

A structure is defined as heterogeneous if at least one of the following conditions is true.

- different types of beads are used for building the structure
- the environment in which lie the beads of the structure is changing within the structure.

Five main control fields need to be defined.

   a) MODIFY
   b) FLAG
   c) POINTER
   d) IDENTIFICATION
   e) PARAMETER

2.3.1 MODIFY field

The MODIFY field is a one bit field preceding every bead of a heterogeneous structure: it is a flag set when followed by one or several control fields of type b, d, or e, which aim at modifying either the environment of data beads or their type. This field has the value:

1 if the attached data bead type and its environment do not change

0 if the attached element is a control field or a sequence of control fields of type b, d, or e specifying a change in type/or environment of following data beads.

2.3.2 FLAG field

When set, the MODIFY field is immediately followed by an 8 bit FLAG field indicating which of the IDENTIFICATION and several possible PARAMETER fields are present; when set to one each individual bit means the following:

bit number

0	IDENTIFICATION field present
1	first parameter field present
2	second parameter field present

6	sixth parameter field present
7	next field is another FLAG field for some more parameters (in case more than 6 parameters may be attached to a bead environment).

2.3.3 POINTER field

The number and nature of pointers to be attached to each bead depends on the structure definition. A given list structure may need one forward pointer. A ring structure may use an additional pointer to the first element. The necessary linkage between beads are defined in the structure definition thereafter the necessary pointer fields automatically added to each data bead. A bead is referenced within a structure by an address relative to the head of the structure. Thus a 16 bit pointer field should be fully sufficient to contain this address.

2.3.4 IDENTIFICATION field

The IDENTIFICATION field is an 8 bit field which identifies a bead type among the list of defined bead types. Standard bead types are numbered from zero up and non-standard bead types are numbered from 255 down. The non-standard types numbering is special to each server program or to a set of server programs. The IDENTIFICATION fields follow a MODIFY field of value 1 whenever the bead type has not been defined all over the structure in the structure root. Identification fields are also used at the level of the head of the structure to specify the type of identical elements (beads or structures) used within this structure.

2.3.5 PARAMETER field

The PARAMETER field gives the list of the environment parameters in which the following string of data beads lies. A PARAMETER field is specific of a bead type; it directly follows the MODIFY field when there is no ambiguity or the type of the next data beads.

Network Working Group
Request for Comments #51

M. Elie
4 May 70

Example: the paraméter field of the standard bead BEAMMVT will contain the following fields.

- a 2 bit field indicating the type of movement generated

    00   do not display   move the beam
    01   display final point   point
    10   display vector   vector
    11   unused

- a 4 bit field indicating beam intensity, by a number from 0 to 15, 0 meaning a null intensity, and 15 the maximum possible intensity.

- a 1 bit field for blinking

    0   off
    1   on

- a 1 bit field for light pen sensitivity

    0   off
    1   on

2.4 Metalanguage definition

A COBOL - report like meta language is used in the examples because of its readibility, as well in the beads as in the structure definitions.

Symbol	Meaning
+	concatanation
{ }	choice
[ ]	optional choice
{ }$^{l \leq n \leq u}$ [ ]$^{l \leq n \leq u}$	repetition

l lower bound on the number of identical items; if omitted l is assumed to be 0.

u upper bound on the number of identical items; if omitted u is assumed to be ∞.

a number alone means: exact number of repetition.

Network Working Group
Request for Comments #51

M. Elie
4 May 70

    :   label for further use <u>within the same rule</u>
    =   assignment
= ⊃   conditional alternative
( )   grouping
' '   indicates a special value given to the following field name

    ⊕   plus
    ⊖   minus

2.5   Proposed standard beads

2.5.1 Alphanumeric beads

    Character: CHAR

A character is composed of one eight bit field (which has the same name). Many special patterns, corresponding to currently used special characters are defined; they are indicated in table 2.5.1, as well as some subsets of CHAR. The basic character code is declared as standard ASCII
                           standard EBCDIC
or by the name   CODE
followed by the 128 characters in this code corresponding to the 128 ASCII characters. If no code declaration is specified, the ASCII code is assumed by default.

    Number representation

Normally the kernel of a program stays in the server's HOST and the user's HOST should have no arithmetic operations to perform on the data. In this case, the principles involved in the arithmetic unit conception of a HOST do not need to be described. But the format of fixed and floating point numbers has to be described.

- in the case when user and server HOST's have the same number representation, for instance the standard representation, the transmission of data in their number representation reduces the data flow between them.

- if the server HOST has a different number representation than the standard representation, depending on the data transmitted, there are two alternatives:

Network Working Group
Request for Comments #51

M. Elie
4 May 70

+ the numerical data is exchanged as decimal numbers in the standard code

+ the fixed and floating point format are defined to the Network Machine and the user HOST performs

> either a direct transcoding from the server binary representation to decimal representation and vice versa.
>
> or a transcoding from the server binary representation to its own binary representation and vice versa.

As most of the numbers exchanged are to be printed in decimal or are given as decimal input, it is felt that when there is incompatibility between binary representations of corresponding HOSTs, exchanges in decimal representation would be the easiest.

Thus are defined:

a) Number in decimal representation which is not a bead but a string of characters (see 2.3.1)

b) Fixed point numbers single precision FXPNUM1
                                  double precision FXPNUM2

Field definition   BYTE   8   SIGN   1
                     SBYTE   7

FXP NUM1 $\leftarrow$ SIGN + SBYTE + $\{BYTE\}^3$
FXP NUM2 $\leftarrow$ FXPNUM1 + $\{BYTE\}^4$

c) Floating point numbers single precision FLPNUM1
                                 double precision FLPNUM2

FLP NUM1 $\leftarrow$ SIGN + SBYTE + $\{BYTE\}^3$

FLP NUM2 $\leftarrow$ FLPNUM1 + $\{BYTE\}^4$

This only expresses the syntax of the floating point number. The semantics should say: in FLPNUM1

SIGN is the sign of the number of format $\{BYTE\}^3$ which is the mantissa

SBYTE is the exponent, and its value is based by a value of 40_{16} to insure positive exponents. In fact, FXPNUM1 and FLPNUM1 differ by their semantics.

Network Working Group
Request for Comments #51

M. Elie
4 May 70

These properties will be expressed by special field definition:

$$EXP \leftarrow SBYTE \oplus {}'40H'SBYTE$$
$$MANT \leftarrow SIGN \oplus \{BYTE\}^3$$

and a floating point number is defined as:

$$FLP = MANT \; 2^{EXP}$$

Network Working Group
Request for Comments #51

M. Elie
4 May 70

1. Special Characters

    Transmission Control Characters

        SOH
        STX
        ETX
        EOT
        ENQ
        ACK
        DLE
        NAK
        SYN
        ETB
        ESC

    Printer Control Characters

horizontal tabulation	HT	←	'0X1' CHAR
vertical tabulation	VT	←	'0BX' CHAR
new line	NL	←	'0AX' CHAR
end of message	EOM	←	'08X' CHAR

    Teletype Control Characters

Carriage return	CR	←	'0DX' CHAR
shift out	SO	←	'0EX' CHAR
shift in	SI	←	'0FX' CHAR
	BS	←	

    Device Control Characters

        DC1
        DC2
        DC3
        DC4

Table 2.3.1

Network Working Group
Request for Comments #51

M. Elie
4 May 70

2. Subsets of Characters

Numeric characters

$$\text{NUM} \leftarrow \left\{ \begin{array}{c} \text{'1'} \\ 2 \\ \cdot \\ \cdot \\ 9 \end{array} \right\} \text{CHAR}$$

Printable characters

$$\text{PRCHAR} \leftarrow \left\{ \begin{array}{c} \text{NUM} \\ \text{ALPH} \\ = \end{array} \right\} \text{CHAR}$$

Intermediate characters

$$\text{ITCHAR} \leftarrow \left\{ \begin{array}{c} \text{'characters'} \\ \text{in column} \\ 2 \end{array} \right\} \text{CHAR}$$

Final Characters

$$\text{FIN CHAR} \leftarrow \text{CHAR} \ominus \text{ITCHAR}$$

Transmission Control Characters*

$$\text{TRACHAR} \leftarrow \left\{ \begin{array}{c} \text{'NUL'} \\ \cdot \\ \cdot \\ \text{DEL} \end{array} \right\} \text{CHAR}$$

Derra Control Characters

$$\text{DCCHAR} \leftarrow \left\{ \begin{array}{c} \text{'DC1'} \\ \text{DC2} \\ \text{DC3} \\ \text{DC4} \end{array} \right\} \text{CHAR} \quad \text{TYCCHAR} \left\{ \begin{array}{c} \text{CR} \\ \text{SO} \\ \text{SI} \\ \text{BS} \end{array} \right\}$$

Teletype control character

Alphabetic characters

$$\text{ALPH} \leftarrow \left\{ \begin{array}{c} \text{'A'} \\ \cdot \\ \text{Z} \end{array} \right\} \text{CHAR}$$

Printer Control Characters

$$\text{PCCHAR} \leftarrow \left\{ \begin{array}{c} \text{HT} \\ \text{VT} \\ \text{NL} \\ \text{EOM} \end{array} \right\} \text{CHAR}$$

Table 2.3.1: Special ASCII characters and groups of ASCII characters.

*see USACII standards

Network Working Group
Request for Comments #51

M. Elie
4 May 70

2.5.2 Graphic Beads

As proposed in RFC #5 by J. Rulifson, the screen of any graphical display is taken to be a square; the coordinates of points are normalized from -1/2 to +1/2 on both axes. The position of the first point of a structure is determined by the deflection from the origin which is the rest point of the beam; following points are determined by their deflections (AX,AY) from the last beam position.

Thus, only two data fields need to be defined:

DEFLECTION   which is a 12 bit field: the deflection is defined by a number between - 1 and +1 with the precision usual to the server.

ANGLE   which is a 15 bit field defining an angle from 0 to 2Π in radians between the horizontal axis and an axis passing through the origin. The first bit of it indicates if the angle must be taken clockwise or counterclockwise.

The data beads are:

MOVE

Depending on the parameters which are set when this bead appears, MOVE may specify:

- an invisible movement of the beam; in this case the beam intensity is null

- a new point: in this case the beam intensity is on only when the beam has reached the new point.

- a vector: in this case thebeam intensity is set to a certain non zero value

$$\text{MOVE} \leftarrow \{\text{DEFLECTION}\}^2$$

Arc of circle: ARC

An arc of circle is defined by its center, followed by its starting point and the angle of its ending axis.

$$\text{ARC} \leftarrow \{\text{DEFLECTION}\}^4 + \text{ANGLE}$$

Network Working Group
Request for Comments #51

M. Elie
4 May 70

2.6 Proposed parameter fields.

2.6.1 Character strings.

In character strings some of the control characters are really parameter fields: they act as an operator on the following string of characters. i.e.:

    lower shift
    upper shift
    new line
    escape
    . . . .

But as the code and use of these characters are determined in the standard codes, they are not included in parameter definition. It may be taken advantage that these characters are in the two left columns of the ASCII or EBCDIC standard code: they correspond to codes with the first three bits null in EBCDIC and the first two bits null in ASCII.

2.6.2 Graphics parameters

The following parameter fields are defined:

scale	SCALE		4
beam intesity	INT		4
light pen sensivity	SENS	←	SWITCH
blinking	BLINK	←	SWITCH
beam	BEAM	←	SWITCH

SWITCH is a 1 bit field which may take the values:

    ON ← '1'   SWITCH
    OFF ← '0'   SWITCH

A switch parameter stays ON, as long as it is not reset to OFF.

The beam intensity is expressed by a number from 0 to 1. 0 is black and 1 as light as the display can go. Numbers in between specify the relative log of the intensity difference. BEAM permits to switch the BEAM on or off without changing the current INT parameter.

2.7 Structures

2.7.1 Structure definition.

The structure definition consists mainly in the specification of the topological relations between data beads:

- sequential relations; no pointer field necessary
- links through a number of pointers.

16

Network Working Group
Request for Comments #51

M. Elie
4 May 70

2.7.2 Standard structure type.

Two basic standard structure types are chosen

VECTOR to represent sequence of data beads (strings, arrays, tables...)

PLEX to represent any kind of directed graph, tree, ring...)

VECTOR $(C;N_1,...N_C)$ ← VECTORHDR + VECTORBODY

VECTORBODY ← $(=C+1:\{defined\ bead\})^{Ni}$ + [VECTORBODY]

VECTORHDR ← 'VECTOR' IDENTIFICATION + C + N_1 + N_2 + ... + N_C

C is the number of parts (columns) in the vector, each part having N_C elements.

It is also probably interesting to define a compressed vector COMPVECTOR in which sequence of the identical elements are transmitted as 1 element + a special bead + the number of identical elements in sequence.

PLEX (M)

The first bit of a pointer field indicates if the pointer points to a terminal element or not. If it is the case, forward <u>pointer fields are not added</u> to the data element.

M is the number of data elements in the structure.

2.8 Objects

2.8.1 object definition.

An object is defined by a semantic rule including, on the right hand side ⎰a name to identify the object
⎱a set of parameters of the object definition.

on the left ⎰operands: name of the beads used as data elements
hand side ⎱operators: parameter fields
⎱structure of the data beads.

i.e. The definition of a new object called SQUARE is: SQUARE ←
(A,L,A∈) ROT∈(ANGLE∈) (VECTOR(1,4) (BEAM'OFF'+
MOVE (A) + BEAM 'ON' + MOVE (0,L) + MOVE (L,0) +
MOVE (0,∈L) + MOVE (∈L,0))

Where ROT refers to a transformation defined in the data manipulation language, and VECTOR is defined as a standard structure.

The identifier of the new structure is SQUARE
The structure type used is VECTOR with dimension 1 and 4 elements
The elements of the VECTOR are standard beads MOVE
The parameters are A, L, and A θ
Parameter fields BEAM 'OFF' and BEAM 'ON' are used.

2.8.2 Alphanumeric standard objects.

Compressed character string (COMSTRING)

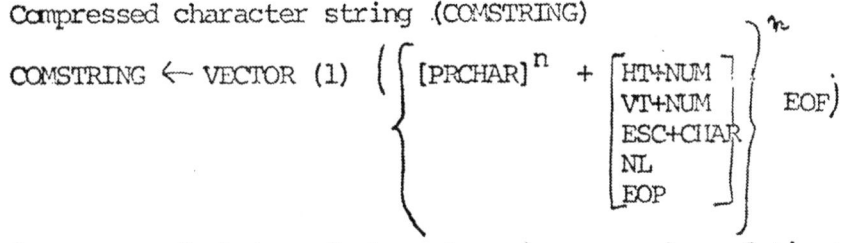

A compressed string of characters is any number of times a string of any number of printable characters followed by one of the following characters

- horizontal tabulation followed by the number of corresponding blanks to be added

- vertical tabulation followed by the number of lines to be skipped.

- escape followed by any character

- new line
- end of page

The compressed string is ended by an EOF character.

- Code table (CODE)
  CODE ← VECTOR (1;128) {CHAR}^{128}

CODE is the name of the translation table assumed for a given program. When defined by the user, he must give from column 1 to column 8 the 8 bit pattern equivalent to the corresponding ASCII code.

Network Working Group
Request for Comments #51

M. Elie
4 May 70

- Binary card image

$$B\ CARD \leftarrow VECTOR\ (1;120)\ \{CHAR\}^{120}$$

Packed decimal number HNUM 4 bits field

$$DSIGN \leftarrow \begin{Bmatrix} A & X \\ C & X \\ E & X \\ F & X \\ B & X \\ D & X \end{Bmatrix} HNUM \qquad PNUM \leftarrow \begin{Bmatrix} 0\ H \\ \vdots \\ 9\ H \end{Bmatrix} HNUM$$

$$PDNUM \leftarrow \{PNUM\}^{1 < n < 31} + DSIGN$$

- Decimal number (unpacked or zoned

$$DNUM \leftarrow \{NUM\}^{1 < n < 31} + D\ SIGN + PNUM$$

PART C
Building the ARPANET

Looking back at the ARPANET effort decades later

by David C. Walden

In late 1968, the Advanced Research Projects Agency (ARPA) of the US Department of Defense announced the award to Bolt Beranek and Newman Inc. (BBN) of a competitively procured contract to develop the backbone of packet switches for the ARPANET.

The ARPANET initially consisted of packet switches called Interface Message Processors (IMPs), lo ng-distance leased telephone circuits between pairs of IMP, and host computers connected to directly to an IMP at the host computer site. Network users were connected to their local host computers and could specify for their local host computer to communicate with a host computer connected to an IMP at another site. A set of communication protocols specified the interface between the hosts and the IMPs and conventions for communicating between a host connected to one IMP and a host connect to another IMP.

Eventually, I think it is fair to say, the ARPANET evolved into what has become the Internet. Thus, the ARPANET activities in 1969 were an important step in the development of what is arguably the most significant societal and technology development since the development of the computer itself. The massive distribution of computation to the desktop that we know today was directly related (a) to the decreasing price and size of computation, and (b) the computer networking advances that followed and to a significant extent grew out of the ARPANET, e.g., Local Area Networking and the connection of these networks together into the internetwork of LANs and WANs that covers the world today.

Many people and institutions were involved in the ARPANET activities in 1969 including ARPA itself, the ARPANET host sites (the first four being at University of California at Los Angeles, Stanford Research Institute, University of California at Santa Barbara and University of Utah), Network Analysis Corporation, and others. By virtue of its contract to develop the packet switches, BBN was a central player during the first ARPANET year, 1969.

BBN's contract from ARPA was a one-year contract to develop and deliver a backbone network of four IMPs, and on August 30, 1969, the first IMP was delivered to UCLA. By the end of calendar 1969 the first four IMPs had been delivered. Naturally, the year of effort at BBN was intense, and I had the good fortune to be part of this invigorating activity.

While I don't remember the exact dates, I think by 1968 Robert Kahn, who was aware that there would be a competitive procurement for the ARPANET backbone of IMPs, had convinced BBN management that BBN should prepare itself to bid on this procurement when it came out. BBN pulled a team together under the supervision of Frank Heart that included Bob, Severo Ornstein, me and perhaps others to think about what we would bid once the Request for Proposal came out from the government. In 1968 the RFP did come out and a number of people from throughout BBN helped draft and review the proposal. Before the proposal was submitted, Will Crowther was recruited from MIT Lincoln Laboratory (where Frank, Severo and I had previously worked) to join our team. By roughly the time the contract was awarded Ben Barker joined us from Harvard where Severo had met him in a class Severo taught. Also, soon after contract award, Bernie Cosell, who had been working on another project at BBN was added to the team. Thus, the primary team that worked on developing the IMP for the first year consisted of:

- Frank Heart (team leader)
- Robert Kahn (communications theorist and the person who did much of the communication with the external world)
- Severo Ornstein and Ben Barker (hardware development)
- Will Crowther, Bernie Cosell and I (software development).

Others from BBN contributed or got added full-time to the project later in the year.

In retrospect, our approach to bidding on the RFP was pretty smart. We had decided to submit a fairly detailed design, including initial hardware designs, a software architecture and fairly detailed initial timing analysis, principles of system operation, and so forth as part of our bid. This level of detail helped us (I suspect) win the procurement. It also left us in a fairly advanced starting position at the beginning of the actual contract. This helped us finish in the specified one year, removed a lot of uncertainty from the beginning of the implementation period (we were sure we could do the design and development on time), and enabled us to begin the actual development period with what was in effect a second design cycle. Often, people talk about developing good designs before starting implementation on complex or difficult implementation projects. It was the inclination of our team to actually do so.

Regardless of how well prepared we were to begin the design and development effort, the year was an intense one, and one that was under intense scrutiny with lots of collaboration from ARPA and the members of the host community. In particular, BBN had contractual commitments to deliver a series of design and specification documents reports during that first year.

Upon rereading some of these reports from the first year (BBN Reports 1763, 1783, 1837, 1890, 1822, and 1928) a few years ago, I was struck by a number of design characteristics.

1. Many features to make the IMPs run reliably and with minimal on-site assistance and with cross-network diagnosis, debugging, and new releases
2. Considerable facilities for network monitoring and measurement
3. No constraints put on the data hosts could exchange over the network
4. Highly successful initial algorithms for IMP-to-IMP communications and network routing (both were changed over time, especially the latter, but they did an excellent job in their time, and provided in the initial implementations in the Internet of a system of positive acknowledgments and time-outs and a distributed algorithm for routing)
5. Much less successful initial algorithms for Host-to-IMP and source-IMP-to-destination-IMP communications-the former was too limited because of the assumption of a direct electrical connection rather than a remote communications interface, and the latter was simply inadequate to the congestion control and multiplexing task it was designed for
6. A design and implementation that was very high performance in terms of use of memory and machine cycles and very reliable in terms of the IMPs not crashing because of coding bugs
7. Generally, this first large-scale demonstration of packet-switching technology dramatically "proved" the technology's viability, leading in no small way to its ubiquitous use in the world today.

Although there were some missteps, the initial IMP design and implementation was quite robust and provided good support for the host experiments and a powerful mechanism for releasing incremental improvements as they were needed. In fact, aspects of our original design can still be seen in how the Internet works today.

As I reflect back to that first year, now so many years ago, I am also struck by the general competence of the effort and the team's certainty of successful completion. Today, nearly forty years later, people often ask me whether I was worried to be a member of a team that had so much to accomplish in only one year. Of course developing that first IMP system was a relatively small project compared to the massive extent of what people think of today when they think of the Internet. We also knew we had a tight schedule, and we worked very hard. However, I didn't see any real worry from any member of the team at any time. We were a small team of highly motivated and, on average, highly experienced people that worked well together during that first year. We were one of those "hot teams" that sometimes get written up in management books. We were very focused—the team was enormously pragmatic and concentrated on getting a system delivered on time that worked "well enough."

Of course, much of the ARPANET development effort happened at other places than BBN—at ARPA, UCLA, SRI, UCSB, the University of Utah, and Network Analysis Corporation. While we at BBN (and I personally) participated intensely in the broader efforts of the ARPANET community, others are better able than I to reflect on the non-BBN parts of the story. I can only say what a joy it was for me to be part of the ARPANET effort.

Dave Walden
East Sandwich, Massachusetts
November 2006

Report No. 1763   Bolt Beranek and Newman Inc

PREFACE

A contract was recently awarded to Bolt Beranek and Newman Inc (BBN) for the implementation of a four-node group of interface message processors (IMPs) for the ARPA computer network. This document describes our preliminary design plans for the IMPs and the network protocol.

Since implementation is only just beginning, some aspects of this design will probably change. This document is for information only and should not be construed as a firm specification.

Cambridge, Mass.
January 6, 1969

Report No. 1763   Bolt Beranek and Newman Inc

TABLE OF CONTENTS

		page
A.	Introduction	1
B.	General Discussion of the IMP	4
C.	Host-Host Protocol and the Notion of Links	6
D.	Messages and Packets: HOST-IMP, IMP-IMP, and IMP-HOST Protocol	10
E.	Acknowledgment Procedures	19
	1. IMP-to-IMP acknowledgment of packets	19
	2. Request-For-Next-Message (RFNM)	21
F.	Examples of Message Flow	23
G.	Word Length Mismatch	26
H.	Hardware Description and Interface Operation	30
	1. The HOST/IMP interface unit	33
	2. The IMP/MODEM interface unit	37
J.	Organization of IMP Storage	41
K.	Buffer Congestion	44
L.	Line Quality Determination and Rerouting	46
M.	Network Introspection	49
	1. Faults	50
	2. Performance measurements	54
	3. Summary of abnormal messages	56
N.	The Operational IMP Program	58
	1. Summary of IMP program routines	64
	2. Timing and space considerations	66
	3. Test programs	68
	4. Utility programs	68
O.	Optional Site Arrangements	69
APPENDIX A		A-1

Report No. 1763 Bolt Beranek and Newman Inc

LIST OF FIGURES

		page
FIGURE 1	IMP CONFIGURATION	5
FIGURE 2	MULTIPLE HOST-TO-HOST LINKS	9
FIGURE 3	MULTIPLEXED HOST-TO-HOST LINKS	9
FIGURE 4	HOST-TO-IMP INFORMATION FORMAT	12
FIGURE 5	ORIGINATING IMP PACKET STRUCTURE	14
FIGURE 6	COMMUNICATION LINE PACKET FORMAT	15
FIGURE 7	PACKET FORMAT AS RECEIVED FROM MODEM INTERFACE	16
FIGURE 8	IMP-TO-HOST INFORMATION FORMAT	18
FIGURE 9	FORMAT OF LAST PACKET OF A MESSAGE	29
FIGURE 10	HOST AND IMP BUFFER FORMAT FOR A TWO-PACKET MESSAGE	31
FIGURE 11	GENERAL VIEW OF A TYPICAL IMP SYSTEM	32
FIGURE 12	LOGIC VIEW OF MODEM	38
FIGURE 13	PACKET BUFFER FORMAT	39
FIGURE 14	IMP PROGRAM CONTROL LOGIC	60

Report No. 1763   Bolt Beranek and Newman Inc

INITIAL IMP DESIGN

A. Introduction

In this report we present our proposed system design. We begin by describing the most important features of the design, followed by a description of the overall hardware configuration of the IMP. The main part of the document is devoted to a detailed description of the process of message communication, including the primary aspects of network message flow and the selected network protocol. We discuss the function of the IMP/MODEM Interface and the IMP/Host Interface. The logical organization of the IMP buffer storage is then described in detail. The potential causes of network congestion are summarized along with the provisions we have included for handling this situation. Next we discuss line quality determination and rerouting. Questions of fault detection, status examination, and reporting procedures are also discussed. The end of the document is devoted to the main program structure and the support software.

Our experience convinced us that it was wrong to plan for an *initial* network that permitted a sizable degree of external and remote control of IMPs. Consequently, as one important feature of our design, we have planned a network composed of highly autonomous IMPs. Once the network is demonstrated to be successful, then remote control can be added, slowly and carefully. Messages are processed by an IMP using information which has been received from other IMPs and Host computers in the network, but special control messages or other external control signals are initially avoided to the greatest possible extent. One specific consequence of this policy is that the IMPs measure performance of the network on a regular basis and report in special messages to the network measurement center (presumably at UCLA).

A second important feature of our design is the provision of a *tracing* capability which permits the operation of the net to be studied in great detail. Any message may contain a "trace bit", and each IMP which handles such a message generates a special report describing its detailed handling of the message; the collection of such special reports permits reconstruction of the history of such messages as they traverse the system. This technique permits highly flexible sampled study of the network.

We have also included an automatic trouble reporting capability which detects a variety of network difficulties such as line quality deterioration, and reports them to an interested Host (perhaps, the network measurement center).

A principal feature of our system is a provision for letting IMPs throw away packets which they have received but have not yet acknowledged. Each IMP transmits packets to other IMPs at its own discretion. Each time an IMP receives *and accepts* a packet it returns a positive acknowledgment to the transmitting IMP. The transmitting IMP retains its copy of the packet until it receives the positive acknowledgment. The transmitting IMP will retransmit the packet if an acknowledgment is not received within a time-out period. It will continue to try transmissions, via a different route if necessary, until such time as a positive acknowledgment is returned. We have explicitly avoided the use of negative acknowledgments which we feel are insufficient and consequently redundant.

We have carefully provided for the preservation of natural word boundaries in transmissions between computers with equal word sizes (a thing which, despite intuition, does not tend to "happen naturally"). We introduce a technique of padding and marking which neatly and generally allows the beginning and end of a message to be clearly indicated to a destination Host without requiring the Host programs to count bits. [Although we have made an effort to provide a network protocol that allows the Hosts a great deal of flexibility, this is a difficult technical area, and we would plan to examine further the problems associated with Host-Host word reformating.]

Another important feature of our design is a hardware modification to the IMP computer that permits the program to set an interrupt. This trick permits *three* levels of priority in the operational program (interrupt routines, urgent task routines, and background), which, in turn, has an important bearing on the IMP Program's ability to handle occasional time-consuming word-rate tasks (such as ASCII conversion, or other data transformation).

The Host computers have a few responsibilities for participation in the network. Specifically, the Host must provide a network-linking Program within its operating system to accept standard format network messages and to generate network messages in accordance with this standard format. The Host message includes identification information that accompanies the message from the source to the final destination. The Host computer must not present a message of over 8080 bits to the IMP. Larger transmissions must therefore be broken up by a Host into a sequence of such messages.

The network is carefully designed to protect and deliver messages from the source Host to the destination Host. The operation is self contained, and does not in any way constrain the procedures a Host may use in communicating with other Hosts.

B. General Discussion of the IMP

The overall configuration of an IMP includes a Honeywell DDP-516 computer, which has a 0.96 µs cycle-time, a 16 bit word length and 12K of memory (expandable), 16 channels of priority interrupts (expandable), a relative-time clock, and a 16 channel data multiplexor as shown in Fig. 1. Also shown are several special interfaces, specifically one to the Host, and one to each modem. A paper tape reader has been included because we feel a very strong need for a device which does not depend upon the network or any Host computer for the loading of an IMP program. We believe that this is a simple, reliable and inexpensive way to read in new versions of a program during the initial phases of network operation. A teletype is required for maintenance of the IMP computer, but is not used by the main program and can be disconnected and removed during normal operation. A specially designed set of status-indicator lights are provided

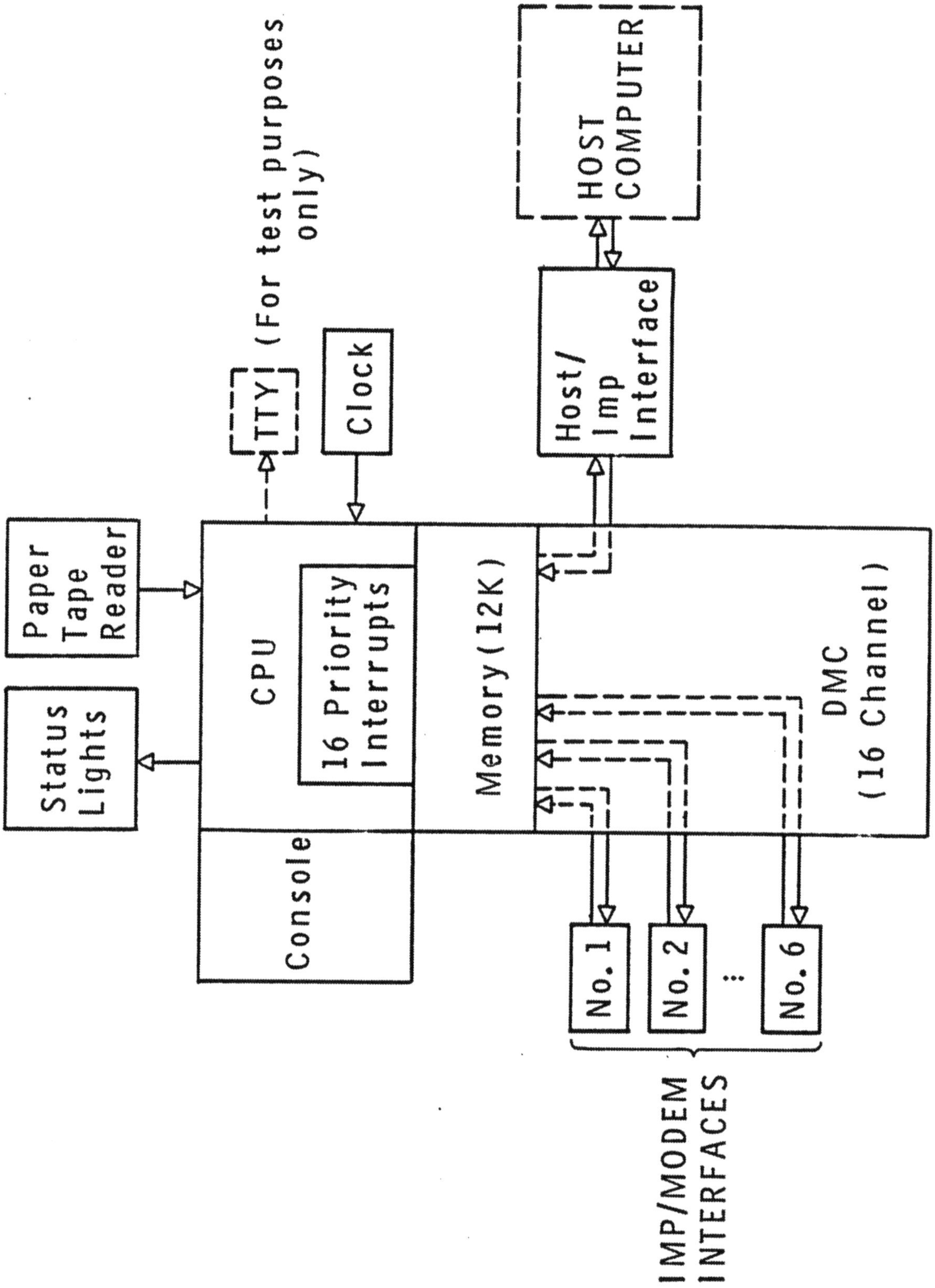

FIG. 1 IMP CONFIGURATION.

for use by the IMP program to report trouble conditions to local Host personnel or to maintenance personnel without necessitating a halt in normal program operation.

The IMPs in the initial network will each have three built-in full duplex modem interfaces, but the interface design is modular and may be extended up to as many as six units, without a change in packaging.

The IMP, including all interface hardware, will be packaged in a single 69" × 24" × 28" rugged cabinet. (See Plate I.)

C. Host-Host Protocol and the Notion of Links

It is important to draw a sharp line between the responsibility of the network facilities in transmitting information and the responsibility of the Host organization for developing and adopting procedures for utilizing this facility. However, in considering the system design, it became clear that we would have to pay some degree of attention to limitations that the network protocol might place on the Host use of the network. We reached the conclusion that a network protocol that satisfactorily achieves the transmission requirement might nonetheless adversely affect the implementation by Host organizations of certain very desirable protocol features.

We considered the problems introduced when a multiplicity of user programs at a given Host installation are concurrently using the network and concluded that provisions for allowing such usage were rather important. The Host computers view the network as a means for passing messages back and forth between

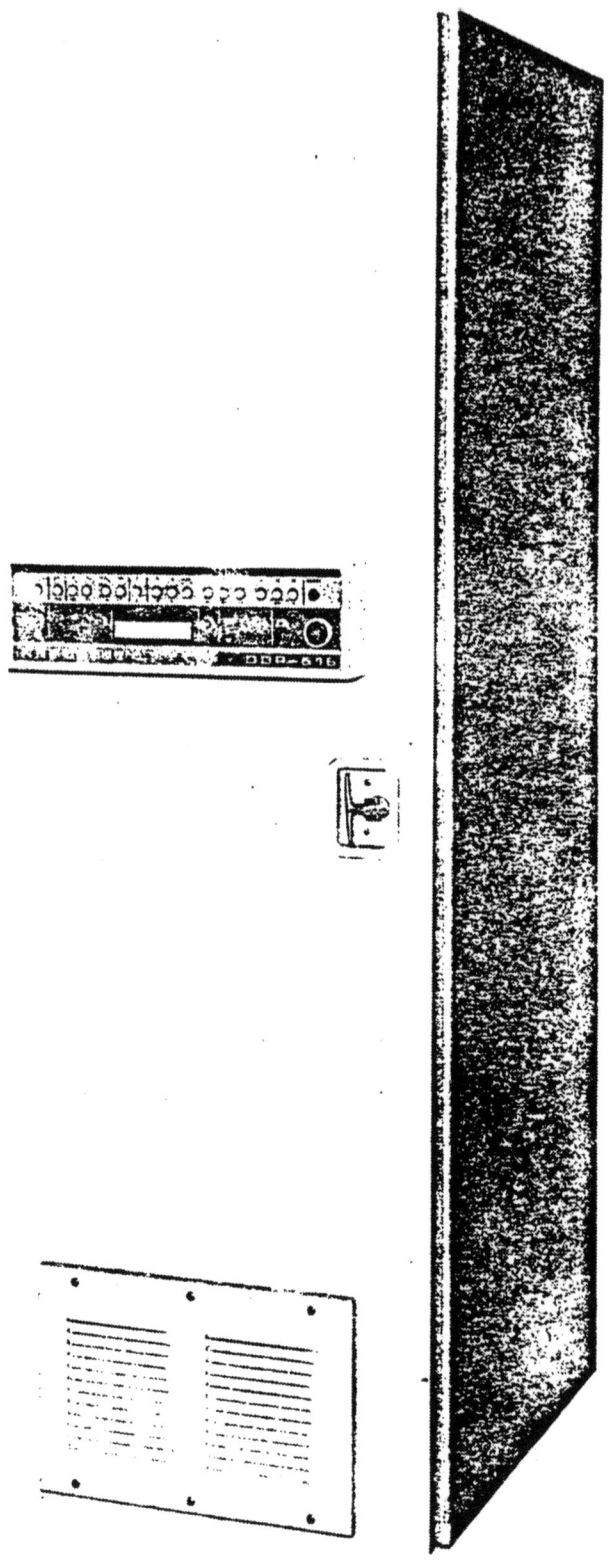

PLATE 1. THE IMP.

parties rather than between pairs of Host computers themselves. We call a logical connection between two parties at remote Host computers a *link*. Many different links may exist simultaneously between a pair of Host computers. As illustrated in Fig. 2, our network protocol permits many concurrent links to time-share the same physical network facilities. These links are established, identified, and maintained by a network program in each Host computer that effectively multiplexes outgoing messages from the parties into the network and distributes incoming messages to the appropriate parties as illustrated in Fig. 3. Writing and maintaining the Host's network program is, of course, the responsibility of the individual Hosts.

An identification number is assigned by each Host computer to each network party in his machine. The party that initiates a link is known as the *caller*. The identification number of the caller is used as an identification number for the link and, in conjunction with the identity of the two Host computers, uniquely identifies the link. Each message which the Host network program presents to the network contains several pieces of information used by the network. One of these is the link identification number. The network uses this number to control the flow of messages and passes it along to the receiving Host.

A message is designated by its link and its direction of travel. (Source and destination are terms which identify the direction of travel.) Thus, complete identification for a message consists of the following four items:

1) Identity of Source Host;

2) Identity of Destination Host;

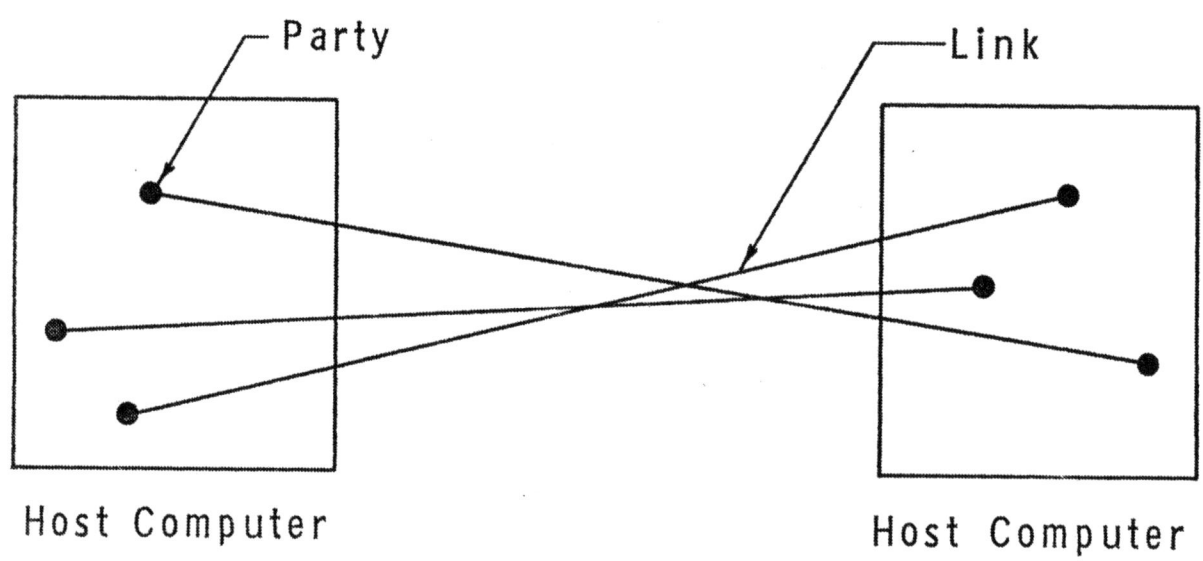

FIG. 2   MULTIPLE HOST-TO-HOST LINKS.

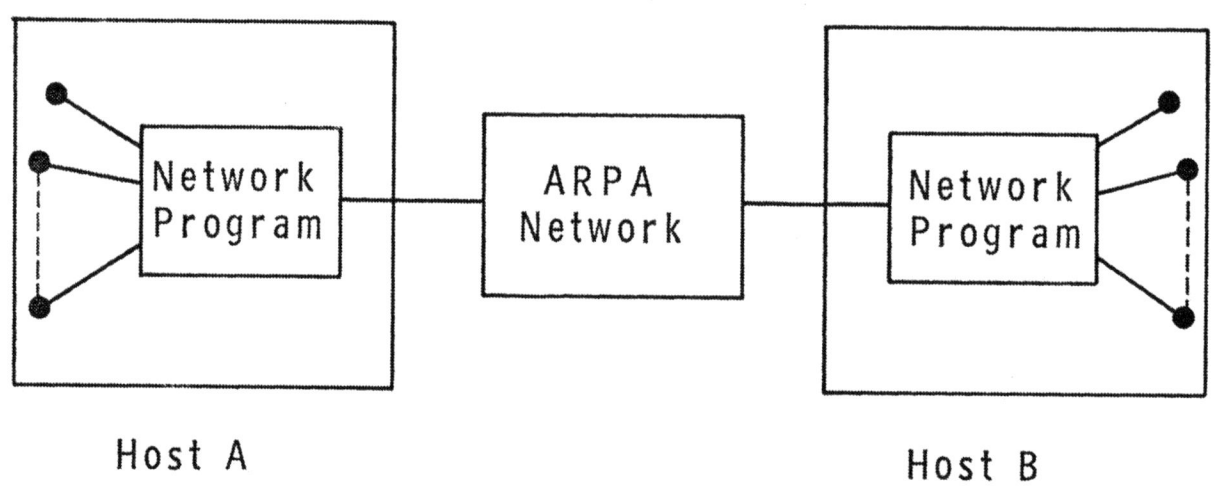

FIG. 3   MULTIPLEXED HOST-TO-HOST LINKS.

3) Link identification number; and

4) Caller location (at source or at destination).

For example, if party n in Host A calls Host B, the message will be identified as going from source A to destination B and the caller for the link will be party n at the source. A return message from Host B on this link is identified as going from source B to destination A and the caller for the link will be party n at the destination.

We introduce the notion of a *link* early in this design discussion primarily because we wish to include the link identification number as an integral part of the identification information passed from Host to IMP, from IMP to IMP in the network, and finally from the destination IMP to the destination Host.

D. Messages and Packets; HOST-IMP, IMP-IMP, and IMP-HOST Protocol

Hosts communicate with each other via sequences of messages. A message is taken into an IMP from its Host computer in segments. These segments are formed into packets and separately shipped out by the IMP into the network. They are reassembled at the destination IMP and delivered in sequence to the receiving Host, who obtains them as a single unit. Thus the segmentation of a message during transmission is completely invisible to the Host computers.

The transmitting Host attaches identifying information to the beginning of each message which it passes to its IMP. The IMP forms a *header* by adding further information for network use. The header is then attached to each segment of the message.

Report No. 1763   Bolt Beranek and Newman Inc

The transmitting hardware computes parity check digits that are shipped with each segment and that are used for error detection. The destination IMP performs an error check, strips off the header from each segment in the course of reassembly and attaches identifying information at the beginning of the reassembled message for use by the destination Host.

A message from a Host is legislatively limited to be less than 8080 bits, and is sent to its IMP via a single block transfer. The hardware interface detects the end of the block transfer. Messages vary in size up to the 8080 bit limit. The first sixteen bits of each message which a Host sends to an IMP for a transmission are prescribed by the standard network protocol as follows:

> Eight bits are allocated to the link identification number, five bits are allocated to identifying the destination Host, one bit is presented for tagging selected messages which are to be traced through the network, and two bits are reserved as spares. The tracing is discussed more fully in a later section. The format for these 16 bits of Host information is illustrated in Fig. 4.

The HOST/IMP Interface transfers bits serially from the Host and forms them into 16 bit IMP words. The IMP program takes groups of successive words in segments and stores them in separate buffer regions until the end of the message has been recognized. The first buffer accepts up to 64 IMP words from the Host (1024 bits including the 16 bits of Host information). Each succeeding buffer accepts up to 63 words (1008 bits). Thus, the maximum Host message of 8080 bits will be taken by the IMP in exactly 8 segments.

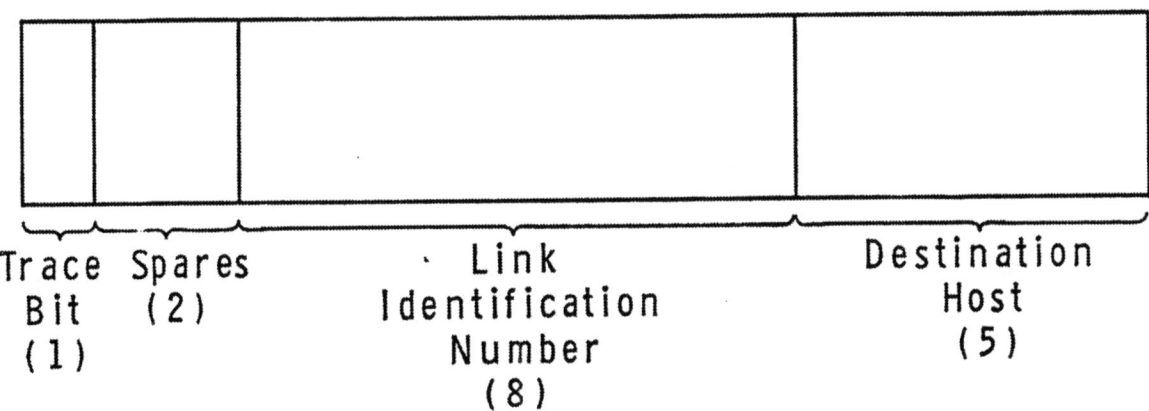

FIG. 4 HOST-TO-IMP INFORMATION FORMAT.

The IMP now formats each segment into a *packet* for transmission into the network. The structure of a formatted packet as it appears in the originating IMP memory is shown in Fig. 5. The output hardware prefaces the packet into the phone line with the character pair DLE STX to mark the packet beginning for the receiving channel hardware. The packet is then transmitted serially over the communcation lines beginning with the left most bit of the first header word and proceeding through the header and the text. The channel hardware computes 24 parity check digits, which it attaches after the packet, immediately following two ASCII control characters DLE ETX to mark the end of the packet for the receiving channel hardware.

A continuous stream of the ASCII control character SYN is transmitted by the channel hardware between packet transmissions. These are used to separate packets and to obtain character synchronization in the receiving channel hardware. Thus the packet appears on the communication line as shown in Fig. 6.

The receiving channel hardware locks into character synchronization on a bit-by-bit search for an 8 bit SYN code. Once synchronization has been obtained, the channel hardware looks for the first occurrence of DLE STX and succeeding characters are fed into the IMP memory until the DLE ETX at the end of the packet is detected. The hardware also computes a 24 bit error check based upon the received data, which should equal zero if no errors have occurred in transmission.

The received data between the STX and the DLE is written into the IMP memory and appears in the buffer as shown in Fig. 7.

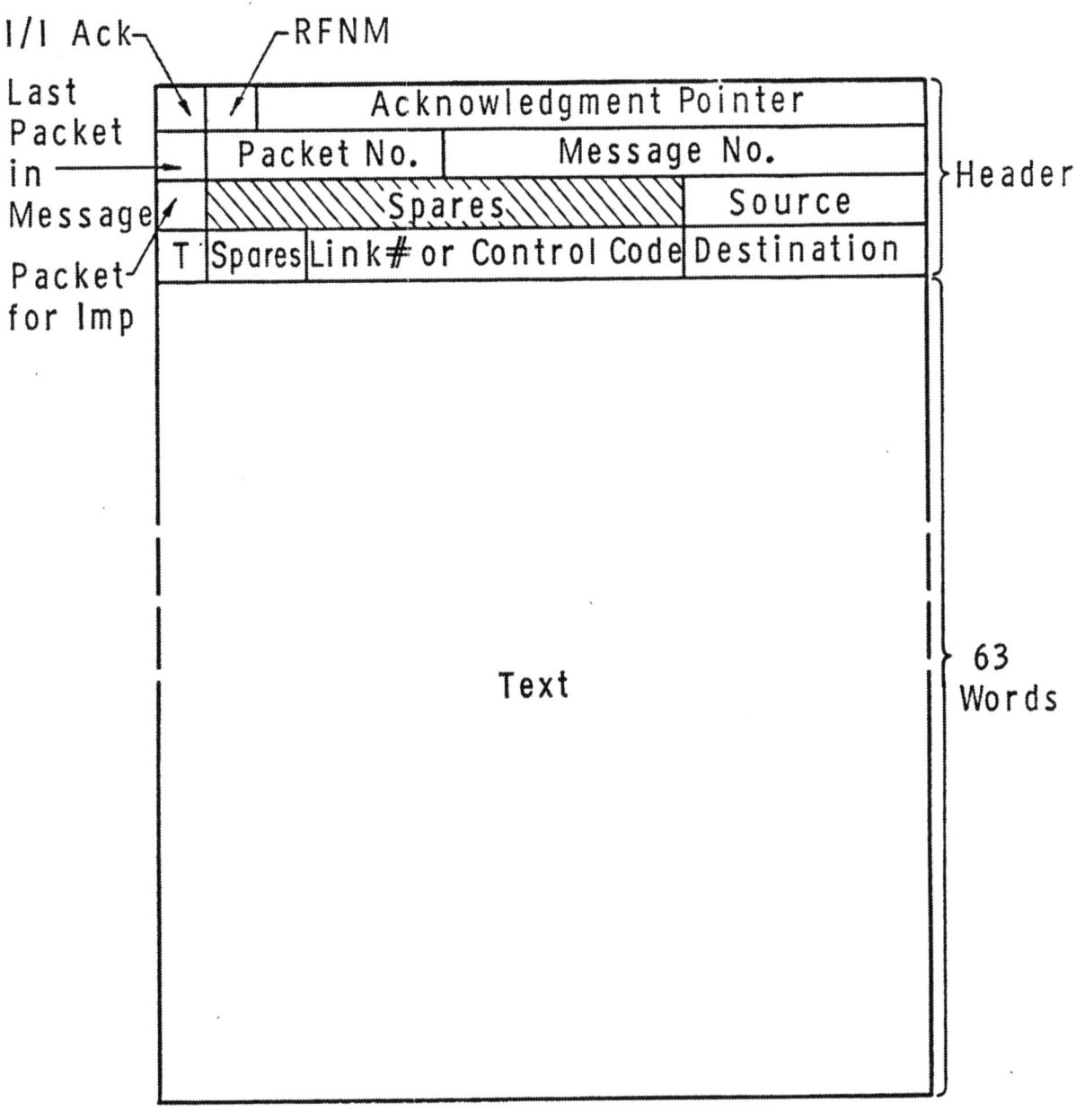

FIG. 5 ORIGINATING IMP PACKET STRUCTURE.

```
      S S D S                    D E C C C S S
··· Y Y L T    Header    Text    L T C C C Y Y ···
    N N E X_____E X 1 2 3 N N
```

FIG. 6 COMMUNICATION LINE PACKET FORMAT.

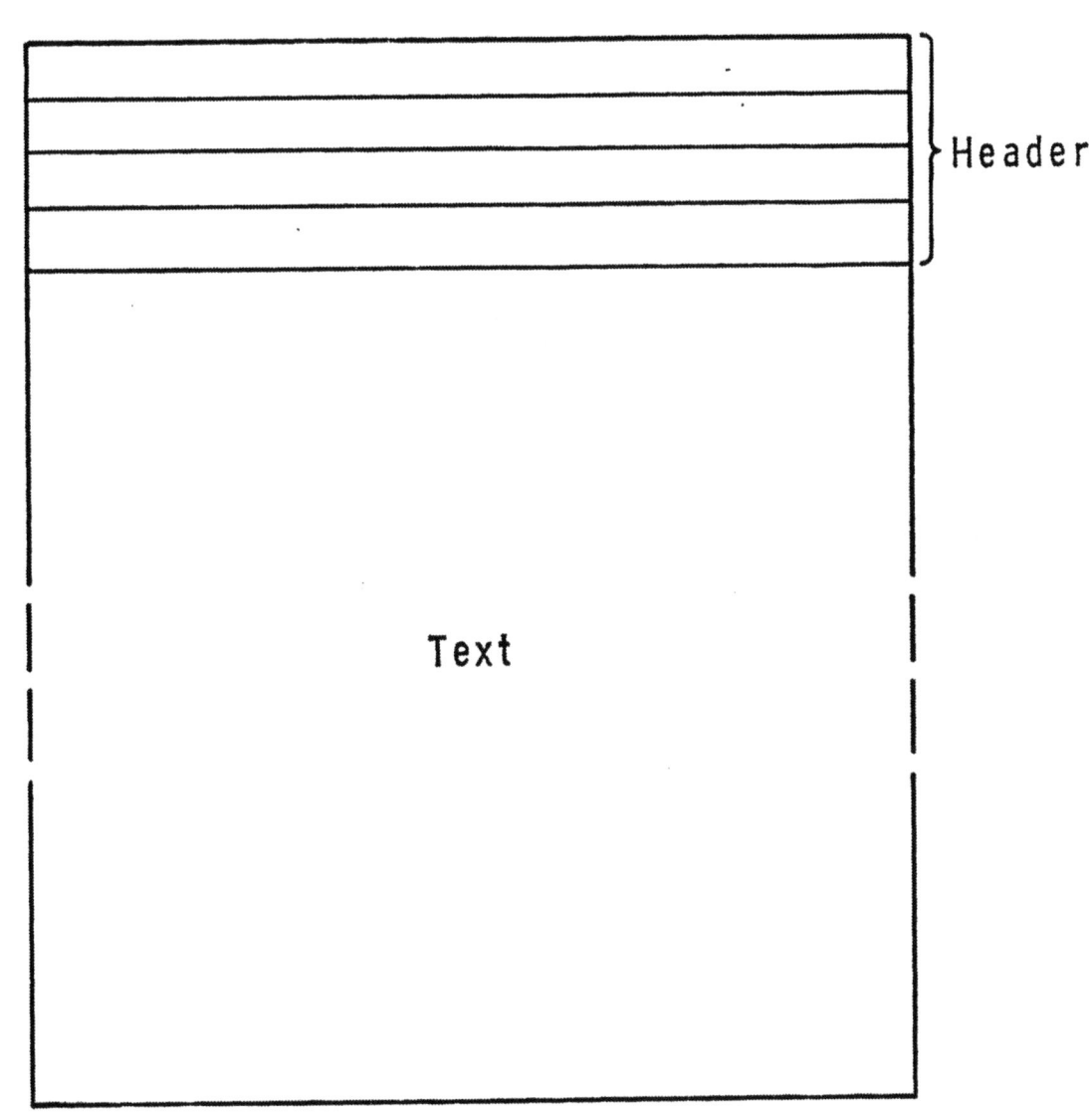

FIG. 7   PACKET FORMAT AS RECEIVED FROM MODEM INTERFACE.

If the receiving IMP is not the final destination, the header and the following text is fed to the appropriate output channel hardware. The channel hardware recomputes 24 parity check digits and appends these as described earlier, together with the DLE STX and the DLE ETX.

Eventually, the packet will arrive at the destination IMP. In fact, eventually all the packets of the message will arrive at the destination IMP, although not necessarily in the order of transmission.

The destination IMP sorts received packets according to the link identification as specified in the header. When all packets of the message have arrived, it delivers them in the proper order to its Host.

Packets within a given message are numbered sequentially by the transmitting IMP in the second word of the header and the last packet is specially marked by an identifying bit in the same word. This allows the receiving IMP to determine the order of the packets and to know when all packets have been received.

The receiving IMP strips off the header from each packet before sending it on to the Host. Furthermore, 16 bits are sent to the Host preceding the text of the first packet. The Host network program uses these bits to identify the link in sorting incoming messages. The format for these 16 bits is shown in Fig. 8.

Thus, the complete message is finally delivered to the destination Host in the same form as it left the transmitting Host, with the source in place of the destination in the Host information.

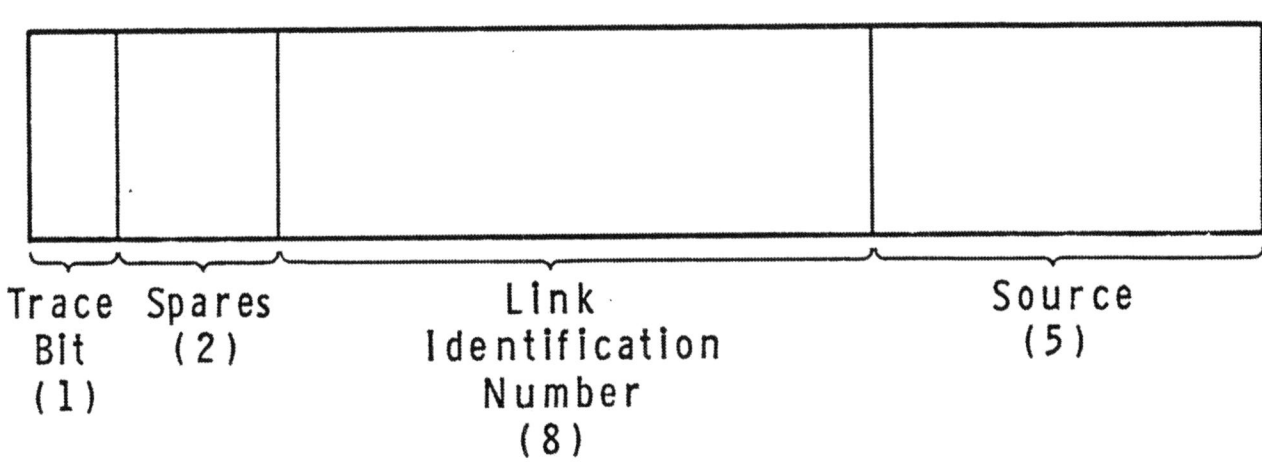

FIG. 8   IMP-TO-HOST INFORMATION FORMAT.

E. Acknowledgment Procedures

We now discuss two kinds of messages which will be used to control flow in the network: "IMP-to-IMP acknowledgments," and end-to-end "Requests For Next Message."

1. IMP-to-IMP acknowledgment of packets

The process of communicating a message from the source to the destination IMP uses the store and forward services of intermediate IMPs. As a packet moves from one IMP to the next, it is stored in each IMP until a positive IMP-to-IMP acknowledgment message is returned from the succeeding IMP. This ackowledgment indicates that the packet was received without error and was accepted. The acknowledgment is returned over the same line on which the packet arrived. A 14 bit acknowledgment pointer, containing the memory address of the first word of the transmitted packet, is included in the header of the packet to simplify the process of releasing that packet when acknowledged. (The packet identity data are checked before releasing the packet; the acknowledgment pointer simply avoids searching.)

To send an acknowledgment of a received packet, an IMP simply returns a packet (without text) whose header is an exact copy of the header of the received packet, but with the first bit of the first word changed to a one. This bit is called the IMP-to-IMP acknowledgment bit and is the first item sensed by the IMP program upon receipt of every packet. (The source and destination do not apply in the usual way to the acknowledgment message itself.)

Once an IMP has accepted a packet and returned a positive acknowledgment, it hangs on to that packet tenaciously until it, in turn, receives an acknowledgment. Under no other circumstances (except Host or IMP malfunction) will an IMP discard a packet after it has generated a positive acknowledgment. However, an IMP is always free to discard a packet by simply not returning a positive acknowledgment. It may do this for any of several reasons: the packet may have been received in error, the IMP may be busy, the IMP buffer storage may be full, and so forth.

Packets which are not recognized by the receiving channel hardware, which incur errors in transmission, or which are not accepted for whatever reason, are not acknowledged. At the transmitting IMP, the situation is readily detected by the absence of a returned acknowledgment within a reasonable time interval. Such packets are simply retransmitted.

Acknowledgments are themselves not acknowledged, although of course they are error checked in the usual fashion. Loss of an acknowledgment results in the eventual retransmission of the packet. The resulting duplication is sorted out at the destination IMP by use of the message number and packet number in the header.

There are no negative acknowledgments in our proposed design. They cannot be relied on to induce retransmission. If a negative acknowledgment is lost, one must resort to a time out procedure, in which case, the negative acknowledgment becomes redundant. Since the time out procedure must, therefore, always be used, we include it in our design.

2. Request-For-Next-Message (RFNM)

A central concern of network protocol is the problem of congestion at a destination IMP. This congestion must be reflected back into corrective quenching of the flow toward that point from other parts of the net. Otherwise, it would give rise to the discard of packets at the destination, blockage of those packets at the contiguous IMPs and the congestion would rapidly propogate back through the network. If the sources of packets for that destination continue sending, this congestion would rapidly affect the flow of other messages within the net.

There are at least two kinds of quenching which could be adopted.

1) We could limit the *degree* of congestion of remote IMPs that can be caused by any particular congested Host or link. For example, if each IMP only accepted, say, two messages for any given destination, the congestion would be limited to that amount and, eventually, the source would be unable to transmit additional new packets toward the troublesome destination.

2) We could try to limit congestion at the source directly by shutting off any new packets directed toward the troublesome destination. This action could be accomplished in either of two ways: a control message could be dispatched when congestion actually has occurred, or successive transmissions could routinely require a "clear-to-send" indication from the destination.

Although we have tried to avoid control messages in our design wherever possible, we decided in this case initially to use the control message technique. *We propose to avert congestion, by only allowing a source IMP to send one message at a time over a given link.* After sending a message over a link, a source IMP must delay sending the next message until a "Request for next message over link X" (RFNM) packet is end-to-end returned from the destination IMP. (Note that all packets of a single message, and/or messages over different links between the same two Hosts, may be sent into the net without delay.) The RFNM is passed along to the Host, who may use it to schedule the servicing of links. This technique only quenches individual links and therefore a limit is placed on the total number of links which a transmitting IMP will accept from its Host.

This technique has several important advantages and two disadvantages. The advantages are:

1) The demand for reassembly storage at the destination IMP for use by a given link is limited to eight packets.

2) When congestion occurs, flow is *automatically* quenched without any control messages. If source IMPs do *not* get new RFNM's, they do *not* send new messages.

3) Since the flow is quenched at the source, large numbers of packets from a given link neither enter the net nor flow about the net trying to get to the congested destination. Thus, congestion of other parts of the net by a single link is avoided.

Obviously, the main disadvantage is that waiting for RFNM packets may reduce the effective rate over a given single link. We have examined this disadvantage and have decided that it is not serious, for the following reasons:

1) Depending upon the number of active links, there may or may not be a reduction of the effective rate between two Hosts. When several links are established in a given Host computer, the messages will be time multiplexed. The RFNM delay in that case may already naturally appear in the system.

2) Since the message length will probably be bi-modal (very short or very long) and since very short packets are probably generated by humans, the RFNM delay is insignificant for processes at human rates. For very long messages, in the worst case of no time multiplexing and an unoccupied line, we estimate the reduction in effective rate to be only 30%.

A second disadvantage is the increase in number of control messages. Since RFNM's are very short, however, we feel that this effect is also not serious.

The use of an RFNM control message is a very clean, simple, and positive way to avoid some nasty and confusing problems. We are not fully satisfied that the doctrine is optimum, but, so far, we have been unable to see a clearly superior alternative. We therefore propose to use RFNM control of congestion in the initial design. During the implementation and testing, we will continue to consider this issue in an attempt to determine whether other alternatives appear to be more advantageous.

F. Examples of Message Flow

The chart on the following pages shows the flow of packets involved in transmitting a message from one Host to another. The

EVENT				STATE OF THE NETWORK				
Comments	Packet	From	To	h1	i1	i2	i3	h3
Host 1 has two packets for Host 3				21				
	1	h1	i1	2	1			
	1	i1	i3	2	1		1	
	2	h1	i1		21		1	
Acknowledgment returned	1a	i3	i1		2		1	
	2	i1	i3		2		21	
	2a	i3	i1				21	
	12	i3	h3				r	21
RFNM goes back to h1	r	i3	i1		r		r	
RFNM also acknowledged	ra	i1	i3		r			
	r	i1	h1	r				
Host 1 has two packets for Host 3				21				
	1	h1	i1	2	1			
	2	h1	i1		21			
	1	i1	i3		21		1	
Packet 1 acknowledgment lost	1a	i3	i1		21		1	
	2	i1	i3		21		21	
	2a	i3	i1		1		21	
Packet 1 rerouted*	1	i1	i2		1	1	21	
	1a	i2	i1			1	21	**
Packet 1 arrives second time	1	i2	i3			1	21	
	1a	i3	i2				21	
	12	i3	h3				r	21
	r	i3	i1		r		r	
	ra	i1	i3		r			
	r	i1	h1	r				

24

EVENT				STATE OF THE NETWORK				
Host 1 has two packets for Host 3				21				
	1	h1	i1	2	1			
Error on line (i.e., Packet 1 does not get to i3)								
	1	i1	i3	2	1			
Packet 1 rerouted*	1	i1	i2	2	1	1		
	2	h1	i1		21	1		
	2	i1	i3		21	1	2	
	2a	i3	i1		1	1	2	
	1a	i2	i1			1	2	
	1	i2	i3			1	12	
	1a	i3	i2				12	
Packets 1 & 2 get sorted	12	i3	h3			r		21
	r	i3	i1		r		r	
	ra	i1	i3		r			
	r	i1	h1	r				

LEGEND:

21 = 12 =	Packet 1 and Packet 2
1	Packet 1
2	Packet 2
1a	Packet 1 acknowledgment
2a	Packet 2 acknowledgment
h1	Host 1
i3	IMP 3
r	Ready for next message
ra	RFNM acknowledgment

*A time out period elapses before Packet 1 is rerouted. In the third example, other events which are not shown (because they are irrelevant for this example) prevent Packet 2 from being transferred from Host 1 to IMP 1 during this interval.

**In this example, the duplicate of Packet 1 merely overlays the one in IMP memory, effectively deleting it. The reassembled message could have entered the Host any time in the bracketed interval, before the arrival of the duplicate packet. In this case, the message number of the duplicate allows it to be discarded.

packets of the message, the acknowledgment packets, and the ready for next message packet are indicated assuming that the message being transmitted contains two packets.

The chart includes three examples: in the first, transmission is completed without any problem; in the second, an IMP-to-IMP acknowledgment for one packet is lost; and in the third, a packet encounters difficulty due to line error. Although the events within the examples are ordered, we emphasize that most of the events occur asynchronously and could be ordered in many other ways. Equal time does not pass between events.

The relevant portion of the network assumed for the examples is:

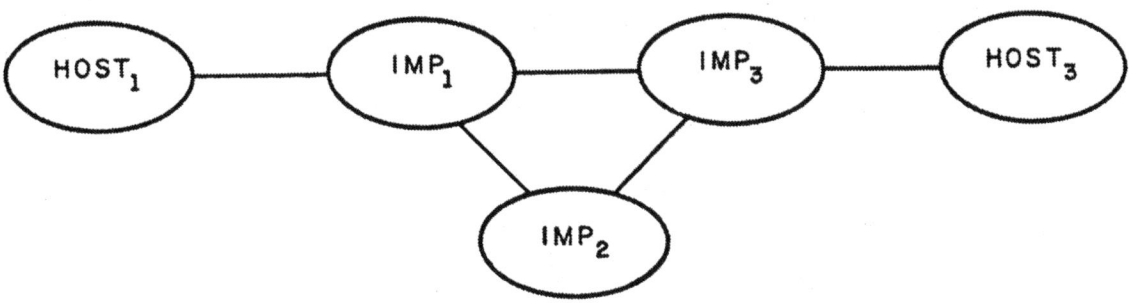

G. Word Length Mismatch

We discuss two aspects of word length mismatch: first, the obvious need for formatting that occurs between computers of different word length; and second, since mismatched words may lead to messages that end in the middle of words, the need for marking the exact beginning and ends of a message to permit unambiguous recognition.

There are several logical ways in which the reformatting of a word length mismatch might conceivably be handled. One may decide upon a word-by-word algorithm, where transfers from long to short machines involve truncation, and where transfers from short to long machines deposit a partial word. Unfortunately, there are many slightly different ways to do this and, worse, it is very undesirable in many applications. A second possibility is to list a number of kinds of reformatting and have a given message carry a code for the required type of reformatting. We feel that such a plan would be unreasonable for a 19 node net. Finally, one may beg the question and just send a bit stream, leaving to the individual Hosts the task of reformatting.

We have decided to adopt almost this latter position. Our design guarantees that between Hosts of identical word length the natural word boundaries are preserved. (This is not as easy as it sounds.) But, reformatting in general will be initially left to the Hosts. At a later time, the IMP program might be used to alleviate further this set of problems.

The second problem is that of recognizing the end of a message at the receiving Host. There are two general solutions to this, one of which is to locate the last bit in the message by counting from the beginning (using either a transmitted count or an agreed upon fixed value). The other general solution requires that the ends be marked in an unambiguous way. We have chosen the latter scheme, which marks the end of the message by appending a "one" followed by zeroes after the last bit in the message. This process is called *padding* and is accomplished by the hardware in the HOST/IMP interfaces. The receiving Host can therefore identify the end of the message.

As a message passes from the transmitted Host to its IMP, the hardware appends a one to the bit string when it receives the end of message signal. This bit may fall, in general, in any position of an IMP word somewhere in the last packet. The hardware then fills any remaining bits of this word with trailing zeros. The format of the last packet of a message as it thus appears in the IMP memory is shown in Fig. 9.

The packet appears in the destination IMP in exactly the same format.

As the last packet is serially shifted into the Host through the interface, the last bit from the IMP (which in our example is the fifth trailing zero in the padding) will fall, in general, somewhere in the middle of the receiving Host's final word. The remaining bits in this word are filled in by the Host's special interface hardware with additional trailing zeros. (Note that a one is purposely omitted here.) Thus the packet appears in the receiving Host with a one immediately following the last bit in the message, followed by a string of zero or more trailing zeros that terminate at a Host word boundary. The last word in the receiving bit stream does not necessarily contain the last bit in the message, as it may contain nothing but padded zeros.

Another occasion for inserting a form of marking data arises at the beginning of a message. The transmitting Host, in general, arranges that the text of a message begins at a word boundary. Since the network protocol requires the first 16 bits of a message to contain Host information, there will thus, in general, be a gap between the end of that identification and the beginning

Report No. 1763 Bolt Beranek and Newman Inc

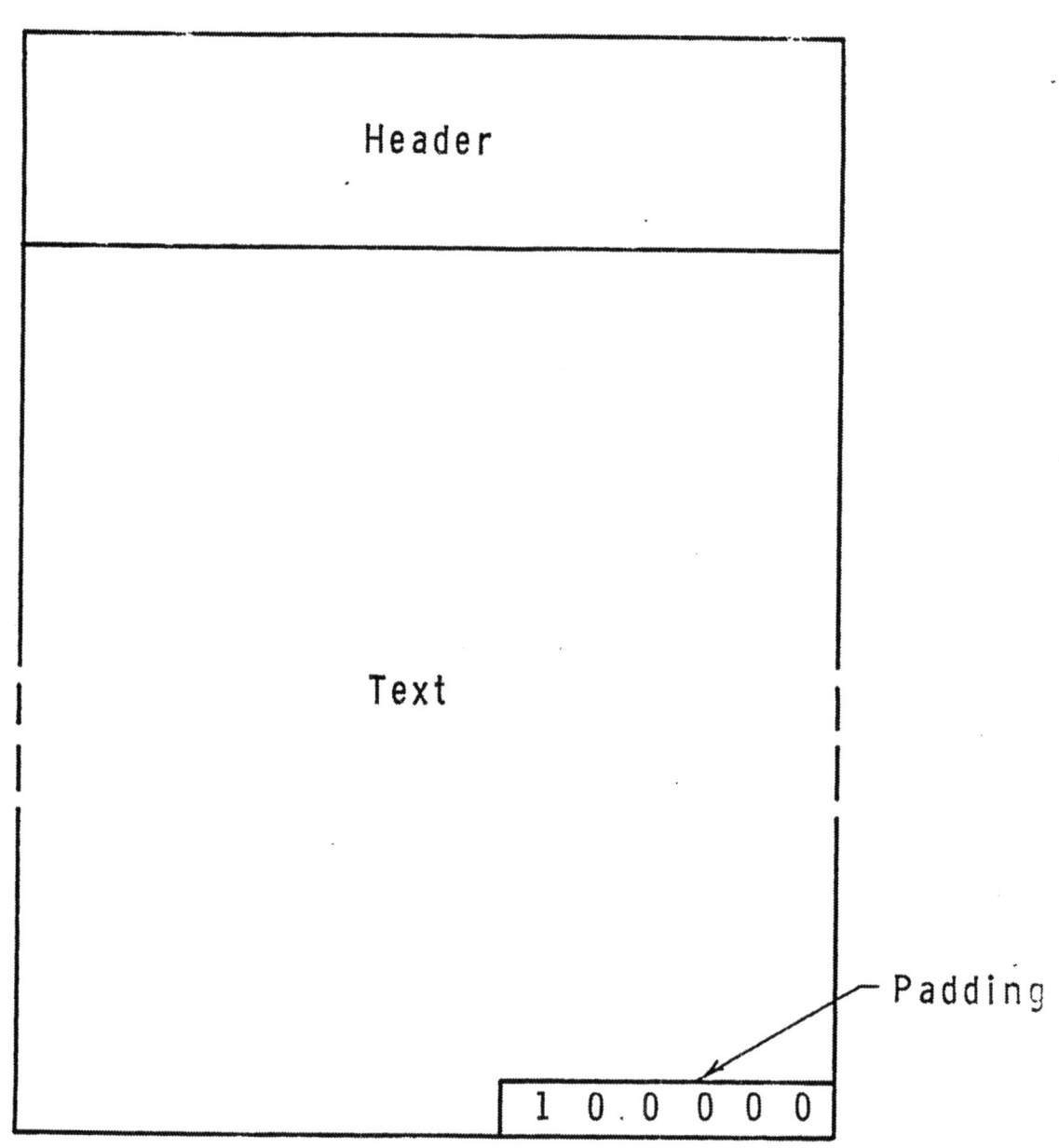

FIG. 9 FORMAT OF LAST PACKET OF A MESSAGE.

of the text. This gap is preserved in transmission to the destination Host and must be marked in a way which the destination Host can recognize as not forming part of the message. This *marking* must be inserted by the transmitting Host's software, and consists of a one preceding the first bit of the text and, in turn, preceded by a zero or more zeros to fill up the gap.

In Fig. 10 we illustrate one complete set of Host and IMP buffers, corresponding to a message of slightly under two full packets. We have selected in our example a 22 bit source Host word length and a 20 bit destination Host. We have specifically indicated both the padding and the marking in the figure.

H. Hardware Description and Interface Operation

A block diagram of the IMP computer and its interfaces to the Host and phone line modems is shown in Fig. 11. The area between the heavy vertical lines shows the IMP system itself; the area to the left is specialized Host equipment; the area to the right is phone line equipment. There are from one to six full-duplex IMP/MODEM interface units and one (or optionally two) HOST/IMP interface unit. The DMC provides the only direct access to and from memory, other than that for the CPU itself. The functioning of these units is described briefly in this section.

The IMP/MODEM Interface Unit is full duplex. It serializes and deserializes data for the Modem to and from memory. In the absence of outgoing messages, it loads a continuous string of SYN characters onto the line. It does special formatting for output, and character sensing for the beginning and end of input

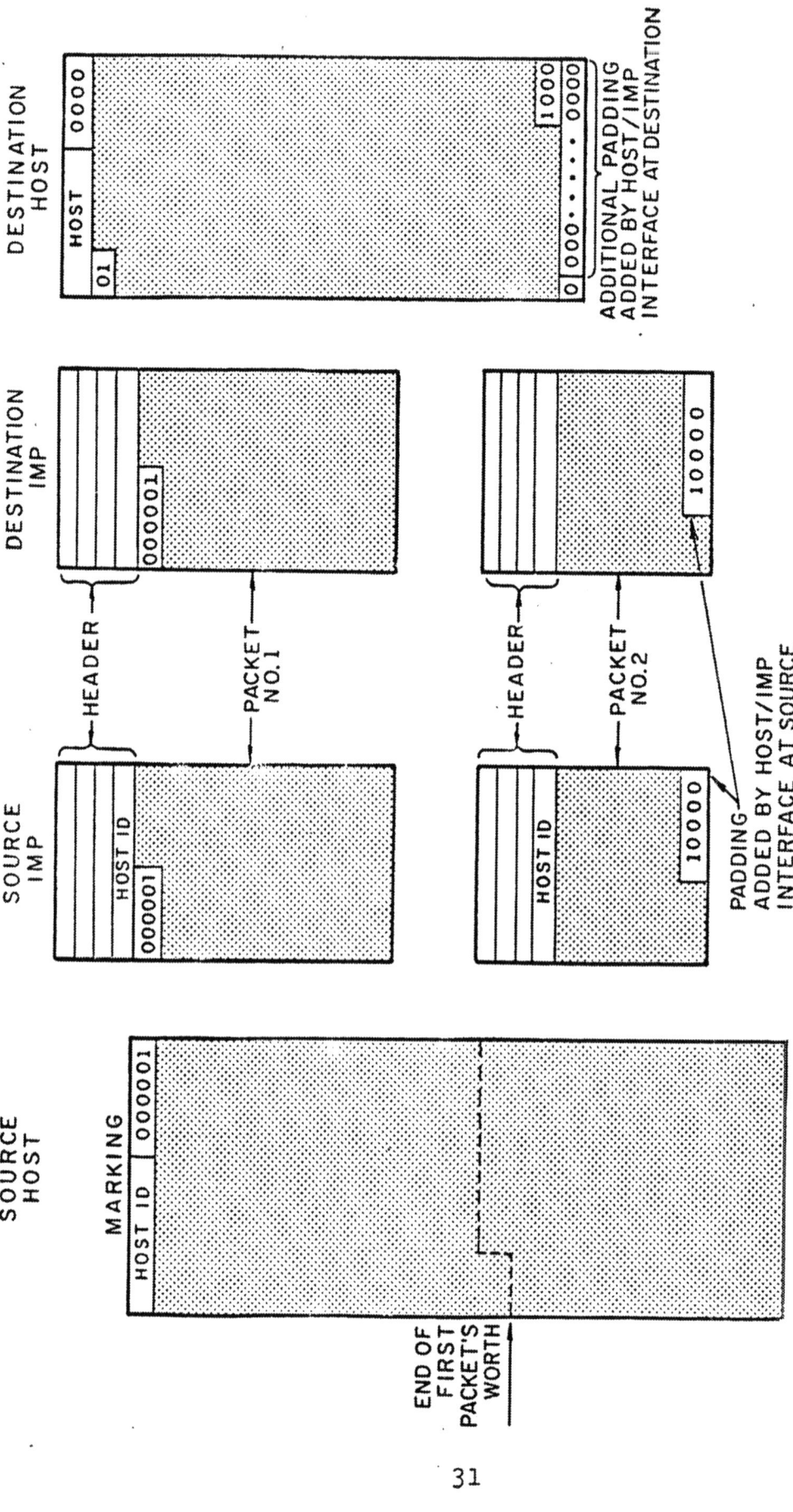

FIG. 10 HOST AND IMP BUFFER FORMAT FOR A TWO-PACKET MESSAGE.

Report No. 1763

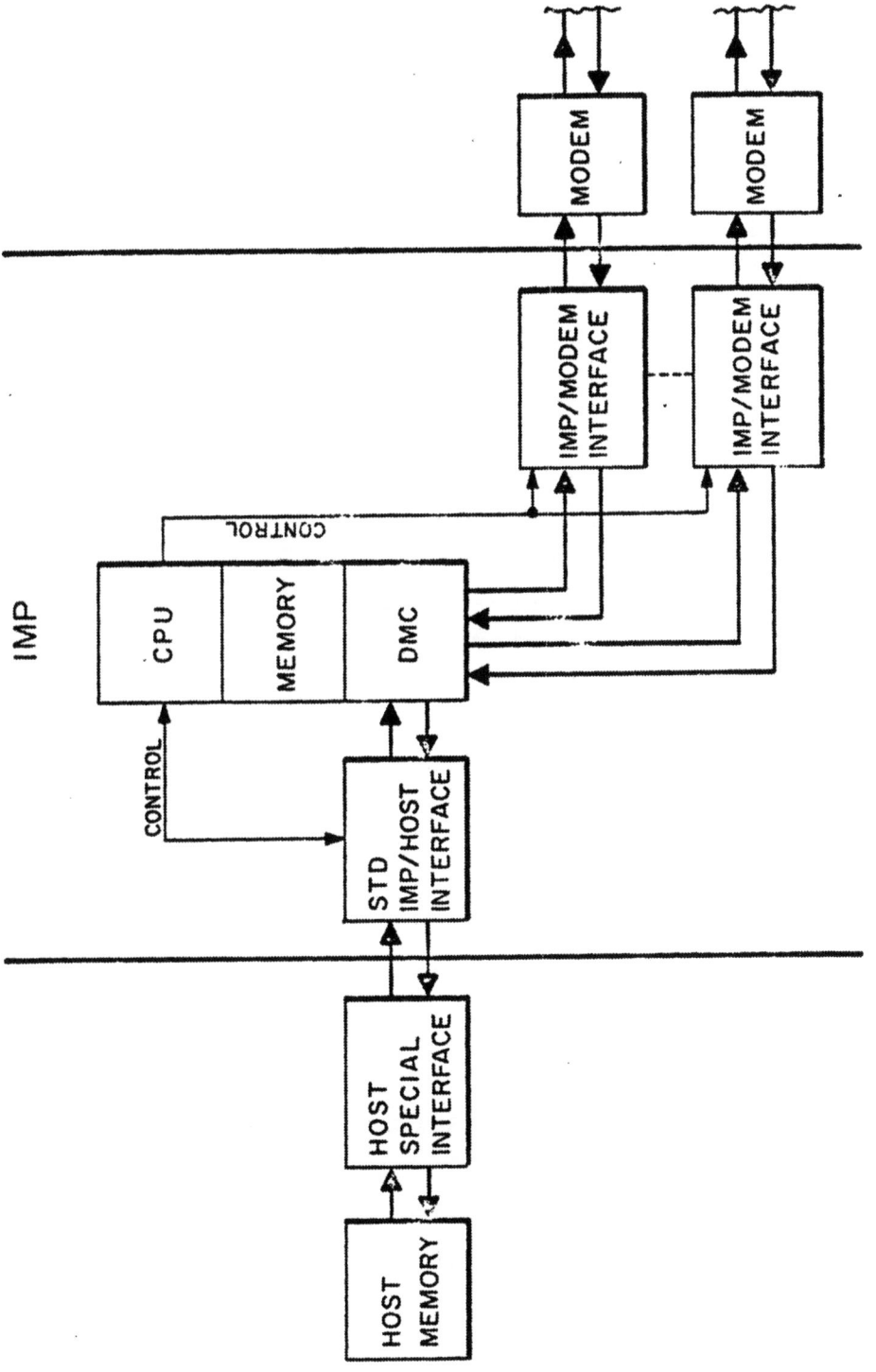

FIG. 11 GENERAL VIEW OF A TYPICAL IMP SYSTEM.

messages. It includes construction and testing of parity check digits and fault detection and reporting. Its timing is controlled primarily by the Modem.

The standard HOST/IMP Interface Unit is full duplex and passes messages bit-serially to and from the Host special interface. It also deserializes and serializes words to and from the IMP memory. Communication across the interface with the Host is asynchronous to allow for maximum flexibility.

The relative-time clock is a 16-bit counter indexed every 20 μs and may be read into the Accumulator. The full clock count repeats approximately every 1.3 sec and an Interrupt is generated on the turnover of an appropriate high order bit. This bit is selected to give an interrupt frequency which is convenient for use by the program in performing time outs for retransmission of packets.

1. The HOST/IMP interface unit

There is no general rule whereby the HOST/IMP Interface Unit can determine in which direction (Host-to-IMP or IMP-to-Host) information will next have to be processed. The equipment must therefore be capable of starting a transmission in either direction. Transmission requests arrive asynchronously for the two directions and, rather than trying to sort them out for processing over a half duplex channel, a full duplex channel is provided. The primary advantage of this is simplicity and it also provides the capability for concurrent transmission in both directions. The HOST/IMP Interface is thus divided logically into two parallel channels — one for either direction — as indicated in the following figure.

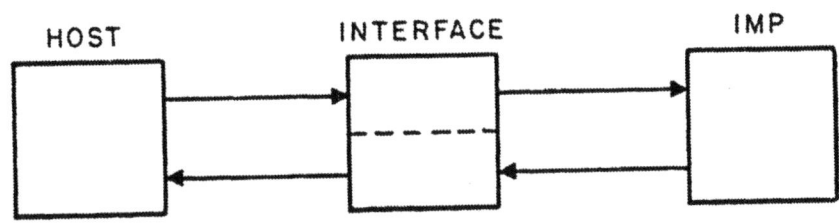

Because Hosts vary in word length, signal forms, and logic for receiving and transmitting information, we further subdivide "vertically" the HOST/IMP Interface, into two separate units:

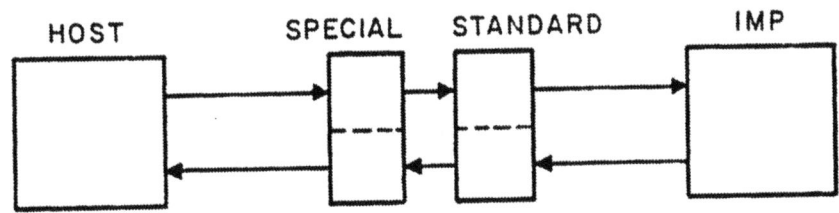

The right hand Unit contains logic that is standard for all HOST/IMP Interfaces. The left hand unit contains the special equipment for interfacing directly to the particular Host. Standard signals pass between these two halves; all special logic and signal adjustments (which vary from Host to Host) are handled in the left hand portion. Power for the standard unit is directly connected to the IMP's power — i.e., its power is turned on whenever IMP power is turned on. Power for the special unit is derived from the Host power system (or a separate supply) and will probably have a separate on/off switch.

Each participating Host will be responsible for the design and building of its own special unit that will mate to the standard unit according to fixed rules. In general, this special unit serves to serialize and deserialize information in whatever manner best suits the particular Host. The IMP-to-Host section of the special unit must perform the "padding with zeros" function discussed earlier.

Two levels of hardware handshaking take place between a Host and its IMP. At the meta-level, each needs to know whether the other is turned on and operational. The standard unit provides to the special unit (and it in turn to the Host in whatever way is appropriate) a signal which indicates that IMP power is up and that the IMP program has turned on a Ready indicator. The special unit presents a similar Host ready signal to the standard unit, and thence to the IMP. Each unit automatically monitors the readiness of the other, and if the other's readiness state changes, the unit will notify its parent computer; in the case of the IMP, by an interrupt. Thus, for example, should the Host computer fail or drop power, the IMP will be interrupted and can take appropriate action. Only when the Host returns to Ready, which requires not only reinstating power but also program turn on of the Host ready indicator in the special unit, will communications with the Host be re-established. Under normal operation, when either computer detects that the other has become ready, it will prepare to receive information. Thus, with both Host and IMP ready, each will be waiting for the other to transmit. As soon as information is provided by either one, it will flow across the Interface.

Thus, when the Host ready indicator comes on, the operational IMP program prepares to receive from its Host by setting up a pair of pointers used by the standard Host-to-IMP interface channel of the DMC. These pointers delineate a packet-sized buffer in the IMP memory. After they have been set, the IMP program issues an ACCEPT* command to the interface. Thereafter, when information becomes available from the Host, the standard interface unit takes it in serially and forms it into 16 bit-IMP words in an input buffer register. These words are stored into successive locations of the IMP memory buffer until the buffer area becomes full or until the message end is indicated by the Host. When either of these happens, information flow ceases and the IMP program is interrupted. In the case where the Host message ends, the hardware appends a trailing "one" followed by any "zeros" necessary to pad out a full 16-bit word. The interrupt routine will normally reset the pointers to another buffer location and restart the interface with a new ACCEPT command. Serial transmission makes the standard unit independent of Host word size, and requires only one data line driver and receiver. The interface unit is designed to accept bits from the Host at 1 MHz maximum rate (5 MHz circuits are used). The Host, of course, can slow this rate by controlling the flow of bits. Memory references in both computers will slow the rate well below the maximum.

When the IMP has set up memory pointers and is ready to transmit a packet into the Host, it starts the transmission via a GO command. The first word is then loaded from the IMP memory into the interface and the Host unit takes the bits serially. Each time 16 bits have been taken in, a new word is fetched from the IMP memory. When the buffer has been emptied, the program is

---

*Control commands to devices are delivered by execution of assigned OCP instructions. These instructions deliver appropriate control signals.

interrupted and normally prepares for the next transmission to the Host if any more buffers are waiting. When the IMP is ready to transmit the last packet of a message, it executes a special END command before starting the transmission with the GO. In this case, when the last bit of the packet is taken into the special Host unit, an end-of-message signal is also sent to the unit. This causes the special Host unit to pad the remaining bits of its final word with zeros before passing it to the Host with the "that's all" indication.

2. The IMP/MODEM interface unit

Each IMP connects to several (up to 6) telephone line modems each of which has a separate IMP/MODEM Interface unit. This unit converts outgoing information into serial form and assembles incoming serial information into 16-bit words which it places in the IMP memory. It also computes 24 parity check bits, which it transmits at the end of a packet and checks upon receiving a packet. As shown in Fig. 12, a modem consists of two logical halves, each producing clock signals and containing a single data line, one in and one out. The interface unit correspondingly contains two logically distinct sections, one dedicated to transferring output from the IMP to the modem and the other dedicated to transferring in the other direction. In the absence of outgoing messages, the output section sends a continuous stream of SYN characters to the modem. Fig. 13 shows a typical packet buffer in the IMP memory from both the output and input points of view. In this presentation, only those elements of particular concern to the hardware are separated out. Thus header and text are not distinguished.

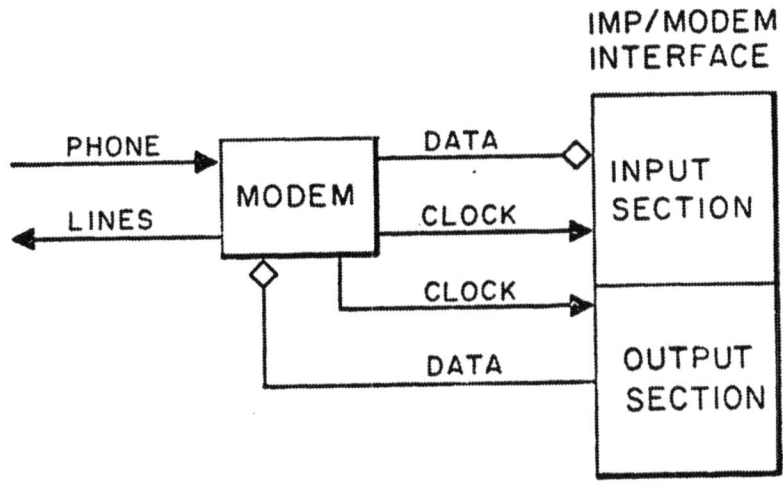

FIG. 12   LOGIC VIEW OF MODEM.

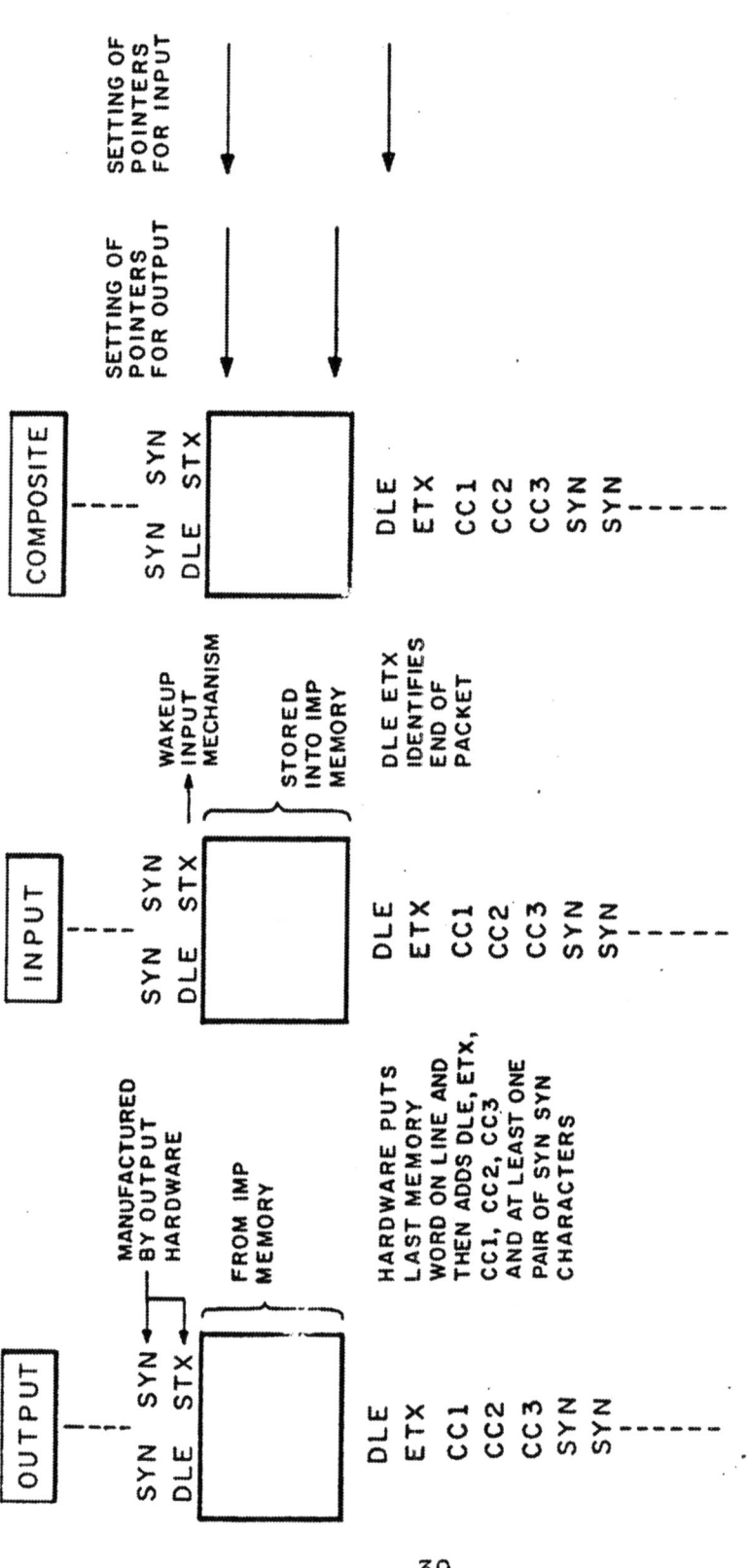

FIG. 13 PACKET BUFFER FORMAT.

After setting the output pointers, as shown, the IMP program notifies the output hardware that a packet is ready to be transmitted. The hardware then sends the character pair DLE STX and follows this with the data words taken from the IMP memory according to the pointers. When the DMC indicates that the entire packet has been sent, the hardware appends the character pair DLE ETX followed by the check digits and at least one pair of SYN characters. A string of SYN characters then follows until another transmission is initiated.

Additionally, the hardware monitors the data from memory for DLE characters and, upon finding one, immediately inserts another character, thus averting confusion resulting from a DLE within the packet. The receiving input unit deletes these extra DLEs. Of course, extra DLEs are not inserted with the hardware-generated DLEs.

The input hardware detects the DLE STX, which marks beginning of a message and loads into the IMP memory all characters between (but not including) the STX and the DLE of the final DLE ETX character pair. The three check digits which follow the DLE ETX are never brought into memory. Any error indicated by the parity check is signaled to the computer. Note that the STX is not itself fed into memory but serves only to cue the input hardware to the start of the packet on the line. The bottom input pointer points to *one location beyond* the point where the last data word of a maximum-sized legal packet would be put. Normally, the input hardware recognizes the end of input by spotting the DLE ETX at the end of the packet. To assure that, if it misses this, input does not proceed to flood the IMP memory, input is cut off if the allocated IMP buffer fills up —

i.e., if *one more* than the expected maximum number of words arrives in a packet. An error is indicated to the IMP program in this case. Since the receiving input unit recognizes when a packet begins and ends by the DLE STX and DLE ETX characters enclosing the packet, there is no possibility of confusing the start or end of a message since DLE STX or DLE ETX character pairs can never occur *within* a message without being preceded by another DLE. The receiving input unit deletes the extra DLE's.

J. Organization of IMP Storage

Message packets are read into buffers in IMP storage as we have already discussed. Each incoming packet is allocated one free buffer selected from a free buffer pool. Pointers are set by the CPU to the beginning and end of the buffer and an input transfer is enabled. When a packet is read into memory, an interrupt signals the program upon completion of the transfer. If an error is detected, the buffer is returned to the free buffer pool. The packet, in effect, is discarded, since the buffer is now free to be overwritten. Otherwise, the packet is assumed to be correct.

Within an IMP, a packet is never moved from one buffer to another. It is read into one location in memory with a set of input pointers and taken out of the same location with a set of output pointers.

Approximately six thousand words of memory will be occupied by programs and the remainder will be available for buffers and program expansion. Each of the buffers contains about 70 words.

One of these is a free word allocated at the end of the buffer to detect the case where the buffer is about to be overflowed, due to the loss of the end of message indication. An interrupt will be generated during input if the moving pointer ever coincides with a pointer to this last cell. Approximately two additional words at the beginning of each buffer are used for holding queue pointers as discussed below.

We distinguish between three types of packets in the IMP which we call store and forward packets, packets for the Host and packets for the IMP. A store and forward packet is one whose destination is another site. A packet for the IMP, defined implicitly, is handled by special IMP routines and does not require lengthy storage since the buffer is quickly released back into the free buffer pool.

The Host computer generates only store and forward packets or packets for its IMP. Packets that arrive over the communication lines may be either store and forward packets, packets for the Host, or packets for the IMP.

A packet for the Host computer may be a single packet message or part of a multiple packet message. Single packet messages, which are uniquely identified by the last-packet-in-message bit on packet number one, clearly require no reassembly and may be directly transmitted to the Host computer. When the first packet is received for a multiple packet message, seven additional buffers are removed from the free buffer pool and reserved. As each additional packet of this message arrives and is stored in a free buffer, one of the reserved buffers is released into the free buffer pool. When all packets of the message have been reassembled, the remaining unused reserved buffers are released and the complete message is sent to the Host. Waiting until the full message is assembled avoids the risk of typing up the channel to the Host in the middle of a message. The storage for these packets is called reassembly storage.

Each communication line has a buffer assigned to it which is unassigned upon receipt of an incoming error-checked packet, whereupon another buffer from the free buffer pool is assigned in its place.

A correctly received store and forward packet is placed on a queue for transmission over the first choice output communication line. An IMP with three communication lines has three such queues, one assigned to each line. Packets on each of the three queues are transmitted sequentially over the communication lines. There is also a similar queue for reassembled messages going to the Host.

We now discuss the maintenance of these queues. Upon arrival, each store and forward packet is placed at the end of a first choice queue which is determined from an entry in a routing table. Each queue is linked in the forward direction and three pointers into the queue are kept. These pointers locate the current service position on the queue, the last entry into the queue, and the position of the packet expected to be acknowledged next. In addition, the last packet in the queue is linked to the first packet, thus forming a circular queue. The last position on each circular queue is defined to be the position just behind the current service position.

There are certain packets which, upon arrival or generation, may be placed at the head of a queue at the current service position where they will be next in line for transmission. These may include all packets for IMPs and all short packets.

K. Buffer Congestion

We now discuss the subject of buffer congestion and the techniques that we have introduced to deal with it. We indicate the principle causes of buffer congestion, describe the kinds of difficulties which are caused by it and develop a number of simple strategies which either attempt to prevent buffer congestion from occurring or ensure the recovery from it.

Certain Host computers will be primary receivers of network messages and their corresponding IMPs will have a substantial portion of the buffer storage containing messages for the Host computer. Other IMPs will function essentially in the store and forward mode, containing significantly fewer messages for their own Host computers than for other IMPs in the network. IMPs such as these, which primarily store and forward messages, are critical links in the network. When they become congested, they affect the overall pattern of traffic flow.

An IMP is said to be congested whenever the contents of the free buffer pool falls below a level equal to the number of communication lines. There are several different causes of buffer congestion, the most serious of which is a malfunction. We discuss the effects of a malfunction later in the chapter. However, congestion can also occur during normal operation of the network due to transmission errors, line concentration, or reassembly.

Line errors may be expected to occur on the order of seconds apart. At 50,000 bits per second and line bit error probability of 10^{-5}, one error is expected every two seconds. However, the errors will undoubtedly be clustered so that the interval between error bursts will probably be over 10 seconds on the average. An IMP stores packets from the time they arrive until an acknowledgment is returned. Sufficient storage has been allocated to handle the reasonable peak loads of offered traffic and to allow for line errors.

Line concentration refers to the situation when messages arrive on several different communication lines and are intended for transmission over the same outgoing channel. Since a packet must be transmitted contiguously in time over a communication line, two packets cannot be simultaneously transmitted and therefore at least one of the packets must wait.

Buffer congestion may also occur if insufficient reassembly storage is available. For example, if 10 network users are logged into one system, all messages have 8 packets, and a buffer is 70 16-bit words, then 5K of core would be needed for reassembly alone, with all users simultaneously being reassembled. We may expect to be confronted from time to time with the situation where the IMP simply does not have enough buffers to do reassembly. Furthermore, if a Host computer does go down or if messages are fed to it over many links, the backup of packets into the rest of the network could cause the entire network to overload. The process of automatic rerouting which takes place when

45

messages fail to get through on a primary route (as discussed in the following section) will tend to alleviate this situation.

In Section E (above) we already discussed the use of RFNM's for averting congestion. We now discuss several more techniques designed for coping with buffer congestion. To prevent buffer congestion from affecting reassembly, we lock in (i.e., reserve) seven more buffers for reassembly at the destination IMP when the first packet of a message arrives. A reassembly packet is accepted only if the addition of the seven additional buffers will not trespass on the 25% minimum store and forward buffer space. Buffer storage is conceptually divided into two sections, one to hold messages to and from the Host computer and the other used for store and forward packets. There is no fixed allocation of buffers into one category or the other. The amount of storage allocated to each is adjusted to meet the network demands. However, some fixed minimum percentage of the total number of buffers is always reserved for store and forward traffic. That is, an IMP is never allowed to block network traffic by assigning all its buffers for reassembly packets and outgoing messages from its Host. The minimum number of buffers that must always be available to the rest of the network for store and forward packets is an IMP program parameter. Initially, we will dedicate at least one quarter of the IMP buffers for such store and forward packets.

L. Line Quality Determination and Rerouting

We define the *quality* (Q) of a line as the time varying relation of received acknowledgments of a line to the total number of packets requiring acknowledgment transmitted over the line. Thus, the quality is a simple and direct measure of transmission success on the line. The quality of a broken line will rapidly drop to a very low value. Similarly, the quality of a line to a congested IMP which does not regularly acknowledge packets will also drop. This quality factor is used in two ways: to detect difficulties with the functioning of a line for statistics gathering and trouble reporting, and *as a criterion for rerouting*. In addition to the line quality, there is an *a priori* weighting of the lines that reflects the desirability of using each line to reach a given destination. This weighting is designated by the letter K. The determination of K for each line to each destination is a complex judgmental matter, reflecting not only the topology of the net but also knowledge, as it is gained, about known average traffic patterns. Such information comes from human analysis of network performance. The values of K are thus selected in advance, loaded into the IMP as required, and kept in a routing table.

Unless a line is disabled, when a packet first arrives in an IMP, ready to be sent to some other IMP, the packet is placed on a queue for the line with largest value of K. The line quality is thus not normally used in the initial transmission, thereby guaranteeing that lines are tried frequently in order to maintain an up-to-date estimate of Q. Of course, routing for *retransmission* is based on both the line quality and the K factor.

Regular checks are made on the status of all entries in the queues as part of a time out procedure, in order to consider the possiblity of retransmission. The algorithm which selects packets for retransmission works as follows: Each buffer on a queue has a "sent" bit which is set to one when the contents of the buffer have been transmitted. The bit is reset to zero if the buffer is to be retransmitted. During each time out procedure, a check is made to determine if a time out has occurred since the packet was last transmitted. If the packet was transmitted but has not timed out, the sent bit is left on. If the packet has timed out, a calculation is made to determine the most desirable route and the packet is routed accordingly. The calculation will be a simple function of the line quality and the preassigned weighting of the line.

We have not attempted to specify the alternate routine algorithm in greater detail at this time for two primary reasons. First, any reasonable algorithm will perform acceptably in the initial net since the connectivity is so limited. Secondly, we did not want to include as part of our proposed design, an *ad hoc* solution to a problem upon which the network performance will be critically dependent under heavy load. We plan to provide an algorithm which is adaptive, free from recurring loops, and reflects our best judgment on this matter.

We have designed and operated a network simulation program on our 940 computer. The program drives a CRT display that may be used to assist in the testing and simulation of various algorithms. This simulation will be a valuable instrument in studying improved routine algorithms. The algorithms can then be tested by actual network experimentation.

Report No. 1763　　　　　　　　　　　　　Bolt Beranek and Newman Inc

M. Network Introspection

As the network operates to service Hosts, it must monitor its own performance to detect faults, take corrective actions as required, and report on its own activity to various points in the network. The reporting function includes urgent messages about malfunctions, prompt comments about changing conditions, and more leisurely periodic summaries of statistical performance. In order to permit such monitoring, fault recovery, and reporting by the program, adequate "test points" must be built into the hardware and the operational software. In addition, decisions must be made as to where reports of various types should be sent: reports might go to a local Host, or to a "special" IMP run by the network contractor, or to ARPA, or to a particular special Host, or to some combination of these places. We do not feel that the choice of destinations is a crucial issue at this time, and for purposes of discussion we have assumed the existance of a "network measurement center" (NMC). This NMC is presumed to be a particular interested Host.

In the remainder of this section, we first discuss detection, reporting, and recovery from three kinds of faults, namely, Host faults, line faults and IMP faults. We then discuss the techniques to be used for gathering detailed information about network performance, and the reporting of that performance; finally we summarize the kinds of abnormal messages which will be generated in these processes.

1. Faults

1.1 Host Faults

If a Host actually goes off the air, either voluntarily or through a traumatic failure such as loss of power, a special Host ready indicator which resides in the IMP/Host Interface will be turned off. Any change of state of this indicator produces an interrupt of the IMP; thus, the IMP program may note the change and take action. If the shutdown was voluntary, the IMP may have been notified previously and therefore suitably modified its tables. If no prior notification has been received, the IMP informs the current remote users. A message saying "My Host is down" will be sent to users who try to login at unavailable Hosts. The normal result of a traumatic Host failure is not only the immediate quenching of additional messages from the sources, but a discarding of all packets in the net addressed to that Host upon their arrival at the destination IMP. When a Host comes back up after a down period, the ready status will change to on and the IMP will note this change. Test messages may also be used in this case to confirm proper operation of the channel to the Host.

A more difficult case occurs when the Host fails in some way which does not change its ready status, but which nonetheless destroys its ability to interact with the network. Such failures, for example, may be caused by software bugs, or minor hardware transients, which can cause programs to loop. In order for the IMP to detect such a situation, it will keep an indicator of the quality of communication with the Host. If normal IMP-Host message flow is greatly diminished for some comparatively long time, the IMP will assume that the Host is down and will take the same action as if the ready indicator had been turned off. To determine when the Host is again available involves the use of test messages from the IMP to the Host. The outage of the Host, even for extended periods, does not in any way affect the IMPs role in storing and forwarding other network messages.

1.2 Line Failures

The normal operational IMP program maintains up-to-date indications of the quality of every incoming and outgoing line. If the estimate of quality on a given line falls below a preset clip level (a program parameter), the IMP will inform local personnel by changing lights in the lights register, and will inform the NMC by producing a trouble report. This provides a relatively straightforward and positive procedure for keeping track of line troubles.

Checks of the lines will also be done during initialization of the IMP program, and also during scheduled and unscheduled maintenance of the line. A special IMP program will be able to cross patch each line under program control and test the Modem and Interfaces of each line. It is conceivable that such cross-patch testing could be built into the operational program at a later stage in the development of the network, but we do not plan to include it initially.

1.3 IMP Faults

Despite the extreme provisions for reliability built into the IMPs, faults will sometimes occur. Detection of these faults is necessary to ensure smooth operation of the network. In some cases (such as total failure), an IMP will be unable to detect trouble itself. Provision must be made for neighboring IMPs (which do detect such failure) to report this. Communication outside the network channel (e.g., by phone) will then be used to inform personnel at the site of the IMP of that IMP's malfunction.

On the other hand, the majority of IMP failures should be able to be detected at the IMP itself by making the operating program periodically reset a timing device. Failure to reset the timer before it times out will set a failure indicator.

This internal failure detector can communicate the failure to the failed IMP or to a maintenance person without resort to external communication. For this reason, we have included an internal failure detector utilizing a time-out period.

Having detected failure, there are several methods for implementating a restart. Certainly the simplest to implement at the outset is to arouse the Host operator with an alarm and allow him to load the system via the paper tape reader following the same *simple* procedure employed in start-up of new program versions. As the system evolves, automatic restart procedures could reduce the outage time caused by transient failure. Ideally, the IMP could restart automatically from an auxillary storage device capable of multiple restarts. Alternatively, one could restart by automatically reloading the IMP from its Host. (We do not favor involving the Host with this task.) Still another alternative is to reload one IMP from another by causing a loader to be put into operation in the failed IMP. This IMP, in turn, requests and checks the reloading of the operational program from a neighboring IMP.

We would tend to order these automatic restart alternatives on the basis of IMP autonomy and simplicity, and would thus tend to favor first an auxillary storage device, followed by restart from a neighboring IMP and, lastly, restart from the Host. The actual choice and implementation of automatic restart should be the subject of further study and experiment in the 4 node network. Initially, the IMPs should be restarted manually with paper tape following a hardware alarm. The 4 node IMP equipment will support experimental investigation of alternative automatic restart methods; the IMP will have a limited amount of protected memory and a suitable timer for this purpose.

An IMP which fails may be a critical node which cuts off some existing links. For example, a destination IMP failure cuts off all links to its Host. The network must respond appropriately to such an outage. All links through the IMP will quickly be blocked since no RFNM messages will get back to the sources. Packts trying to get through a down IMP will circulate in the system, trying to circumvent it. When the IMP comes back on the air, the messages will eventually reach the destination and be discarded.

Should an IMP be down for an extended period, some sort of mechanism is required to purge the system of undeliverable packets. We have not settled on a particular technique but have considered two possibilities. The first of these is to include in each packet a handover number that would increase on every IMP-to-IMP transfer and that would allow a discard of the packet when a (high) clip level is reached. An alternate approach is to have a Host generate special messages for this purpose.

2. Performance measurements

We propose two main techniques for gathering performance information on the operation of the network: (1) Regular measurement by each IMP of its internal performance; and transmission of that information on a periodic basis to the NMC and (2) the tracing of messages through the system, resulting in the generation of report packets about that message proceeding to the NMC for reconstruction of the message path.

a) Regular Data Gathering

Each IMP will include in its operational program a routine that will be run on a clock interrupt. Thus the program will run periodically independent of the load on the IMP at that time. This program will sample some program parameters and either save the values or running averages of these values. The following list provides examples:

1. Empty buffer count
2. Number of messages being reassembled
3. Queue length of output queues
4. Number of sent but not acknowledged buffers in each queue
5. Quality measures
6. Rate of inputs

The list of sample parameters will then be included in a special report message directed to the NMC. We believe that this regular technique of reporting will provide a comprehensive history of what the IMPs are doing. It naturally assumes some attention on the part of the NMC, but obviously remains a matter of choice.

b) Tracing

The other data gathering facility, which we believe will be exceptionally useful, we call tracing. A common notion in computer programming, tracing allows one to obtain either a small amount of information or a large amount of information as the trace proceeds. We believe that our network trace feature has the same extremely desirable flexibility.

Any or all messages may include a trace bit in the header. Messages with trace bits may be initiated by the NMC or by other Hosts. For example, trace bits could be put in some set fraction of each Host's messages. In fact, we can think of a number of techniques whereby trace bits could be added to messages on a sample basis. To give one more example, each IMP could be asked to include a trace bit in every mth IMP message. We believe this technique will permit occasional sampling or complete tracing of messages in the network.

When an IMP receives a message that includes a trace bit, it incurs the additional task of noting in detail how it handles that particular message. When the IMP has finally released that message, it must generate the special report about that message and send the report to the NMC. The NMC will thus receive a

55

sequence of report messages for each message that contains a trace bit. It should then be possible for the NMC to generate a good representation of the path taken by that message, or by a group of messages in the network.

3. <u>Summary of abnormal messages</u>

Results of the introspection discussed above are transmitted by "abnormal" messages that are generated by IMPs for these special purposes; these abnormal messages are not part of the normal flow of data between Hosts. We believe that there will be a large number of packets of this type, but it is impossible to list them now with any confidence. However, we can distinguish between several kinds of packets, and provide an initial estimate of what types might exist.

We group the class of special packets into three categories. The first category contains those packets which only cross IMP/MODEM Interfaces and contain all IMP-to-IMP messages. The second category contains those messages which only cross an IMP/HOST Interface. The third category defines messages which cross one HOST/IMP Interface and one or more IMP/MODEM Interfaces. (If two HOST/IMP Interfaces are crossed, the message is a Host-to-Host message and considered to be part of the Host protocol.)

We list some of the special messages in each of these three categories:

1. Across IMP/MODEM INTERFACES
   a. Query
   b. Response

Report No. 1763   Bolt Beranek and Newman Inc

      c. IMP going down
      d. IMP back up
      e. Acknowledgment
      f. Ready for next message
      g. My Host is down

2. ACROSS IMP/HOST INTERFACES
      a. Query
      b. Response
      c. I am going down
      d. Ready for next message

3A. IMP TO REMOTE HOST
      a. Fault detected
      b. Report generation

  B. HOST TO REMOTE IMP
      a. Change routing table

The above list contains some entries such as "My Host is down." In connection with messages such as these, we wish to here introduce the notion of busy signals. In making a telephone call, there is no indication, at the telephone and before the call is tried, that a line will be busy, out of order, or not answered. We feel that this is a powerful concept as applied to the network. For example, when an actual user at a Host site tries to use the network to call some other Host, *at that time* the network should try the call and then send back a message, finally reaching that user, which says, "Sorry, the Host you just tried to call is down." This arrangement has the advantage that as a given Host goes up and down it is not necessary for large numbers of control messages to flow around the network. To keep everyone informed of the instantaneous status of that

57

Host. Instead the status is made available "on request." This approach can be applied to many situations within the network, and we propose to apply it where possible. Naturally some status information will, in fact, be kept distributed, but we will try to minimize the number of different kinds of status tables that must be kept up-to-date.

N. The Operational IMP Program

Inasmuch as the operational program implements the strategy and protocol of the network, some discussion of general philosophy and its significant features is in order.

Because of the experimental nature, the diffuse geography and the multiplicity of Host types of the network, it is essential that the program be simple and crisp. The program should be divisible into clearly defined functional units with as few interconnecting pathways as possible. This approach will greatly simplify the debugging of the software. Since the network will evolve as we learn more about networks and their uses and constraints, the program must be designed to allow for changes and modifications.

To cope with a wide range of real-time data rates, particular attention must be paid to timing requirements. In addition, since much of the IMP memory is given over to buffer storage (both to and from the local Host and for store and forward), the program must be as compact as possible. Of the 12K of memory, we expect the program will eventually occupy approximately one-half to two-thirds. The network software is outlined in this section.

Report No. 1763   Bolt Beranek and Newman Inc

We feel that the only sensible language in which to write the IMP software is DDP-516 assembly language. This will enable the IMP programs to be as compact and efficient as possible, which is something a higher level language typically subverts. Optimum efficiency is essential here; when a program must deal with low level hardware considerations in real time, a high level language becomes more of a nuisance than a convenience. Although a high level language makes programs more readable and easier to debug, we do not feel we can afford the luxury.

Figure 14 is a schematic diagram outlining the control logic of the operational program. It has five basic pieces: an initialization routine, interrupt routines, task routines, shared subroutines, and background routines. The program is started at the initialization routine, which first goes through a machine and interface checking routine. It then sets up inputs for all input channels (from Host and phone line Modems) such that, when an input is complete, an interrupt will occur. It also enables the clock interrupt and does all other initialization that is necessary and then turns control over to the background loop.

The routines of the background loop are cycled through repeatedly until an interrupt switches control to some other routine. When all interruptions have been serviced, control is returned to the instruction in the background routine which was about to be executed when the first interrupt occurred.

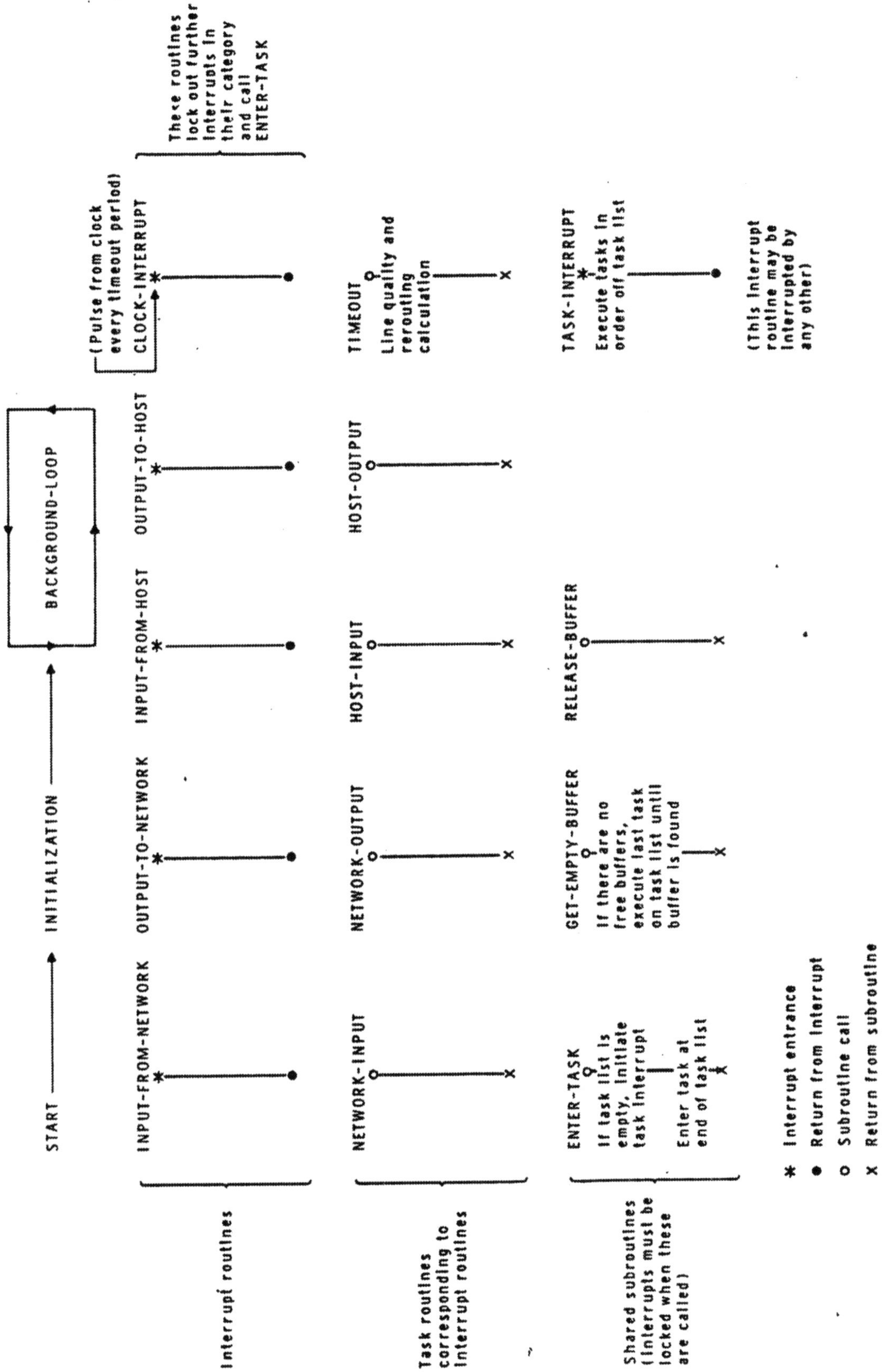

Report No. 1763　　　　　　　　　　　　　　Bolt Beranek and Newman Inc

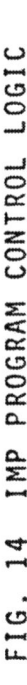

FIG. 14　IMP PROGRAM CONTROL LOGIC

When an interrupt occurs, a call to the routine associated with that interrupt is executed. This call saves the point of interruption so that control can later be returned to the proper place. The interrupt routine also saves the state of the machine for restoration upon return. An example of an interrupt condition is the completion of the input of a packet from a neighboring IMP. The input hardware calls the interrupt routine, which sets up another input, rearms the interrupt line and designates the received packet for subsequent processing. The input interrupt routines are indicated just below the initialization routine in the diagram. These interrupt routines prohibit calls *of themselves* while they are running by locking out further interrupts of the same kind upon entry to the routines.* Consequently, these routines must be very fast so that interrupts can be re-enabled quickly and not be missed. Most of the time-consuming work is taken out of the interrupt routines by having them merely stack calls to other routines (called task routines) on a task queue which will be executed in what is, in some sense, high priority background time. This allows some time buffering of packet handling if the handling routines take more than real time for a short period.

The question arises as to how the tasks contained in the task queue are ever processed, since the interrupt routines return control to another interrupt routine (if interruption occurred there) or to the background routines when all interrupts have been serviced. This is done as follows: each time a task is entered onto the task list, a check is made to see whether there

---

*The DDP-516 provides for this with a convenient interrupt selection mask and enable scheme.

are any previous tasks on the queue. If not, a special hardware feature is used for a program-initiated interrupt (called the "task interrupt"), which is set so that, when the "normal" interrupt routine returns to the background loop and re-enables interrupts, the "task interrupt" will take control and allow entries to be processed in the task queue. (The ENTER-TASK and TASK-INTERRUPT routines are shown in the bottom left and the bottom right of Fig. 14.) When the task list is empty, control is returned to the point of interruption in the background loop. The interrupt routine which executes tasks can be interrupted by any other interrupt routine but will never interrupt itself. Because calls of the task routines are executed sequentially, there is no need to make the task routines reentrant and indeed this is the fundamental reason for queueing tasks. Appendix F includes an example of the use of task and interrupt routines.

There remains a set of routines called the shared subroutines. These are the routines that make entries on the task list, the routines that handle empty buffers, etc. Other interrupts which may call these routines are locked out when these routines are called.

In summary, then, there are really three levels of priority, each corresponding to programs which perform a particular type of function:

1) interrupt routines that interrupt task routines and background routines and even some other interrupt routines;

2) task routines which (in some sense) interrupt the background routines; and

3) background routines.

The interrupt routines for the interfaces are activated as buffers fill, or are emptied. In general these routines reset pointers, make entries in the task queue for handling filled buffers and releasing emptied ones, and reactivate the interface in question. The clock interrupt routine indexes a higher order clock counter which is maintained in core memory and adds to the task list the task that tests for packet time out. Some of the task routines are: allocating and reclaiming empty buffer storage; handling short buffers with high priority; timing out for IMP-to-IMP acknowledgments and retransmitting (when appropriate); processing end-to-end Requests-For-Next-Message; locating the next buffer to send; identifying incoming messages and placing them on the proper queue for transmittal either to the Host or into the proper output line; transmitting IMP-to-IMP acknowledgments; reassembling messages for the local Host and transmitting Requests-For-Next-Message after reassembly is complete; breaking off destination information from the top of messages from the local Host and fabricating and attaching link identification; and other header information to outgoing packets of a message.

The concept of three priority levels, and the availability of the background loop permits the IMP to perform much more extensive computations on an occasional basis. This is particularly important if the need arises for word-rate jobs on occasional packets. If Host-peculiar programs are required for ASCII conversion, or for other data transformation tasks, such jobs may be accomplished without disrupting the tight timing of the interrupt routines or the task queue. Background programs also include such jobs as transmitting and checking received network test messages and miscellaneous statistics gathering.

Report No. 1763   Bolt Beranek and Newman Inc

1. <u>Summary of IMP program routines</u>

Initialization

    Checks hardware of machine and interfaces, sets up initial inputs, enables interrupts, and does other necessary initialization.

Background loop

    Set of routines executed cyclicly, in order when not interrupted.

Execute task

    Executes entries on task list in order.

Input from network

    Answers interrupt, sets up new input from network line, and enters task on task list.

Output to network

    Answers interrupt and enters task on task list.

Input from host

    Answers interrupt and enters task on task list.

Output to host

    Answers interrupt and enters task on task list.

Timeout

    Answers interrupt and enters task on task list.

} Interrupt Routines

Input from network
> Puts acknowledgment on output queue and dispatches* to the input processing routines.

Output from network
> Finds next unused buffer, marks it sent and sets up output.

Input from Host
> Appends header to buffer, etc., puts buffer on output queue, and sets up new input.

Output to Host
> Sets up output to next buffer to Host.

Timeout
> Searches output queues for any unacknowledged buffers and reroutes them.

} Task Routines

Enter task
> If task list is empty, initiates program interrupt and enters task on task list.

Get empty buffer
> Calls Execute task if no empty buffers remain and returns buffer.

Return empty buffer

Rerouting

} Shared Subroutines

---

*These routines do most of the work of IMP program.

We feel that the program structure just described meets the goals discussed earlier. The program is constructed of functional modules that are logically independent, thus giving them a simplicity that will make their coding, debugging, and understanding easy. Such modularity also enables natural and easy addition and deletion of functional modules.

Recursion (i.e., reentrancy), which is costly in time, is eliminated through use of the task list that also provides a single consistant manner of calling and passing arguments to subroutines. Speed is also attained by moving pointers rather than buffers and by keeping buffers on doubly linked lists for easy insertion and deletion from queues.

While the proposed program structure does not waste space, it is not designed to be as short as possible. We feel it is not worth the additional complexity that results from routines which share short pieces of common code, especially since the routines run on interrupts and interrupt each other. Of course within a routine we will use all of the cleverness at our disposal.

2. Timing and space considerations

In this section we estimate the running time of the crucial routines of the IMP program, review the consequences of these times, and estimate the storage requirement of the IMP program.

A study of the various IMP program routines yields our timing estimates. We first consider in detail the running time of the INPUT-FROM-NETWORK interrupt routine (we actually coded sample routines).

The coding requires 40 instructions with an average time of 2.5 μs/instruction. We next estimate quite closely the running time of the NETWORK-INPUT task routine, including the STORE-AND-FORWARD input processing routine which we feel approximates an average path through the NETWORK-INPUT task routine. This we also estimate to be 40 instructions.

We also estimate that the OUTPUT-TO-NETWORK interrupt routine and the NETWORK-OUTPUT routine will each take about 20 instructions.

The time required to handle the Host is under the IMP's control and is also down by a factor of four from the time required to handle the four modem lines and may thus be temporarily discounted; rerouting happens rarely, as it is clocked.

Thus, the bulk of the work may be tabulated:

- 40 instructions — INPUT-FROM-NETWORK
- 40 instructions — NETWORK-INPUT
- 20 instructions — OUTPUT-TO-NETWORK
- 20 instructions — NETWORK-OUTPUT

Since the number of instructions required to pass a packet into an IMP is 80 and the number of instructions required to pass a packet out is 40, we take the average number to handle a packet to be 60 instructions. Adding a factor of one-half to take into account things we have forgotten (overheads of various types, Host routines, and a share of the rerouting time for each packet), we arrive at an estimate of ninety instructions required, on the average, to pass a packet across an IMP boundary.

Using these numbers, Appendix A draws the following conclusions: assuming the RFQ model (i.e., 4 links, 15Kb lines, 344 bit packets, etc.), 14% of the machine time is used. Assuming the RFQ model, but with all 50Kb lines, 43% of the machine time is used.

We finally estimate, based on experience rather than actual coding, that the storage necessary for the main IMP program outlined in this section — the program which does the hard, fast, "necessary" work — will fit in 2000 words of DDP-516 storage. The remainder of the program (the background routines, the special IMP-TO-HOST message routines, etc.) is much less well defined but we estimate that it will occupy somewhere around 4000 words. This leaves about 6000 words for buffers and program expansion.

3. Test programs

Typically, many of these programs are short and simply pump test patterns through the interfaces for observation on an oscilloscope. Programs for loop and inter-computer tests in general will not involve complex error analysis although they will include error detection. The more sophisticated test programs transmit and receive (in loop or inter-computer configuration) random patterns, checking for identity upon receipt. No program means exists for generating errors in the cyclic check mechanism of the hardware, but failure can be introduced by temporarily disabling check character generation in the sending hardware.

4. Utility programs

The DDP-516 comes with an assembler, a primitive editor, a program loader and an octal debugger. Assembly of programs will be done

Report No. 1763   Bolt Beranek and Newman Inc

at the test facility on a 516 which will have a high-speed punch. Programs will be composed and edited on BBN's PDP-ld computer under time-sharing and will be punched in ASCII for the 516 assembler. This requires the construction of no additional sophisticated utility programs, allows multiple users access to program composition facilities, and causes no disturbance of the standard DDP-516 assembly and debugging system.

O. Optional Site Arrangements

We have given some consideration to three special sorts of site installations: one with two hosts to be served, one in which the IMP acts as a terminal controller, and one in which the IMP services the Host as a data concentrator. For the site with two hosts, two IMP/HOST hardware interfaces will be required. While the standard interface is modular in nature and two such interfaces can be installed in an IMP, this installation creates a special situation. First of all, either additional priority interrupts will be required or some of the normal priority interrupt channels will have to be reassigned. In either case, some special tailoring of the standard program will be required, at the very least, to enable it to handle the interrupts properly. The 16 channels of the DMC are sufficient to cover this case. However, we feel that generalizing the standard program in such a way as to make it directly suitable for either a one or two host installation is not sensible: the additional required sorting and routing is simply too expensive in terms of time and space to warrant its inclusion in the standard version. On the other hand, the program is amenable to modifications that will enable it to handle the two host situation — but with some degradation of performance.

If a proposed network node does not have a Host computer, it may be useful to put into the IMP those functions of a Host computer that allow users at Teletypes to converse with distant nodes.

To do this, one might first conceptually partition the IMP computer into two parts — one for the IMP network program and one for a program similar to the Host network program which each normal Host has. This partition is easy to make since both programs will run asyncronously on interrupts. Additionally, a Teletype scanner must be attached to the I/O channel for the pseudo-Host network program. This program maintains an input and an output buffer for each Teletype line and gathers characters for the buffers as the scanner collects them. When a buffer is full, it is passed to the IMP network program as a packet. The IMP program which normally deals with the Host interface is now no longer necessary.

This scheme subtracts from the time available for the IMP network program to service store and forward packets. The method does not detract from the space available for buffers, since the pseudo-Host program replaces the IMP Host interface program, and the pseudo-Host program shares buffer storage with the IMP network program.

If there is a Host computer at a network node, it might be feasible to use the IMP as a data concentrator for the Host. In this case, the pseudo-Host program described above is still necessary; instead of passing packets to the IMP network program, the program passes them to the Host. The Host can arrange to process these special packets as, for example, line-at-a-time Teletype input to the standard Host operating system.

Once again, no timing problems occur since the separate IMP programs are run asynchronously on interrupts, but the additional IMP program does subtract from the available space since the IMP/Host interface program cannot be omitted.

We have not investigated these issues in any real detail. There are many other possible, perhaps better, methods of simultaneously using an IMP for a data concentrator or terminal.

Report No. 1763   Bolt Beranek and Newman Inc

APPENDIX A: TIMING COMPUTATIONS

A central computation in the design and evaluation of the network is the determination of the actual amount of IMP processing time. It affects the selection of the IMP computer, the performance and utilization of the chosen computer, and forms a basis for the model calculations. It also strongly affects the design of the hardware interface and, in conjunction with the chosen computer, forms a principal measure of the expansion capability of the network.

However, this computation cannot be performed without making some estimate of the traffic which an IMP is expected to handle. The results which are obtained are extremely sensitive to the initial assumptions. In this appendix we will discuss two sets of assumptions which we label as A and B.

Assumption A: This is the assumed traffic in the RFQ model. Each channel carries 15 kilobits/sec and the Host line carries 20 kilobits/sec. The average packet size on a channel is 344 bits and the average packet size on the Host line is 576 bits. There are four channels and one Host line.

Assumption B: This corresponds to a "reasonable" peak load condition and is identical to assumption A except that all channels as well as the Host line are assumed to carry 50 kilobits/sec.

We determine the total number of bits per second, R, and the average number of packets per second, P, that cross an IMP interface in any direction.

A: $R = 8 \times 15{,}000 + 2 \times 20{,}000 = 160{,}000$ bits/sec

$$P = \frac{120{,}000}{344} + \frac{40{,}000}{576} = \sim 420 \text{ packets/sec;} \qquad (1)$$

B: $R = 10 \times 50{,}000 = 500{,}000$ bits/sec

$$P = \frac{400{,}000}{344} + \frac{100{,}000}{576} = \sim 1325 \text{ packets/sec.} \qquad (2)$$

There are two primary components to the calculation of the IMP processing time, namely the time required for I/O transfers and the time required for internal packet processing. We first consider the total cycle time, T_T, required to do input-output transfers.

We assume four cycles per I/O transfer (core counters are assumed instead of hardware counters for reasons of economy) and set

     W = Word length in bits
     C = Cycle time in µs
     I = Instruction time in µs.

A: $T_T = \dfrac{160{,}000}{W} \times 4C$ µs/sec;   (3)

B: $T_T = \dfrac{500{,}000}{W} \times 4C$ µs/sec.   (4)

Within each IMP, the bulk of the processing is performed on a per packet basis. We have estimated the average number of instructions required in the IMP program to process these packets. There are four basic components of the processing.

INPUT INTERRUPT ROUTINE - 40 instructions ⎫ 80 for
INPUT TASK PROCESSING   - 40 instructions ⎭ input

OUTPUT INTERRUPT ROUTINE - 20 instructions ⎫ 40 for
OUTPUT TASK PROCESSING   - 20 instructions ⎭ output

We average these quantities to obtain a figure of 60 instructions/packet in crossing an IMP boundary. We further estimate that all additional tasks will average another 30 instructions/packet. Therefore we use the figure of 90 instructions/packet as the average number of instructions which must be performed by the IMP program to process each packet which crosses the IMP boundary. Note that a packet which *traverses* the IMP is thus assigned a total of 2 × 90 = 180 instructions.

The total program instruction time, T_I, is given by

A: $T_I = 420 \times 90I = \sim 38,000I$ μs/sec;   (5)

B: $T_I = 1325 \times 90I = \sim 120,000I$ μs/sec.   (6)

We now wish to estimate the individual instruction time, I, for a small sized computer. It is reasonable to assume that in a hypothetical 20 bit machine, indirect addressing should never be required to access any word of memory (in a typical IMP configuration of less than 16K). We assume that such a 20 bit machine requires an average of 2 cycles per instruction and that a machine with a shorter word length, W, will require approximately 2 × 20/W cycles/instruction due to an increasing frequency of indirect addressing with decreasing word size.

Thus, we have the following expression for the instruction time

$$I = \frac{20}{W} \times 2C \text{ µs}$$

and the total program instruction time, T_I, for handling packets is

A: $\quad T_I = 38{,}000 \times \frac{20}{W} \times 2C = 1.52 \times 10^6 \frac{C}{W}$ µs/sec; $\quad\quad$ (7)

B: $\quad T_I = 120{,}000 \times \frac{20}{W} \times 2C = 4.8 \times 10^6 \frac{C}{W}$ µs/sec. $\quad\quad$ (8)

On adding Eq. 3 to Eq. 7 and 4 to 8 we obtain an estimate, $T = T_T + T_I$, of the total cycle time required to handle the IMP traffic.

A: $\quad T = 6.4 \times 10^5 \frac{C}{W} + 1.52 \times 10^6 \frac{C}{W} = 2.2 \times 10^6 \frac{C}{W}$ µs/sec;

$\quad\quad\quad\quad\quad\quad\quad\quad\quad\quad\quad\quad\quad\quad\quad\quad\quad\quad\quad\quad\quad\quad$ (9)

B: $\quad T = 2 \times 10^6 \frac{C}{W} + 4.8 \times 10^6 \frac{C}{W} = 6.8 \times 10^6 \frac{C}{W}$ µs/sec. $\quad\quad$ (10)

From this point we will simply assume that

$$C = 1$$
$$W = 16$$
$$I = \frac{20}{W} \times 2C = 2.5 \; ,$$

since these are the appropriate values for the DDP-516, and proceed with the computation of the timing and the model.

Report No. 1763 Bolt Beranek and Newman Inc

A: $\quad T = 2.2 \times 10^6 \times \frac{1}{16} \cong 0.14 \times 10^6$ μs/sec *or 14% of capacity*; (11)

B: $\quad T = 6.8 \times 10^6 \times \frac{1}{16} \cong 0.43 \times 10^6$ μs/sec *or 43% of capacity.* (12)

Therefore, under assumption A, only 14% of the machine capacity is used, while at the "reasonable" peak loads of condition B approximately 43% of the machine capacity is used.

UNCLASSIFIED
Security Classification

DOCUMENT CONTROL DATA - R & D
(Security classification of title, body of abstract and indexing annotation must be entered when the overall report is classified)

1. ORIGINATING ACTIVITY (Corporate author)	2a. REPORT SECURITY CLASSIFICATION
Bolt Beranek and Newman Inc 50 Moulton Street Cambridge, Massachusetts 02138	UNCLASSIFIED
	2b. GROUP

3. REPORT TITLE

INITIAL IMP DESIGN

4. DESCRIPTIVE NOTES *(Type of report and inclusive dates)*

5. AUTHOR(S) *(First name, middle initial, last name)*

Bolt Beranek and Newman Inc

6. REPORT DATE	7a. TOTAL NO. OF PAGES	7b. NO. OF REFS
January 1969	80	
8a. CONTRACT OR GRANT NO. DAHC 15-69-C-0179	9a. ORIGINATOR'S REPORT NUMBER(S)	
b. PROJECT NO.	BBN Report No. 1763	
c. (not yet known)	9b. OTHER REPORT NO(S) *(Any other numbers that may be assigned this report)*	
d.		

10. DISTRIBUTION STATEMENT

Unlimited

11. SUPPLEMENTARY NOTES	12. SPONSORING MILITARY ACTIVITY
	Advanced Research Projects Agency Washington, D.C. 20301

13. ABSTRACT

The basic function of the IMP computer network is to allow large existing time-shared (Host) computers with different system configurations to communicate with each other. Each IMP (Interface Message Processor) computer accepts messages for its Host from other Host computers and transmits messages from its Host to other Hosts. Since there will not always be a direct link between two Hosts that wish to communicate, individual IMPs will, from time to time, perform the function of transferring a message between Hosts that are not directly connected. This then leads to the two basic IMP configurations —— interfacing between Host computers and acting as a message switcher in the IMP network. The message switching is performed as a store and forward operation. Each IMP adapts its message routine to the condition of those portions of the IMP network to which it is connected. IMPs regularly measure network performance and report in special messages to the network measurement center. Provision of a tracing capability permits the net operation to be studied comprehensively. An automatic trouble reporting capability detects a variety of network difficulties and reports them to an interested Host. An IMP can throw away packets that it has received but not yet acknowledged, transmitting packets to other IMPs at its own discretion. Self-contained network operation is designed to protect and deliver messages from the source Host to the destination Host.

DD FORM 1473 (PAGE 1)
S/N 0101-807-6811

UNCLASSIFIED
Security Classification

UNCLASSIFIED
Security Classification

14. KEY WORDS	LINK A		LINK B		LINK C	
	ROLE	WT	ROLE	WT	ROLE	WT
Computers and Communication						
Store and Forward Communication						
ARPA Computer Network						
Honeywell DDP-516						
IMP						

DD FORM 1473 (BACK)
1 NOV 65
S/N 0101-807-6821

UNCLASSIFIED
Security Classification

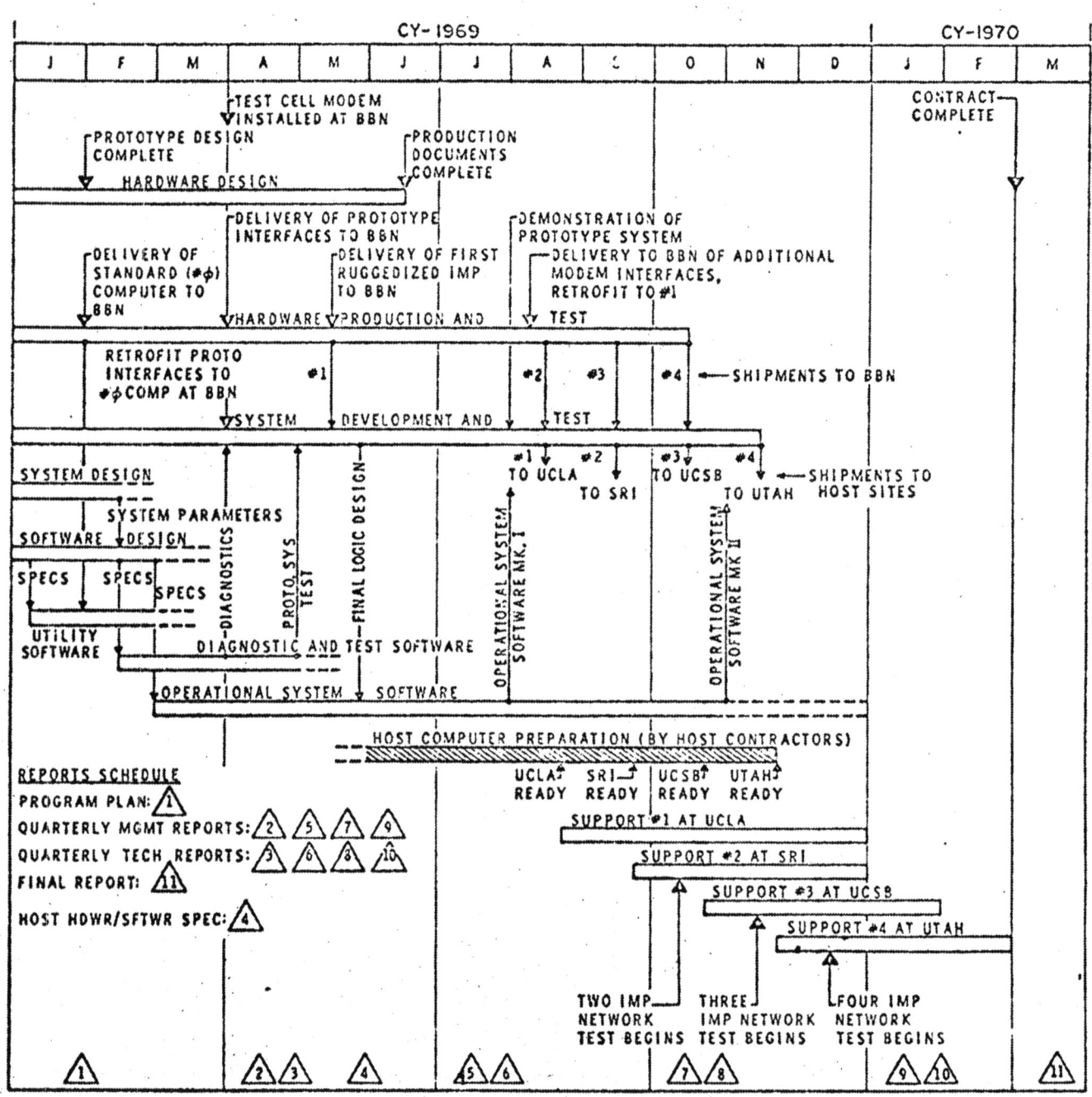

FIG. 1 IMP PROGRAM SCHEDULE

Report No. 1783　　　　　　　　　　　　　　　　　Bolt Beranek and Newman Inc

INTERFACE MESSAGE PROCESSORS FOR
THE ARPA COMPUTER NETWORK

QUARTERLY TECHNICAL REPORT No. 1
2 January 1969 to 31 March 1969

Principal Investigator:　Mr. Frank E. Heart

Sponsored by
Advanced Research Projects Agency
ARPA Order No. 1260

Submitted to:
Advanced Research Projects Agency
Washington, D.C. 20301
Attn:　Dr. L.G. Roberts

Report No. 1783   Bolt Beranek and Newman Inc.

TABLE OF CONTENTS

Section 1.   INTRODUCTION.....................................1
        2.   HARDWARE DESIGN..................................2
        3.   SOFTWARE DEBUGGING...............................5
        4.   MULTIPLE HOSTS...................................7
        5.   ROUTING ALGORITHM...............................10

Report No. 1783　　　　　　　　　　　　　Bolt Beranek and Newman Inc

1. INTRODUCTION

A contract has been awarded to Bolt Beranek and Newman (BBN) to design, fabricate and install interface message processors (IMPs) for the ARPA computer network. Work on this contract began on 2 January 1969 and is proceeding according to schedule: initial field installations will take place in the Fall of 1969. This Quarterly Report No. 1 describes several aspects of our technical progress during the first quarter of 1969. [BBN Report No. 1763 describes the initial IMP design and we assume a general familiarity with that document. Since we have adhered quite closely to the initial design plans, we have therefore included in this report only new material and modifications to the initial design.]

Work is proceeding on both the hardware and the software design. Section 2 describes the status of the hardware design. Intensive work has also begun on the software package. In the first quarter, we placed some emphasis on building software *tools* as well as the main program. In Section 3 of this report, we describe our plans for software debugging. A stand-alone debugging program (DDT) has been written and will be modified to run in conjunction with the operational IMP program and to assist in *network* debugging.

We have made provision for the connection of up to four Hosts to a single IMP by enlarging the number of Host tables, by expanding the Host routines, and by a change in the method of handling links. We discuss these multiple Host provisions in Section 4.

Report No. 1783   Bolt Beranek and Newman Inc

We have designed, and are currently implementing, a routing algorithm. Each IMP regularly estimates the minimum delay path through the network to each destination and stores the information in an updated routing table. This algorithm and its implementation are discussed in Section 5.

Report No. 1783　　　　　　　　　　　　Bolt Beranek and Newman Inc

2. HARDWARE DESIGN

The prototype interface hardware is now complete. The IMP/Host and the IMP/Modem interface designs that have been realized by Honeywell are functionally identical to those described in our initial design. We have made modifications to the hardware at a detailed level to permit its construction using standard Honeywell micro-pacs.

Some additional protective features have been added. For example, in order to protect against noise in the Modem clock signal, we have inhibited clock transitions from occurring too frequently. Special test and crosspatching features incorporated into the hardware design permit the operational program to perform loop tests on each interface and to indicate detected error conditions.

In addition to the interfaces, several other features have been defined and incorporated into the design:

1) Memory protection, under switch control, has been provided for a 1000 (octal) word block of the memory and for the two specific memory locations associated with the Watchdog timer (see 2 below) and power fail interrupts.

2) The Watchdog timer is normally held off by a periodic command from the program. Should the program fail in such a way as to stop issuing these commands, the timer will run out, causing a "program failure" interrupt via a

protected location (see 1 above) into a special restart routine in the block of protected memory. When the timer runs out, it will restart itself. After four successive time-outs occur without a successful program restart, an alarm will be presented and the computer will be shut off.

3) A set of 24 status indicator lights has been provided on the front of the machine.

4) Provision has been made for a program-generated interrupt.

5) A relative time clock has been provided. The program can enable or disable the clock and can also read the time into the accumulator. The clock causes a program interrupt to facilitate program event timing.

6) Upon the return of power following a power failure, an automatic restart feature will restart the program. In combination with the regular power failure interrupt (which stops the program "cleanly"), the auto restart feature should permit the resumption of normal duties after a power outage, without the need for human intervention.

Report No. 1783　　　　　　　　　　　　　　　Bolt Beranek and Newman Inc

3. SOFTWARE DEBUGGING

We have begun intensive work on the software package. Organization and function of the operational program is essentially as described in our initial design. One part of the software package which has already been built is a stand-alone debugging program (DDT) that will be used as a tool for debugging IMP programs.

The stand-alone DDT program will be used in the initial debugging phase. It occupies approximately 600 registers and can be used to examine and modify storage registers in the IMP or to start programs. To provide maximum isolation between itself and the IMP programs, the stand-alone DDT program runs without interrupts. Teletype input and output are handled by direct testing of the Teletype interface hardware.

We felt that it was also desirable to have a debugging program from which the operational program could be run. Consequently, we have made a provision to incorporate the stand-alone DDT into an operational DDT program that can run in conjunction with the operational IMP program.

This operational DDT program will include most of the stand-alone DDT program along with a Teletype interrupt routine and a software interface with the operational program. The interface will provide a mechanism for transferring characters in both directions between the operational IMP and DDT programs.

The operational DDT program will provide debugging assistance at a single location and, in addition, may be used in *network* testing and in *network* debugging and maintenance. Using DDT a programmer at the IMP Teletype will have complete control over the operational program and, in particular, he will be able to modify unprotected registers while the operational IMP program is running. More important, a programmer will be able to construct a packet within the IMP and place it on an output queue. *This packet need not necessarily conform to a standard packet format;* for example, it could be a test packet specifically constructed to contain one or more format errors. However, it also could be a packet intended for the operational DDT program at another IMP. With this last capability, it will be possible to display on the Teletype at one IMP the contents of storage registers at another IMP. To accomplish this, an appropriate packet would be sent by the DDT program at one IMP to the DDT program at the other IMP, whereupon a packet containing the desired information would be returned. In a similar fashion, it would be possible to modify the contents of storage registers at other IMPs.

We are aware of the risks associated with such powerful debugging tools and we will attempt to restrict access to the DDT when the system is in operational use.

Report No. 1783　　　　　　　　　　　　　　Bolt Beranek and Newman Inc

4. MULTIPLE HOSTS

Our initial design incorporated a single Host and a maximum of six communication channels. The operational program has now been modified to accept a maximum of *four* Hosts connected to a single IMP. Since each Host will require a separate Host/IMP interface to replace one IMP/Modem interface, an IMP with four Hosts can have no more than three communication channels.

We thoroughly reconsidered the program timing and organization for the cases of one to four Hosts, and, for each case, we determined that the program timing is still satisfactory, although program size and complexity increases with the number of Hosts.

Timing primarily depends on the maximum rate at which interrupts must be handled. An increase in the number of effective I/O channels increases the maximum rate at which interrupts can arrive. Since each additional IMP/Host interface replaces one IMP/Modem interface, the maximum number of effective I/O channel is unchanged and the program does not encounter substantially different timing conditions than it did in the one-Host case.

The increase in program complexity is due primarily to a change in the method of handling links and to an expansion of the Host routines for disabling interrupts, maintaining multiple tables and for otherwise insuring the ability of the Host routines to be shared. The increase in program size is primarily due to the need for additional tables.

A separate pair of ASCII conversion tables are being considered for each Host. All Host packets marked with a special ASCII bit will be placed on the appropriate input or output ASCII queue to await conversion in the "background". A limit will be placed on the total number of packets allowed on the ASCII queues.

We have changed the method of handling links to avoid placing a constraint on the ability of the ARPA network to grow and to increase the number of available links at a multiple Host site. The initial method considered for the handling of links was to maintain in each IMP a sparsely filled link table with 32 links to each destination. For 16 IMPs, this table occupied 512 words of core. However, additional IMPs in the network would have required a corresponding increase in the size of the table. For four Hosts at a single site, the number of links on which a given Host could receive packets was reduced from 32 by a factor of 4. This number of links could have remained at 32 via a fourfold increase in the size of the link table to over 2000 words of core; however, this size was considered too large a portion of memory to be allocated to this function in a machine with only 12K of core. Moreover, we considered 8 links per Host at a four-Host site only marginally sufficient, especially since it is still unclear how the Hosts might decide to use the links.

Consequently, the new method selected for handling links avoids placing any internal constraints, such as table size, on the number of IMPs that a network may have and also provides a large *pool* of links which may be shared among all the Hosts at each Host site.

A table will be allocated to handle 64 transmit links and 64 receive links at each IMP. These links are for the combined use of all Hosts at the site and may form a common pool or be legislatively apportioned by the Hosts among themselves. The link number contains eight bits. Thus, at a four-Host site, 64 unique link numbers could be assigned to each Host if desired. The IMP will accept any 8-bit link number that the Host includes at the beginning of a message and establish that link in its transmit link table. The link is identified in the table by the link number, the destination IMP, and the destination Host.

A link is established in the receive link table of the destination IMP when the first packet on that link arrives. The only limitation placed on the Hosts is that at any one time they may not combine to use a total of more than 64 links for transmitting packets, nor may they receive a combined total of more than 64 links at any one time.

If an established link is not used for a given period of time (currently planned to be 5 or 10 minutes), a procedure will be initiated to delete it from the transmit and receive link tables. Of course, if the link subsequently reappears in use, it will be automatically reestablished — provided fewer than 64 links are then established in the link table.

A Host may request and will receive link status information from its IMP. The Host will have the option to delete transmit links, although there appears to be no need for it to exercise this option under normal circumstances.

A provision has also been made to indicate up to four dead Hosts at a given site. In effect, a dead Host simply means that messages to that Host will be discarded. A dead Host at a multiple Host site will not affect the status of other Hosts at that site.

Report No. 1783 Bolt Beranek and Newman Inc

5. ROUTING ALGORITHM

A routing algorithm has been designed for the ARPA network to direct each packet from its source to its destination along a path for which the total estimated transit time through the network is smallest. A path originates at a source IMP, terminates at a destination IMP, and may include one or more intermediate IMPs. A path is therefore composed of one or more IMP-to-IMP segments called legs. Each IMP estimates the best route from itself to a given destination and selects the corresponding leg.

A path is constructed for each packet one leg at a time, beginning at the source IMP. If the first leg terminates at the destination IMP, the packet encounters no intermediate IMPs and the routing is completed. If the first leg terminates at an intermediate IMP, a second leg is selected by that IMP upon receipt of the packet, and the packet is transmitted along that new leg. Each intermediate IMP, in turn, selects the next leg of the path until one leg finally terminates at the destination IMP and the routing is completed.

At each IMP, the next leg is determined straightforwardly by a fast and simple table lookup procedure. For each possible destination, an entry in the table designates the appropriate next leg to be selected. This table is called the routing table.

Each IMP constructs its own routing table. The entries for this table are determined from information transmitted to the IMP from its neighbors and from estimates of its own internal delay. The information from its neighbors consists of delay information, connectivity information, and dead Host information, which have propagated backward into the network from each destination. The connectivity and dead Host information are monitored for status changes. The received delay information is stored in a table, called the "neighbor's delay table" (NDT), and is used to construct a "minimum delay table" containing minimum delay estimates to each destination.

The NDT at the IMP is the set of minimum delay tables that are transmitted to it by its neighbors. An updated minimum delay table is transmitted (asynchronously) by each IMP to all its neighbors approximately every half second during a time-out routine. Upon arrival, this new table is used to overwrite a portion of the NDT. The entries in the minimum delay table are updated, as are the entries in the routing table, just prior to this transmission.

The routing table is dynamically updated to adjust for changing traffic conditions in the network. For each leg and destination, an estimated delay is formed from two components, namely an estimated delay along the leg and an estimated delay from the end of the leg to the final destination. The sum of the two components is simply called the *delay* for the particular leg and destination and, for each destination, the smallest of the delays is entered into the minimum delay table. The second of the two components is contained in the NDT. The IMP program computes the first component at kD where k is a scale factor and D the solution to the equation

$$D = Q_D(1-P_r) + (100+D+Q_D)P_r \quad ,$$

for which Q_D is the queue delay in milliseconds with no retransmission; P_r is an estimate of the probability of retransmission; and 100 msec is the elapsed time between retransmission attempts. The above equation may be solved for D to yield

$$D = \frac{Q_D + 100P_r}{1 - P_r}.$$

The estimate for the quantity Q_D is taken to be 20L, where L is equal to the length of the output queue awaiting transmission on that line. The estimate for P_r is E/20 where E is equal to the recorded number of retransmissions among twenty consecutive packets transmitted on that line. L is updated with every packet and E is updated every twenty packets. If E equals 20, the value for 19 is used to avoid dividing by zero.

One or more IMPs are disconnected from the rest of the network when no path exists between them and the other IMPs. This condition may be attributed to the presence of dead lines that connect the IMPs with the rest of the network. A *dead line* is defined by the sustained absence on that line of either received messages or acknowledgements. If no packets arrive on a line for approximately two and a half seconds, the line is defined to be dead and no outgoing packets will be routed onto it. In addition, any packets still remaining on the queue for that line will be rerouted to another queue.

A dead line may reflect trouble in either the communication facilities, in the IMP hardware, or possibly in the IMP itself. Normal outages on a line due to dropouts, impulse noise, or other error conditions are not expected to result in a dead line since they typically last only a few milliseconds, and only occasionally last as long as a few tenths of a second. Therefore, we expect that a line will be defined as dead only when serious trouble conditions occur.

In the absence of regular packets to transmit over a line, the IMP program transmits *hello* packets at half second intervals. The acknowledgement for a hello packet is called an *I heard you* packet.

A dead line must remain dead long enough for all the IMPs to learn of the condition, since a dead line may cause one or more IMPs to be disconnected from the rest of the network. When thirty consecutive *hello* packets have been acknowledged (an event which consumes at least 15 seconds), the line will be defined to be alive once again and will subsequently be included in the normal routing procedure.

After a line is defined to be dead, it is not permitted to be used as the next leg of a path. Subsequent entries into the composite delay table are generated without reference to routing information from that line. Routing tables in the network are adjusted automatically to reflect the loss of a line as the composite delay tables are continually transmitted between neighboring IMPs.

If every path leading to a destination IMP contains one or more dead lines, it is impossible for packets to reach that IMP and they will therefore be discarded. The routing table will be modified to indicate no path to such an IMP.

Report No. 1783 Bolt Beranek and Newman Inc

Disconnected IMPs can not be rapidly detected from the delay tables that arrive from neighboring IMPs. Consequently, additional information is transmitted between neighboring IMPs to help detect this condition. Each IMP transmits to its neighbors the length of the shortest existing path from itself to each destination. To the smallest such received number per destination, the IMP adds one. This incremented number is the length of the shortest path from that IMP to the destination. If the length ever reaches 15 to any destination, the destination is assumed to be unreachable, all packets to that destination are discarded.

Messages intended for dead Hosts (which are not the same as dead IMPs) cannot be delivered and therefore require special handling to avoid indefinite circulation in the network and possible spurious arrival at a later time. Such messages are purged from the network either at the source IMP or at the destination IMP.

Information that identifies dead Hosts is regularly transmitted between IMPs, accompanying the routing information. A Host computer is only notified about another dead Host when it attempts to send a message to that Host.

BOLT BERANEK AND NEWMAN INC

CONSULTING · DEVELOPMENT · RESEARCH

Report No. 1837
July 1969

INTERFACE MESSAGE PROCESSORS FOR
THE ARPA COMPUTER NETWORK

QUARTERLY TECHNICAL REPORT NO. 2
1 April 1969 to 30 June 1969

Principal Investigator: Mr. Frank E. Heart
Telephone (617) 491-1850, Ext. 470

Sponsored by
Advanced Research Projects Agency
ARPA Order No. 1260

Contract No. DAHC15-69-C-0179
Effective Date: 2 January 1969
Expiration Date: 28 February 1970
Contract Amount: $1,077,727.00

Submitted to:
Advanced Research Projects Agency
Washington, D.C. 20301
Attn: Dr. L.G. Roberts

CAMBRIDGE   NEW YORK   CHICAGO   LOS ANGELES

Report No. 1837　　　　　　　　　　　　　　　Bolt Beranek and Newman Inc.

TABLE OF CONTENTS

　　　　　　　　　　　　　　　　　　　　　　　　　　　　　　　page

SECTION 1.　INTRODUCTION. . . . .　1

　　　　 2.　OPERATIONAL PROGRAM DESIGN. . . . .　2
　　　　　　　A.　Program Organization. . . . .　3
　　　　　　　B.　Buffer Allocation and Queues. . . . .　5
　　　　　　　C.　Program Routines. . . . .　7

　　　　 3.　NETWORK MEASUREMENTS. . . . .　11
　　　　　　　A.　Measurement Facilities. . . . .　11
　　　　　　　B.　Tracing . . . .　14

Report No. 1837   Bolt Beranek and Newman Inc.

1.   INTRODUCTION

   This Quarterly Technical Report No. 2 describes several aspects of our progress on the ARPA Computer Network during the second quarter of 1969. During this quarter, the specifications for interconnecting a Host and an IMP were documented in BBN Report No. 1822, which was distributed to all the participating Hosts. The report, which was made available in loose leaf form, is divided into four sections: an introductory section; a section describing the physical apparatus and the requirements for its installation; a section devoted to software protocol and message formatting; and a section detailing the standard Host/IMP interface, the electrical signals on the Host cable, and the requirements for the design of the Host's special hardware interface.

   Early in this quarter, we completed the hardware design and received a prototype IMP. This unit contains one IMP/Modem interface and one IMP/Host interface, as well as a normal complement of the other special features (real-time clock, watchdog timer, etc.). The prototype was checked out and has since been operating reliably.

   The software design has been substantially completed and the implementation of the initial operational IMP program is well underway. In this report we describe the organization of this program and present our preliminary plans for obtaining measurements.

Report No. 1837   Bolt Beranek and Newman Inc.

2. OPERATIONAL PROGRAM DESIGN

An initial operational IMP program has been designed and is being implemented for use in the ARPA network. The overall function and organization of this program is based upon the IMP design and the network protocol, as described in BBN Report No. 1763. The current program design is decribed below.

The system software has been specially designed (for the modified Honeywell D.D.P.-516 computer) to maximize packet throughput, to provide maximum autonomy for each IMP, and to maximize the available buffer space by using as little core memory for the program as possible.

The principal function of the program is the processing of packets. This processing includes segmentation of Host messages into packets for transmission, building of headers, receiving and transmitting of store and forward packets, reassembling of packets received at a destination into messages for transmission to the Host, and generating of RFNM's and acknowledgements.

Another important function of the IMP program is network monitoring, which helps to maintain reliable communication. Network monitoring includes detecting adjacent lines that have gone dead and detecting and discarding duplicate packets. In addition, information received from its neighbors at half second intervals is used to identify unreachable destinations (dead or inaccessible sites) and to inform the IMP of the minimum expected delay to each destination.

Our preliminary plans for providing measurement facilities incorporate the taking of synchronized network snapshots, the accumulating of histograms, the tracing of packets through the network, and the recording of actual packet arrival times on an input channel. These measurement facilities are discussed in Section 3.

The program currently occupies approximately 6000 registers of core, which is half of the available memory.* The other half of memory will be used for buffer storage (except that a portion of this buffer space will be used for the operational DDT program early in the network operation).

A. Program Organization

The program is composed of five main pieces: a *task routine* that performs the major portion of the IMP packet processing; the Modem routines (IMP to Modem and Modem to IMP) that handle interrupts and resetting of buffers for the Modem channels; the Host routines (IMP to Host and Host to IMP) that not only handle interrupts and resetting of buffers for the Host channels but also build packet headers during input and construct RFNMs that are returned to the source Host during output; a *timeout routine* that maintains a software clock, activates certain deferred tasks, and attends to infrequent events; and a *background routine* that handles all jobs of sufficiently low priority that the exact time of their execution is relatively unimportant. The background routine also includes an initialization routine that is used during startup.

The transfer of program control from one routine to another is completely governed by the occurrence of priority interrupts. After the initialization routine is executed, program control remains in the background routine, which is cycled through repeatedly until an interrupt occurs causing control to be transferred to another routine. Each routine has associated with it a priority that allows it to interrupt any other routine situated below it in the hierarchy. The hierarchy of program control is shown in Fig. 1 below.

---

*The IMP cabinet has space for an additional 4000 words of core.

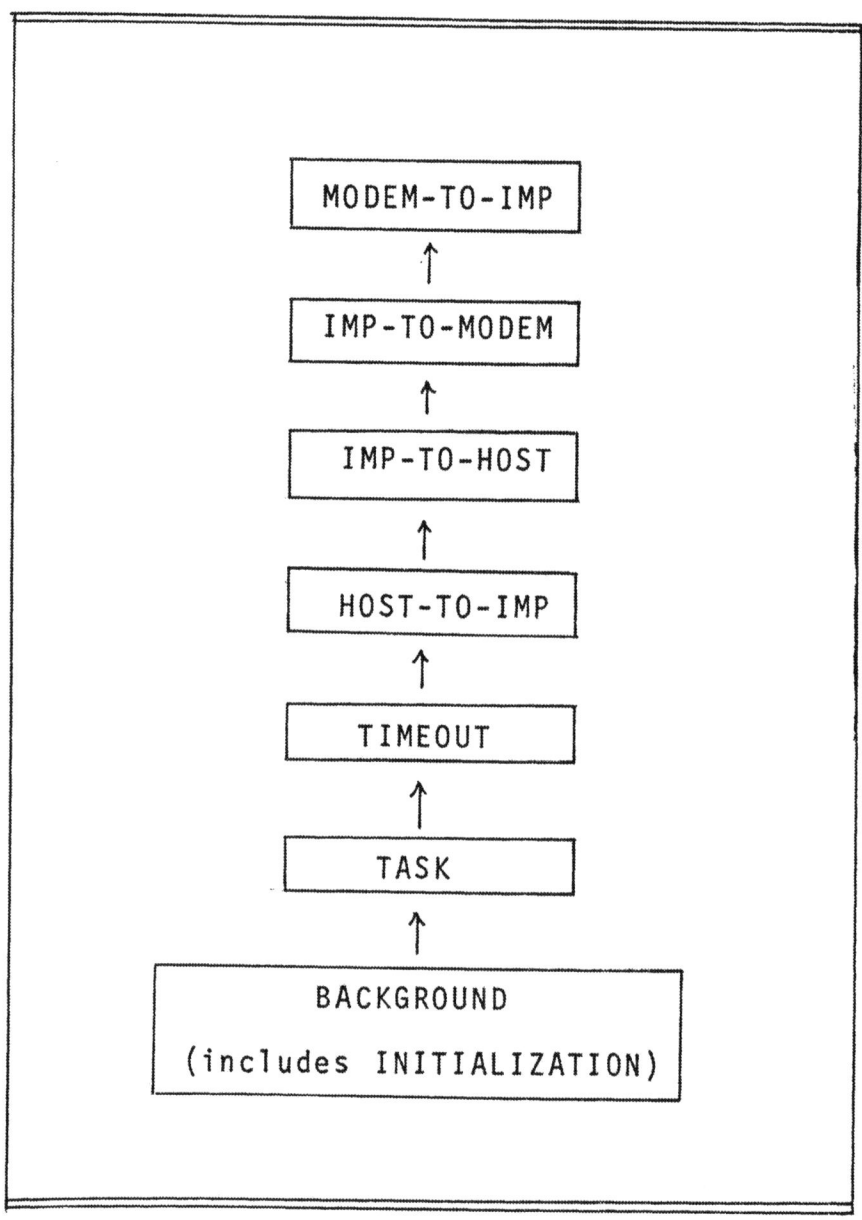

Figure 1. Program Control

When all interrupts have finally been serviced, control is again returned to the background routine, which resumes at the instruction that was about to be executed when the first interrupt occurred.

B. Buffer Allocation and Queues

A large fraction of core memory is partitioned into fixed size buffers, each of which is used for storing a single packet. A buffer in which no packet is stored is said to be free, and all free buffers are chained together on a free buffer list. A buffer is removed from the free buffer list and set up for input each time a buffer is needed to store the next packet from a Host or Modem channel or to store an internally generated packet. Buffers that are not located on the free buffer list either are set up to store an incoming packet, are having their contents transmitted on one of the output channels, are being processed by the IMP program, or have been dispatched to one or more system queues for subsequent processing.

There are seven principal system queues:

Task Queue

The task queue is organized into a Host task queue and two Modem task queues. Packets received on Host channels are placed on the Host task queue. All received acknowledgements, dead Host and routing information, I Heard You and Hello packets are placed on a fast Modem task queue. All other packets from the Modems are placed on a regular Modem task queue. The fast Modem task queue will be serviced first. The IMP program currently services the Host task queue before the regular Modem task queue, but this latter arrangement is not yet considered final.

Output Queues

A separate output queue is constructed for each Modem channel and each Host channel. All packets waiting their turn for transmission on a given channel are chained together on the queue for that channel. Each Modem output queue is divided into an acknowledgement queue, a priority queue, a RFNM queue, and a regular message queue, which are serviced in the indicated order. The Host output queue is divided into a control message queue, a priority queue, and a regular message queue, which are also serviced in the indicated order.

Sent Queue

A separate sent queue for each Modem channel contains packets that have already been transmitted on that line but for which no acknowledgement has yet been received.

Retransmission Queue

If a received acknowledgement frees a buffer that is not first on the sent queue, all the skipped buffers are placed on the retransmission queue.

Reassembly Queue

The reassembly queue contains those packets that are being reassembled into messages for the Host.

Conversion Queues

The conversion queues consist of an input queue of fully reassembled messages, which are intended for the Host and are awaiting the application of the Host specified unique transformation, and an output queue of packets, which have just been received from the Host and are awaiting transformation.

C. Program Routines

Modem to IMP

The Modem to IMP routine is executed whenever a packet arrives on a Modem channel. This routine sets up a free buffer for storing subsequent input on that channel and places the buffer containing a correctly received packet on a Modem task queue. If no free buffers are available, the first buffer is removed from its place on the regular Modem task queue. Should no such buffer be available, the last received packet is discarded by setting up its buffer for input.

IMP to Modem

The IMP to Modem routine is executed each time a packet transmission is completed. Buffers containing a RFNM, a priority, or a regular message are placed on the sent queue, and the next buffer on the output queue is set up for transmission. If no packets are present on the output queue, this routine will be restarted when another buffer is placed there.

IMP to Host

The IMP to Host routine is executed whenever the transmission of a packet to the Host is completed. This routine removes the next buffer from the output queue to the Host and sets the buffer up for transmission to the Host. In addition, it builds a RFNM packet and places the RFNM on the Host task queue. If the output queue is empty, a next buffer is not set up and the routine is restarted when the queue is no longer empty.

Host to IMP

The Host to IMP routine is executed whenever the Host finishes its input or the Host input buffer is filled. The routine builds a header into the buffer, which is then placed on the end of the Host task queue. A free buffer is then set up for additional input from the Host. This routine will discard the filled Host buffer, if the Host Error flip flop went on during the transmission; in addition, all succeeding packets will be discarded until an end-of-message signal is detected. This routine also checks the message type for validity, verifies that the destination is not dead and that the link table is not full or the link blocked.

Timeout

The timeout routine is started every 25.6 ms by a clock interrupt. Timeout is used to increment a 16-bit software clock and to insure the occurrence of events that either are expected to be infrequent, or must occur at regular intervals, or have been marked for execution by the timeout routine.

The timeout routine is divided into a fast, medium, and slow timeout routine. The slow timeout routine is run every 25 clock interrupts. The medium timeout routine is run every fifth interrupt, except when the slow routine runs. In all other cases the fast routine is run.

The software clock is updated during each timeout routine. During the medium timeout routine, buffers on the retransmission queue are routed onto an output queue; buffers that are on the sent queue and that have timed out are routed onto an output queue for retransmission, as are all buffers on an output queue for a Modem channel that has just gone dead. During the slow timeout routine, the following tasks are performed.

- One dead line, if any, will be located and marked.
- A flag will be set if the Host ready line is off.
- A new routing table will be built and placed on each output queue to the Modems.

- Counters that might normally overflow are reset.
- A flag is set for each link that has timed out.
- A flag is set for each message that has timed out in reassembly.

Task

The task routine removes the next packet from the top of the task queue for processing and then either discards it or places it at the end of one of the system queues. If the first task is an acknowledgement, its four header words are compared against the header entries on the sent queue. If no match occurs, the buffer is released to the free buffer list and the next task is obtained. If a header match is obtained with the first entry, the buffer is removed from the sent queue and both buffers are freed. If a match occurs at other than the first entry, all the skipped entries are placed on the retransmission queue.

Buffers containing received routing and dead Host information are copied and then released. If a buffer contains an I Heard You packet, a flag will have been reset and the buffer will simply be released. If it is an Hello packet, a flag is set to send an I Heard You packet and the buffer is released.

When a packet reaches its destination the task routine checks the message number and determines whether sufficient buffer storage is available. The buffer is then either placed on the reassembly queue, on the output queue to the Host, or else is discarded.

If sufficient buffer storage is available, store and forward packets are routed onto an output queue to a Modem. If buffer storage is insufficient, the packets are discarded. Discarded packets are not acknowledged and will eventually be retransmitted.

Background

The background routine performs all the low priority processing. It handles all packets that are generated at the IMP teletype or destined for it, all completed trace and statistics buffers, all buffers on the conversion queues, as well as all packets generated by or intended for the operational DDT program. The background routine cannot interrupt any other routine, and, therefore, operates only when no other processing remains to be done.

The initialization routine, which is included in the background, builds and initializes all tables, builds the initial queue pointers, builds the free buffers, and creates a free buffer list. It also creates a list of free trace buffers and a list of free reassembly slots and then starts up all the output routines.

3. NETWORK MEASUREMENTS

As a vehicle for experimentation and study, the ARPA network is intended to provide a continuing supply of data to aid in understanding network performance. Two sources of this data are the direct measurement by the IMP program of its activities and the tracing of selected packets within the network.

In this section we present our preliminary plans for the design of these data gathering facilities. These plans are still subject to change, but in the next quarter we expect to finalize them and to complete our work on the measurement software. At that time we will prepare a separate document describing these facilities in detail.

A. Measurement Facilities

Each measurement facility may be activated or deactivated independently through the use of Host generated control messages. If all the facilities are activated at the same time, the system may experience a substantial measurement load, which might affect the flow of traffic and, consequently, the measurements themselves.

We have also provided for synchronization of the software clocks throughout the network. The clock in each IMP is synchronized to the clock of the IMP (that is not dead) with the lowest destination number. Each IMP transmits the reading of its 16 bit software clock to its neighboring IMPs every 1/2 second along with the routing information. The IMP uses the received time from the neighboring IMP, which is nearest the time reference, to adjust its own clock.

Periodic Snapshots

Once every half second, the IMP program will record the following information (referred to as *snapshots*) and transmit it to the measurement center.

- Length of the free buffer list
- Length of each Modem output queue
- Length of each Host output queue
- Length of the sent queue
- Length of the retransmission queue
- Length of the conversion queues
- Length of the background queue
- Number of messages in reassembly
- Number of transmit links in use
- Number of receive links in use
- Delay table (delay/HOP/Dead Hosts)
- Routing table (lines)
- Number of transmit characters converted
- Number of receive characters converted
- Received time from each neighboring IMP
- Own time

Snapshots at all IMPs will be synchronized to occur at approximately the same time.

Accumulated Histograms

Histograms are accumulated over an interval of ten seconds and then transmitted to the measurement center. Certain histograms are actual counts of number of occurrences of a particular event, while other histograms actually approximate a distribution. Specifically, the following information is recorded.

a. Per Modem

- Total number of regular and priority message words on each output line.
- Number of output Hello packets.
- Number of output RFNM packets.
- Number of output acknowledgement packets.
- Number of transmitted packets with: 1   word of text

      2–3 words of text

      4–7 words of text

      8–15 words of text

      16–31 words of text

      32–63 words of text.
- Number of input I Heard You packets.
- Number of input packets in error.
- Number of good packets on input line.
- Number of good packets discarded because of no free buffers.
- Number of regular Modem task buffers liberated on input.
- Number of acknowledgements on input line.
- Number of retransmitted packets.

b. Per Host

- Number of messages on the input line with: 1   word of text

      2–3 words of text

      4–7 words of text

      8–15 words of text

      16–31 words of text

      32–63 words of text.
- Number of messages on the input line with: 2 packets

      3 packets

      4 packets

      5 packets

      6 packets

      7 packets

      8 packets.

- Number of messages on the output line with: 1   word of text
  2-3 words of text
  4-7 words of text
  8-15 words of text
  16-31 words of text
  32-63 words of text
- Number of messages on the output line with: 2 packets
  3 packets
  4 packets
  5 packets
  6 packets
  7 packets
  8 packets.
- Number of words to Host.
- Number of words from Host.
- Number of control messages from Host.
- Number of control messages to Host.
- Number of input messages to each destination.

c. Other
- Number of trace messages generated.
- Number of packets handled for each destination.

Interarrival Times

Upon command from the measurement center the IMP will record, for use in modeling the interarrival time distribution on the lines, the times at which the input interrupts on a given line occurred. A table containing approximately 60 IMP words will be used for this purpose. If more than 60 interrupts occur within 1/2 second, the measurements will be temporarily suspended for the remainder of the half-second interval and then automatically resumed.

B. Tracing

In the leader of each Host message is a trace bit which, if set to a one will cause that particular message to be traced through the network. Each IMP that handles the packets of that message will record the following information and transmit it to the network measurement center.

- Packet header.
- Time packet arrives at IMP.
- Time packet (buffer) is placed on the output queue.
- Time packet (buffer) is set up for transmission.
- Time the acknowledgement is returned or the time the buffer is placed on the retransmission queue. (For Modem Channels).
- Time the transmission is completed (For Host Channels).
- Output channel.
- Acknowledged or retransmitted.

To enable its tracing mechanism, an IMP must receive a command from the measurement center. This command will include the destination to which the trace packets should be sent and a link number for the IMP to use. If the tracing mechanism is not enabled, the IMP will ignore the trace bit. Once enabled, though, a second control message is needed to disable the mechanism.

Report No. 1890   October 1969

INTERFACE MESSAGE PROCESSORS FOR
THE ARPA COMPUTER NETWORK

QUARTERLY TECHNICAL REPORT NO. 3
1 July 1969 to 30 September 1969

Principal Investigator: Mr. Frank E. Heart
                           Telephone (617) 491-1850, Ext. 470

Sponsored By
Advanced Research Projects Agency
ARPA Order No. 1260

Contract No. DAHC15-69-C-0179
Effective Date: 2 January 1969
Expiration Date: 28 February 1970
Contract Amount: $1,077,727.00

Submitted to:

Advanced Research Projects Agency
Washington, D.C. 20301
Attn: Dr. L.G. Roberts

Report No. 1890　　　　　　　　　　　　　　Bolt Beranek and Newman Inc.

TABLE OF CONTENTS

		page
SECTION 1.	INTRODUCTION	1
2.	HARDWARE CHECKOUT AND INSTALLATION	2
	A. Test Program Development	2
	B. Test Cell Activity	2
	C. Initial Installation Activity	4
3.	SOFTWARE DEVELOPMENT	5
	A. Network Failure Recovery	5
	B. IMP Failure Recovery	6
	C. Stopping an IMP	7
4.	PROJECTED IMP PERFORMANCE	9
	A. Capacity in Connected Lines	9
	B. IMP Throughput	9

Report No. 1890   Bolt Beranek and Newman Inc.

1. INTRODUCTION

This Quarterly Technical Report No. 3 describes several aspects of our progress on the ARPA computer network during the third quarter of 1969. During this period, the first IMP was delivered to UCLA on schedule with an operational program. The IMP successfully communicated with the UCLA Host computer (a Sigma 7).

In Section 2, we describe the test programs developed, the testing procedure used, and the technical problems encountered in installing the initial IMP. In Section 3, we outline several new features that have been incorporated into the operational IMP program described in our Quarterly Technical Report No. 2 (BBN Report No. 1837). We will soon make these features available in a second version of the operational program. We have begun a preliminary study of the IMP program in an attempt to understand its performance. A few projected measures of program performance are presented in Section 4.

Documentation during this quarter consisted of two minor revisions of the Host specification (BBN Report No. 1822).

2. HARDWARE CHECKOUT AND INSTALLATION

During this quarter, we tested the IMPs intensively. After being tested separately, the IMPs were combined into small networks of two or three locally connected IMPs and then retested. Upon installation at UCLA, the IMP was tested further.

A. Test Program Development

An extensive program has been developed for checkout and testing of the IMP. The program consists of two parts: first, a section that performs one-time tests on several special IMP features (watchdog timer, automatic restart, memory protection, power-fail interrupt, etc.); and second, a loop that repeatedly drives a selectable data pattern through the interfaces to compare incoming data with outgoing data for errors. The data can be driven through a crosspatched interface, through a locally looped modem, through a phone line looped at a remote location, or to another IMP performing an identical test.

The tests have uncovered bad cables and logic packs, a number of wiring deficiencies, two minor interace design errors, and a design problem in the DDP-516 data-channel hardware. We are preparing a manual that describes verification, test, and installation procedures and discusses the test program in detail.

B. Test Cell Activity

During this quarter, Honeywell delivered IMPs Number 2 and 3. As with IMP No. 1, these machines contained a considerable number of faults which were debugged and corrected in the Test Cell.

A small temporary hardware patch to the Modem interfaces in IMPs 1 and 2 made possible the direct connection of these interfaces, thereby removing the need for intervening modems. This modification allowed for the construction of a three node pseudo-network as shown in Figure 1 below:

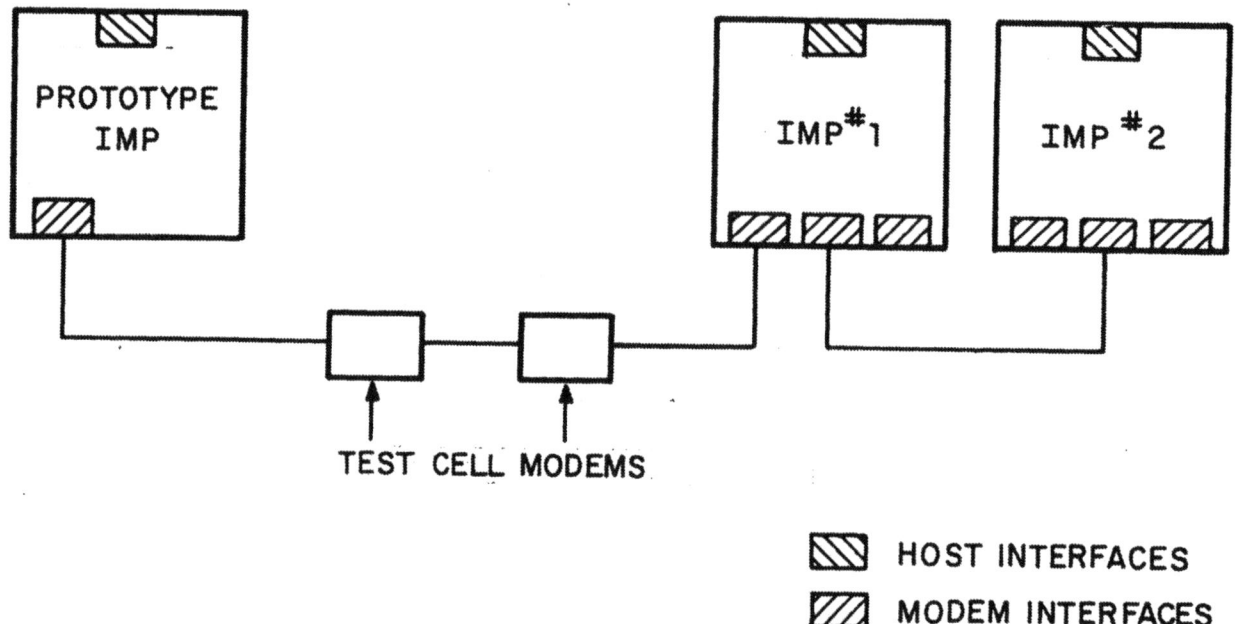

FIG. 1

This configuration provides a reasonably sophisticated setting for hardware testing and also allows for debugging of configuration dependent features (e.g., routing) of the operational program. An equivalent configuration was constructed using IMP No. 3 to replace IMP No. 1 after the latter had been shipped to UCLA.

C. Initial Installation Activity

Within a few days of its delivery to UCLA on Saturday, August 30, the IMP was connected to and operating with both the Sigma 7 and the phone company equipment. Intensive testing revealed a minor design error in the IMP's standard Host interface and a minor design error and some bad components in the Host's special interface. After these errors were corrected, tests were conducted with the UCLA-SRI phone line looped at the SRI end, and messages were successfully sent around this loop. During installation, we decided that we would like to test the phone company equipment but we found that the program used in the BBN Test Cell was not appropriate for studying phone-line error characteristics. We are presently writing a program for this purpose.

At the time of installation, we recognized a need for the Sigma 7 Host to have its own test program for communication with its IMP. A cooperative UCLA-BBN effort resulted in a simple program to send and receive character strings between the IMP and Host teletypes. This approach proved so successful that we plan to encourage the use of similar programs in all future installations.

We found the phone company installations at UCLA and SRI to be inconsistent with regard to physical configurations of voice circuits cabinetry, original design, etc. These difficulties were reported to the telephone company.

Report No. 1890   Bolt Beranek and Newman Inc.

3. SOFTWARE DEVELOPMENT

The software effort during this quarter was devoted to implementing the program design described in our Quarterly Technical Report No. 2. Version 1 of the operational program was delivered to UCLA with the first IMP. At this time, implementation is almost complete.

During this implementation period, new software features involving error-recovery procedures have been added to the program. These procedures handle the failure of an IMP or a Host, with consequent loss of whole or partial messages from the network. We feel that after a reasonable period, on the order of many minutes, all trace of such an event should be eliminated from the network and that the user should be informed of the occurrence.

Error-recovery procedures fall into two categories: the response of the network to an IMP or a Host failure and the response of an IMP to its own failure.

A. Network Failure Recovery

An IMP may detect a network failure in one of three ways:
1. A packet expected for reassembly of a multiple packet message never arrives.
2. A link in the link table of the transmit IMP is never unblocked.
3. The Host does not take a message from its IMP.

If a message is not fully reassembled in 15 minutes, the system presumes a failure. The message is discarded and a RFNM returned with a "transmission incomplete" bit set. This

5

RFNM, in turn, is passed along to the transmitting Host as Error Message Number 9.

If the Host has not taken a message after 15 minutes, the system presumes that it will never take the message. Therefore, as in the previous case, the message is discarded and a RFNM with the incomplete transmission bit is returned to the source Host.

If a link remains blocked for longer than 20 minutes, the system again presumes a failure, perhaps a lost RFNM or a lost message. The link is unblocked and an incomplete transmission error message is sent to the source Host. The delay is slightly longer for this failure so that the other failure mechanisms will have a chance to operate and unblock the link.

All three failures involve an event that takes much longer that it should. For the present, we have tried to pick reasonable time limits for each case; as we discover more about the behavior of the network, we will be able to define these limits more exactly.

In all three cases, Error Message No. 9 is given to the transmitting Host. We expect that failures of this sort will be infrequent enough to permit the human operator controlling the Host transmission to determine how to proceed.

B. IMP Failure Recovery

An IMP can recover from its own failure in two ways. In the event of power failure, a hardware feature permits the IMP to turn off the program before the program destroys itself. When power returns, the IMP restarts automatically. We considered several possibilities for handling the packets found in an IMP during a power failure and concluded that no plan to salvage the packets was both practical and foolproof. For example, we cannot know whether the packet in transmission at the time of failure successfully left the machine before the power failed. Should that packet be reintroduced into the network after a lengthy delay, it might actually be delivered twice! Therefore, we decided simply to discard all the packets and restart the IMP program.

The second recovery mechanism is the "watchdog timer", which transfers control to protected memory whenever the program neglects this timer for about one minute. Everything unique to a particular IMP must reside in its protected memory. Only one register (containing the IMP number) currently differs from IMP to IMP.

We presume that the program in unprotected memory is destroyed either through a hardware transient or software failure. The program in protected memory sends a reload request down a phone line selected at random. The neighboring IMP responds by sending a copy of its whole program back on that phone line. A normal IMP would discard this message because it is too long, but the IMP in trouble can reload its program. The process of reloading from the network takes only a few seconds and can be repeated until successful. This feature of loading from the network would permit delivery and incorporation of a new version of software through the network. However, we still view paper tape as the primary input medium.

C. Stopping an IMP

Care must be taken to stop a working IMP without introducing network failures. Therefore, we have implemented a "clean stop" feature (a special switch) that shuts down the IMP without losing messages. The program initiates the following sequence of events when the IMP is taken down cleanly:

1. Sends the Host an "IMP going down" message.
2. Waits 5 seconds to let the Host finish network transactions.
3. Refuses messages from the Host and notifies the network that the Host is dead.
4. Waits 5 seconds to let other Hosts learn that this Host is dead.
5. Refuses messages from the network.
6. Waits 5 seconds to allow its IMP to empty of store and forward messages.
7. Stops.

Report No. 1890   Bolt Beranek and Newman Inc.

4. PROJECTED IMP PERFORMANCE

During the last quarter we began to study the projected performance of the IMP. This study was based upon a recent version of the operational program and provides only preliminary data. The IMP has not yet been tested under heavy load conditions and consequently no experimental data is available. In the following paragraphs, we present a few conclusions about IMP performance.

A. Capacity in Connected Lines

The amount of traffic flowing on a fifty kilobit line fully loaded with store and forward packets is adopted as a unit traffic load on the IMP. We call this unit an *effective channel*. Thus, a fifty kilobit line offers at most one effective-channel load, while a 230.4 kilobit line offers at most a load of 4.6 effective channels. Conveniently, the processing time for a message on the Host line is about equal to the processing time for the same message on a phone line; thus, Host lines and phone lines are equal with regard to effective-channel traffic.

The computational capacity of the IMP is a function of message length. For a load consisting only of short messages (one word), the capacity is seven effective channels. For the longest messages (eight packets), the capacity is nineteen effective channels.

B. IMP Throughput

We adopt the IMP throughput in bits/second as a measure of IMP performance. The throughput is the maximum number of

9

Host data bits that may traverse an IMP each second. The actual number of bits entering the IMP each second is somewhat larger than the throughput because of such message overhead as headers, RFNMs and acknowledgements. Each packet on the phone lines contains seventeen characters of overhead, thirteen of which are removed before the packet enters an IMP.

The maximum IMP throughput of approximately 700,000 bits/second is achieved with large (8 packet) messages on nineteen effective channels. A curve of maximum throughput as a function of message length is shown in Figure 2. The difference between the throughput curve and the line traffic curve represents overhead.

BOLT BERANEK AND NEWMAN INC

CONSULTING · DEVELOPMENT · RESEARCH

Report No. 1928   January 1970

INTERFACE MESSAGE PROCESSORS FOR
THE ARPA COMPUTER NETWORK

QUARTERLY TECHNICAL REPORT NO. 4
1 October 1969 to 31 December 1969

SUBMITTED TO:

Advanced Research Projects Agency
Washington, D.C. 20301

Attention: Dr. L.G. Roberts

This research was supported by the Advanced Research Projects Agency of the Department of Defense under Contract No. DAHC15-69-C-0179.

CAMBRIDGE   NEW YORK   CHICAGO   LOS ANGELES

Report No. 1928　　　　　　　　　　　Bolt Beranek and Newman Inc.

TABLE OF CONTENTS

　　　　　　　　　　　　　　　　　　　　　　　　　　　　page

SECTION 1.　INTRODUCTION 1

　　　　2.　SOFTWARE DEVELOPMENT 2

　　　　3.　HARDWARE DEVELOPMENT 6

　　　　4.　PHONE LINE TEST PROGRAM 7

　　　　5.　HOST PROTOCOL 8

Report No. 1928   Bolt Beranek and Newman Inc.

1. INTRODUCTION

This Quarterly Technical Report No. 4 describes several aspects of our progress on the ARPA computer network during the fourth quarter of 1969. During this period, the installation of a four-node initial network connecting UCLA, UCSB, SRI, and Utah was completed on schedule. A second version of the operational IMP program which replaced the earlier version was released on November 2. The continuing software development activity is described in Section 2. Work was also completed on the implementation of a hardware add-on to the standard Host/IMP interface unit to drive a 2000-foot Host cable. This work is described in Section 3.

An initial version of a phone line test program was written during this quarter in order to obtain data on the performance of the wideband communication circuits. This program and our initial experience in using it is described in Section 4. A slight modification to the IMP's RFNM mechanism resulted from our discussions with the Hosts in the initial network. Our participation in the effort to develop a sensible Host protocol is described in Section 5.

Report No. 1928   Bolt Beranek and Newman Inc.

2. SOFTWARE DEVELOPMENT

During this quarter, version two of the operational program was delivered to the sites. This new version incorporates most of the features previously described in our technical reports, such as a complete set of measurement facilities, and includes a new status reporting feature.

In order to incorporate these measurement facilities, we made a substantial effort to utilize the existing program routines. As a result, it was decided that the IMP should use the Host/IMP and IMP/Host routines to handle messages generated by or destined for an IMP and thus to treat these IMP messages as if they were Host messages.

An IMP message is distinguished from a Host message by a digit 1 in the FOR IMP or FROM IMP bit in the leader of the message. A message from an IMP is identified by a 1 in the FROM IMP bit position in the leader; likewise, a message to an IMP is identified by a 1 in the FOR IMP bit position of the leader. The particular *type* of IMP message is designated by the two Host bits in the leader. The RFNM mechanism works in the usual fashion for IMP messages. A detailed description of the formats for communication between a Host and an IMP will be incorporated into BBN Report No. 1822, the Host Specification. A typical Host will ordinarily have little need to communicate directly with an IMP.

The various types of messages to and from an IMP are illustrated in Figure 1 and are described below:

1) TELETYPE — FOR IMP messages of type 0 are printed out on the IMP teletype. FROM IMP messages of type 0 are generated at the IMP teletype.

2) DEBUG — DEBUG messages are used to examine, modify, and report the contents of registers in core. Messages to and from DEBUG are designated by type 1. The IMP software prevents the unauthorized use of the DEBUG program.

3) TRACE — When this feature is activated (using PARAMETER CHANGE), the IMP program records and transmits information about packets that have been marked for tracing. This FROM IMP information is designated by type 2.

4) STATISTICS — When this feature is activated, the IMP program performs measurements on network activity and transmits this information to a designated destination. This FROM IMP information is designated by type 3.

5) PARAMETER CHANGE — An authorized Host can send a message to an IMP that causes preselected IMP parameters to be modified. This FOR IMP message should be of type 2.

6) DISCARD — The IMP program will discard any FOR IMP message of type 3.

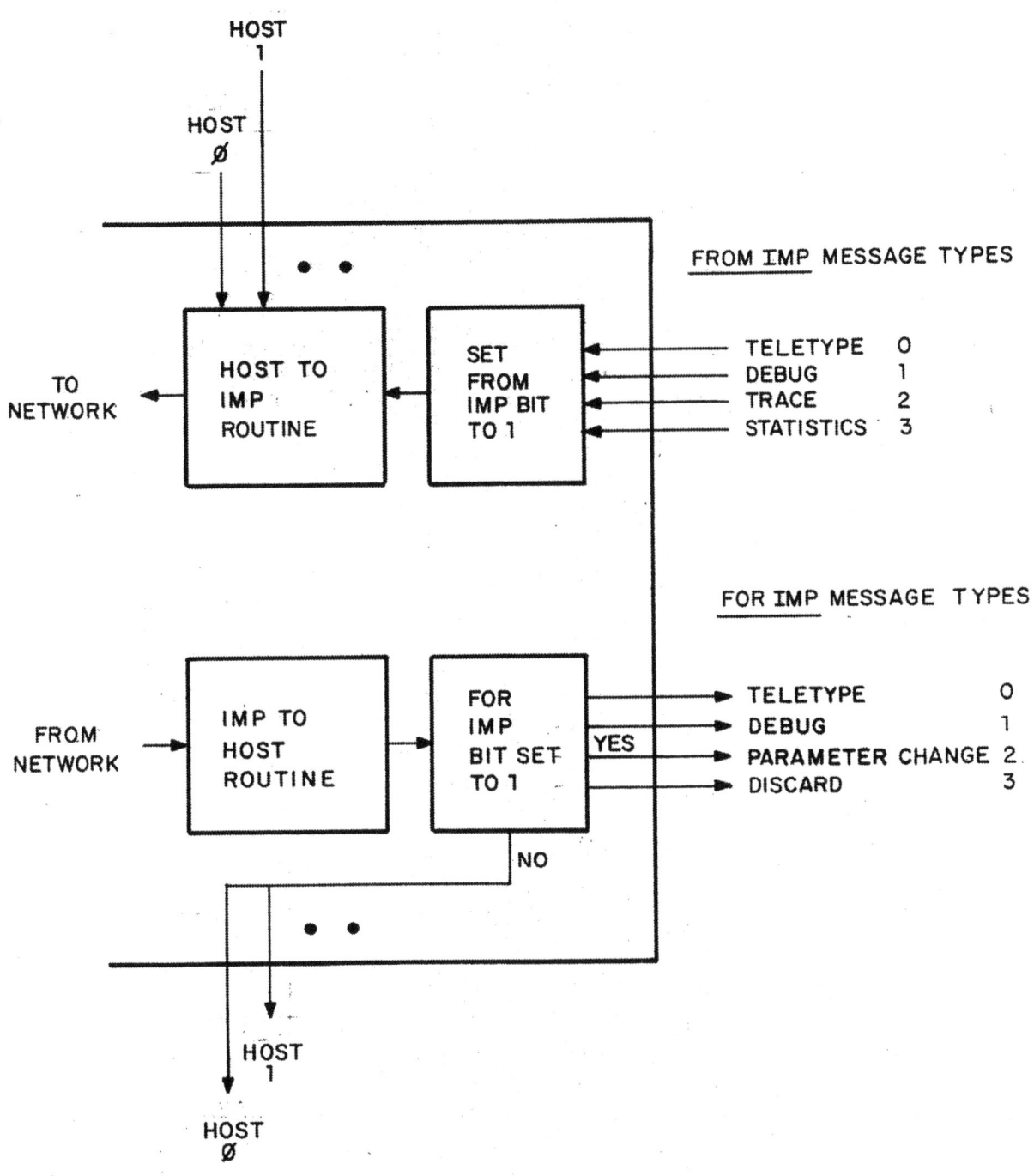

FIG. 1. COMMUNICATION WITH AN IMP.

Report No. 1928   Bolt Beranek and Newman Inc.

The status reporting mechanism provides current information about the condition of the network. When activated at a given IMP, this mechanism periodically forms a message that records the status of the Host, the phone lines, and the sense switches. A new status message is formed and transmitted every ten minutes to the control center and also whenever live/dead status changes occur. These messages are printed on the IMP teletype at the control center in the following form:

IMP #	HOST STATUS	LINE 1 STATUS	LINE 2 STATUS	LINE 3 STATUS	SENSE SWITCH STATUS

The Host and line status entries denote the respective live/dead conditions. In addition, the line status entries also denote the number of retransmitted packets on that line in the last twenty recorded tries. The sense switch status entry records the position of each sense switch. The format will be modified to include additional lines and hosts as needed. An up-to-date record of the network status is thus available at the control center whenever this feature is activated.

3. HARDWARE DEVELOPMENT

During the last quarter, we developed a prototype distant Host driver that may be added to the standard interface to permit connection of a Host to an IMP at distances up to 2000 ft. The inclusion of a distant Host driver does not change the logical operation of the Host interface, although the actual line signals are different from those of a local Host connection.

The distant Host driver performs two functions. It accommodates a shift in ground potential between two distant systems and it provides a signaling method having sufficient power and noise resistance to communicate over a 2000-foot separation. The reference level for the logic signals is shifted in the driver unit from the IMP signal reference to the Host signal reference by transformer coupling. The Host reference is then carried to the distant Host driver through the cable shield. Within the distant Host cable, signals are transmitted on twisted pairs as balanced differential signals that permit rejection of induced common mode noise.

A prototype driver has been successfully tested on a 2000-foot cable loop and production versions will be available early in the spring.

Report No. 1928   Bolt Beranek and Newman Inc.

4. PHONE LINE TEST PROGRAM

In the last quarter, we designed and implemented a test program to obtain data on the performance of the fifty kilobit communication circuits. This particular test program continuously transmits short packets (88 bits) on each phone line and keeps track of arriving packets in a way that allows the real time occurrence of packet errors to be recorded on the console teletype. In addition, it records, for arriving packets, a burst length histogram of successive correct packets and successive packets in error.

The basic operation of the program is as follows. The program sends out in each packet one word of data that contains a 16-bit count. The count is incremented by one for each transmitted packet. When a packet arrives without error, the new count is compared with the last received count and any difference greater than one is taken to indicate an error burst.

Two different types of line test can be run. A two-way line test may be run whenever the remote modem is looped back. Two one-way line tests may be run whenever the remote modem is not looped and another copy of the test program is running the neighboring IMP.

Preliminary two-way test data, obtained during a 27-hour period on the UCSB-SRI line (looped back at SRI), indicates approximately one packet per 20,000 in error. However, subsequent tests have uncovered a 100% variation in this number — apparently due to many unusually long periods of time (on the order of hours) with no detected errors. The distribution of error bursts appears to be concentrated in the range between one and seven packets.

5. HOST PROTOCOL

Under this contract, the primary BBN responsibility has been the implementation of an IMP subnet and the related connection of the subnet to the Host computers. In addition to this development effort, the utility of the ARPA Network is dependent upon the formulation of sensible Host protocols. The difficulty of this task reflects the basic underlying research problem of how local and remote computer programs should interact. Informal efforts to generate a Host protocol have been in progress for some time, and an informal "Network Working Group" exists as one forum for discussions. In the last quarter, BBN has increased its participation in these efforts* and we expect to continue this participation in the next quarter.

It is apparent that the development of a Host protocol involves some interaction between BBN and the Hosts on the subject of IMP protocol. As one result of this interaction, a minor change is being made in the RFNM mechanism to simplify an aspect of Host/Host traffic control. A Host that wishes to stop the flow of incoming traffic on a given link, or on all links, simply notifies its IMP via a control message. The IMP then sets a special control bit in the next RFNM it returns on that link. It is the responsibility of the transmitting Host to interpret this information and stop the flow of traffic. The IMP will not enforce this blockage, as the IMP will unblock the link as soon as the RFNM returns. A Host-to-Host message is required to restart the flow on this link. We anticipate other cases where small IMP protocol changes will be useful and we will try to be responsive to such needs.

---

*Much of our discussion has been with S. Crocker of UCLA and we acknowledge his contribution.

More generally, we have been participating in the consideration of several Host protocol issues. For example:

1. While we have come to believe that the IMP should not do character set conversions, there is still an immediate need for a network-wide teletype character set into and out of which each Host translates his messages. The choice is arbitrary, and the need for a decision has become urgent (already we see Hosts converting to the language of the destination). We recommend the adoption of 8-bit ASCII with the 8th bit (checksum bit) set to a 1, which is the IMP's internal character set. This choice has the small additional advantage that Hosts may send messages to local or remote IMP teletypes without an additional conversion. As network use develops, other standards (such as a display language) will be needed.

2. With regard to the user level of message control, we recommend the notion of user *ports* whereby a user may request to establish a port with a specific port number. The user may request to send messages from one port to another, or to receive messages at a port from either a specific port or from any port. Standard programs in each Host (the logger, the message box, etc.) would have standard published numbers and would be generally available for use. We hope to participate in further detailing of this approach.

3. A potential conflict exists over how to handle echoing. Local echoing is troublesome for systems that do not always echo the input; remote echoing is both troublesome for systems whose hardware automatically echoes and may introduce undue echoing delay. This topic deserves further study.

Report No. 1928   Bolt Beranek and Newman Inc.

At this point the initial network is installed and operational. New Hosts will be entering the network at a rate of one a month for the next several months. There is thus an urgent need for further work on Host protocol and for documents specifying formats and procedures for Host-to-Host communication.

APPENDIX

Reprints from *Matrix News*

"And They Argued All Night…"

… over whose claim was right: first at which, and for what, and with whom.

M.A. Padlipsky <map@multiscans.org>

Despite my stated views on the futility of "doing" technohistory, I can scarcely find it in what's left of my heart to decline Peter Salus' invitation to take a turn in his *Lest They Forget/Be Forgotten* series, especially since I've been itching for at least a couple of years to have an excuse to dispute various self-serving claims of Fathers of this and Inventors of that now that the 'Net is the darling of the mediaocrities. And the best place to start is almost certainly with a restatement of why I think technohistory can't be done (lifted from *The Elements of Networking Style and Other Essays and Animadversions on the Art of Intercomputer Networking*, with permission of, and indeed by, The Author):

> Around [20, by now] years ago I ran into an Old Network Boy friend (Gary Grossman, actually) I hadn't seen for a while. We got to reminiscing about the good old days five or so years previously on the "New" Telnet [. . .] working group and I said, "You know, I always liked your IAC trick." (a fairly important second-order mechanism of the ARPANET's second-pass Virtual Terminal Protocol.) "Wait a minute," he replied, "IAC was one of yours." *[Page 24, if you're curious about the fuller context.]*

He was right, by the way. The neat ideas zipped around the design meetings at a great rate of speed (and volume, usually; in both senses of the term).

Even before we all hit at best EarlyMiddleage (and I fear I crossed over into MiddleMiddleage last May; most of the others still have a few years to go though, damn them) we didn't really remember who'd come up with which neat notion. Indeed, over at least a 22-year period before the untimely and intensely lamented death of Jon Postel, he and I had frequent conversations trying to reconstruct the origins of a number of neat notions and we almost never succeeded, even on many of the ones I was fairly sure had been his (which, in fact, was most of them). And before the 'Net became big business, it was fairly easy for us to shrug it off; things had worked out, and what did it matter whether he, or I, or Gary, or even one of the BBN guys—who always seemed to get to write the histories and hence always seemed to have claimed to have invented everything, anyway, perhaps because BBN was the only "for-profit" to furnish key members of the original Network Working Group (NWG)—had actually been the first to enunciate an idea that was almost always implicit in the discussion to begin with?

Now, however, there seems to be at least some celebrity value attached to that sort of thing, if not indeed some financial value. There might even just possibly be a minute amount of value to be attached to "historical accuracy", or "intellectual integrity", or some other hopelessly pre-GenX ab-

---

[Over the 15 years from 1971 through 1985, Mike Padlipsky authored over 20 RFCs. He ran the Networking Group for the Multics machine at MIT during the early years of the ARPANET, among other things. His The Elements of Networking Style and Other Essays and Animadversions on the Art of Intercomputer Networking *(Reprint Edition ISBN: 0-595-08879-1) remains the best book on OSI. —PHS.] Article copyright ©2000 by the author, edited and condensed for this compilation. The original is available at <http://firstmap.googlepages.com/allnight.html>.*

straction, but it would doubtless be a tactical error to espouse that sort of thing. Besides, as indicated, some of the current claims stick in my craw, and Peter did ask me to "write something" and didn't get at all specific as to what, so . . .

Let's start with the one I'm in fact quite certain I was the inventor of, especially because I can't recall which of the BBN guys is claiming it and so I can put off the delicate question of whether I want to name names for a while longer: "anonymous login". I remember pretty clearly, despite being somewhat unsure as to who the other person in the conversation was (Dirk, maybe?), being at SRI for some sort of meeting sometime around 1973 and being told that "the NIC" (or at least Jake *[=Elizabeth Feinler - PHS]*) was worried about this idea to put the RFCs on-line, because they'd have to establish all sorts of accounts so people could FTP them. "That's easy," I said, "just use my NETML trick." By which I meant, and went on to explain, that just as I'd had to propound a conventional universal "dummy" id and password so that netmail (as we'd called it when we were inventing it, but I'll get to that soon enough) could work via FTP without causing grave harm to the security (and accounting) mechanisms of at least some of the Hosts (mainly Multics, of course, since I was the Multics Network Technical Liaison at the time), all the NIC needed to do was establish a single, known account everybody could use to slurp the RFCs from. "'guest' would be a perfectly fine id," I went on, "and the password should be 'anonymous', since we'd gain some measure of security in that people'd have to know how to spell it and of course not everybody does." Or words very close to that, and to exactly that effect, even if I actually gave the id and password values in the reverse order. *[The NETML trick was enunciated in RFC 491, in case you care—and in case it ever gets scanned in so you can care. —MAP]*

Now, EarlyMiddleAgedMemory (EMAM) being what it was, and MiddleMiddleAgedMemory (MMAM) being what it is, naturally I don't recall whether I read that one of the BBN guys was laying claim to "anonymous login" the other year or saw it on one of those overly-coy little "courses" PBS (the P is for Pious, I like to observe) has taken to showing, before I decided they annoyed me so much I won't watch any more. (Even if I were on one? Irrelevant question. I didn't get rich, nor did I get my claims to've invented things into "the literature" early enough, because my company didn't get commissioned to write the "First 10 Years" report and wind up being visited first by the Internet history book writers.) But I submit that anybody who knows me knows that the crack about security has to be one of mine, and MMAM insists that whoever was laying the claim gave it as his own, which makes me suspect that the charitable explanation of parallel evolution doesn't apply and it was either his EMAM in play or just plain theft of intellectual property. Fortunately, anonymous login isn't really anything to be proud of—especially since it was exploited for a famous security breach when it was misimplemented on a certain highly popular Host type—so I can rise above.

Digression on Internet History Books
I'm not ready to name names yet, but I do want to offer a thought or two about this business of who gets talked to first by the historians. The authors of a couple of Internet history books did, one way or another, happen to get in touch with me during their "research" phases. Both had been in touch with BBN first. One of the authors did do me the courtesy of not buying the BBN version of the anonymous login story when the topic came up during our e-conversations. The other author apparently "bought into" the BBN version of just about everything (I've been warned by several friends not to read the book, in deference to my G.I. Woe), and on happening to meet me a couple of years after canceling out on a scheduled interview, said "You don't look at all like what I'd expected" and then wandered away, without even letting me explain why my reply had been, "You mean because I'm not 7 feet tall?". Maybe I'm wrong, but the only explanation I could come up with was that the BBN guys had described me with about the same degree of objectivity as Shakespeare had applied to Richard III, and the cognitive dissonance—is embarrassment over having been duped too much to hope for? Probably—was more than could be dealt with.

There might be some other reason for the apparent personal slight, and I'm taking care not to identify the author in question, but the fact still remains that enormous bias can be introduced into all history books, much less technohistory ones, based on whom the authors talk, or refer, to first . . . and whom they find agreeable, of course. (Hey, at least the first author kinda liked me.)

(By the way, the "7 feet tall" crack came from the time I once got a telephone call at work from a programmer who worked for Univac who'd been astute enough to have figured out that I was the right person to ask about the design intent of the Telnet Protocol, and when it came out in the course of the conversation that I'm not above average height she said, quite unsarcastically I believe, "But you write as if you're seven feet tall!")

Back to the Main Thread, Such as it Is
OK, here goes. It'd be not only disingenuous but downright cowardly not to name a couple of names. So first off, I don't believe Ray Tomlinson invented "e-mail". And not because of the quibble that we called it netmail originally, though that does offer an excuse to observe that I personally find the term "e-mail" awfully cutesy, and references to "sending an e-mail" syntactic slime. Nor because of the semi-quibble that "mail" had been around intra-Host on several of the Host operating systems since well before anybody realized they were Hosts, though that one has a great deal of abstract "historical" appeal. No, it's because I have a completely clear memory that Ray wasn't even at the FTP meeting where we decided to add mail to the protocol. Granted, one of the BBN guys mentioned that Ray had done a TENEX to TENEX mail hack already, and that he'd used the "@" between id and host name for the addresses, but that was after somebody had said, "Hey, why don't we send mail via FTP?" And for all I know, that somebody might have been me. (Or "been I", I imagine . . . if you're a fanatic Syntactic Puritan.) I'm not saying it was, but I don't know it wasn't. What I am sure of is that I was one of the strongest proponents of doing it, whoever broached the idea, and that I could have vetoed the famous "@", but didn't.

Vetoed it? Huh? Well, it takes a little, um, er, history to explain that one. When the "TIP" (or Terminal IMP, the ancestral terminal support machine, and at least weakly arguably the grandfather of the "ISP") was introduced—and MMAM assures me EMAM had long believed it was at the 1971 Network Working Group meeting in Atlantic City, though both could be wrong, as usual—the BBN guys announced, with grins, that the "intercept character" was going to be the "at-sign" and all looked at me. The reason was that on Multics, the at-sign was the reserved line-delete character. I thought about it for a second or two (being much younger and quicker of wit then) and said something very much along the lines of, "I guess. After all, everybody hits it a few times to be sure it takes, and you tell me doubling it will let it get through, so it shouldn't be that hard to remember that if we're TIPping to Multics we need to hit it an odd number of times when we want it intercepted but an even number of times when we want Multics to get it." And with that in mind, since in those days we tended, or pretended, to subscribe to the "all researchers together" myth, I had one coming, and could have insisted that it was too inconvenient for Multics users to have to type \@ when sending netmail, so let's pick another character. Or even use the more Multicsy syntax of "-at". But since it was the at sign—even though I could swear it was called the "commercial at sign" in my high school typing class, just to pick a nit now that I might well have picked then, too—and since I am a Semantic Puritan, I couldn't bring myself to argue that it wasn't appropriate, and let it pass.

So when it comes to who invented e-, or net-, mail, I submit: that as usual it was a group thing; that Ray wasn't at the meeting where it became part of the 'Net, although, granted, he was, as far as I know, the first person to send mail from one computer to another over a network, even though they were like computers, which isn't particularly interesting or challenging even if the world's most over-"capped" corporation can't seem to do consistently better than that these days, and for all I know somebody at the National Physical Laboratory in England had already done at least the same, and maybe even used unlike operating systems (the Brits turn out to have better claims to've invented a surprising number of things, I've noticed over the years, but apparently the historians' travel budgets are never adequate . . .)—and he did have the insight to realize that "@" is commonly pronounced "at", of course; and that if I really wanted to I could always pretend to be sure I'd been the one to propose doing mail via FTP at the meeting and I don't think anybody who was there and who is intellectually honest could gainsay me, but I don't really want to because I'm simply not sure who proposed it. I am, however, completely sure that it was implicit in what we were doing, so in a fairly real sense we all invented it.

One other thing about mail: Realize that FTP-based mail required the other Host to be up at the time (though people did come up with queuers for delayed sending if it wasn't), and it's arguable that what made "e-mail" really take off was when the model was changed so that that was no longer the case. The change came with SMTP. Jon was, of course, the author of that protocol, and knowing him he probably was the one who proposed it at the meeting, but I wasn't at the meeting so I don't know, but I'm perfectly content to assert that his claim to inventing "e-mail" is as good as anybody's.

"It's a Wise Child that Knows Its Own Father"

Or is it "It's a wise father that knows his own child"? (Or, in PC—for Philologically Corrupt—contempobabble: It's a wise child that knows their own father, maybe. Let's hope it wouldn't have to be their own parent in PCorruption of the first version, anyway, which MMAM does think is the original: the use of "their" with a singular antecedent to avoid choosing between "him", "her", or "him or her" is nauseating enough; if They insist on destroying the sense by ignoring that motherhood is a matter of fact, fatherhood is the one that's a matter of conjecture, They're not even worth trying to talk to.) Anyway, let's get to this "Father of the Internet" crap.

Normally, I'd say "In my humble but dogmatic opinion", but I don't want to be misunderstood. In my considered opinion, Len Kleinrock's claim to be the father of the Internet is . . . no, don't get "personal", make it, I know: unfounded. And/or lacking in merit. And/or utterly unfounded. And/or utterly lacking in merit. And/or . . . get the picture?

Now, between the word count Peter asked me to live with and the fact that my carpal tunnels are on the brink of cave-in after some 37 years of "keyboarding", I'm not going to go into much detail as to why I think a number of people's claims for that fundamentally meaningless but emotively compelling title are better than Len's, though I'll touch on some of them briefly. And perhaps surprise you by not including myself among them. But for Clio's sake, if she was the Muse of History, or for x's sake assuming Peter will fill in the x for me *[Clio is correct. —PHS]*, all Len was was the faculty guy who got the grant from ARPA to do the Network Measurement Center (NMC), where the first IMP happened to be installed. That doesn't even make him the father of the ARPANET, which ISN'T the Internet, if you're not a mediaocrity and care something about technical accuracy as opposed to "selling papers". Granted, three people who worked for him have good claims to the title—far, far better claims, imhbdo—but that would at best let him claim to be the grandfather, or more accurately great-grandfather, not the father. And depending upon how you define "the Internet", it's eminently arguable that their claims aren't as good as those of three other guys, whose efforts led to Len's getting the grant. (There's a fourth guy who worked at the NMC, who's still a good friend, whose claims to netpaternity are no better than my own non-existent ones, but he was also an important "player" in the early days and he's so incensed by Len's claim that in his honor I'm spending more time, and subjecting my wrists and fingers to more wear and tear, on this point than I might otherwise have done. However, the "all Len was" point just made is, at some level, sufficient refutation.)

By the way, I left out one strikingly negative (imhbdo) contribution Ray made in order not to get "personal", and I'm leaving out two (ditto) Len made for the same reason; but I'm not anywhere near noble enough not to mention that I'm doing so. But wait: I've belatedly realized that I also left out an amusingly discreditable sidelight on the second "history book's" author, so I fear nobility has nothing at all to do with it, it's just that I seem to be getting soft, in my MMA. Not soft enough, after due deliberation, to omit mention of one other craw-sticker, though, namely the . . . interesting aspect of the BBN "corporate culture" which led the nominal author of the "New" Telnet RFC to effusively acknowledge the assistance of his BBN colleagues in the document and totally ignore the fact that not only had I edited it extensively but around a quarter of the actual words printed were mine. (Not that I choose to offer him the publicity of mentioning his name, of course, but he's also the one who declined to co-sign my Host-Front End Protocol RFC despite the fact that 20-some others in the NWG did and he'd privately told me he agreed with it, on the stated grounds that "it wouldn't be good for the company" to admit publicly to being for something that would make more work for the IMP—which tells us some more about the corporate culture, I'd say. Indeed, MMAM belatedly assures me that for a number of years I was quite fond of saying that we'd done the 'Net despite BBN, not because of it, but I'm already over the word-count as I add this and probably couldn't remember enough of the points on which that was based anyway, so will let it go at that.)

"Historically speaking", let's touch on the three without whom Len wouldn't have gotten his grant in the first place: J.C.R. Licklider, Bob Taylor, and Larry Roberts. Lick is usually credited with having had the germ of the idea to network computers, and I liked him so much personally I can't be objective: if there must be a "the" Father of the 'Net to satisfy the mediaocrities, then as They seem to non-define the 'Net, Lick's the one. Period. Bob Taylor, whom I didn't know personally but as his wife happened to tell me at a party at Bob Metcalfe's apartment in 1978 did pick up the torch from Lick and hired Larry Roberts to run with it, has a very good claim too. (Speaking of Metcalfe, a non-PBS show I made the mistake of watching recently semidemihinted that he, as the acknowledged "father" of Ethernet, might have some claim to the Internet title as well. I don't think he admitted the soft impeachment, as it were, but just for the record the Internet wasn't built to link together only Ethernets, but in fact various and sundry comm subnet "technologies", nor did Bob have anything to do with developing IP, as I recall, so that's a non-starter.) And Larry was introduced at the '71 NWG meeting with the phrase "And now a word from Our Sponsor", so to those of us doing the work of building the ARPANET, Larry's claim feels pretty good, too—especially to those of you who weren't fortunate enough to've worked in the same building as Lick for what, five or six years, one or two of which he was your boss's boss's boss.

Nor, turning to the three who originally worked at the NMC, should we overlook the person who was chairing the meeting and introducing Larry: Steve Crocker. Steve was hired by the ARPA office to run the NWG, and deserves full credit for getting things going w/r/t the 'Net, even unto writing RFC #1. I don't feel at all filial about his role, but his claim still strikes me as better than Len's. Then there's Vint Cerf's role. He, too, started at the NMC and went on to the ARPA office. The difference is that if you define the Internet at all strictly, Vint's participation in the "invention" of TCP/IP coupled with his role in coordinating the contracts and contractors who implemented the protocol suite makes me feel that if he chose to say "I was the Father of the Internet" on his "web site" I might flinch a bit but I certainly wouldn't sneer. Finally, we shouldn't overlook Jon Postel, the way almost everybody did until we lost him and then people suddenly noticed how important, how central, how vital his participation had been all the long. He was the only one of the Old Network Boys whose views I took with fewer grains of salt than I took my own, of course, but the real point is that almost all the protocol RFCs were under his authorship, and not because he was that slick a writer. It's because he understood how the protocols had to work better than any of us, usually because the ideas they embodied were his, even when he wouldn't acknowledge that, after the fact.

At the risk of getting a bit sloppy here, and almost certainly committing a metaphor that should have been blocked, I simply can't resist observing that it's not particularly interesting who the "father" of the Internet was, because what really matters is who its "mother" was, in the sense of whose labor gave it birth. And if you need me to spell the rest of it out for you, I assume you wouldn't understand it anyway . . .

Come to think of it, though, if that's all a bit too equivocal for you, maybe we should remember our Time Enough for Love (and if you haven't read everything Heinlein wrote at least twice, it's your loss) and consider how the fleshly version of the computer "Minerva" came to be: a chromosome pair from Justin Foote for math, a chromosome pair from Lazarus Long presumably for longevity, and so on. So maybe the Internet wasn't fathered or mothered but rather created out of Lick's genes for inspiration and, I dunno, charm, and Jon's genes for call it technical intuition or brilliance and maybe composure, or whatever it was that enabled him to forge consensus among all us prima donnas, and Vint's gene for, I suppose, leadership, and . . . so on. (Gee, maybe that way even I'd get a piece of the action myself, since I'd like to think that my gene for, what, righteous indignation? Constructive Snottiness? belongs in the mix, too, for being willing to take up the cudgels in public against the ISORMite idiocy—a/k/a "OSI" for those who haven't read The Book—probably did help, some.)

"In Conclusion Bear in Memory"
Keep the password in your mind . . . Oops, wrong song (but a wonderful one; do searchengineer it if you don't know it—provided anybody's bothered to webulate it, of course). No, what to keep in mind is that from my point of view it's all rather moot, when you get right down to it:

Jon's been taken from us, after all, so sticking up for his "rights" is merely an exercise in sentimentality—though not, one hopes, futility. . . .

And I, after all, went into de facto retirement years ago, when I left the second job in a row over not being allowed to smoke in my own office, so I've got nothing to gain from winning any technopaternity suits. (Not even the mild egoboo of a cameo on one of the tellyjoke shows, since I'd insist on approval of the final cut lest I be accorded the same gratuitously snotty treatment Ted Nelson—eminently arguably the "Father of the Web", by the way—was, and clearly that'd never be granted.) Unless . . . gee, what if The Book reprint'd be a best-seller if it were advertised as being by the Father of . . . ? Nah, anybody who read it would still need to be able to deal with real sentences, and there are far too few of us left.

So unless some or all of the over-"capped" companies that owe their existence to us (cisco, Network Solutions, and, save the mark, AOL come immediately to mind) were to decide to give chunks of stock to the Fathers of this and Inventors of that in appreciation, all that's at stake is another one of those hopelessly pre-GenX abstractions: "for the record". (Actually, what I think would be far more seemly would be to award, say, 1,000, but even a couple of hundred would be nice, shares per RFC to the authors of all substantive [i.e., non-repetitive, in the sense of the monthly reports on Host traffic or even the every-hundred indexes] RFCs with numbers under 1000 [inspired by the time Interop gave out t-shirts to the authors of the first thousand RFCs, even if they only allowed us to pick one RFC number to have printed on it, which led some of us to agonize a lot]. That'd be nice. And Jon's lion's share of the shares could go to funding the Old Programmers Home, as we discussed when I first had the idea . . . the day I heard Netscape's stock was over 150, to which I'd also will the proceeds of my own 20-some lots. Of course, with my usual luck if they did do it the market'd make October of '29 look like a mere blip before I could convert to tax-frees anyway, so it's all still moot, isn't it.)

Meanwhile, what price "resource sharing"? The Bandwidth Bandits reign, even turning off "autoload images" doesn't spare one from slithering signs, everybody's committed to being HTML-trendy, "browsers" are bigger than operating systems need to be, and the main difference between "the Web" and the Sunday paper is that the p-ads can be used for wrapping fish . . .

Let at least one tradition be upheld, though: we conclude with the usual

cheers, map

Response to Padlipsky

Les Earnest <les@cs.stanford.edu>
Copyright © 2000 by the author.

In an article titled "And They Argued All Night..." http://www.mids.org/mn/1002/mike.html, Mike Padlipsky writes:

> Normally, I'd say 'In my humble but dogmatic opinion', but I don't want to be misunderstood. In my considered opinion, Len Kleinrock's claim to be the father of the Internet is ... no, don't get 'personal', make it, I know: unfounded. And/or lacking in merit. And/or utterly unfounded. And/or utterly lacking in merit. And/or ... get the picture?

Speaking as one who was peripherally involved in ARPANET/Internet development from the beginning, the picture I get is that Mike is missing part of the picture. As we know, success has many fathers. Len Kleinrock played a significant role in bringing ARPANET into existence, as discussed below.

Further on Mike gets more specific, saying:

> all Len was was the faculty guy who got the grant from ARPA to do the Network Measurement Center, where the first IMP happened to be installed. That doesn't even make him the father of the ARPANET, which ISN'T the Internet, if you're not a mediaocrity and care something about technical accuracy as opposed to 'selling papers'.

In fact, during the early 1960s Len Kleinrock laid the theoretical foundations for what came to be called packet switching, which made the ARPANET and Internet work. All that happened before Mike stumbled onto the scene. The first entry in Larry Roberts' "Internet Chronology" http://www.packet.cc/ says:

Jul-61 First Paper on Packet Switching Theory, Leonard Kleinrock, 'Information Flow in Large Communication Nets.', RLE Quarterly Progress Report. This was the theoretical work that convinced Roberts that packets could be used for the Internet.

A later entry in Roberts' chronology says "Oct-68 Network Measurement Center at UCLA contracted by Roberts at ARPA to Leonard Kleinrock at UCLA to undertake ARPANET measurement. Kleinrock was chosen because of his previous queuing theory work on networks and his ability to then measure the real network and from this verify or fix the theory. A sound, proven theory was critical for future networks." That decision was apparently based in large part on Kleinrock's book published in 1964 on *Communication Nets: Stochastic Message Flow and Delay*, McGraw-Hill (New York).

In a SIGCOMM Presentation in Boston on August 31, 1999, Roberts stated that:

> Packet switching was new and radical in the 1960s. In order to plan to spend millions of dollars and stake my reputation, I needed to understand that it would work. Without Kleinrocks work of Networks and Queuing Theory, I cold never have taken such a radical step. All the communications community argued that it couldnt work. This book was critical to my standing up to them and betting that it would work.

While it is understandable that Mike Padlipsky might not be aware of how the theoretical foundations of packet switching were developed, it is foolish of him to make unqualified assertions about ARPANET origins given that he wasn't involved when that work was being done.

COMPUTER HISTORY BOOKS *from Peer-to-Peer*

April Fool's Day RFCs
Compiled by Thomas A. Limoncelli and Peter H. Salus, *Editors*

For over 35 years, the Requests for Comment have been the guidelines and standards of the Internet. But squirreled away within the over-4000 RFCs are a number of mock items, generally (not always) issued on April Fools' Day.

This all-in-one collection not only reprints the RFCs in their original ASCII graphic greatness but also enriches them with commentaries by Tom and Peter and Forewords by Brad Templeton, Scott Bradner, and Mike O'Dell.

"The Complete April Fools' Day RFCs is a nigh-perfect geek reader for the top of your favorite nerd's toilet tank...engineer humor at its finest — geeks making up stuff to amuse other geeks" —Cory Doctorow, *Boing Boing*

Find out how to distinguish good stuff from malware, how to use pigeons as packet carriers, how the Roman addressing system works . . . 45 edifying and entertaining essays in all.

PAGES: 390 pages
ISBN-13: 978-1-57398-042-5
PRICE: $24.95 US; $29.95 CAN
Published April 2007

COMPUTER HISTORY BOOKS *from Peer-to-Peer*

Unix Review's 1996 Book of the Year

Lion's Commentary on UNIX

"The Lions book", the underground classic cherished by UNIX hackers and widely circulated as a photocopied bootleg document since the late 1970's, is really two works in one:
- The complete source code to an early version of the UNIX operating system, a treasure in itself (this is basically the pristine code which earned Dennis Ritchie and Ken Thompson, the two earliest developers of UNIX, the Turing award).
- A brilliant commentary on that code by Prof. John Lions

Lions' marriage of source code with commentary was originally used as an operating systems textbook, and it remains ideally suited for that purpose (MIT was still using it as a text in 2005!). As a self-study UNIX conceptual tutorial, it has informed and inspired computer professionals and advanced operating system students for over twenty years.

An international "who's who" of UNIX wizards, including Ritchie and Thompson, have contributed essays extolling its merits and importance. Besides being as chic as a computer book can be, "The Lions book" remains the most respected operating system book ever published.

AUTHOR: John Lions
PAGES: 254 pages
ISBN-10: 1-57398-013-7
ISBN-13: 978-1-57398-013-5
PRICE: $39.95 US, $57.95 CAN

www.ingramcontent.com/pod-product-compliance
Ingram Content Group UK Ltd.
Pitfield, Milton Keynes, MK11 3LW, UK
UKHW051301180426
11947UKWH00020B/1840